D0930106

THE PIE BOOK

OVER **400** CLASSIC RECIPES

Louis P. De Gouy

DOVER PUBLICATIONS, INC.
MINEOLA, NEW YORK

THIS BOOK IS FONDLY DEDICATED
TO THE MEMORY OF
LOUIS P. DE GOUY
(1876–1947)
BY HIS DAUGHTER
JACQUELINE S. DOONER

Bibliographical Note

This Dover edition, first published in 2018, is an unabridged republication of the work originally published by Greenberg Publisher, New York, in 1949.

International Standard Book Number

ISBN-13: 978-0-486-82455-0
ISBN-10: 0-486-82455-1

Manufactured in the United States by LSC Communications
82455101   2018
www.doverpublications.com

CONTENTS*

*The beginning numbers refer to the recipe numbers

CHIFFON PIE RECIPES, 327

CAN SIZE CONVERSION CHART

No. 1 picnic	1¼ cups	10½ to 12 ounces
No. 300	1¾ cups	14 to 16 ounces
No. 303	2 cups	16 to 17 ounces
No. 2	2½ cups	20 ounces
No. 2½	3½ cups	27 to 29 ounces
No. 3	5¾ cups	51 ounces
No. 10	3 quarts	6½ pounds to 7 pounds and 5 ounces

CONVERSION TABLES

DRY INGREDIENTS

Ounces		Grams	Grams		Ounces	Pounds		Kilograms	Kilo-grams		Pounds
1	=	28.35	1	=	0.035	1	=	0.454	1	=	2.205
2		56.70	2		0.07	2		0.91	2		4.41
3		85.05	3		0.11	3		1.36	3		6.61
4		113.40	4		0.14	4		1.81	4		8.82
5		141.75	5		0.18	5		2.27	5		11.02
6		170.10	6		0.21	6		2.72	6		13.23
7		198.45	7		0.25	7		3.18	7		15.43
8		226.80	8		0.28	8		3.63	8		17.64
9		255.15	9		0.32	9		4.08	9		19.84
10		283.50	10		0.35	10		4.54	10		22.05
11		311.85	11		0.39	11		4.99	11		24.26
12		340.20	12		0.42	12		5.44	12		26.46
13		368.55	13		0.46	13		5.90	13		28.67
14		396.90	14		0.49	14		6.35	14		30.87
15		425.25	15		0.53	15		6.81	15		33.08
16		453.60	16		0.57						

LIQUID INGREDIENTS

Liquid Ounces		Milli- liters	Milli- liters		Liquid Ounces	Quarts		Liters	Liters		Quarts
1	=	29.573	1	=	0.034	1	=	0.946	1	=	1.057
2		59.15	2		0.07	2		1.89	2		2.11
3		88.72	3		0.10	3		2.84	3		3.17
4		118.30	4		0.14	4		3.79	4		4.23
5		147.87	5		0.17	5		4.73	5		5.28
6		177.44	6		0.20	6		5.68	6		6.34
7		207.02	7		0.24	7		6.62	7		7.40
8		236.59	8		0.27	8		7.57	8		8.45
9		266.16	9		0.30	9		8.52	9		9.51
10		295.73	10		0.33	10		9.47	10		10.57

Gallons (American)		Liters	Liters		Gallons (American)
1	=	3.785	1	=	0.264
2		7.57	2		0.53
3		11.36	3		0.79
4		15.14	4		1.06
5		18.93	5		1.32
6		22.71	6		1.59
7		26.50	7		1.85
8		30.28	8		2.11
9		34.07	9		2.38
10		37.86	10		2.74

INTRODUCTION

Pastry-making began in ages so remote that no records remain of the earliest recipes and formulas. Where did the pastry originate? Legend says from Greece, where an ancient Greek pastrycook with primitive handmade tools and utensils produced delicious honey cakes, fimbria, nubes, esculentas, etc.

From Greece the art of pastry-making was introduced into Italy. Good living was unknown to the Romans as long as they were fighting to secure their independence. But when their conquests were extended to Africa and Greece (they had feasted at the expense of the vanquished in those countries where civilization was more advanced), they brought back to Rome the art of preparing delicious pastry. Dishes of attractive flavors were invented by them to flatter the palate without loading the stomach. The Romans prided themselves on having beautiful gardens where they cultivated not only fruits already known a long time, such as pears, apples, figs, grapes, etc., but also those which were brought from different countries—the apricot from Armenia, peach from Persia, quinces from Sidon, strawberries from the valleys of Mount Ida, and the cherries (the conquest of Lucullus) from the kingdom of Pontus. With these they made delicious pastries and desserts—wafers with tender and flaky crusts; tortes; spicy artologamus, the dough of which was made of wine, milk, olive oil, and spices; the scribilta, a kind of delicious cheese cake; the placenta, made of oat flour, cheese and honey, etc.

The Romans were the inventors of ice cream and its countless variations. We might fill pages describing the development of pastry and dessert-making in Italy. Old chronicles of Italian authors are full of these delicious preparations in which Italians became, and remain, masters.

From Italy the art of pastry-making went to Gaul. The first Capetian kings had at their court an officer called "Patissier-Bouche" and four assistant pastrycooks. The first corporation, or trade union, of pastry-makers was created in Paris in 1270 and extended all over the French kingdom. The final status, granted by the king in 1566, gave to all its members the title of "Master Pastrycook," with franchise and privileges, as well as severe and rigorous by-laws. Before the Revolution of 1789, the Trade Union of Master Pastrycooks was divided into several branches or specialties, such as wafer-makers (oublieurs), cream-makers (darioleurs), etc., and each branch or specialist did not have any right to encroach upon or usurp the specialties of another.

Real pastry as it is known today was created about 1790 but was not developed to its present-day standard of proficiency until the beginning of the nineteenth century. Pastry-making was introduced in America by the Pilgrims and has progressed to such an extent that the story of pastry-making in the United States—as, of course, that of cookery—is closely related to the traditions, customs, and progress of the nation.

The catalogue of all our native delicacies and of those from across the seas is a long one and runs through the courses of a dinner for a sophisticated American. But pass over all the meats, fowl, and game, the razor-back and sugar-cured hams of the South, and all the sea foods of Baltimore and New Orleans, and picture for yourself a bit of still life on the buffet: an English tart or trifle, a plate of Copenhagen confections; some British and Vienna symphonies of almond paste, glacé fruits, sugar and puff paste; a glittering Gâteau St. Honoré from Paris; and a little bit back, at one side, four pies by an American pastrycook—apple, mince, pumpkin, and lemon meringue. Then, if you are an honest person, what shall the answer be?

Louis P. De Gouy

TECHNICAL DATA

(1) WEIGHING AND MEASURING

The system is avoirdupois, sixteen ounces to the pound. Weighing is more accurate than measuring, but it is slower, and the measuring can be made sufficiently accurate for most daily work. Weighing is necessary in the cookery of large pieces and in the preparation of large quantities of pastry. The measures in common use are ¼ teaspoon, ½ teaspoon, teaspoon, tablespoon, the ½ pint measuring cup (1 cup), the pint (2 cups), quart (4 cups), and gallon of liquid measure.

It is necessary to know the relation of these different weights and measures to each other. The following abbreviations are short cuts in reading:

oz. = ounce or ounces	pt. = pint or 2 cups
lb. = pound	qt. = quart or 4 cups
tsp. = teaspoon	gal. = gallon
Tbsp. = tablespoon	pkg. = package
c. = cup	

(2) HOW TO MEASURE DRY INGREDIENTS

To measure 1 teaspoon, 1 tablespoon, or any part thereof, or 1 cup or fraction of a cup, or a pint or a quart of any dry ingredient such as sugar, meal, flour, or cereal, fill the utensil full by *lifting* the material, by means of spoon or cup, into the cup, pint, or quart and level off by passing the edge of a straight knife or spatula over the top. Fractions of a teaspoon or tablespoon are measured as follows: To measure ½ teaspoon, or ½ tablespoon, fill the spoon with the ingredient, level off and divide the spoon lengthwise in half. To measure ¼ teaspoon or ¼ tablespoon, fill the spoon with the ingredient, level off with a knife or spatula, divide lengthwise in halves, then crosswise in fourths. Scrape off the unused portion. (Measuring spoons are available for ½ and ¼ teaspoons.)

(3) HOW TO MEASURE FLOUR

Pastry flour is generally used in pastry-making because of the larger proportion of starch. Some pastry chefs claim, however, that bread flour gives a more flaky crust, and it is generally used in making Puff Paste (No. 41). A blend of the two flours is preferred by some, as indicated for No. 66, Winter Wheat Crunchy Semi-Puff Paste Flaky Pie Crust, which, however, may be used for both one-crust or two-crust pastry.

Two methods of filling a cup or quart measure have been found to give very good results. One is to sift the flour gently, bringing it up heaping full, and putting it into the cup or quart measure with almost as light a touch as though it were an explosive likely to blow up if jarred, then leveling off the top with the edge of a spatula—not the flat surface, for here there is a tendency to use pressure. By this method, the variation in the weight of any number of measurements of a given sample of flour need not run much, if any, higher than the equivalent of ½ tablespoon per cup, or about 2 tablespoons per quart. Another method of measuring flour is to sift it directly into the cup or quart slightly overful and then level off the surface with the edge of a spatula. However, the modern baker knows that there is just one procedure to be followed in measuring flour, and that is: *sift, measure, sift.* Flour which has been standing for several days may be so closely packed that a cup of it is really 1 cup plus 5 or 6 tablespoons, while the flour that has just been delivered in the bouncing truck of the dealer will give only 14 tablespoons to the cup instead of the usual 16.

As a result of variation in flour particle size and differences in methods of measuring, it is difficult to give exact figures for the weight of a cupful of flour. The following figures are used by a number of research workers:

1 cupful sifted bread flour	= 112.0 grams
1 cupful sifted all-purpose flour	= 110.0 grams
1 cupful sifted cake flour	= 96.0 grams
1 cupful sifted pastry flour	= 100.0 grams
1 cupful stirred whole-wheat flour	= 120.0 grams

(4) HOW TO MEASURE BROWN SUGAR

Pack sugar firmly into the spoon, cup, pint or quart, then level off with a straight knife or spatula. If lumpy, roll and sift before measuring.

(5) HOW TO MEASURE LIQUIDS

Fill the utensil to the point where it is completely full without overflowing.

(6) HOW TO MEASURE FATS

In measuring fats, a real difficulty is encountered—that is, the tendency for large air spaces to form. This is greater if the fat is cold. Let us take lard as an example, which is plastic and easily packed. A cupful measured immediately after it is taken from the refrigerator is found to be $6\frac{2}{5}$ oz., whereas the same measure of this lard, when allowed to come to the temperature of the room, weighs $7\frac{2}{3}$ oz., which is the correct value. The difference of $1\frac{4}{15}$ oz., between the two measurements assumes considerable significance when thought of as almost 2 tablespoons.

Butter, being harder and less plastic than lard, shows an even greater resistance to packing when cold and a greater tendency to slip and slide around when one tries to pack it down into the utensil.

Another difficulty met with in measuring fats is the resistance to leveling off. If one is not careful, the top is still rounded after passing the spatula over it. A rounded surface would, of course, tend to compensate for air spaces and therefore might appear to be desirable in measuring cold fats; but since no two cups of fat with air spaces and rounded tops are likely to weigh the same, it is better to pack solid and to level off the top to a flat surface.

The difficulty in measuring fats can be much lessened by taking the fat out of the refrigerator for a few minutes in hot weather—an hour or so in cold—before it is to be measured; but even then a special effort must be made to see that the pack is solid, with no air spaces.

For all solid fats: Measure by tablespoons for amounts of ¼ cup or less. To measure a spoonful of fat, pack it solidly into the spoon, then level off with a spatula or knife. To measure by cup, pack the shortening in so solidly that it will hold the shape of the cup (or other measure) when turned out; then level off. For fraction of cup, pack solidly or level off at the desired fraction, if cups in fractional sizes are used; or use the *water displacement method.* For example, for ½ cup of shortening, fill cup half full of cold water, add shortening until the water reaches the top of the cup, being sure that all the shortening is kept under the level of the water, then drain off water carefully. The remaining shortening measures the correct amount. This method may be used for any fraction of a cup, pint, or quart. To *measure from a pound print* (as for packaged butter or lard), is an easy matter if one is familiar with the relation between a pound and cup. One pound is equivalent to 2 cups. One-half pound equals 1 cup; a ¼ pound stick equals ½ cup.

To resume: Any difficulties which are encountered by measuring fats by the cupful are easily overcome by the purchase of a scale of suitable size to weigh the amount of shortening called for in the recipe.

For melted shortening: The solid shortening may be measured and leveled off with knife or spatula, then melted, or it may sometimes be more convenient to melt the shortening before measuring. The amount should be the same.

(7)   STANDARD MEASURES

Standard measuring cups, graduated to read ⅓ and ⅔ on one side, and ¼, ½ and ¾ on the other, and sets of measuring spoons consisting of 1 tablespoon, 1, ½ and ¼ teaspoons are available for accuracy in measuring. Some measuring cups designed for liquid have an extra rim for the 1 cup mark, but these should not be used for measuring ingredients which must be leveled off.

(8)   FATS OR SHORTENINGS

Under the term *shortening* are included all fats which are used with flour and other ingredients to make breads, cakes, and pastries tender, long, or short. Fats or shortenings are the only materials in pie crust which are not dissolved in the water nor wet by the water. They are not changed during the baking process and thus produce tenderness by preventing the flour, sugar, and other non-fatty materials from combining into a hard, brittle, continuous mass. Water as a liquid, for example, does not act in this manner. Fats or shortenings also prevent the products from drying out quickly.

(9)   BUTTER

The butter in pies, although it adds flavor, is very expensive. Even in hotels and restaurants, pastry made with butter is extremely rare.

Butter's chief value is its flavor. When substituting butter for lard or any other shortening in pastry, remember that butter is not 100 per cent fat, and so more butter should be used than is stated in the recipe. In general, 2 tablespoons of butter should be added for each cup of pure fat required. Butter is only 81 per cent pure fat, the rest of the contents being casein, salt, and water. When butter is used in pastry, the moisture present develops the gluten of the flour and makes a tough pastry. However, when butter is washed to remove all buttermilk, it gives a tender pastry with a flavor not obtained by the use of any other shortening. Some bakers prefer to melt the butter, remove the curds which settle, cool the remaining butter fat, and use it in a semi-solid condition. This is practised by the French and Italian pastry makers. Others recommend using lard or hydrogenated fat to mix with the flour; then when this pastry has been dampened and rolled out, spread on butter, fold and roll again. This method produces what is called semi-puff paste.

(10)   MARGARINE

Margarine, as produced at the present time in the United States, is a combination of highly refined vegetable oils (more than 90 per cent of the oils used are cottonseed oil and soybean oil; other oils include corn, peanut, sunflower, seed oil, and meat fats, to a limited degree) pasteurized and cultured skim milk, salt and Vitamin A. The term *oleomargarine*, indicating the use of "oleo," is no longer a true description of modern margarine. The original product, made largely from beef fat, was invented in 1870 by a French chemist, Mege-Mouriet, who discovered that beef fat from particular portions of the bullock would melt at the same temperature as butter, and would keep longer without becoming rancid. Like butter, margarines are not used to any extent in pie crust in the baking trade, hotel, restaurant, and home.

(11)   # LARD

The consistency of lard is extremely soft, and lard is not always uniform, since it is a natural fat and its qualities depend to a large extent on the feed of the animals. Quite often, a very plastic shortening such as lard tends to separate from the dough and work out on the board or bench, requiring the use of considerable dusting flour, which, of course, tends to produce an inferior crust. Some lards, such as hydrogenated lards, have been improved for baking and have better keeping qualities than others. Shortenings used for pie crust should be able to resist oxidation at oven temperature. If shortenings used for pie crust oxidize at oven temperature, they give the crust a disagreeable rancid taste and odor. This is not generally true of the hydrogenated lards.

The following kinds of lards are available on the market: (a) kettle-rendered leaf lard; (b) kettle-rendered lard; (c) prime steam, or steam-rendered lard; (d) hydrogenated lard.

(a) *Kettle-rendered leaf lard* is made from the leaf fat, or the internal fat of the abdomen of the hog, excluding that adherent to the intestines. It is rendered in an open kettle, which is steam-jacketed, at a temperature of 230° to 250°F. This method of making lard is similar to the home method; it is light in color, slightly grainy with firm texture, has a mild and pleasing flavor and has excellent keeping qualities.

(b) *Kettle-rendered lard* is made from leaf and back fat and is rendered in a steam-jacketed open kettle at a temperature of 240° to 260° F. Kettle-rendered lard is light in color, but somewhat darker than leaf lard, slightly grainy in texture, is of very good keeping quality, and has a very pleasing flavor.

(c) *Prime steam lard* is made from killing and cutting fats, rendered in direct contact with steam in a closed tank under a pressure of 30 to 50 lbs., or at a temperature of about 285° F. It is usually cooled rapidly over a chill roll or refrigerator drum, which produces a very smooth texture. It is whiter and has a different flavor from kettle-rendered lard (a). This kind of lard represents 80 per cent of the commercial product. The keeping qualities are satisfactory, and the cost is usually less than that of the kettle-rendered lards. Of course, none of the above mentioned lards has as good keeping qualities as hydrogenated lard or hydrogenated vegetable shortenings.

(12) # HYDROGENATED LARD

By the processes of hydrogenation, addition of antioxidants, deodorization, caustic refining, and plasticizing, new so-called "hydrogenated lards" are on the market. This type of lard will keep firm at room temperatures, not needing refrigeration, has increased stability, more uniform and firmer consistency than other lards, and improved baking characteristics. Some brands on the market have a smoking point of 420° F. and can be kept fresh for fourteen to sixteen months.

(13) # ALL-HYDROGENATED VEGETABLE OIL SHORTENINGS

In the manufacture of all-hydrogenated shortenings, every particle of vegetable oil used is subjected to the hydrogenation process. The properties of the original oil are changed so that a shortening with more desirable properties is produced. The hydrogenation process is controlled during manufacture so that finished shortenings have the desired consistency or body.

After the oils are hydrogenated to the proper body, they are further processed to give them a bland and neutral flavor, and to give the smoothness and feel which are characteristic of this type of shortening. Hydrogenated shortenings do not impart any objectionable fatty flavors to the crust. In addition, they resist breakdown and the development of "off" flavors at normal baking temperatures. The body of hydrogenated shortenings is just right to blend readily with the flour in order to produce a tender crust. Furthermore, hydrogenated shortenings maintain distribution in the dough and do not bake out of the crust.

Hydrogenated shortenings permit the production of any type of crust which may be desired—from the very mealy crust to a crust with a maximum flakiness. They have a desirable creamy white color, smooth texture, and a bland or neutral flavor. They keep well and longer than any other shortenings.

(14) # STANDARD SHORTENINGS

Standard shortenings are vegetable oil shortenings made by blending, for example, refined, bleached, vegetable oil with sufficient vegetable stearine to produce the desired consistency. Vegetable stearine is vegetable oil hydrogenated to a high melting point. The vegetable stearine and hydrogenated oil are liquified and mixed together; when cooled, the vegetable stearine hardens the unhydrogenated vegetable oil. From this point on, the mixture is processed in much the same manner as the all-hydrogenated shortenings.

Standard shortenings have excellent consistency for pie crust and have good flavor, but they are inferior to hydrogenated shortenings in keeping qualities and in their ability to resist break-down at high temperature.

(15) CHICKEN FAT OR OILS, SOUR CREAM, BACON FAT, SUET

These products may be used in the manufacture of pie crust, but in my opinion their use is so limited and so impractical that the use of better shortenings is preferred.

(16) FLOUR

Flour may be ground according to two classes: (1) The kinds of wheats from which they are made—(a) *durum wheat*, (b) *hard wheats* and (c) *soft wheats*. (2) The uses for which they are milled. Different types and varieties of wheat may be blended to yield flours that are particularly well adapted to special uses. (a) *Macaroni flours*. These, as the name implies, are designed for the making of macaroni and related products. They are milled from durum wheats, which are high in protein. The flours are quite granular and usually creamy in color. (b) *Bread flours*. These are milled from blends of hard spring and hard winter wheats. They are fairly high in protein and somewhat granular to the touch. They may be bleached or unbleached. Bread flours are milled primarily for bakers. (c) *General- purpose, or family flours*. As the name implies, these flours are of such composition that they may be used satisfactorily for all household cookery purposes. In the hard wheat producing areas they are usually a blend of hard wheats. They are lower in protein content than bread flours. They do contain enough protein for making good yeast breads, but not too much for good quick breads and cakes. In soft wheat areas, all-purpose flours are usually a blend of soft wheats. Although both "northern" and "southern" all-purpose flours give good results in any type of product, the "northern" variety makes especially good yeast breads, while the "southern" variety makes especially good quick breads. Either of them gives good results in all types of home-baked products, except perhaps the finest cakes, which are best made from cake flour. (d) *Pastry flours*. These may be made either of hard or soft wheat, although usually of the latter. They are fairly low in protein and are finely milled, though they are not so fine as cake flour. They are especially milled for making pastry, and are used chiefly by bakers. (e) *Cake flours*. These are milled from soft wheats. They are short patents, representing the most highly refined flour streams of the mill. The granulation is uniform and very fine, and the protein content is low.

(f) *Self-rising flour.* This is flour to which calcium acid phosphate or monocalcium phosphate, bicarbonate of soda, and salt have been added.

(17)   SELECTING FLOUR FOR BAKING

How good a flour is for a given purpose depends, of course, on many factors—the quantity and quality of the protein; the size of the flour particles; the size of the starch granules, so tiny that nature may pack thousands of them into one microscopic particle of flour; the sugar content; the crude fibre of branny particles; the kind and quantity of enzymes; the fatty substance; the mineral, or ash, content; and finally, the skill of the baker using the flour, and the accuracy of his recipe.

Each of the above points is important. Yet the proteins are often considered the most important constituent of flour, since of all the cereal grains only wheat contains the kind of proteins which enable the flour from it to make a smooth, satiny dough.

Of the several proteins that flour contains, the chief ones are gliadin and glutenin. Together these may make up a large part of the proteins in flour. Gliadin may be present in larger quantity than is glutenin, but the latter substance is the protein which makes wheat flower unique as the chief bread-baking cereal of the world. Other cereals, such as rye and corn, contain gliadin, but none besides wheat contains glutenin in large enough quantity to possess good baking qualities.

(18)   GLUTEN

When wheat flour is moistened, the gliadin and glutenin combine to form a substance called gluten. Gluten makes the framework of bread, biscuits, cakes, and most other baked products.

A simple way to examine some of the qualities of gluten is to put a cupful of flour into a bowl, add enough water to make a stiff dough, mix thoroughly, and then knead the dough until it is smooth and satiny (10 minutes). Then, under a stream of cool running water, or in a deep bowl, wash the dough, kneading it constantly. The kneading develops the gluten, and the washing removes the starch. When the wash water is no longer cloudy, an elastic, grayish mass remains. This is crude gluten. It may be shaped into a smooth, moist ball, put on a sheet of heavy paper or on a pan and baked for an hour in a hot oven (450° F.). The heat causes steam to form so that the gluten first expands and then becomes firm, for gluten is very elastic; and because it is protein, it is coagulated or hardened by heat.

Different kinds of flour yield different amounts and different kinds of gluten. Bread flour yields more gluten than cake flour. Moreover, strands of gluten from bread flour are more elastic, thicker and less tender than those from cake flour. The gluten from soft wheat all-purpose flour is more delicate and less tenacious than that from hard wheat all-purpose flour. Long ago it was found that when a small amount (½ of 1 per cent) of calcium acid phosphate was added to all-purpose flour made from soft wheat, the gluten became slightly more tenacious and its performance in baking was improved. For this reason, in many sections of the South where soft wheat is grown and milled, phosphated flours are commonly used.

Aside from expanding and holding its shape when baked, gluten also has the property of absorbing much water. Just how much of the moisture-absorbing capacity of a given flour is dependent on its gluten and how much on its starch seems to be an unsettled question. Certain it is that flours differ greatly in this property, bread flour in general absorbing more than the pastry. This difference in moisture-absorbing capacity gives trouble when one changes from one type of flour to the other in a given recipe, a fact which is especially noticeable in biscuit dough. Obviously, if one flour absorbs much more liquid than the other, we cannot use the same proportions of the two for a given volume of liquid. Provided there is the right proportion, however, it does not seem to make much difference which type of flour we use for muffins and biscuits. But pastry flour seems necessary for pies and cakes if they are to be at their best.

(19)   # BAKING PROCEDURES

The different amounts as well as different kinds of gluten developed are responsible for the different cookery procedures recommended when various types of flour are used. Yeast breads, for example, can be made from either hard or soft flours. But the method of making is changed slightly. Hard wheat flour, with its strong gluten, requires a longer fermentation time during which the gluten becomes softened and tender. The gluten of soft wheat flour is already soft and tender, so it needs only enough fermentation to generate carbon dioxide for leavening and to develop the delicious flavor characteristic of yeast breads. Consequently, when yeast breads are made from soft wheat flour, the amount of yeast is increased; the fermentation time is kept short, and the dough is handled gently so as not to injure the gluten meshwork that has been built up.

On the other hand, in making quick breads, which are best when the gluten remains somewhat underdeveloped, the procedure is just the opposite. When soft wheat flour is used, the batter may be stirred or the dough kneaded with less danger of developing a tough product than when hard wheat flour is used.

Although flours differ in protein content and particle size, the fact is that any good flour makes good products, provided the ingredients are properly proportioned and the method of mixing is adapted to the kind of flour used. For special types of baking, flours milled for specific purposes obviously give the finest type of products.

(20)   STORAGE OF FLOUR

The place where flour is stored must be moderately dry, well lighted, airy, never exposed to a freezing temperature or to excessive heat. An even temperature of 70° to 75° F. is best if it is to be used within six months; that to be held longer should be kept cooler.

Whether in a barrel or sack, flour should always be placed on a rack at least two inches from the floor, in order to allow a current of air to pass under and prevent dampness from the floor; and it should *never* be placed in contact with grain or other substances which are liable to generate heat.

Flour is peculiarly sensitive to atmospheric influences—hence it should never be stored in a room with any material which emits an odor. Any smell perceptible to the human sense will be absorbed by it. A damp cellar, or a close attic or loft is especially unsuitable.

(21)   FOOD INGREDIENT SUBSTITUTES

1 square of chocolate for ¼ cup of cocoa in pudding, pies, cakes, icings, or beverage. ¼ cup of cocoa for 1 oz. or square of chocolate in cake—take out 2 tablespoons of flour. In cakes and cookies add 1 teaspoon of shortening.

1 cup bread flour, less 2 tablespoons, plus 1½ tablespoons cornstarch for 1 cup of pastry flour.

1 tablespoon of cornstarch for 2 tablespoons of flour—for thickening.

1 cup of pearl tapioca for ¾ cup of quick-cooking tapioca.

1 teaspoon of baking powder for ¼ teaspoon baking soda and ½ teaspoon of cream of tartar.

⅞ cup chicken fat, hydrogenated fats, lard or oil, equivalent to 1 cup of butter in fat content.

2 to 2¼ cups heavy cream, equivalent to 1 cup of butter in fat content. Make allowance for difference in liquid. 1 cup of 40 percent heavy cream equals 1/3 cup of butter plus ¾ cup milk.

1 cup of milk for ½ cup of condensed milk and ½ cup water—omit sugar in recipe.

1 cup of milk for ½ cup of evaporated milk and ½ cup of water.

1 cup of milk for 4 tablespoons of powdered milk and 1 cup of water.

Sour milk for sweet, by using ½ teaspoon of baking soda for each cup of milk; cut down baking powder by 1½ teaspoons.

Sweet milk for sour, by adding 1 tablespoon of vinegar to each cup of milk, letting stand 20 minutes.

½ teaspoon of baking soda neutralizes 1 cup sour milk, or buttermilk and leavens 1 cup of flour.

½ teaspoon of baking soda neutralizes ½ to 1 cup of molasses and leavens 1 cup flour.

(22)   THICKENING AGENTS

Thickening agents which thicken hot liquids as they cook are (a) flour, (b) cornstarch, (c) ground tapioca (or tapioca flour), (d) rice flour, (e) potato flour, (f) arrowroot, and (g) eggs.

Junket added to lukewarm milk, pectin added to fruit juice, stiffen these liquids as they cool.

Gelatin when hydrated (soaked in cold water) and dissolved in any heated cooking liquids, *except* fresh pineapple juice, stiffens the liquid on cooling.

Cornstarch, arrowroot, rice flour have twice the thickening power of flour. They give a clearer cooked mixture than flour.

1 level tablespoon of flour thickens 1 cup of liquid for a thin sauce.

2 level tablespoons of flour thicken 1 cup of drippings or liquid for gravy or sauce, or for a medium sauce.

4 level tablespoons (¼ cup) of cornstarch thicken 1 pint (2 cups) of liquid for cornstarch filling.

1 level tablespoon of granulated gelatin will stiffen 1 pint (2 cups) of liquid, cooled on ice in 2 to 4 hours.

3 eggs thicken 1 pint of milk for custard (cup or pie).

1½ eggs or 2–3 yolks thicken 1 cup of milk for cup custard.

(23)   FRESH FRUIT PREPARATION

Fresh Peaches. To remove skins from fresh peaches, proceed as follows: For every two gallons of water used, dissolve ¼ lb. bicarbonate of soda and bring this to a boil. Add the fresh peaches and slowly bring back to a boil. Let boil 2 minutes, or until skins begin to slip off. Drain at once, cover with cold water. The skins will rub off easily without losing any flavor, and the peaches will not discolor. Use only firm, well-ripened peaches, as the skins of partly green peaches are rather difficult to remove by any method, except by peeling with a knife. Discard bruised or over-ripe peaches.

Strawberries. In washing strawberries, raspberries, and the like, don't let the water from the faucet play on them. They are too tender to stand such treatment. Instead, put them in a large bowl of warm water and then lift them out of the water with fingers somewhat apart to act as strainer. The sand and soil on the berries will settle to the bottom of the container. For that reason, don't pour the water off the berries. Unless they are quite dirty, two such rinses are usually sufficient. Above all, don't let berries stand in water to lose color and flavor.

Should you be against washing berries, here is a dry method: Tie one end of a large piece of cheesecloth, hammock fashion, to the side of a sturdy table. Hold the other end in your hand. Now drop berries into the center; raise and lower the free end of the cloth and allow the berries to roll back and forth its length. Shake them a little as they roll. The porous cheesecloth will catch all the particles of sand and soil and remove them from the berries. Do this a few times and the berries will be thoroughly free from foreign matter.

Banana Discoloration. Following are several methods to prevent darkening of this popular fruit:

(a) When preparing bananas for pie filling, proceed as rapidly as possible.

(b) When slicing bananas for pies or any kind of dessert, try using a wooden knife, which you can whittle yourself, of hard wood, making a thin blade. You can also buy one ready made in almost any kind of house furnishing store.

(c) Sprinkle bananas with a solution of water and lemon juice; use 2 tablespoons of lemon juice or ¼ tsp. powdered ascorbic acid for each quart of water and drop banana slices into this solution; do not allow the bananas to remain in this solution longer than 10 or 15 minutes. Drain thoroughly and use at once.

(d) Pile sliced bananas immediately into pie shell, and cover at once with either cream, meringue, or glaze.

(e) Better yet, marinate sliced bananas in a mixture of lemon and orange and a very little lime juice, sweetened with honey. But drain well before using for pie.

(24)   **DRIED FRUIT PREPARATION**

Today, dried fruits are by no means shriveled fruits, or withered fruits, as they once were when less efficient handling methods were employed. Strictly speaking, they should be considered fresh fruits from which the water has been evaporated—or evaporated fruits, if you will.

Apricots, apples, dates, figs, peaches, pears, prunes, and raisins—fresh fruits all, but evaporated—are ready to cook, ready to save store or pantry space, and present no other storage problem.

Mention has just been made of the better handling and other factory processes which now permit the evaporated fruit to more closely approximate fresh fruit. There is also the better packaging in airtight cartons which do everything possible to continue to keep the fruit moist. The result is that these new evaporated fruits are not "dried" or desiccated—and this fact quite radically affects their cooking or preparing processes.

In the old days when evaporated fruits were indeed dried and withered, it was necessary to "soak overnight" or at least eight hours. But today this is not only unnecessary but *decidedly wrong.* Quick cooking is the secret of success with these tender, delicate fruit pulps, and quick cooking *must be practiced.* It is really entirely up to the cook whether or not these fruits shall be whole, shapely, and delicious, or whether they shall come out an unsightly broken or mashed mass of a dark or yellow, unpleasant color. *Quick cooking,* and *practically no soaking,* must be the rule.

Another point is that too many pieces of fruit should not be cooked at the same time. After all, isn't this exactly what we do when we cook all fresh fruits, like fresh peaches, or plums, or cherries, or strawberries? If we put a few pieces at a time into the water or syrup, then each piece has room in which to simmer down but still retain its shape; whereas, if we dump a whole mass of pieces into the kettle, then we must expect little else than a shapeless mixture to result. Strange, that while so many cooks follow this sensible rule when cooking fresh fruits, they do just the opposite when they handle evaporated fruits.

Here are the rules for dried fruit preparation:

APPLES (Absorb enough water to make their cooked bulk five times the original lb.)	Remove particles of core. Rinse, cover with water, and boil 40 minutes. For fresh apple flavor, omit sugar; or if desired, or directed, allow ¼ cup sugar for each cup fruit. Added flavor may be obtained with few grains salt.
APRICOTS (Double in weight when cooked)	Rinse, cover with water, and boil 30 minutes. Allow, if directed, ¼ to ½ cup sugar for each cup fruit, to taste, added 5 minutes before cooking is completed.
FIGS (Double in weight when cooked)	Rinse, cover with water and boil 20 to 30 minutes, depending on condition of fruit. Allow 1 tablespoon sugar for each cup fruit and add for last 5 minutes of cooking.

PEACHES (Triple in weight when cooked)	Rinse, cover with water, boil 5 minutes, and remove skins. Cover with fresh water and boil 45 minutes. Allow ¼ cup sugar for each cup fruit, added 5 minutes before cooking is completed.
PEARS (Triple in weight when cooked)	Rinse, remove cores, cover with water, and boil 35 minutes. Allow ¼ cup sugar for each cup fruit, added 5 minutes before cooking is completed
PRUNES (Double in weight when cooked)	Rinse, cover with water, and boil 45 minutes to 60 minutes, depending on condition of fruit. Sugar is not needed, but from 1 to 2 tablespoons for each cup prunes may be added, if desired, the last 5 minutes before cooking is completed.
RAISINS (Double in weight when cooked)	Rinse. Allow 1 cup water for each cup raisins, boil 10 minutes, and add ¼ to ½ tablespoon sugar for each cup fruit, the last 5 minutes before cooking is completed.

Practically all foods shrink during the cooking process, but the dried fruits are a notable exception.

Raisins, dates, currants, and figs blend better with other ingredients if they are soaked for 5 minutes in a little boiling water. Use 2 tablespoons boiling water for each ½ cup of fruit.

(25)

NUT CHART

Nut	How Purchased	Weight	Measure by cups
ALMONDS			
Hard shell	In shell	1 lb.	1 cup meats
Soft shell	In shell	1 lb.	2 cup meats
Jordans	Meats	1 lb.	3 cup meats
Valencias	Meats	1 lb.	3 cup meats (generous)
Salted	Meats	1 lb.	3½ cup meats (generous)
Butter	Glass jar	5 ozs.	⅓ cup meats (generous)

Nut	How Purchased	Weight	Measure by cups
BRAZIL NUTS	In shell	1 lb.	1½ cup meats (generous)
BUTTERNUTS	In shell	1 lb.	½ cup meats (generous)
CASHEW NUTS	Salted	1 lb.	4 cup meats (generous)
CHESTNUTS	In shell	1 lb.	2 cup meats (generous)
COCONUT			
Shredded	Bulk	1 lb.	6 cup meats (generous)
Shredded	Paper carton	¼ lb.	1⅓ cup meats (generous)
Shredded	Paper carton	½ lb.	2⅔ cup meats (generous)
Shredded	Tin can	4 ozs.	1½ cup meats (generous)
Shredded	Tin can	10 ozs.	3¾ cup meats (generous)
Whole	In shell	per nut	2 cup meats (chopped)
FILBERTS			
Shelled	Meats	1 lb.	3½ cup meats (chopped)
	In shell	1 lb.	2⅔ cup meats (chopped)
HICKORY	In shell	1 lb.	1 cup meats (chopped)
PEANUTS			
Jumbo	Salted	1 lb.	3 cup meats
Spanish	Salted	1 lb.	3⅓ cup meats
Roasted	In shell	1 lb.	2½ cup meats
Peanut butter	Glass jar	6½ ozs.	¾ cup meats
PECANS			
Paper shell	In shell	1 lb.	2 cup meats
Hard shell	In shell	1 lb.	1 cup meats
Meats	Meats	1 lb.	3½ cup meats
PINE NUTS	Meats	1 lb.	4 cup meats
PISTACHIOS	In shell	1 lb.	2 cup meats
WALNUTS (black)	In shell	1 lb.	⅔ cup meats
Shelled	Meats	1 lb.	4 cup meats
WALNUTS (English)			
Hard shell	In shell	1 lb.	1⅓ cup meats
Soft shell	In shell	1 lb.	1⅔ cup meats
Halves	Meats	1 lb.	4½ cup meats
Halves	Tin can	8 ozs.	2 cup meats
Broken pieces	Meats	1 lb.	3 cup meats

(26)   # MERINGUE TOPPING

The recipe depends upon the type of meringue to be used. If you wish it to tower to the skies and to be dry, 1 tablespoon sugar should be used to each well-beaten egg white. If you prefer a sweeter and more flavorful topping, you may use from 2 to 3 tablespoons of sugar for each egg white. In general, 2 tablespoons of fine granulated sugar per egg white give best results.

With a small amount of sugar, you will have a fluffy meringue, although it will not rise as high as when 2 tablespoons of sugar are used. With a larger amount (especially when made with ultrafine sugar), the result will be a frosting type of meringue which will keep soft and shiny and which is more delicious, although not so spectacular as the others.

There is one other point which must also be considered in making the perfect meringue of any type. The oven temperature must be low (325°–350° F.). Like other rules, this one has one exception. When you are making a baked Alaska—that combination of cake, ice cream, and meringue—you must use a hot oven (400°–425° F.), as the ice cream will not hold up during the longer time necessary for the browning.

When making a meringue for topping, use the correct proportion of sugar and egg whites. Beat egg whites to a foam; add sugar gradually. Beat constantly until the mixture is very smooth. Have egg whites at room temperature; they whip to a greater volume. Beat until they are stiff enough so that they stand up in points as the rotary beater is removed. Another test is to invert the bowl; the whites should not run out. Do not let them reach the "dry" stage, however. A little salt or ¼ teaspoon of cream of tartar per egg white may be added during the beating; this increases the tenderness of the egg white. Flavoring may be used if desired or directed in recipe.

If you use or need a large amount of meringue, place the egg whites in electric beater and beat in second speed with the wire beater. Beat to a medium dry stiffness, to the point where they start to pull away from the bowl sides; then, if making an uncooked meringue, add the required amount or weight of sugar, gradually, very slowly, while the machine is still beating the whites in second speed.

Remember, too little sugar to each egg white tends to give a less fluffy, less-tender meringue and one lacking in sweetness. Too much sugar tends to give a gummy crust or one containing sugar crystals, though the amount of sugar that can be used to obtain a desirable meringue depends on the fineness of the sugar and on its rate of solution. A temperature below 325° F. causes the meringue to shrink after being removed from the oven, and it dries out too much. Too high temperatures toughen the meringue.

Hot Syrup Meringue. Proceed as indicated for large amount of meringue, and substitute a syrup for sugar. This syrup should be hot and poured in very slowly, in just a heavy threadlike stream, while the machine is still beating the whites in second speed. This hot meringue increases the volume almost to double that of the cold method. Let the machine beat the mixture one minute or so after all the syrup has been added. This kind of boiled meringue is very appropriate for butterscotch, custard, sabayon and brandied fruit pies, as well as the chocolate pie class. You may flavor, according to direction, with the desired flavoring extract, just before the beaten egg whites are removed from the machine. If used on citrus pies, such as lime, lemon, grapefruit, or orange pies, the flavoring may be the juice of the fruit used in the pie.

This kind of meringue will appear somewhat softer than the plain sugar meringue, but it will become firm and dry after it is placed on the pies. Another advantage of this boiled meringue is that it is foolproof against leaking, cracking, or shrinking. Again, like other rules, this method has an exception. It should be baked in a hot oven or at 425°–450° F., as it will not keep fluffy long, and should be used at once. Spread the meringue immediately on the pies, being sure that it touches the rim of the crust on all sides. Do not have, unless desired, the meringue with a smooth, even surface but rather what has been described as "mountain and valley" effect; or you may force the meringue through a pastry bag; or a fork or spoon may be worked through the meringue to make an attractive but not fussy appearance.

(27) A FEW POINTERS AND HINTS ABOUT MERINGUE

If you wish really to set your meringue-topped pies in a very delicious way, follow the pointers and hints below:

(a) Two tablespoons sugar per egg white is the average proportion and twelve to fifteen minutes in a rather slow oven (325°–350° F.) allows penetration of heat to all parts of the meringue. For a firmer type, 4 tablespoons sugar per egg white is the rule and bake at 250° F. For a soft one use one tablespoon per white and bake 15 to 20 minutes at 300° F.

(b) A teaspoon of cold water added to the white of each egg will make it whip more easily, and increase the volume of the meringue.

(c) Meringue will always stand up high and perfect if a generous pinch of baking soda is added to beaten egg whites.

(d) Pie meringues become flat when too much sugar is used in them, if they are baked in too hot an oven, or they are not baked enough. A fourth of a teaspoon of cream of tartar mixed with each egg white helps to keep the meringue firm.

(e) Egg whites separate from the yolk easily when the egg is cold, but they whip better when at room temperature.

(f) Meringue should be added without removing pastry from the oven, unless directed to do so.

(g) General direction for one-crust pies which take a meringue or whipped cream topping: Instead of covering the entire filling, pipe a "collar" of the meringue or whipped cream around the outer edge. This leaves a bit of the filling exposed to view, and presents a most attractive appearance.

(h) Grated orange peel gives a delightful flavor to meringue.

(i) Grated apples often are used in meringues. Peel the apples whole, then press them onto a regular grater, turning the apple around in your hand until everything but the core has been grated.

(j) Try sprinkling shedded cocoanut (which may be tinted) over the meringue before browning in oven.

(k) Do you ever make berry pies with a meringue on top instead of a top crust? Blueberry pies, for example, done this way are worth a king's ransom— or almost.

(28)   WHIPPED CREAM TOPPINGS

A few pointers about whipped cream

(a) Very fresh cream is not good for whipping. Cream for whipping should be at least twelve hours old.

(b) It is best to whip no more cream than is necessary at a time. Chill bowl and beater, if using small amount. If the cream is beaten in a warm bowl in a warm place it is apt to turn to butter.

(c) For fluffiness you may combine equal parts of whipped cream and equal parts of stiffly beaten egg whites. It's economical, too.

(d) One quart (refers to unwhipped cream) when whipped will give 50 rounded tablespoons.

(e) Cream which is hard to whip will whip quickly by adding a few drops of lemon juice, and flavor is added too.

(f) Grated orange peel gives a delightful flavor to whipped cream.

(g) Try adding a teaspoon of strained honey to whipped cream to give it a delicious new flavor.

(h) Chopped nuts—walnuts or Brazil—added to whipped cream is something to try. Whipped cream is not *chewable*. Nuts are.

(i) Ever try flavoring whipped cream with cinnamon and sugar?

(j) Drop some black walnut flavoring into the whipped cream you are using for topping on your pies, especially chocolate pies, and see if it doesn't make the most delicious combination.

(k) For a sauce for deep dish apple pies, try whipped cream with brown sugar and flavored with nutmeg. It's great.

(1) Gingerbread split, filled with any of the above flavored whipped cream, fresh or sour, and sliced large berries, or bananas, with cream and fruit on top, is delicious.

(m) Whip sour cream; when thick and smooth, pour over a mound of sugar and surround open berry pies or tarts with it for a delicate flavor.

(29) SPECIAL WHIPPED CREAM FOR CHIFFON AND ONE-CRUST FRUIT PIES

NOTE: the use of dry, white pectin in whipped cream has the advantage of giving firmness, body, and consistency to the resulting product, especially when the whipped cream is used as a first layer in chiffon, berry or heavy fruit pies and tarts. A heavy cream (40 per cent) gives best results, and here is how to proceed:

Place 1 quart heavy cream in beating machine and beat until stiff. Meantime, sift together 3½ cups, or 1 lb. powdered sugar and ½ cup or 4 oz. powdered white pectin. To the whipped cream, add half of the sugar-pectin mixture, and continue beating 4 or 5 revolutions, or until mixture is well blended; then add remaining sugar-pectin mixture and again give 4 or 5 revolutions. (Topping for 5 pies.)

(30) HOW TO WHIP EVAPORATED MILK

Pour the indicated quantity of evaporated milk into top part of double boiler. Heat uncovered over boiling water until hot (scalding point—150° F.). Add to the hot milk, granulated gelatin *which has been soaked in cold water 5 minutes* (see table of proportion below). Stir until dissolved. Pour into chilled bowl and chill until ice cold (45° F.) before whipping, either in a bowl or beating machine. Whip until stiff with rotary egg beater if using a bowl, or in the beating machine (electric beater); then sweeten to taste as directed.

IMPORTANT: Do not remove the film of milk solids that forms on top of the hot milk. It will whip up like the rest of the milk. The bowl should be large, according to amount of milk to be whipped.

GELATIN PROPORTIONS FOR EVAPORATED MILK

MILK	GELATIN	WATER
½ cup	¼ teaspoon	1 teaspoon
¾ cup	½ teaspoon (scant)	1½ teaspoons
1 cup	½ teaspoon	2 teaspoons
1½ cups	¾ teaspoon	3 teaspoons

Another simple method for whipping evaporated milk is as follows:

Place one (or several) unopened can of evaporated milk in the freezing compartment of refrigerator for at least 1 hour. Empty into a well-chilled bowl (or electric beating machine) and whip in the usual way. This takes but a few minutes. Or, pour a can (or several) of evaporated milk into one of the ice trays of the electric refrigerator and set the control for quick freezing. When partly frozen (mushy), whip in the usual way.

There is yet another method similar to the one mentioned at the beginning of this section, but without the use of gelatin, which is as follows:

Pour the amount of evaporated milk called for into top part of double boiler and heat over boiling water to scalding point. Do not discard the film of milk solids that forms on top of the hot milk: stir it in; then chill the milk by placing it in a pan containing either cracked ice or very cold water. Chill in refrigerator and whip in the usual way. Or place the unopened can (or cans) of evaporated milk into a saucepan and cover with very cold water. Boil 5 long minutes, after boiling actually begins. Cool in running cold water and whip in the usual way.

The main point to remember in whipping evaporated milk is that the milk must be thoroughly chilled, either in refrigerator or with the can (or cans) placed in a large bowl and surrounded and covered with cracked ice.

(31)   PIES—PLAIN PASTRY (PIE CRUST)
CHARACTERISTICS OF GOOD PIE CRUST

In appearance, good pie crust is flaky, that is, its surface has a rough, blistered appearance, rather than a smooth, firm one. Moreover, it is tender enough to cut easily with a fork, but not so tender that it crumbles. It is a golden brown color around the edge, a somewhat lighter brown on the bottom; and, even though containing a filling, it is crisp on the bottom as well as along the edge.

(32)   MANIPULATION OF INGREDIENTS

The "secret" of making good, flaky pastry appears to be largely a matter of not overmixing the ingredients. If once the fat, flour, and liquid are all divided into tiny particles and these intimately mixed with one another, they tend to stay that way and give a smooth, solid, tough crust which is impervious to heat and browns unevenly, if at all.

(33)   FAT AND FLOUR ADDITIONS

Care in mixing the ingredients should begin with adding the fat to the flour. When a large proportion of fat is used, it is easy for the inexperienced person to keep on working the ever warming fat into the flour until the grains of the latter become so coated with grease that they will not take up enough water to make the pastry flaky. *The particles of fat should be coated with flour,* and that is accomplished if the combining process is not overdone. There is little danger of doing this, however, if one starts with cold fat, works quickly, and uses a pastry blender or knives rather than the fingers in mixing the fat with the flour.

⁽³⁴⁾ # WATER

The ticklish business of adding the water to the flour-fat mixture would be somewhat simpler if we could give an exact measure of water which could be counted on to give just the right degree of dampness for a given weight of fat and flour. This, however, we cannot do, for the amount varies with the temperature and the fineness of division of the ingredients and the rate of adding it. It is less for warm than for cold ingredients, less for finely divided particles than for coarse ones, and *more* when the water is added slowly rather than quickly.

Less water tends to give a crust which is crumbly rather than flaky, while any appreciable increase makes for toughness. We can stay within the desirable limits easily enough if we keep the ingredients cool and take time to add the water. Remember, the ingredient directly responsible for the tenderness of your pie crust is *the water*. Of course, the mixing of the flour-shortening is also important, but is secondary to the addition of the water.

If the room is cool and you work quickly, you take no special precaution regarding the temperature of the ingredients other than to keep the fat in the refrigerator until you are ready to use it, and to have the water ice-cold. If, however, the room is hot and damp, set the fat-flour mixture in the refrigerator to chill before adding the ice-cold water; if necessary, chill the dough before rolling it. In other words, keep the mixture so cool that the fat shows no tendency to melt.

In adding water, what you try to do is to give each fat-flour particle *just enough* water to dampen it to the point where it will stick to its neighbor. So to distribute the water evenly, sprinkling is almost obligatory. The water should be very cold—ice-cold. To determine when you have added enough water, press the dampened particles gently to see if they tend to stick together, by pushing the small lumps of dough, gathered together, to one side, as the water is sprinkled over the next layer, and so on.

Remember that a stirring motion will develop the gluten of the flour and make a tough pastry, while a cutting-in or chopping-in motion or as it is usually called in pastry terms, "lifting in" motion with a wooden utensil (fork or spoon), tends to produce a light and tender pastry. The less the shortening and flour are mixed, the more water the dough will take.

If the process has been successfully carried out thus far, you will now have a ball of dough which is easy to handle, being neither sticky because of too much water nor crumbly because of too little, and one which will yield tender, flaky pastry. If not, there is nothing to do. Remodeling a dough at this stage simply does not work. The extra cutting-in motion required is almost certain to give a tough, rubbery crust in place of the tender, flaky one.

Should you desire a crust which browns better, you may use part cold milk and part ice water.

In certain parts of the United States, as in Alabama for example, certain pastry makers use the so-called "Hot Water Pastry," which is made by distributing the fat in hot water, then beating the mixture until creamy. This is then added to the sifted flour with salt and sometimes baking powder. The mixture is then thoroughly chilled before using. The baking powder makes the pastry lighter, but careful handling of flour and shortening should be observed; then the product will be a light, flaky, excellent pastry.

(35)   ROLLING OF CRUST

There is a difference of opinion as to the best rolling surface; some bakers prefer smooth hardwood, some canvas, and others a marble slab. The latter is very satisfactory because it remains cold and is easily cleaned. A wooden or glass rolling pin is generally used, although a very clever restaurant manager has invented one of bakelite with gauges at either end to control the thickness of the crust. Some bakers use a cloth cover over rolling pin to prevent sticking.

The board or marble slab should be floured lightly. The dough should be pressed lightly into a disk, not into a ball. There should be no cracks in the edges. Do not knead or pat the dough. With a light, as light as possible, springy motion, roll from the center to the edge, then in the opposite direction, and lastly crisscross; every particle should be rolled evenly. If the dough begins to stick, that is, if it does not spread out from the center when rolled, loosen it with pastry scraper or spatula. Never turn pastry over during rolling process, as there is danger of rolling in too much flour, and the surface may not be smooth. The upper crust is rolled in the same way and may be folded, in order to lift it easily into the pan. Roll to ⅛ of an inch in thickness, for both under and upper crusts.

(36)   PLACING PASTRY ON PAN

After dough has been rolled to the desired thickness, that is ⅛ inch, fold one half over the other, forming a semi-circle. Lift carefully to pan; lay crease in center and unfold so that it covers the entire surface; have the bottom crust about 2 inches larger than the pie pan. If the crust has a tendency to break, it may be lifted on a rolling pin. *Do not grease pan!* Remember, "good pastry greases its own pan." With the right hand, press the pastry to the pan so that it fits like the proverbial paper on the wall. The left hand should lift the pastry to the pan to let out any air which will cause bulging of the crust. *Never stretch pastry;* take enough in the beginning to insure covering the entire pan. Then drop pastry-lined pan onto table to allow pastry to settle.

From now on the treatment of the crust will depend upon the type of pie in which it is to be used; each, therefore, will be described separately.

(37)   FOR A TWO-CRUST PIE

The dough for the bottom crust should be about 2 inches larger than the diameter of the top of the pan. After it has been placed on ungreased pan, as described above (No. 36) it should be trimmed 1 inch from edge by running a knife or scissors around the outer rim of pan. Do not trim too close, or pastry may not cover edge of pan when filling is put in, particularly if the pastry has been stretched or has not been fitted properly into the pan. Roll top crust in same way, allowing 1 inch more than diameter of pan rim. Put in filling. Add butter, if recipe calls for it. Fold one half over other, and with a sharp knife cut several slits in crust top to act as steam vents. Just before placing upper crust on pie, dampen edge of lower crust with pastry brush (using water or milk). Lay upper crust gently and carefully on pan so that it will completely cover pie when unfolded. Put it on loosely and do not stretch. Press edges firmly together and trim off surplus pastry. (A good pastry cook will have few trimmings left. If there are any, the left-over crust and trimmings may be used for pastry snacks. These scraps of pastry, if used in pies, should be worked into lower crusts). To finish the edges, press together with the tines of a fork or a pastry roller or trimmer; the most common method of crimping is by pressing the edge between the thumb and forefinger of left hand. Brush top with ice water, milk, cream, or beaten egg if desired. The temperature for baking will depend upon filling and will be discussed further.

(38)   FOR A ONE-CRUST PIE OR SHELL
(Baked separately)

Roll dough to ⅛ inch thickness and allow 3 inches more than the diameter of top of pan. Fit pastry snugly to pan, leaving no air underneath. Drop onto table to let pastry settle. The edge may be folded, fluted and rimmed in one operation, thus:

With the left hand fold the rim of the pastry at the outer edge of pan, using forefinger of right hand to make crinkly edge, as the forefinger of left hand presses down the edge of pan the surplus pastry breaks off. Prick pie shell with fork to remove air, which causes it to bulge when baking. If the surface puffs up it may be pricked again. If you prefer, a pan may be placed inside the shell during the first part of baking, then removed to brown surface. Shell may also be baked on an inverted pie pan, but must be pricked carefully before baking. For one-crust pie or shell, bake separately in a very hot oven (450° F.) 15–20 minutes.

(39)   FOR ONE-CRUST PIE
(Unbaked)

For one-crust pies when shell is not baked before filling is added, the problem is how to avoid a soggy undercrust. The rolling is the same as No. 35 and 38 above. Any one of these suggestions may help to keep filling from soaking: (1) let shell stand for at least 1 hour or overnight in refrigerator before filling is added; (2) brush surface with slightly beaten egg white and place in oven until egg sets; (3) brush a little flour over bottom of crust before filling is added.

The rim may be brushed with milk or cream before baking to insure a brown edge.

(40)   FOR CRISSCROSS PIES

Prepare the bottom crust of a two-crust pie. Roll pastry to ⅛ inch in thickness in a long strip; then cut into scant ½-inch strips. Put filling into crust and add butter, if directed in recipe. Brush rim with milk or water. Lay strips across parallel and one scant inch apart. Press ends of strips tightly to rim, brush strips with milk or water, then lay the same number of strips at right angles to first and same distance apart. Place a long strip of pastry around rim to cover ends and make a rim, which may be pressed with a fork or fluted. Brush with milk or water again and bake in hot oven (400°–450° F.) for 10 minutes; then finish baking according to time required for filling.

If you want a crisscross lattice-top pie a little different from the ordinary, simply start the strips of pastry in the center and carry them, French style, to the outer edge, twisting them slightly for a curled effect. Fasten the edges with four-leaf clovers cut with tiny cookie cutter; better to use puff paste. Any fruit pie can be easily decorated in this attractive manner.

(41)   PUFF PASTE

Puff Paste is not difficult to make but is more expensive than plain pastry. It also requires more care in handling. There are two kinds of paste: (1) the French Puff Paste, and (2) the Italian Puff Paste. The type known as Italian Puff Paste requires only time. The result, while not as sturdy or high rising as the traditional French Puff Paste, is beautifully flaky, tender, and well flavored. It is fine for pastry Napoleons, fancy baked dumplings, or the crust of any shortcake. For patty shells, regular French Puff Paste is usually preferable. For both types of pastry, bread flour gives better results. Both keep very well for a long time when wrapped in a damp cloth and placed in the refrigerator. Keep away from food with strong odors.

(42)   FRENCH PUFF PASTE TECHNIQUE

INGREDIENTS	AMOUNT OR WEIGHT	
Bread flour, sifted	3 qts.	3 lbs.
Shortening (preferably butter)	6 cups	3 lbs.
Salt	1 Tbsp.	½ oz.
Eggs, well beaten	2	3 oz. (about)
Ice Water	3 cups or thereabouts	

Sift flour and salt together three times. If butter is used, wash it in cold water until it is waxy; press into a cake and squeeze out all water. Work 3 oz. of this washed butter into flour. Combine well-beaten eggs with water and add to butter-flour mixture, making a stiff dough. Turn onto slightly floured board and knead vigorously for 10 minutes or until it is soft and pliable. Chill in refrigerator for 5 long minutes. Put on slightly floured board, roll, and pat to ¼ inch in thickness and a rectangular shape. Now divide the remaining butter into four equal parts and cut it into very thin slices.

Place 1 part of butter in center of rectangular pastry. Fold over the two ends; press edges together with rolling pin to enclose as much air as possible. Chill for 5 minutes. Repeat with other 3 parts of butter, folding and chilling 5 minutes each time. Be careful to use very little flour on board and handle as lightly as possible. When all the butter has been used, fold both ends of pastry to center, envelope-shape; fold again to make four layers. Cover paste with damp towel to prevent surface drying and shortening breaking through. Let stand in refrigerator overnight. Next day, remove from refrigerator, roll and fold twice, and chill before final rolling.

Cut into desired shapes, place them in a baking sheet lined with heavy, unglazed paper. Chill in refrigerator 15 minutes before putting in oven. Bake at 500° F. for 10 minutes, then reduce heat to 350° F. and continue baking for 5 or 10 minutes. The secret of French Puff Paste is having the dough very cold and the oven very hot. This delicate paste may be used for top crusts for pies, or for small individual tartlets, Napoleons, patty shells, etc.

(43)   # OVEN TEMPERATURE

Before science took a hand in things pertaining to baking, temperature was a matter of guesswork. Cooks and bakers depended upon their instincts—or thought they did—to tell them when their oven was just hot enough to turn out a well-baked cake or pie. Really they were depending upon long experience, the cost of which in time and wasted materials no modern cook or baker need pay.

Various kinds of cooking thermometers were evolved to supply this need. Today we have thermometers which standardize the measurement of heat for baking, deep-fat frying, roasting, even candy making. Each one lends to our cooking a certain assurance, and helps to make successful products—not just occasionally, but each and every time.

Of course, we are used to hearing that correct temperatures are important. But have you ever stopped to think just what happens to your cake or your pie if the oven heat soars far beyond the proper temperature? Tough texture, coarse grain, heaviness, cracks on top crust of cake, toughness, burned edges of pie crust, etc.—all these are some of the ills known to befall the products baked at too low or too high temperature. Consequently, knowing your oven temperature is the first principle for successful baking.

Practical oven temperature tests may be made which correspond to these thermometer ranges. Set a pan sprinkled with flour in the oven. If it becomes a delicate golden brown in 5 minutes, the oven is moderate (350° F. to 375° F.); if it turns a deep, dark brown in 5 minutes, the oven is hot (400° F. to 450° F.); if it turns a deep, dark brown in 3 minutes, the oven is very hot (475° F. to 550° F.). These same tests may also be done with white tissue paper or white, unglazed paper.

OVEN TEMPERATURE TESTS

For pie shells	450° F. for 15 minutes
For tart shells	450° F. for 10 to 15 minutes
For berry and fruit (canned or fresh) pies	450° F. for 10 to 15 minutes
and then	350° F. for 20 to 30 minutes
For custard, pumpkin, etc., uncooked mixture baked in uncooked pastry.	450°F. for 10 to 15 minutes
and then	350° F. for 20 to 25 minutes
For dried fruit	425 to 450° F. for 10 to 15 minutes
and then	350° F. for 25 to 30 minutes

In general, all pastry should be baked in a hot oven (450° F.) for 10 to 15 minutes; then the heat should be reduced to medium (350° F.) and baking finished according to indicated time for each. The weight of bottom dough for a 9-inch tin should be between 5½ and 6 oz. before baking, that of the top dough 5½ oz. before baking, making a total weight of dough for a double pie-crust between 11 and 12 oz.

Tart shells may be baked on inverted muffin tins.

Two or 3 minutes after you have started your gas or electric oven, open the door a second or two to let out the damp air. The oven will then heat in a much shorter time.

OVEN TEMPERATURE CHART

OVEN	
Slow	300°–325°F.
Moderate	350°–375°F.
Hot	400°–450°F.
Very Hot	475°–550°F.

(44) SUMMARY OF SOME IMPORTANT POINTS ON PASTRY, PIES, AND PIE FILLINGS

(a) In general, the secret of good pastry lies in the use of the right amount of weight and kind of flour and shortening, in not overmixing or overhandling the ingredients, in enclosing as much air as possible while mixing, and in using as little water as possible.

(b) *Tenderness* of pastry depends much upon the kind of flour, the amount of shortening and handling.

(c) *Flakiness* is determined largely by the method of combining these ingredients.

(d) *Turning Pastry.* Do not turn pastry. Lift from board, table, or cloth with a spatula if it sticks. Turning pastry works in too much flour and often makes a rough surface.

(e) *Shrinkage.* To allow for shrinkage in upper crust, leave upper crust 1 inch larger than the pan. Shape into rim with lower crust.

(f) *Air Bubbles.* To prevent air bubbles in a baked pastry shell, drop pastry-lined pan on table once or twice before trimming. Prick bottom and sides of crust with a fork before placing in oven to bake.

(g) *To glaze* pie crust, brush with milk, cream, or warm melted butter. This will add to the appearance and flavor. For browner glazing, brush with combined melted butter and egg. Always allow the glazing to dry before baking the pie.

(h) *Main Causes for Toughness in Pie:*
    (1) Too much water added to the dough when mixing. Too much moisture will shrink the dough, toughen it, and prevent browning.
    (2) Too little water causes cracking and splitting.
    (3) Too little fat in proportion of flour.
    (4) Too much flour used for dusting, when rolling out.

(i) *Rolling out.* Before you roll pie dough to fit into pie plate, chill dough thoroughly. Doing so makes it easier to handle. Then roll out just enough dough for one pie or two pies at a time. Work quickly, and roll from the center to the outside. Try to keep the shape as round as possible.

(j) *Sifting.* Salt, sugar (if any), flour and spices (if any) are usually sifted together before using.

(k) *Proportion.* Proportion of flour to shortening varies but is usually 3 or 4 to 1 by volume, or 2 to 1 by weight. Three quarts (3 lbs.) of sifted flour with 3 cups (1½ lbs.) shortening will give twelve shells or six two-crust 9-inch pies.

(1) *Pastry Flour.* Made from winter wheat and excellent for pies and pastries. Always use the same kind of flour when dusting the board or working table for pastry rolling.

(m) *Shortening.* When using half shortening and half butter in pastry, cut the chilled shortening into the flour with two knives or pastry blender, until the mixture looks like meal. Then add chilled butter and continue cutting or blending until the pieces of butter are about the size of a small pea.

For a flaky texture, shortening should be evenly distributed and the mixture kept light and airy, not matted down.

The shortening should never be too fine. When a recipe calls for melted shortening, measure after melting.

Since butter and margarine have milk and salt incorporated in them they have more flavor than the other shortenings mentioned. Therefore, they should be used when flavor is an important factor. Unless butter, margarine, or oil is specifically listed among the ingredients of the following recipes, the unflavored solid shortenings are very suitable for pies, cakes and cookies.

(n) *Water.* Always use ice water, preferably as little as possible, and handle lightly. If you do not add *just enough* ice water when mixing, your dough will tear and break when rolling out. This will also happen when dough is insufficiently mixed, or overmixed.

(o) *Cream Filling.* When making cream filling to use in pies, as in Boston Cream Pie, Cream Puffs, Eclairs, etc., do not leave the finished product to cool in the pan in which it has been cooked. Transfer it as soon as possible into a shallow, cold container. This method will prevent souring or separating, especially in summer.

Another good method of preventing souring or separating creams, custards, etc., used for filling, is to beat into recipe cream filling (when lukewarm) a meringue made of 2 egg whites stiffly beaten and sweetened with 3 Tbsps. of powdered sugar beaten into the whites until whites keep their shape (peaks). For one gallon of filling, use 2 cups of egg whites and ½ lb. powdered sugar. This method increases the lightness of the cream filling, helps to prevent souring and separating, and does not in the least affect the consistency or flavor of the filling, because the air cells which have been introduced into it disappear when mixture is cool.

It is not advisable to cool pie fillings by refrigeration, although after they are cold they can be kept in the refrigerator for a limited time. If kept too long in a refrigerator, they are apt to turn cloudy; moreover, the starch has a tendency to reset, resulting in a lumpy filling.

(p) *Fruit juice.* To prevent liquid from berry or any other juicy pies from running out in the oven, place three or four pieces of macaroni about 3 inches in length, upright in the slits cut in top of pie crust. This forms a funnel or outlet and allows the juice to bubble up in the macaroni but not run out.

(q) Another fool-proof method, one of my own creation, is as follows: The bottom crust is rolled, as usual, about 2 inches larger than the pie pan. When the pastry has been fitted into the pie pan and filled, the edges are turned back over the filling, taking a pleat here and there to make it fit. Then a small round piece of pastry is cut to fit the opening. The edges are pressed together with the tines of a fork and a little design is marked in the center. I call this "Tam O'Shanter Pie Crust." The advantages of this method are three fold: (1) it takes less pastry than the usual crimped edge, (2) eliminates juice running out into the oven, and (3) does away with the heavy pastry rim which so many people do not eat.

(r) To prevent fruit filling from soaking into bottom pie crust, dust the bottom crust with a little flour mixed with equal parts of granulated sugar, before pouring in the fruit. You may also brush bottom and sides of crust with unbeaten egg white.

(45)   # CHART OF INGREDIENT

PASTRY AND CRUST	Bread or Pastry Flour				Butter, Lard or Shortening				Salt				Fruit Juice Milk or Water				Granulated brown or Powdered sugar				Bread crumb		
	1 pie A	W	5 pies A	W	1 pie A	W	5 pies A	W	1 pie A	W	5 pies A	W	1 pie A	W	5 pies A	W	1 pie A	W	5 pies A	W	1 pie A	W	5 p A
Alabama Pie Crust (Hot water crust)	1-1/2 c	6 oz.	7-1/2 c	1-7/8 lb.	1/2 c	4 oz.	2-1/2 c	1-1/4 lb.	1/4 t	1/24 oz.	1-1/4 t	5/24 oz.	1/4 c	2 oz.	1-1/4 c	10 oz.							
Bread Crumb Crust					1/4 c	2 oz.	1-1/4 c	10 oz.	1/8 t		5/8 t						2 T	1 oz.	10 T	5 oz.	1 c	1-7/9 oz.	5 c
Cheese Pastry	2 c	1/2 lb.	2-1/2 qts.	2-1/2 lb.	1/2 c	4 oz.	2-1/2 c	2 oz.	1/2 t	1/12 oz.	2-1/2 t	5/12 oz.	6 T	3 oz.	1-7/8 c	15 oz.							
Gingerbread Pie Crust	1/2 c	2-1/8 oz.	2-1/2 c	10-5/8 oz.	2 T	1 oz.	10 T	5 oz.	1/8 t		5/8 t		1/4 c	2 oz.	1-1/4 c	10 oz.	2 T	1 oz.	10 T	5 oz.			
Gingersnap Pie Crust					1/3 c	2-2/3 oz.	1-2/3 c	13-1/3 oz.	1/8 t		5/8 t						1 T	1/2 oz.	5 T	2-1/2 oz.			
Graham Cracker Pie Crust	7/8 c	3-1/2 oz.	4-3/8 c	17-1/2 oz.	1/3 c	2-2/3 oz.	1-2/3 c	13-1/3 oz.	3/4 t	1/8 oz.	3-3/4 t	5/8 oz.	2 T	1 oz.	10 T	5 oz.							
Lemon Juice and Egg Pie Crust	3 c	12 oz.	15 c	3-3/4 lb.	1 c	1/2 lb.	2-1/2 c	1-1/4 lb.	1 t	1/6 oz.	5 t	5/6 oz.	6 T	3 oz.	1-7/8 c	15 oz.							
Long Flaky Pastry	2 c	1/2 lb.	2-1/2 qts.	2-1/2 lb.	1/2 c	4 oz.	2-1/2 c	1-1/4 lb.	1/2 t	1/12 oz.	2-1/2 t	5/12 oz.	6 T	3 oz.	1-7/8 c	15 oz.							
Mealy Pastry	2 c	1/2 lb.	2-1/2 qts.	2-1/2 lb.	1/2 c	4 oz.	2-1/2 c	1-1/4 lb.	3/4 t	1/8 oz.	3-3/4 t	5/8 oz.	5 T	2-1/2 oz.	1-5/8 c	12-1/2 oz.							
Nut Pastry																	3 T	1-1/2 oz.	15 T	7-1/2 oz.			
Pastry Mix			8 c	2 lb.			2-1/4 c	18 oz.			1 t	1/2 oz.							6 T	3 oz.			
Peanut Butter Pastry					1/4 c	2 oz.	1-1/4 c	10 oz.	1/3 t	1/18 oz.	1-2/3 t	5/18 oz.					3 T	1-1/2 oz.	15 T	7-1/2 oz.			
Potato Pastry	2 c	1/2 lb.	2-1/2 qts.	2-1/2 lb.	1/2 c	4 oz.	2-1/2 c	1-1/4 lb.	1 t	1/6 oz.	5 t	5/6 oz.											
Rice Pie Crust					1/3 c	2-2/3 oz.	1-2/3 c	13-1/3 oz.									2 T	8/9 oz.	10 T	4-4/9 oz.			
Rich Pie Crust	1 c	4 oz.	5 c	1-1/4 lb.	6-1/8 T	3-1/6 oz.	1-7/8 c	15-5/6 oz.	1/4 t	1/24 oz.	1-1/4 t	5/24 oz.	2 T	1 oz.	10 T	5 oz.							
Short Flaky Pastry	2 c	1/2 lb.	2-1/2 qts.	2-1/2 lb.	1/2 c	4 oz.	2-1/2 c	1-1/4 lb.	1/2 t	1/12 oz.	2-1/2 t	5/12 oz.	6 T	3 oz.	1-7/8 c	15 oz.							
Special Semi-Sweet Pie Crust	1-1/4 c	5 oz.	6-1/4 c	25 oz.	1/3 c	2-2/3 oz.	1-2/3 c	13-1/3 oz.	1/4 t	1/24 oz.	1-1/4 t	5/24 oz.	2-1/2 T	1-1/4 oz.	12-1/2 T	6-1/4 oz.							
Special Short Paste Crust			8 c	2 lb.			2 c	1 lb.			1 T	1/2 oz.							2-1/2 c	1 lb.			
Special Spicy Pastry	2 c	1/2 lb.	2-1/2 qts.	2-1/2 lb.	1/2 c	4 oz.	2-1/2 c	1-1/4 lb.	1/2 t	1/12 oz.	2-1/2 t	5/12 oz.	6 T	3 oz.	1-7/8 c	15 oz.							
Western Pie Crust	3 c	3/4 lb.	3-3/4 qts.	3-3/4 lb.	1 c	8 oz.	5 c	2-1/2 lb.	3/4 t	1/8 oz.	3-3/4 t	5/8 oz.	1/4 c	2 oz.	1-1/4 c	10 oz.							
Winter Wheat Crunchy Semi-Puff Paste Flaky Pie Crust	1 c	4 oz.	5 c	1-1/4 lb.	5 T	2-1/2 oz.	1-1/2 c	12-1/2 oz.	3/4 t	1/8 oz.	3-3/4 t	5/8 oz.	1-1/2 T	3/4 oz.	7-1/2 T	3-3/4 oz.							
Zwieback Pie Crust																	2 T	1 oz.	10 T	5 oz.			

SYMBOLS:—(t) teaspoon; (T) tablespoon; (c) cup; (oz.) ounces, (qt.) quart; (pkg.) package; (eg.) egg. (y) egg yolk, (lb.) pound.

OR PIE CRUSTS

	Cheese				Nutmeg / Cinnamon / Ginger				Gingersnap / Graham cracker / Zwieback				Egg				Nut or peanut butter				Baking powder / Baking soda / Powdered milk				Mashed potatoes or Rice				Corn syrup / Molasses or egg yolk			
	1 pie		5 pies		1 pie		5 pies		1 pie		5 pies		1 pie		5 pies		1 pie		5 pies		1 pie		5 pies		1 pie		5 pies		1 pie		5 pies	
	A	W	A	W	A	W	A	W	A	W	A	W	A	W	A	W	A	W	A	W	A	W	A	W	A	W	A	W	A	W	A	W
		3-1/5 oz.	5 c	1 lb.																												
					1/2 t	1/24 oz.	2-1/2 t	5/24 oz.					1 eg.	2 oz.	5 eg.	10 oz.					1/4 t	1/32 oz.	1-1/4 t	5/32 oz.					2 T	1-1/2 oz.	10 T	7-1/2 oz.
									1-1/2 c	12 oz.	7-1/2 c	3-3/4 lb.																				
									1/3 c	2-2/3 oz.	1-2/3 c	13-1/3 oz.	1 eg.	2 oz.	5 eg.	10 oz.																
																	1-1/2 c	3/4 lb.	7-1/2 c	3-3/4 lb.												
									1 c	8 oz.	5 c	2-1/2 lb.					1/4 c	2 oz.	1-1/4 c	10 oz.									2 T	1-1/2 oz.	10 T	7-1/2 oz.
																					2 t	16/51 oz.	10 t	1-29/51 oz.	1 c	5 oz.	5 c	25 oz.				
																									2-1/2 c	5 oz.	7-1/2 c	25 oz.				
																					1/16 t		5/16 t									
																					1-1/4 t	1/8 oz.	6-1/4 t	5/8 oz.					1 t	1/4 oz.	5 t	1-1/4 oz.
													6 eg.	12 oz.																		
					2 t	1/6 oz.	10 t	5/6 oz.																								
					1/4 t	1/48 oz.	1-1/4 t	5/48 oz.																								
																													2 y	2 oz.	10 y	10 oz.
									1/2 pkg.	6 oz.	2-1/2 pkg.	1-7/8 lb.																				

(46)

TABLE OF EQUIVALENTS O

	INGREDIENT	Am't. (tsp.)	Weight (oz.)	Amount (tbsp.)	Weight (oz.)	Am't. (1/4 cup)	Weigh (oz.)
1	Apple (whole, fresh, medium)						
2	Apple (fresh, sliced or cubed)	1	1/6	1	1/2	1/4	
3	Applesauce	1	1/6	1	1/2	1/4	
4	Apricots (dried, uncooked)			1	1/3	1/4	1-1
5	Apricots (dried, cooked)			1	2/9	1/4	8/
6	Baking powder	1	8/51	1	24/51	1/4	1-15
7	Baking soda	1	1/8	1	3/8	1/4	1-1/
8	Banana (whole, unpeeled)						
9	Banana (peeled, sliced, or cubed)					1/4	1-1/
10	Blackberries (fresh)			1	1/6	1/4	2/
11	Blueberries (fresh)			1	2/7	1/4	1-1/
12	Bread crumbs (day old, crumbed)			1	1/9	1/4	4/
13	Bread (day old, broken)			1	1/9	1/4	4/
14	Bread (toasted, sieved)	1	1/2	1	1/4	1/4	
15	Butter	1	1/6	1	1/2	1/4	
16	Cake (crumbs)					1/4	3/
17	Cheese (American, grated)			1	1/5	1/4	4/
18	Cheese (baker's pot cheese)					1/4	1-3/
19	Cheese (cream)	1	1/6	1	1/2	1/4	
20	Chocolate (grated)	1	1/9	1	1/3	1/4	1-1/
21	Chocolate (melted)	1	1/6	1	1/2	1/4	
22	Cocoa	1	1/12	1	1/4	1/4	
23	Coconut (shredded)			1	1/5	1/4	4/
24	Coffee (medium ground)					1/4	6/
25	Cornmeal (when cooked)			1	1/3	1/4	1-1/
26	Cornstarch	1	1/9	1	1/3	1/4	1-1/
27	Crackers (graham, meal)					1/4	7/
28	Cranberries (fresh)			1	1/5	1/4	4/
29	Cream (heavy)					1/4	2-3/3
30	Cream of tartar	1	1/3	1	3/8	1/4	1-1/
31	Currants (dried)	1	1/12	1	1/4	1/4	
32	Dates (dried)			1	2/5	1/4	1-3/
33	Egg (one, whole, medium)			3	1 egg unbeaten		
34	Eggs (4-6, whole, medium)					1/4	
35	Egg (white, one, medium)						
36	Egg (whites, 8-10, medium)			1	1/2	1/4	
37	Egg (yolk, one, medium)			1	1		
38	Egg (yolks, 12-16, medium)					1/4	
39	Extracts (flavorings)	1	1/6	1	1/2	1/4	
40	Figs (dried)			1	1/3	1/4	1-1/3

MATERIAL USED IN BAKING

Amount (1/2 cup)	Weight (oz.)	Amount (3/4 cup)	Weight (oz.)	Amount (1 cup)	Weight (oz.)	Number of cups per lb.
						3 apples
1/2	4	3/4	6	1	8	2
1/2	4	3/4	6	1	8	2
1/2	2-2/3	3/4	4	1	5-1/3	3
1/2	1-7/9	3/4	2-2/3	1	3-5/9	4-1/2
1/2	3-13/17	3/4	5-11/17	1	7-9/17	2-1/8
1/2	3	3/4	4-1/2	1	6	2-2/3
						3 bananas
1/2	2-1/4	3/4	3-3/8	1	4-1/2	3-5/9
1/2	1-1/3	3/4	2	1	2-2/3	6
1/2	2-2/7	3/4	3-3/7	1	4-4/7	3-1/2
1/2	8/9	3/4	1-1/3	1	1-7/9	9
1/2	8/9	3/4	1-1/3	1	1-7/9	9
1/2	2	3/4	3	1	4	4
1/2	4	3/4	6	1	8	2
1/2	1-1/2	3/4	2-1/4	1	3	5-1/3
1/2	1-3/5	3/4	2-2/5	1	3-1/5	5
1/2	3-1/2	3/4	5-1/4	1	7	2-2/7
1/2	4	3/4	6	1	8	2
1/2	1-2/3	3/4	4	1	5-1/3	3
1/2	4	3/4	6	1	8	2
1/2	2	3/4	3	1	4	4
1/2	1-3/5	3/4	2-2/5	1	3-1/5	5
1/2	1-5/7	3/4	2-4/7	1	3-3/7	4-2/3
1/2	2-2/3	3/4	4	1	5-1/3	3
1/2	2-2/3	3/4	4	1	5-1/3	3
1/2	1-3/4	3/4	1-5/8	1	3-1/2	4-4/7
1/2	1-3/5	3/4	2-2/5	1	3-1/5	5
1/2	4-3/16	3/4	6	1	8-3/8	1-61/67
1/2	3	3/4	4-1/2	1	6	2-2/3
1/2	2	3/4	3	1	4	4
1/2	3-1/5	3/4	4-4/5	1	6-2/5	2-1/2
						2 oz. per egg
1/2	4	3/4	6	1	8	2
						1 oz. per egg white
1/2	4	3/4	6	1	8	2
						1 oz. per egg yolk
1/2	4	3/4	6	1	8	2
1/2	4	3/4	6	1	8	2
1/2	2-2/3	3/4	4	1	5-1/3	3

(46) Continued

TABLE OF EQUIVALENTS O

INGREDIENT	Am't. Weight (tsp.)	(oz.)	Amount (tbsp.)	Weight (oz.)	Am't. Weigh (1/4 cup)	(oz.)
41 Flour (bread, unsifted)					1/4	1-3/1(
42 Flour (bread, sifted)					1/4	1-1/1(
43 Flour (cake, unsifted)					1/4	1-1/1(
44 Flour (cake, sifted)	1	1/12	1	1/4	1/4	1
45 Flour (graham, unsifted)			1	2/7	1/4	1-1/7
46 Flour (pastry, unsifted)					1/4	1-1/16
47 Flour (pastry, sifted)	1	1/12	1	1/4	1/4	1
48 Flour (rye, unsifted)					1/4	1-1/31
49 Gelatin (granulated)	1	1/12	1	1/4	1/4	1
50 Hominy (raw)	1	1/8	1	3/8	1/4	1-1/2
51 Honey (liquid)	1	1/4	1	3/4	1/4	3
52 Lemon (grating)	1	1/8	1	3/8	1/4	1-1/2
53 Lemon (juice)	1	1/6	1	1/2	1/4	2
54 Marshmallows					3-1/4 pieces	
55 Milk (evaporated) (can 14-1/2 ozs. net)					1/4 can	3-5/
56 Milk (fresh)	1	1/6	1	1/2	1/4	2
57 Milk (malted)					1/4	1-3/16
58 Milk (powdered)					1/4	1-3/16
59 Molasses	1	1/4	1	3/4	1/4	3
60 Oats (rolled)					1/4	16/19
61 Oatmeal	1	1/8	1	3/8	1/4	1-1/2
62 Oil			1	8/17	1/4	1-15/17
63 Oranges (whole, medium)						
64 Orange (grating)	1	1/8	1	3/8	1/4	1-1/2
65 Orange (juice)	1	1/6	1	1/2	1/4	2
66 Peach (dried)			1	1/3	1/4	1-1/3
67 Peach (fresh)			1	1/5	1/4	4/5
68 Pears (fresh)			1	1/5	1/4	4/5
69 Prune (dried, whole, uncooked)			1	2/5	1/4	1-3/5
70 Prune (dried, whole, cooked)			1	2/9	1/4	8/9
71 Pumpkin					1/4	3-1/4
72 Raisins (seeded)			1	2/5	1/4	1-3/5
73 Raisins (seedless)	1	1/9	1	1/3	1/4	1-1/3
74 Raspberries (fresh)			1	2/7	1/4	1-1/7
75 Salt	1	1/6	1	1/2	1/4	2
76 Shortening (lard)	1	1/6	1	1/2	1/4	2
77 Shortening (hydrogenated)					1/4	1-3/4
78 Shortening (margarine)	1	1/8	1	3/8	1/4	1-1/2
79 Spices (miscellaneous)	1	1/12	1	1/4	1/4	1
80 Stabilizer	1	1/8	1	3/8	1/4	1-1/2
81 Strawberries (fresh)			1	2/7	1/4	1-1/7
82 Suet (chopped)			1	2/9	1/4	8/9
83 Sugar (brown)	1	1/9	1	1/3	1/4	1-1/3
84 Sugar (granulated)			1	8/17	1/4	1-15/17
85 Sugar (powdered)	1	2/21	1	2/7	1/4	1-1/7
86 Syrup (corn)	1	1/4	1	3/4	1/4	3
87 Syrup (maple)	1	1/4	1	3/4	1/4	3
88 Water	1	1/6	1	1/2	1/4	2

MATERIAL USED IN BAKING

Amount (1/2 cup)	Weight (oz.)	Amount (3/4 cup)	Weight (oz.)	Amount (1 cup)	Weight (oz.)	Number of cups per lb.
1/2	2-3/8	3/4	3-9/16	1	4-3/4	3-7/19
1/2	2-1/8	3/4	3-3/16	1	4-1/4	3-13/17
1/2	2-1/8	3/4	3-3/16	1	4-1/4	3-13/17
1/2	2	3/4	3	1	4	4
1/2	2-2/7	3/4	3-3/7	1	4-4/7	3-1/2
1/2	2-1/8	3/4	3-3/16	1	4-1/4	3-13/17
1/2	2	3/4	3	1	4	4
1/2	2-2/31	3/4	3-3/31	1	4-4/31	3-7/8
1/2	2	3/4	3	1	4	4
1/2	3	3/4	4-1/2	1	6	2-2/3
1/2	6	3/4	9	1	12	1-1/3
1/2	3	3/4	4-1/2	1	6	2-2/3
1/2	4	3/4	6	1	8	2
7-1/2 pieces	2	15 pieces	4	30 pieces	8	60 pieces per lb.
1/2 can	7-1/4	3/4 can	10-7/8	1 can	14-1/2	1-2/3 per can
1/2	4	3/4	6	1	8	2
1/2	2-3/8	3/4	3-9/16	1	4-3/4	3-7/19
1/2	2-3/8	3/4	3-9/16	1	4-3/4	3-7/19
1/2	6	3/4	9	1	12	1-1/3
1/2	1-13/19	3/4	2-10/19	1	3-7/19	4-3/4
1/2	3	3/4	4-1/2	1	6	2-2/3
1/2	3-13/17	3/4	5-11/17	1	7-9/17	2-1/8
						2 oranges per lb.
1/2	3	3/4	4-1/2	1	6	2-2/3
1/2	4	3/4	6	1	8	2
1/2	2-2/3	3/4	4	1	5-1/3	3
1/2	1-3/5	3/4	2-2/5	1	3-1/5	5
1/2	1-3/5	3/4	2-2/5	1	3-1/5	5
1/2	3-1/5	3/4	2-4/5	1	6-2/5	2-1/2
1/2	1-7/9	3/4	2-2/3	1	3-5/9	4-1/2
1/2	6-1/2	3/4	9-3/4	1	13	1-3/13
1/2	3-1/5	3/4	4-4/5	1	6-2/5	2-1/2
1/2	2-2/3	3/4	4	1	5-1/3	3
1/2	2-2/7	3/4	3-3/7	1	4-4/7	3-1/2
1/2	4	3/4	6	1	8	2
1/2	4	3/4	6	1	8	2
1/2	3-1/2	3/4	5-1/4	1	7	2-2/7
1/2	3	3/4	4-1/2	1	6	2-2/3
1/2	2	3/4	3	1	4	4
1/2	3	3/4	4-1/2	1	6	2-2/3
1/2	2-2/7	3/4	3-3/7	1	4-4/7	3-1/2
1/2	1-7/9	3/4	2-2/3	1	3-5/9	4-1/2
1/2	2-2/3	3/4	4	1	5-1/3	3
1/2	3-13/17	3/4	5-11/17	1	7-9/17	2-1/8
1/2	2-2/7	3/4	3-3/7	1	4-4/7	3-1/2
1/2	6	3/4	9	1	12	1-1/3
1/2	6	3/4	9	1	12	1-1/3
1/2	4	3/4	6	1	8	2

PASTRY AND CRUST RECIPES

(47)
SHORT FLAKY PASTRY
STANDARD PIE CRUST RECIPE

Flour based on sifted pastry flour.

For one 9-inch pie
- Shortening: ½ cup
- Flour: 2 cups
- Salt: ½ tsp.
- Water: 6 Tbsp. (more or less)

For five 9-inch pies
- Shortening: 2½ cups or 1 lb. 4 oz.
- Flour: 2½ qt. or 2½ lbs.
- Salt: 2½ tsps. or 5/12 oz.
- Water: 1⅞ cups or 15 oz. (more or less)

Mix half the shortening with all the sifted flour and salt until no flour spots are evident, or until mix is thoroughly blended. The mix should be cream-colored. Add remainder of shortening and mix to the "pebbly" stage as in first method. The mixing at this point will not toughen the dough, provided that the first mix (half shortening and all the flour) has been thoroughly incorporated. Add water as indicated for No. 34. Chill thoroughly before rolling out ⅛-inch thick.

....

(48)
LONG FLAKY PASTRY
STANDARD PIE CRUST RECIPE

Flour based on sifted pastry flour.

NOTE: This method, which is very popular, requires that the fat and all other ingredients be thoroughly chilled before blending. The cutting in of the fat should be done rapidly, but lightly, being sure that the fat is evenly divided, the mix resembling peas in size. There is a knack to this method of mixing when using the hands—it should be done very quickly, because the heat of the hands may melt the fat. Of course, pastry blenders, chopping knives, and similar utensils may be used. But the hand work seems to be the best method. The fat particles are rubbed through the hands so that the fat is flattened between layers of flour, rather than squeezed together. More air is incorporated in this way. Of course, you should not try to make too large a batch; but 5 pies may be thus mixed. The trick is to work quickly, but not to over-mix. The water should be added very rapidly, lest the dough toughen.

For one 9-inch pie
- Flour: 2 cups
- Salt: ½ tsp.
- Shortening: ½ cup
- Water: 6 Tbsps. (more or less)

For five 9-inch pies
- Flour: 2½ qts. or 2½ lbs.
- Salt: 2½ tsps. or $5/12$ oz.
- Shortening: 2½ cups or 1 lb. 4 oz.
- Water: $1^7/8$ cups or 15 oz. (more or less)

Sift flour and salt, and cut in the chilled shortening, quickly but lightly. Rapidly add water; chill before rolling out to ⅛-inch thickness.

....

(49)   # MEALY PASTRY
STANDARD PIE CRUST RECIPE
Flour based on sifted pastry flour.

NOTE: Mealy pastry results when the shortening is soft so that it is partly dissolved in the mixing. The water used should be the least possible. When oils or semi-liquid fats are used, the pastry is of this type. However, it is possible to obtain the same result by blending a hard or plastic fat, such as lard or vegetable shortening, with flour, using the entire amount of shortening with half the required amount of flour, then blending until mixture is like coarse meal (corn meal or similar); add remainder of flour and as little water as possible. Chill before rolling lightly.

Of course, there are many variations of pie pastry, which will be found in later recipes.

For one 9-inch pie
- Shortening: ½ cup
- Flour: 2 cups
- Salt: ¾ scant tsp.
- Water: 5 Tbsps. (more or less)

For five 9-inch pies
- Shortening: 2½ cups or 1 lb. 4 oz.
- Flour: 2½ qts. or 2½ lbs.
- Salt: 3¾ tsps. or $5/8$ oz.
- Water: $1^5/8$ cups or 13 oz. (more or less)

Allow the shortening to get soft, but not liquid. Cut in with half the amount of sifted flour and salt, cutting in a little longer than for Short or Long Pastry (No. 47 and No. 48, respectively); then blend until mixture is like coarse meal; add remainder of flour-salt mixture, and as little water as possible. Chill well before rolling out lightly to ⅛-inch thickness.

(50)

ALABAMA PASTRY
HOT WATER PASTRY

Flour based on sifted pastry flour.

For one 9-inch pie
- Hot water: ¼ cup
- Vegetable shortening: ½ cup
- Flour: 1½ cups or 6 oz.
- Salt: ¼ tsp. or 1/24 oz.

For five 9-inch pies
- Hot water: 1¼ cups or 10 oz.
- Vegetable shortening: 2½ cups or 1 lb. 4 oz.
- Flour: 7½ cups or 1⅞ lbs.
- Salt: 1¼ tsps. or ⁵⁄₂₄ oz.

Pour boiling water over shortening (you may use shortening made from cotton seeds, if desired), which should be very firm. Stir well until melted; add gradually the flour and salt sifted together, stirring vigorously after each addition. Mix well and handle as little as possible. Chill thoroughly and roll out ¹⁄₈-inch thick.

....

(51)

BREAD CRUMB CRUST
ONE-CRUST PIE

Bread crumbs based on fine, dry crumbs.

For one 9-inch pie
- Fine, dry bread crumbs: 1 cup
- Butter (softened): ¼ cup
- Salt: ¹⁄₈ tsp.
- Sugar (granulated): 2 Tbsp.

For five 9-inch pies
- Fine, dry bread crumbs: 5 cups or 8⁸⁄₉ oz.
- Butter, softened: 1¼ cups or 10 oz.
- Salt: ⁵⁄₈ tsp.
- Sugar (granulated): 10 Tbsp. or 5 oz.

Mix crumbs with softened butter, salt, and sugar and pat firmly against the sides and bottom of a generously buttered (no other shortening should be used) pie pan. Rolled corn flakes, rice flakes, or similar cereal may be substituted for crumbs if desired. Bake in hot oven (425° F.) for 10 minutes. Cool before filling.

(52)
CHEESE PASTRY
TWO-CRUST PIE
Flour based on sifted pastry flour.

For one 9-inch pie
- Flour: 2 cups
- Salt: ½ tsp.
- Shortening: ½ cup
- Grated American cheese: 1 cup
- Water: 5 to 6 Tbsp. (more or less)

For five 9-inch pies
- Flour: 2½ qts. or 2½ lbs.
- Salt: 2½ tsp. or ⁵/₁₂ oz.
- Shortening: 2½ cups or 1 lb. 4 oz.
- Grated American cheese: 5 cups or 1 lb.
- Water: 1⅞ cups (more or less)

Sift flour and salt together. Cut in shortening until size of small peas; blend in grated cheese gently with a fork. Add just enough water to hold mixture together. Roll out ⅛-inch thick on lightly floured board. Brush bottom crust with melted shortening, egg white, etc., to prevent soaking.

(53)
CINNAMON BREAD CRUMB CRUST
Bread crumbs based on fine, dry crumbs.

Double the amount of ingredients for Bread Crumb Crust No. 51, adding 1 generous teaspoon of ground cinnamon to the crumbs when mixing with other ingredients.

Graham cracker crumbs, corn flakes, rice flakes, or similar cereal may be substituted for dry, fine bread crumbs, if desired.

You may also substitute ground Brazil nuts, pecans, walnuts, or almonds for crumbs, omitting butter and using 3 tablespoons sugar. The nuts are rich and more successfully used in individual pies or tartlets. Another combination consists of ¼ ground nut meats and ¾ rolled crumbs, crackers or breakfast cereal crumbs, which give a less rich crust.

(54)

GINGERSNAP PIE CRUST

Appropriate for gelatin and chiffon pies, (pre-baked)

For one 9-inch pie
- Gingersnap cracker (rolled): 1½ cups
- Butter (softened): ⅓ cup
- Sugar: 1 Tbsp.
- Salt: ¹⁄₁₆ tsp.

For five 9-inch pies
- Gingersnap cracker (rolled): 7½ cups or 2 lbs. 5½ oz.
- Butter (softened): 1⅔ cups or 13⅓ oz.
- Sugar: 5 Tbsp. or 2½ oz.
- Salt: ⁵⁄₁₆ tsp.

Crumble and roll gingersnaps very fine; mix with remaining ingredients. Line bottom and sides of a 9-inch pie pan (generously buttered) with the mixture, pressing firmly in an even layer. Bake 10 minutes in a hot oven (425° F.). Cool before pouring in filling.

....

(55)

GRAHAM CRACKER PIE CRUST

Appropriate for lemon, orange, and almost any kind of cream pies.
May be unbaked or pre-baked, according to use.

For one 9-inch pie
- All-purpose flour (sifted): ⅞ cup
- Salt: ¾ tsp.
- Shortening: ⅓ cup
- Water: 2 Tbsps. (more or less)
- Graham cracker crumbs: ⅓ cup

For five 9-inch pies
- Flour (sifted): 4⅜ cups or 1 lb. 1½ oz.
- Salt: 3¾ tsp. or ⅝ oz.
- Shortening: 1⅔ cups or 13⅓ oz.
- Water: 10 Tbsps. or ½ cup plus 2 Tbsps. or 5 oz.
- Graham cracker crumbs: 1⅔ cups or 8⅓ oz.

Combine flour and salt and sift twice. Cut in shortening, mixing well; then gradually add water, using sprinkling method, while mixing thoroughly until mixture is smooth. Let this stand in refrigerator overnight to set and mellow. Next day, sprinkle a heavy coating of rolled, sieved graham crackers on an unfloured pastry board and roll pastry out to ⅛-inch. The finely sieved crackers should be only on the bottom side of the dough. Arrange pastry, crumb side down, on pie pan. Crimp, fold or flute, and trim according to directions given for No. 39, One-Crust Pie, and allow the shell or shells to set for one hour before pouring in the filling. Bake 20 minutes in a hot oven (425° F.).

(56) # LEMON JUICE & EGG PIE CRUST
TWO-CRUST PIE

Flour based on sifted pastry flour.

For one 9-inch pie
- Flour: 3 cups
- Salt: 1 tsp.
- Butter or margarine: 1 cup
- Egg (slightly beaten): 1
- Lemon juice: 3 Tbsps.
- Ice water: 3 Tbsps. (more or less)

For five 9-inch pies
- Flour: 3¾ qts. or 3¾ lbs.
- Salt: 5 tsps. or ⅚ oz.
- Butter or margarine: 5 cups or 2½ lbs.
- Eggs (slightly beaten): 5
- Lemon juice: 15 Tbsps. or 7½ oz.
- Ice water: 15 Tbsps. or 7½ oz.

Mix and sift flour and salt. Work in butter or margarine; add slightly beaten egg mixed with lemon juice. Add just enough water to hold dough together. Roll out to ⅛-inch thickness and place in pie pan. Fill with desired filling, and bake 25 minutes in a hot oven (375° F.).

....

(57) # NUT PASTRY
UNBAKED SHELL

Appropriate for chiffon pie or pies with fruit filling.

For one 9-inch pie
- Ground nut meats (any kind): 1½ cups
- Sugar: 3 Tbsps.

For five 9-inch pies
- Ground nut meats (any kind): 7½ cups or 1 lb. 14 oz.
- Sugar: 1 cup less 1 Tbsp. or 7½ oz.

Mix the nut meats with the sugar in pie pan. Press this mixture with the palm of the hand against sides and bottom of the pie pan and add filling. Chill well before serving.

You may, if desired, add a little cream cheese to the mixture before pressing against pie pan.

(58)

OATMEAL PASTRY MIX
BAKED SHELL OR SHELLS

Appropriate for chiffon pie or fruit, or cream pies. Flour based on sifted pastry flour.

For one 9-inch pie
- Oatmeal (uncooked): 1½ cups
- Flour: 1 cup
- Salt: ¾ tsp.
- Shortening: ⅔ cup
- Ice water: 5 to 6 Tbsps.

For five 9-inch pies
- Oatmeal (uncooked): 7½ cups or 1 lb. 5¼ oz.
- Flour: 5 cups or 1¼ lbs.
- Salt: 3¾ tsp. or ⅝ oz.
- Shortening: 3⅓ cups or 1 lb. 10⅔ oz.
- Water: 1⅞ cups or 15 oz.

Put oatmeal through food chopper, then through a fine sieve. Combine sifted flour and salt with oatmeal. Cut in shortening as for No. 47, Short Flaky Pastry, and sprinkle over enough ice water to hold dough together. Roll out to ⅛-inch in thickness. Arrange on pie pan; put in the filling and bake 10 to 15 minutes in a hot oven (425° F.), reducing heat to suit filling until filling is cooked. Cool thoroughly before serving. Or bake shell and add filling.

NOTE: You may proceed as indicated for No. 55, Graham Cracker Pie Crust, if a quicker bake is desired, and use the shell for custard or pumpkin or pie or pies.

....

(59)

PASTRY MIX

NOTE: For unforeseen occasions and to have on hand as a foundation for pastry. It needs only to have the proper amount of water or fruit juice added, when ready to mix a pie, or pies, tarts, and the like.

- Flour: 8 cups or 2 lbs.
- Salt: 1 Tbsp. or ½ oz.
- Shortening: 2¼ cups, or 1⅛ lbs.

- Water: about 5 to 6 Tbsps. or 3 oz. (more or less)

Mix and sift flour and salt. Cut in shortening with pastry blender, a little at a time, until mixture resembles corn meal in consistency. Store in refrigerator until wanted.

For pastry shells, use only 1¼ cups of this Pastry Mix; for a twocrust pie or pies, use 2½ cups. Add the necessary water or, still better, strained fruit juice to the mix; roll; arrange on pie pan and bake, or fill and bake, according to the requirements. This will make a reserve of pie crust for 10 shells or 5 two-crust pies, or 20 individual pies or 55 to 58 tart shells.

Store in covered container in refrigerator. This will keep several weeks.

....

(60) # PEANUT BUTTER GRAHAM CRACKER PIE CRUST
BAKED SHELL OR SHELLS

Appropriate for lemon, banana, chocolate, chiffon or any kind of cream pie or pies.

NOTE: You may proceed either as indicated for No. 55, Graham Cracker Pie Crust, or as follows (corn syrup is substituted for water):

For one 9-inch pie
- Graham cracker crumbs: 1 cup
- Sugar: 3 Tbsps.
- Salt: ⅓ tsp.
- Peanut butter: ¼ cup
- Butter or margarine: ¼ cup
- Corn syrup: 2 Tbsps.

For five 9-inch pies
- Graham cracker crumbs: 5 cups, or 1 lb. 9 oz.
- Sugar: 15 Tbsps. or 7½ oz.
- Salt: 1⅔ tsps. or ⁵⁄₁₈ oz.
- Peanut butter: 1¼ cups or 12½ oz.
- Butter or margarine: 1¼ cups or 10 oz.
- Corn syrup: ⅝ cup, or 7½ oz.

Roll graham crackers; then force through sieve and mix with sugar and salt in mixing bowl. Cut in blended peanut butter and butter or margarine with pastry blender (do not use hands) until thoroughly blended and mixture resembles corn meal. Add corn syrup and mix well. Press firmly to ⅛-inch thickness over bottom and sides of pie pan. Bake 20 minutes in moderate oven (350° F.). Cool before adding filling.

(61)

POTATO PASTRY
TOP CRUST FOR MEAT PIES

Flour based on sifted pastry flour.

For one 9-inch pie
- Flour: 2 cups
- Salt: 1 tsp.
- Baking powder: 2 tsps.
- Shortening: ½ cup
- Mashed potatoes: 1 cup
- Cold milk: Enough to make a soft dough

For five 9-inch pies
- Flour: 2½ qts. or 2½ lbs.
- Salt: 5 tsps. or ⅚ oz.
- Baking powder: 3⅓ Tbsps. or scant 1⅔ oz.
- Shortening: 2½ cups or 1¼ lbs.
- Mashed potatoes: 5 cups or 2½ lbs.
- Cold milk: Enough to make a soft dough

Mix and sift flour, salt, and baking powder. Work in shortening with tips of fingers. Add cold, smooth mashed potatoes alternately with enough cold milk to make a soft dough. Turn out on floured board; pat and roll to fit the top of a 9-inch meat pie dish (or individual ones, if desired) that has been filled with the meat mixture. Place on pie; make several incisions with a sharp knife in top and bake 10 to 15 minutes, or until golden brown, in a moderately hot oven (375° F.–400° F.).

---

(62)

SPECIAL SHORT PASTE CRUST FOR TARTS AND TORTES
PRE-BAKED SHELLS—FOR 60 TART SHELLS

Flour based on sifted pastry flour.

- Flour: 8 cups or 2 lbs.
- Salt: 1 Tbsp. or ½ oz.
- Sugar (powdered): 2½ cups or 1 lb.
- Butter or margarine: 2 cups or 1 lb.
- Eggs (whole) 6 or about 10 oz. (slightly beaten)

Sift flour, salt and powdered sugar twice; cut in butter or margarine; blend well; then add the slightly beaten whole eggs, all at once, and mix thoroughly. Turn dough on to lightly floured board, and toss and roll out into a thin sheet (⅛-inch in thickness). Fit closely into individual tart tins, or place over inverted tart tins; crimp or flute edges (No. 38, For A One-Crust Pie). Place on a baking sheet and bake 18–20 minutes in a hot oven (400° F.). Chill well before filling.

(63) SPECIAL SEMI-SWEET PIE CRUST FOR PUMPKIN OR SQUASH PIE OR CUSTARD PIES

Flour based on sifted pastry flour.

For one 9-inch pie
- Flour: 1¼ cups
- Salt: ¼ tsp.
- Powdered skimmed milk: 1¼ tsp.
- Corn syrup: 1 tsp.
- Water: 2½ Tbsps.
- Shortening: ⅓ cup

For five 9-inch pies
- Flour: 6¼ cups or 1 lb. 9 oz.
- Salt: 1¼ tsps. or about ¼ oz.
- Powdered skimmed milk: 6¼ tsps. or ⅝ oz.
- Corn syrup: 5 tsps. or 1¼ oz.
- Water: ¾ cup plus 2 tsps. or 6¼ oz.
- Shortening: 1⅔ cups or 13⅓ oz.

Sift pastry flour and salt twice. Combine powdered skimmed milk, corn syrup, and water; stir until dissolved and thoroughly blended. Cut in shortening, then quickly rub between the hands until it is as fine as corn meal. Sprinkle water mixture over the dough and mix well. Toss upon lightly floured board and roll out to ⅛-inch in thickness. Do not chill. Fit a 9-inch pie pan with the dough and mix well. Toss upon lightly floured board and roll out up to the brim and bake 25 minutes in a hot oven (450° F.). Chill before serving.

....

(64) SPECIAL SPICED PASTRY FOR EITHER PIES OR TURNOVERS

Proceed as indicated for either No. 47, Short Flaky Pastry; No. 48, Long Flaky Pastry; or No. 49, Mealy Pastry, adding the following ingredients to flour before sifting with salt:

For one 9-inch pie
- Cinnamon: 1 tsp.
- Nutmeg: 1 tsp.

For five 9-inch pies
- Cinnamon: 5 tsps. or ⁵/₁₂ oz.
- Nutmeg: 5 tsps. or ⁵/₁₂ oz.

and proceed as indicated for cutting in shortening and adding water.

(65)   ## VANILLA WAFER PIE CRUST

Appropriate for chiffon, fruit filling and cream filling pies. For one 9-inch pie

Roll enough vanilla (or chocolate) wafers to make ¾ to 1 cup of crumbs. Cut enough vanilla (or chocolate) wafers in halves to stand around edge of a 9-inch pie pan. Cover bottom of pie pan with crumbs and fill in spaces between halved wafers. Pour in filling as usual. Chill thoroughly before serving.

....

(66) ## WINTER WHEAT CRUNCHY SEMI-PUFF PASTE FLAKY PIE CRUST
ONE-CRUST PIE SHELL

Appropriate for chiffon, fruit, gelatin and cream pies.
Flours based on equal parts of sifted bread and pastry flour.

For one 9-inch pie
- Flour (soft winter wheat): ½ cup
- Flour (bread flour): ½ cup
- Salt: ¾ tsp.
- Lard: 2½ Tbsp.
- Hydrogenated shortening: 2½ Tbsps.
- Lemon juice: 1½ Tbsps.

For five 9-inch pies
- Flour (soft winter wheat): 2½ cups or 10 oz.
- Flour (bread flour): 2½ cups or 10 oz.
- Salt: 3¾ tsps. or ⅝ oz.
- Lard: generous ¾ cup or 6¼ oz.
- Hydrogenated shortening: generous ¾ cup or 6¼ oz.
- Lemon juice: scant ½ cup or 3¾ oz.

Sift both flours with salt twice; combine both shortenings, blending thoroughly, and place in refrigerator overnight. Next day, cut chilled shortening mixture into flour mixture, until dough lumps the size of an olive, or thereabouts, sprinkling while mixing with well-chilled lemon juice. Blend well without breaking the lumps. Roll out to a generous ¼-inch in thickness, upon lightly floured board, shaping into rectangular form. Now, fold this dough into three layers, bringing both ends to the middle. Chill for 40 minutes and repeat the rolling and folding motion three times, chilling after each rolling and folding; the last time, chill 1½ hours. Then the dough is ready to be rolled out in the usual way, about ⅛-inch in thickness. Place on ungreased pie pan, crimp or flute as indicated for No. 38, For A One-Crust Pie, trimming at the same time. Prick bottom with the tines of a fork; bake in a hot oven (425° F.) for 20 minutes. Fill when thoroughly cooled.

(67)
ZWIEBACK PIE CRUST
BAKED SHELL

For cooked fillings and chiffon pies. For uncooked filling, do not bake. The result will be a caramel-flavored crust. Based on dry, packaged, rolled, then sieved, zwieback.

For one 9-inch pie
- Zwieback: ½ package
- Sugar: 2 Tbsps.
- Butter (melted): ¼ cup

For five 9-inch pies
- Zwieback: 2½ packages or 15 oz.
- Sugar: ⅝ cup or 5 oz.
- Butter (melted): 1¼ cups or 10 oz.

Roll zwieback and force through sieve. Combine with sugar, mixing thoroughly. Melt butter until well browned, but not burned, and stir in (off the heat) the zwieback-sugar mixture. Press over bottom and sides of pie pan firmly and bake 10 minutes in a slow oven (325° F.). Cool before filling.

(68)
GINGERBREAD PIE CRUST
BAKED SHELL

Appropriate for gelatin or chiffon pies. Flour based on sifted bread flour.

For one 9-inch pie
- Egg (small): 1
- Sugar: 2 Tbsps.
- Bread flour: ½ cup
- Salt: ⅛ tsp.
- Ginger: ½ tsp.
- Molasses: 2 Tbsps.
- Soda: ¼ tsp.
- Hot water: ¼ cup
- Shortening (melted): 2 Tbsps.

For five 9-inch pies
- Eggs: 5 eggs or 7½ oz.
- Sugar: ⅝ cup or 5 oz.
- Bread flour: 2½ cups or 10 oz.
- Salt: ⅝ tsp.
- Ginger: 2½ tsp. or scant ¼ oz.
- Molasses: ⅝ cup or 7½ oz.
- Soda: 1¼ tsp.
- Hot water: 1¼ cups or 10 oz.
- Shortening (melted): ⅝ cup or 6 oz.

Beat a small egg until light; gradually add sugar, continuing beating until mixture is lemon-colored. Combine bread flour, salt and ginger and sift twice. Add half of flour mixture to egg mixture and beat until smooth. To this, add ⅔ of the molasses, alternately with remaining flour mixture, and blend thoroughly. To the remaining molasses, add the baking soda and stir until foamy, adding, while beating, the hot (not boiling) water and mix well. Lastly add the melted shortening. Add the flour mixture and blend. Arrange one circle of heavy paper, generously greased, in bottom of a 9-inch pie pan, the paper circle being ½-inch larger than the pie pan, and spread gingerbread mixture evenly to fit the circle to a depth of ¼-inch in thickness. Bake 5 minutes in a hot oven (400° F.). Cool before filling.

....

(69)   # WESTERN PIE CRUST

Appropriate for almost any kind of two-crust pie. Flour based on sifted pastry flour.

For one 9-inch pie
- Flour: 3 cups
- Salt: ¾ tsp.
- Ginger: ¼ tsp.
- Sugar (very fine): ¼ cup
- Butter or margarine: 1 cup
- Egg yolks, beaten: 2
- Pineapple juice (strained): ¼ cup

For five 9-inch pies
- Flour: 3 qts. and 3 cups or 3¾ lbs.
- Salt: 3¾ tsps. or ⅝ oz.
- Ginger: 1¼ tsps. or scant ⅛ oz.
- Sugar: 1¼ cups or 10 oz.
- Butter or margarine: 5 cups or 2½ lbs.
- Egg yolks (beaten): 10 or ¾ cup (about)
- Pineapple juice: 1¼ cups or 10 oz.

Mix flour, salt, ginger and very fine granulated or powdered sugar and sift twice. Blend butter carefully, forming mixture like corn meal. Then blend in the well-beaten egg yolks alternately with strained pineapple juice. Roll out to ⅛-inch in thickness upon lightly floured board; fit pastry into pie pan; add filling; adjust top crust and make several holes in the center with a fork; brush all over with diluted egg yolk and milk and bake in a 375°–400° F. oven for 40 to 45 minutes. Dust with powdered sugar when serving.

(70)

RICH PIE CRUST
ONE-CRUST PIE

Appropriate for almost any kind of one-crust pie—chiffon, cream,
fruit and gelatin fillings. Flour based on sifted pastry flour.

For one 9-inch pie
- Flour: 1 cup
- Salt: ¼ tsp.
- Baking powder: $1/16$ tsp.
- Lard: $1/3$ cup (generous)
- Water: just enough to moisten
- Butter: 1 Tbsp.

For five 9-inch pies
- Flour: 5 cups or 1¼ lbs.
- Salt: 1¼ tsps. or scant ¼ oz.
- Baking powder: ½ scant tsp. or $1/16$ oz.
- Lard: $1\,2/3$ cups or $13\,1/3$ oz.
- Water: just enough to moisten
- Butter: 5 Tbsps. or 2½ oz.

Mix and sift dry ingredients; cut in lard until mixture resembles corn meal; add just enough ice water (use fruit juice, if desired) to moisten. Roll out on lightly floured board to $1/8$-inch thickness; cover with butter cut in small pieces. Fold dough over butter and roll out. Repeat the rolling three times, chilling 15 to 20 minutes after each rolling. Last time, place on pie pan; crimp or flute, if desired, and perforate with a fork. Bake 10 minutes at 450°F. Cool before adding filling.

....

(71)

RICE PIE CRUST—CREOLE STYLE
ONE-CRUST PIE

Appropriate for custard, uncooked fillings such as cream fillings and the like.
Also for gelatin and chiffon pies (for these pies the crust should not be baked).

For one 9-inch pie
- Cold boiled rice: 2½ cups
- Butter or margarine (melted): $1/3$ cup
- Brown sugar: 2 Tbsps.

For five 9-inch pies
- Cold boiled rice: 7½ cups or 14 oz. (about)
- Butter or margarine (melted): $1\,2/3$ cups or $13\,1/3$ oz.
- Brown sugar: $5/8$ (generous) cup or $3\,1/3$ oz

Force rice through a sieve, add melted butter or margarine, alternately with brown sugar. Mix well and place evenly in a generously buttered pie pan. (You may add a few grains of nutmeg, if desired.)

PIE
RECIPES

(72) A FEW FACTS ABOUT APPLES FOR PIES

Fresh, canned, or dried apples may be used in pie-making, as well as apple sauce, either freshly made or canned. If fresh fruit is used, only certain apples are suitable for pie-making. A tart, juicy apple makes the best pie.

The amount of sugar will vary according to the kind of apple used: from ¼ cup to 1¼ cups per quart of peeled, cored apples. They should be peeled, sliced thin rapidly and put into the pie; or dropped immediately into salted water with lemon juice added until ready to use, to prevent discoloration. Don't keep too long, lest they become soggy.

Remember that size has very little to do with apple quality, and definite savings are to be added by buying apples in quantity. Compare the price of a bushel of apples which weighs about 48 pounds with what you would have to pay if you purchased the fruit pound by pound. Do the same for a box of apples, which weighs about 44 pounds, or a barrel, which holds 140 pounds of apples.

Apples with mealy or brown flesh mean wastage. Of course, you can't always tell from the outside of the apple whether it is brown, but those that feel soft or bruised should be rejected. As the apple season moves into the winter months, this defect becomes more common on account of faulty storage. Apples that have been frozen or bruised soon turn brown, become watersoaked, and their skins take on a leathery look. Although a mild freeze may not injure the apple's eating quality, it will damage its keeping quality.

Store in a cool place with good circulation of air. Choose a dark spot away from exposure to sunlight. The cooler the storage room, or space, the better, so long as it doesn't get below 32° F.

And it is worth remembering that a good deal of the mineral content of fruits (and vegetables also) lies near the skin. Consequently, do not discard apple peelings and corings, but cook them in as little water as possible, over slow heat; then when soft, taste, and add whatever amount of sugar is necessary. Force through a sieve, cool and serve with meat, such as pork, or with any kind of smoked meat. The color will not be like sauce made from the fresh pulp—it will be a little reddish—but the full flavor of the apple will be there.

IMPORTANT: The wide variation in flavor and texture of canned apples demands careful sampling before buying in quantity. Canned fruit which has remained in the can over the season has a tendency not only to lose its lustre and color, but its flavor as well.

Here are a few hints and pointers for apple pie:

(a) When apple pie is two-thirds baked, sprinkle grated cheese over the top. Return to the oven and continue baking. This adds much to the flavor of the pie.

(b) An apple pie with a foreign flavor is the same dear dessert as ever—e.g. a little orange marmalade and chopped crystallized ginger added.

(c) The flavor of an apple pie is greatly improved if the juice of half a lemon, or an equal amount of pineapple juice, is sprinkled over the apples after they have been placed on the lower crust.

(d) Try marinating apple slices in a mixture of lemon and orange and a very little lime juice, slightly sweetened with honey. Drain well before putting on the lower crust.

---

(73)

APPLE PIE I
TWO-CRUST PIE

For one 9-inch pie
- Flour: 1½ Tbsp.
- Salt. A few grains
- Cinnamon: ⅛ tsp.
- Nutmeg: ⅛ tsp.
- Sugar (granulated): ⅘ cup
- Apples (fresh, sliced thin): 1 qt.
- Butter: 1 Tbsp., melted
- Pastry: For 1 two-crust pie

For five 9-inch pies
- Flour: 6 Tbsp. or 1½ oz.
- Salt: 1 tsp. or ½ oz.
- Cinnamon: ½ tsp. or ¹/₁₂ oz.
- Nutmeg: 1 tsp. or ¹/₁₂ oz.
- Sugar (granulated): 4 cups or 2 lbs.
- Apples (fresh, sliced thin): 5 qts. or 15 lbs.
- Butter: 5 Tbsps. or 2½ oz., melted
- Pastry: For 5 two-crust pies

Mix flour, salt, cinnamon, and nutmeg, and sift once. Combine with sugar. Put apple slices into a pastry-lined pie pan; arrange the apples in packed ring around the rim, then pile others loosely in center; be careful to have center higher than edge. Sprinkle sifted dry ingredients over the apples and sprinkle melted butter over. Wet edge of crust with water; adjust top crust and perforate with a fork; brush with milk or cream and bake 10 minutes in a very hot oven (450°F.); reduce to 350°F., and continue baking 40 minutes longer, or until crust is done and apples are tender. Serve warm or cold, with cheese, a la mode or with whipped cream.

(74)
APPLE PIE II
TWO-CRUST PIE

For one 9-inch pie
- Apples: 1 #2 can
- Sugar (granulated): ⅗ cup
- Cinnamon: ⅛ tsp.
- Nutmeg: ⅛ tsp.
- Salt: ¼ tsp.
- Tapioca: 1⅕ tsp., reground
- Butter (melted): 1⅕ tsp., melted
- Pastry: For 1 two-crust pie

For five 9-inch pies
- Apples: 1 #10 can, sliced, or 5 lb. 15 oz.
- Sugar (granulated): 3 cups or 1½ lbs.
- Cinnamon: ½ scant tsp.
- Nutmeg: ½ tsp.
- Salt: 1¼ tsp. or 5/24 oz.
- Tapioca: 2 Tbsps. or 1 oz., reground
- Butter (melted): 2 Tbsps. or 1 oz.
- Pastry: For five two-crust pies

Combine all the ingredients, except pie crust and butter, and mix thoroughly. Let stand for 1 hour to allow the reground tapioca (the size of fine granulated sugar) to expand. Then fill pastry-lined pie pan as for No. 73, Apple Pie I (using fresh, thinly sliced apples); sprinkle melted butter over apple mixture, wet edge of crust with water; adjust top crust, fluting if desired; perforate top crust with a fork; brush with milk or cream and bake 10 minutes in a very hot oven (450° F.); reduce to 350° F., and continue baking 40 minutes longer, or until crust is done and apples are tender. Serve warm or cold, with cheese, a la mode or with whipped cream.

···

(75)
APPLE PIE III —DUTCH METHOD
ONE-CRUST PIE

For one 9-inch pie
- Pastry: For 1 one-crust pie
- Flour: 1 Tbsp.
- Sugar: 1 cup
- Apples: 5 medium-sized, or about 1¼ lbs.
- Butter: 2 teaspoons
- Nutmeg: ¼ tsp.
- Salt: A few grains

For five 9-inch pies
- Pastry: For 5 one-crust pies
- Flour: 5 Tbsps. or 1¼ oz.
- Sugar: 5 cups or 2½ lbs.
- Apples: 3 qts. or 6½ lbs.
- Butter: 3⅓ Tbsps. or 1⅔ oz..
- Nutmeg: 1¼ tsps.
- Salt: ½ tsp. or 1/12 oz.

Line a deep dish with pastry. Sprinkle with flour and ¼ cup of sugar. Peel and quarter apples, removing cores, and place in the shell, cut side down. Cover with remaining sugar; dot with butter and sprinkle with nutmeg; add salt. Bake in moderate oven (350° F.) for 35–40 minutes, or until apples are baked and a rich syrup has formed. Serve warm or cold.

In certain parts of the country, they serve this delicious apple pie cold, topped with whipped cream.

---

(76)   ## APPLE PIE IV—FRENCH METHOD
CRISSCROSS PIE

For one 9-inch pie
- Apples: 4 medium-sized or 1 lb.
- Raisins (seedless): ¾ cup
- Cherries (red sour, pitted): ¾ cup
- Sugar: ¾ cup
- Lemon juice: 1 tsp.
- Cinnamon: ⅛ tsp.
- Salt: A few grains
- Pastry: For 1 crisscross pie
- Streusel, No. 475: As required

For five 9-inch pies
- Apples: 20 medium-sized or 5 lbs.
- Raisins (seedless): 3¾ cups or 1 lb. 4 oz.
- Cherries (red sour, pitted): 3¾ cups or 1 lb. 4 oz.
- Sugar: 3¾ cups or 1 lb. 14 oz.
- Lemon juice: 5 tsps. or ⅚ oz.
- Cinnamon: ⅝ tsp.
- Salt: 1 tsp. or ⅙ oz.
- Pastry: For 5 crisscross pies
- Streusel, No. 475: As required

Pare, core, and quarter apples; put in enough cold water to barely cover; add ½ cup sugar, then cook over low heat until apples are soft but not mushy (rather underdone). Remove from the heat and cool. Cook raisins with enough water to barely cover and put in the remaining sugar (see No. 24, Dried Fruit Preparation). The water should be completely evaporated, or else drain whatever remains; add lemon juice, cinnamon, and salt, stir well to blend, and allow to cool. Do not cook cherries. You may use either fresh, frozen, or canned cherries, but they should be thoroughly drained, lest they discolor the apples. Line a pie pan with pastry rolled ⅛-inch thick; add the filling, cover with pastry strips as For Crisscross Pies (No. 40) and fill open spaces with Streusel (No. 475). Bake 35 minutes in a hot oven (425° F.). Serve cold without any accessories.

You may omit the crisscross and cover the entire surface of the open pie with Streusel, if desired.

(77)   APPLE PIE V—SOUTHERN METHOD
ONE-CRUST PIE

For one 9-inch pie
- Pastry: For 1 one-crust pie
- Apples: 4 large ones, or 1½ lbs.
- Sugar: ¾ cup
- Salt: ¼ tsp.
- Cinnamon: ½ tsp.
- Butter (melted): 2 Tbsps.
- Coconut (shredded): 1 cup

For five 9-inch pies
- Pastry: For 5 one-crust pies
- Apples: 3¾ qts. or 7½ lbs.
- Sugar: 3¾ cups or 1 lb. 14 oz.
- Salt: ¼ tsps.
- Cinnamon: 2½ tsps. or scant ¼ oz.
- Butter (melted): ⅝ cup or 10 oz.
- Coconut (shredded): 5 cups or 1 lb.

Line a 9-inch pie pan with pastry, rolled ⅛-inch thick, allowing pastry to extend 1 inch beyond edge. Fold edge back to form standing rim; flute with fingers. Fill pie shell with apples thinly sliced. Cover with mixture of sugar, salt, and cinnamon; sprinkle with melted butter. Bake in hot oven (450° F.) for 15 minutes; then decrease heat to 375° F., and bake 25 minutes longer. Quickly top with coconut and continue baking 5 or 6 minutes longer, or until coconut is delicately browned. Serve cold.

....

(78)   APPLE PIE VI—MIDDLE WEST METHOD
TWO-CRUST PIE

For one 9-inch pie
- Pastry: For 1 two-crust pie
- Apples: 5 large or 1¾ lbs.
- Sugar (granulated): ¼ cup
- Sugar (brown): ½ cup
- Cinnamon: ½ tsp.
- Lemon peel (grated): 1 tsp.
- Salt: ⅛ tsp.
- Nutmeg: ¼ tsp.
- Butter: 1 Tbsp.

For five 9-inch pies
- Pastry: For 5 two-crust pies
- Apples: 4⅜ qts. or 8¾ lbs.
- Sugar (granulated): 1¼ cups or 10 oz.
- Sugar (brown): 2½ cups or 1 lb. 2 oz.
- Cinnamon: 2½ tsps. or ¼ oz.
- Lemon peel (grated): 1⅔ Tbsps. or ⅝ oz.
- Salt: ⅝ tsp.
- Nutmeg: 1¼ tsps. or about ⅛ oz.
- Butter: ⅓ cup or 2½ oz.

Line a 9-inch pie pan with pastry, rolled ⅛-inch thick. Moisten edges with cold water, and fill with apples, thinly sliced. Sprinkle with mixture of sugars, cinnamon, lemon peel, salt, and nutmeg and dot with bits of butter. Adjust top crust and slit to allow escape of steam. Brush pastry top with milk. Bake 15 minutes in hot oven (450° F.); decrease heat to 375° F., and continue baking for 25–30 minutes. Serve warm with cheese.

....

(79)   # APPLE BUTTERSCOTCH PIE I
TWO-CRUST PIE

For one 9-inch pie
- Sugar (brown): 1 cup
- Cream (heavy): ⅓ cup
- Corn syrup: 3 Tbsps.
- Lemon (grated rind): ½ tsp.
- Lemon juice: 1 tsp.
- Apples (sliced thin): 4½ cups
- Pastry: For 1 two-crust pie
- Flour: 2 Tbsps.
- Salt: ⅛ tsp.

For five 9-inch pies
- Sugar (brown): 5 cups or 1 lb. 10⅔ oz.
- Cream (heavy): 1⅔ cups or 13¾ oz.
- Corn syrup: 1 scant cup or 11¼ oz.
- Lemon (grated rind): 2½ tsps. or ⁵⁄₁₆ oz.
- Lemon juice: 1⅔ Tbsps. or ⅚ oz.
- Apples (sliced thin): 5⅝ qts. or 11¼ lbs.
- Pastry: For 5 two-crust pies
- Flour: ⅝ cup or 2½ oz.
- Salt: ¾ to 1 tsp. or ⅛ to ⅙ oz.

Combine sugar, cream, syrup, and lemon rind. Place in top of double boiler and cook over boiling water for 30 minutes, stirring frequently. Remove from heat and add lemon juice. Blend well. Put layer of apples in unbaked pie shell and sprinkle with mixed flour and salt. Pour ⅓ of the cream sauce mixture over apples. Repeat once, reserving ⅓ sauce. Cover with top crust, sealing edges together; slit to allow escape of steam; make a small slash in center, and bake in a hot oven (425° F.) for 40–45 minutes. Remove from oven and immediately pour remaining cream sauce mixture, heated, through slash in center of pie. Serve warm or cold.

(80)
APPLE BUTTERSCOTCH PIE II– HOME METHOD
ONE-CRUST LATTICE PIE

For one 9-inch pie
- Sugar (brown): 1½ cups
- Water: ⅔ cup
- Lemon juice: 1 Tbsp.
- Apples (sliced): 3 cups
- Flour (sifted): 3 Tbsps.
- Sugar (granulated): ¼ cup
- Vanilla: 1 tsp.
- Cinnamon: 1 tsp.
- Salt: ¾ tsp.
- Butter: 3 Tbsps. or 1½ oz.
- Pastry: For 1 one-crust pie and latticing

For five 9-inch pies
- Sugar (brown): 7½ cups or 3 lb. 5⅓ oz.
- Water: 3⅓ cups or 1 lb. 10⅔ oz.
- Lemon juice: 5 Tbsps. or 2½ oz.
- Apples (sliced): 3¾ qts. or 7½ lbs.
- Flour: scant cup or 3¾ oz. (sifted)
- Sugar (granulated): 1¼ cups or 10 oz. or ⅝ lb.
- Vanilla: 5 tsps. or ⅚ oz.
- Cinnamon: 5 tsps. or 5/12 oz.
- Salt: 3¾ tsps. or ⅝ oz.
- Butter: 1 scant cup or 7½ oz.
- Pastry: For five one-crust pies and latticing

Mix the brown sugar and water in a heavy saucepan; add the lemon juice and apples. Cover and cook until the apples are tender. Remove the apples and add the mixed flour, sugar (granulated) to the syrup; cook, stirring until blended, or about 3 minutes. Add vanilla, cinnamon, salt, butter and cooked apples. Blend well. Cool. Line a 9-inch pie pan with pastry rolled ⅛-inch thick; fill with the apple mixture; arrange pastry strips, lattice fashion, over the top. Place in a hot oven (450° F.) and bake for 10 minutes; reduce heat to moderate (350° F.) and continue baking 35 minutes longer. Serve cold.

(81) APPLE COBBLESTONE PIE
ONE-CRUST PIE

For one 9-inch pie
- Apples: 4 large or 1½ lbs.
- Pastry: For 1 one-crust pie
- Butter: 1½ Tbsps.
- Sugar (granulated): 1 cup
- Salt: ¼ tsp.
- Nutmeg: ¼ tsp.
- Cinnamon: ½ tsp.

For five 9-inch pies
- Apples (large): 20 or 7½ lbs.
- Pastry: For 5 one-crust pies
- Butter: 7½ Tbsps. or scant ½ cup or 3¾ oz.
- Sugar (granulated): 5 cups or 2½ lbs.
- Salt: 1¼ tsps. or $^5/_{24}$ oz.
- Nutmeg: 1¼ tsps. or $^5/_{48}$ oz.
- Cinnamon: 1¼ tsps. or $^5/_{48}$ oz.

Wash, pare and cut apples in quarters; remove the cores. Line a 9-inch pie plate with your favorite pastry rolled ⅛-inch thick; pinch with fingers to make a fancy edge, and arrange the apple quarters into it to represent cobblestones. Dot apple quarters with butter, then sprinkle over the combined sugar, salt and spices, being sure to cover the entire surface of apple quarters. Bake 10 minutes in a hot oven (450° F.); reduce heat to 350° F., and continue baking 20 minutes longer, or until apples are tender. Serve cold.

(82) APPLESAUCE CRUNCHY ANGEL FOOD PIE
ONE-CRUST PIE

For one 9-inch pie
- Egg whites (stiffly beaten): 4
- Salt: ¼ tsp.
- Sugar (powdered): ¾ cup
- Ginger (ground): ⅛ tsp.
- Applesauce (canned): 1 cup
- Heavy cream: 1 cup
- Salt: ⅛ tsp.
- Vanilla extract: ½ tsp.
- Nut meats (ground): 1 cup

For five 9-inch pies
- Egg whites (stiffly beaten): 20 or 1¼ lb.
- Salt: ¼ tsps. or $^5/_{24}$ oz.
- Sugar (powdered): 3¾ cups or 1½ lbs.
- Ginger (ground): ⅝ tsp.
- Applesauce (canned): 5 cups
- Heavy cream: 1¾ qts. or 5 cups
- Salt: ⅝ tsp.
- Vanilla extract: 2½ tsps. or $^5/_{12}$ oz.
- Nut meats (ground): 5 cups or 2½ lbs.

Beat egg whites until almost stiff. Gradually add salt mixed with ½ of the powdered sugar, and continue beating, adding the ground ginger, until smooth and egg whites hold their peaks. Line a 9-inch pie pan, shaping into form of the pan, and bake 25 to 35 minutes in a slow oven (300° F.), or until slightly browned. Remove from the oven and cool. Just before serving, spread applesauce in bottom of meringue shell as evenly as possible; top with whipped cream to which remaining powdered sugar, salt, vanilla and nut meats (any kind) have been added. Sprinkle top of cream with a little ground nuts.

These shells, unfilled, will keep a long time in a cool, dry place.

NOTE: There are many variations in these rich pies, such as substituting apricot puree, or pineapple, or peach, etc. for applesauce. Berries may be substitutes for nuts. When substituting pineapple (crushed), be sure it's well drained. The whipped cream should be spread only just before serving.

....

(83)
APPLE CRANBERRY PIE
CRISSCROSS PIE

For one 9-inch pie
- Sugar (granulated): 1 cup
- Flour: 2 Tbsps. or ½ oz.
- Salt: ⅛ tsp.
- Apples (sliced thin): 3 cups
- Cranberries (whole): 1½ cups
- Pastry: For 1 one-crust pie
- Nutmeg: ⅛ tsp.
- Butter (melted): 1 tsp.

For five 9-inch pies
- Sugar (granulated): 5 cups or 2½ lbs.
- Flour: ⅝ cup or 2½ oz.
- Salt: ⅝ tsp.
- Apples (sliced thin): 3¾ qts. or 7½ lbs.
- Cranberries (whole): 7½ cups or 1½ lbs.
- Pastry: For 5 one-crust pies
- Nutmeg: ⅝ tsp.
- Butter (melted): 1⅔ Tbsps. or ⅚ oz.

Mix sugar, flour, and salt together, and combine with prepared apples and washed, drained, whole fresh cranberries. Let stand 30 minutes to mellow. Line pie pan with pastry rolled to ⅛-inch thickness; put in the fruit mixture as evenly as possible; sprinkle with nutmeg and butter. Place crisscross strips of pastry over the fruit mixture, proceeding as indicated for No. 40, For Crisscross Pies. Bake in a very hot oven (450° F.) for 20 minutes; then reduce heat to 350° F., and continue baking 20 minutes longer.

APPLE CREAM PIE—
MIDDLE WEST METHOD
ONE-CRUST PIE

(84)

For one 9-inch pie
- Apples (chopped): 1 #2½ can or 1 lb. 10 oz. pkg. frozen apples
- Sugar: ¾ cup
- Flour: 2 Tbsps.
- Salt: ⅛ tsp.
- Eggs (beaten slightly): 2
- Cream (whipped): 1 cup
- Vanilla extract: ½ tsp.
- Pastry: For 1 one-crust pie

For five 9-inch pies
- Apples (chopped): 1 #10 can apples or 6 lbs. frozen apples
- Sugar: 3¾ cups or 1 lb. 14 oz.
- Flour: ⅝ cup or 2½ oz.
- Salt: ⅝ tsp.
- Eggs (beaten slightly): 10 or 1 lb. 4 oz.
- Cream (whipped): 5 cups or 10½ oz.
- Vanilla extract: 1⅔ Tbsps. or ⁵/₁₂ oz.
- Pastry: For 5 one-crust pies

Mix sugar, flour, and salt together; then add eggs, alternately with whipped cream and vanilla. Combine this with coarsely chopped apples. Blend well. Line a 9-inch pie pan with pastry rolled to ⅛-inch thickness; turn in the apple mixture as evenly as possible (you may brush the bottom of the shell with egg white, if desired, to prevent soaking). Bake 10 minutes in a very hot oven (450 F.); reduce the heat to 350° F. and continue baking 25–30 minutes longer. Remove from the oven and sprinkle over Streusel Topping made as indicated for No. 475. Serve cold without any accessory.

APPLE CRUMB PIE
ONE-CRUST PIE

(85)

For one 9-inch pie
- Pastry: For 1 one-crust pie
- Apples (sliced): 4 cups
- Granulated sugar: 2 Tbsps.
- Cinnamon: ½ tsp.
- Lemon juice: 2 Tbsps.
- Brown sugar: ½ cup
- Flour: ½ cup
- Shortening: 2 Tbsps.
- Butter: 2 Tbsps.
- Nuts (chopped): ½ cup

For five 9-inch pies
- Pastry: For 5 one-crust pies
- Apples: 5 qts. or 10 lbs.
- Granulated sugar: ⅝ cup or 5 oz.
- Cinnamon: 2½ tsps. or scant ¼ oz.
- Lemon juice: 19 Tbsps. or 5 oz.
- Brown sugar: 2½ cups or 13⅓ oz.
- Flour: 2½ cups or 10 oz.
- Shortening: 10 Tbsps. or 5 oz.
- Butter: 10 Tbsps. or 5 oz.
- Nuts (chopped): 2½ cups or 13½ oz.

Line pie pan with pastry rolled to ⅛-inch thickness and fill shell with sliced apples. Mix together granulated sugar, cinnamon, and lemon juice, and sprinkle over the apples. Mix brown sugar and flour. Cut in combined shortening and butter until mixture is like corn meal. Add nuts and blend well. Sprinkle this mixture over the apples, and bake for 1 hour in a hot oven (400° F.). Serve with chilled Lemon Meringue Topping, recipe No. 451.

(86)
APPLE CUSTARD PIE—
MERINGUE TOPPING
ONE-CRUST PIE

For one 9-inch pie
- Apples (thinly sliced): 4 cups
- Sugar (granulated): ⅔ cup
- Nutmeg: A few grains
- Lemon juice: 1 Tbsp.
- Pastry: For 1 one-crust pie
- Egg yolks: 3
- Milk (evaporated): 1 cup
- Salt: A few grains
- Egg whites: 3
- Sugar (granulated): ¼ cup

For five 9-inch pies
- Apples (thinly sliced): 5 qts. or 10 lbs.
- Sugar (granulated): 4 cups or 2 lbs.
- Nutmeg: ⅔ tsp.
- Lemon juice: 5 Tbsps. or 2½ oz.
- Pastry: For 5 one-crust pies
- Egg yolks: 15 or 15 oz.
- Milk (evaporated): 5 cups or 2 lb. 11½ oz.
- Salt: 2½ to 3 tsps. or ½ oz.
- Egg whites: 15 or 15 oz.
- Sugar (granulated): 1¼ cups or ⅔ lb.

Mix apples with combined sugar and nutmeg. Sprinkle over lemon juice and carefully toss to blend well. Turn this into pastry-lined pie pan. Now mix slightly beaten egg yolks with undiluted evaporated milk and salt, and pour over the apples. Bake in a very hot oven (450° F.), for 15 minutes; reduce to 325° F., and continue baking for 20 to 25 minutes. Just before the apples are tender and the custard is set, cover with a meringue made by beating 3 egg whites, gradually adding 4 or 5 tablespoons sugar. Return to oven, and bake 15 minutes in a slow oven (300°–325° F.). Applesauce may be used instead of apples.

(87)
APPLE DATE PIE—CHEESE CRUST
TWO-CRUST PIE

Proceed as indicated for recipe No. 73, Apple Pie I, using the same amount or weight for each pie, mixing with the sliced apples 8 pitted dates cut lengthwise. Bake as indicated. Serve with cheese.

(88) APPLE DELIGHT PIE—HOME METHOD
ONE-CRUST PIE

For one 9-inch pie
- Pastry: 1 baked pie shell
- Currant jelly: ¼ cup
- Shredded almonds: 3 Tbsps.
- Apples (pared, cubed): 4 cups
- Orange rind (coarsely grated): 1 Tbsp.
- Lemon rind (grated): ½ tsp.
- Water (cold): ½ cup
- Sugar (powdered): ¼ cup
- Sugar (brown): ⅓ cup
- Heavy cream: 1 cup (whipped)

For five 9-inch pies
- Pastry: 5 baked pie shells
- Currant jelly: 1¼ cups or 12½ oz.
- Shredded almonds: 1 cup or 3 oz.
- Apples (pared, cubed): 5 qts. or 10 lbs.
- Orange rind (coarsely grated): 5 Tbsps. or ⅞ oz.
- Lemon rind (grated): 2½ tsps. or 5/16 oz.
- Water: 2½ cups or 1¼ lbs.
- Sugar (powdered): 1¼ cups or 5 5/7 oz.
- Sugar (brown): 1⅔ cups or 8 8/9 oz.
- Heavy cream: 5 cups (whipped) or 2½ lbs.

In the bottom of baked pastry shell spread combined currant jelly and blanched, shredded almonds. Set aside. Combine apple cubes, orange rind, lemon rind and cold water and cook until apples are tender, but not mashed (rather underdone), about 12 to 15 minutes, adding combined sugars after 5 minutes of cooking (slow cooking process will insure a good result). Cool a little, and add to pastry shell. When cold, spread top with whipped cream, forced through a pastry bag with a fancy tube. Serve cold.

(89) APPLE HONEY PIE
TWO-CRUST PIE

Proceed as indicated for recipe No. 73, Apple Pie I, using the same amount or weight of ingredients for each pie. Bake as directed. As soon as the pie is removed from the oven, slowly pour ⅔ cup of warmed (not boiled) strained honey, or 6⅖ oz. per pie, into the slits in the crust. Let the pie stand at least 30 minutes before serving, if served warm. If a spicy apple pie is wanted, add a piece of ginger root and a small stick of cinnamon to the honey when warming it. Serve with whipped cream topping.

(90)
APPLE MARSHMALLOW PIE— HOME METHOD
ONE-CRUST PIE

NOTE: In this delicious recipe, the apples must steam, covered with an inverted pie pan, for about 15 minutes, or more, until tender.

For one 9-inch pie
- Pastry: For 1 one-crust pie
- Butter (creamed): 2 Tbsps.
- Apples (sliced): 3 cups
- Brown sugar: 1 cup
- Salt: 1/8 tsp.
- Cinnamon: 1 tsp.
- Marshmallows (halved): 16

For five 9-inch pies
- Pastry: For 5 one-crust pies
- Butter (creamed): 5/8 cup or 5 oz.
- Apples (sliced): 3¾ qts. or 7½ lbs.
- Brown sugar: 5 cups or 1 lb. 10⅔ oz.
- Salt: 5/8 tsp.
- Cinnamon: 4 tsps. or 5/12 oz.
- Marshmallows (halved): 80 or 1 lb. 4 oz.

Line pie pan with pastry rolled ⅛-inch thick, building a rim along edge. Spread or brush bottom and sides with half of the creamed butter to prevent soaking of the crust during baking process. Fill pie pan with coarsely sliced apples. Mix brown sugar with salt and cinnamon and sprinkle over the apples. Cover the pie with an inverted pie pan and bake in a hot oven (425° F.); remove inverted pie pan after 15 minutes and continue baking for 25 minutes longer. Remove from oven; reduce the heat to 325° F.; cover apple filling with marshmallow halves, pressing them lightly into the apples. Return to oven and bake until marshmallows have melted slightly and browned lightly, or about 5 minutes. Cool slightly and serve lukewarm.

(91)

APPLE MERINGUE PIE—
SOUTHERN MANNER
ONE-CRUST PIE

For one 9-inch pie

- Applesauce (unsweetened): 1½ cups
- Lemon rind (grated): 1 lemon
- Cinnamon: ½ tsp.
- Nutmeg: ¼ tsp.
- Salt: ¼ tsp.
- Sugar: ¾ cup
- Cornstarch: 2 tsps.
- Egg yolks (slightly beaten): 2
- Milk: 1¼ cups
- Pastry: For 1 one-crust pie
- Meringue topping

For five 9-inch pies

- Applesauce (unsweetened): 7½ cups or ¾ lbs.
- Lemon rind (grated): 5 lemons or ⅝ oz.
- Cinnamon: 2½ tsps. or scant ¼ oz.
- Nutmeg: 1¼ tsps. or scant ⅛ oz.
- Salt: 1¼ tsps. or ¼ oz. (scant)
- Sugar: 3¾ cups or 1 lb. 14 oz.
- Cornstarch: 3⅓ Tbsps. or 1⅑ oz.
- Egg yolks: 10 or 10 oz.
- Milk: 6¼ cups or 3 lb. 2 oz.
- Pastry: For 5 one-crust pies
- Meringue topping

To applesauce, add lemon rind, cinnamon, nutmeg, salt and sugar and cornstarch. Blend well. Combine egg yolks with milk and add to applesauce mixture and mix thoroughly until smooth and free from lumps. Turn into 9-inch pie pan lined with pastry rolled ⅛-inch thick and bake in a hot oven (450° F.) for 10 minutes; reduce to 350° F. and continue baking for 25 to 30 minutes. Cover with selected meringue (either Ginger Honey or Lemon Meringue Topping); return to oven to brown meringue.

(92)   APPLESAUCE CUSTARD NUT PIE
ONE-CRUST PIE

For one 9-inch pie
- Sugar: ⅔ cup
- Constarch: 3 Tbsps.
- Applesauce (unsweetened): 1 #2½ can
- Salt: ½ tsp.
- Butter: 2 Tbsps.
- Milk (scalded): 1 pint
- Egg yolks (slightly beaten): 2
- Brazil nuts (finely chopped): ¾ cup
- Pastry: For 1 one-crust pie

For five 9-inch pies
- Sugar: 3⅓ cups or 1 lb. 10⅔ oz.
- Cornstarch: 1 scant cup or 5 oz.
- Applesause (unsweetened): 1 #10 can or 6 lb. 10 oz.
- Salt: 2½ tsps. or ⁵/₁₂ oz.
- Butter: ⅝ cup or 5 oz.
- Milk (scalded): 2½ qts. or 5 lbs.
- Egg yolks (slightly beaten): 10 or 10 oz.
- Brazil nuts (finely chopped): 3¾ cups or 2½ lbs.
- Pastry: For 5 one-crust pies

Combine sugar and cornstarch. Add applesauce, salt, butter cut into small pieces, and scalded, cooled milk. Blend thoroughly, adding egg yolks gradually. Sprinkle half of finely chopped nut meats in unbaked pastry shell; turn in applesauce mixture, and top with remaining half of chopped nut meats. Bake in a hot oven (450° F.) for 15 minutes. Reduce heat to 350° F. and continue baking 25 to 30 minutes longer. Serve cold.

....

(93)   APPLE AND PEACH PIE— GEORGIA MANNER
TWO-CRUST PIE

For one 9-inch pie
- Pastry: For 1 two-crust pie
- Canned apples: 1 #2½ can
- Canned peaches: 1 #2½ can
- Sugar: ¾ cup
- Flour: 2 Tbsps.
- Cinnamon: ½ tsp.
- Nutmeg: ¼ tsp.
- Butter: 1 Tbsp.

For five 9-inch pies
- Pastry: For 5 two-crust pies
- Canned apples: 1 #10 can or 6 lbs.
- Canned peaches: 1 #10 can or 6 lbs. 8 oz.
- Sugar: 3¾ cups or 1 lb. 14 oz.
- Flour: ⅝ cup or 2½ oz.
- Cinnamon: 2½ tsps. or scant ¼ oz.
- Nutmeg: 1 tsp. or ¹/₁₂ oz.
- Butter: 5 Tbsps. or 2½ oz.

Line 9-inch pie pan with pastry rolled ⅛-inch thick and fill with alternate layers of apples and peaches, well-drained. Mix sugar, flour, cinnamon and nutmeg thoroughly and sprinkle over the fruit. Dot with butter; cover with pastry in the usual way, seal edges and bake in a hot oven (400° F.) for 35 to 40 minutes. Serve cold with either cheese or whipped cream.

....

(94)

APPLE POT CHEESE PIE— FINNISH MANNER
ONE-CRUST PIE

For one 9-inch pie
- Apples (thinly sliced): 2½ cups
- Pot cheese: 1 lb.
- Bread crumbs: ½ cup
- Grated orange rind: 2 tsps.
- Eggs (slightly beaten): 3
- Cream (heavy): 1 cup
- Sugar: 1 cup
- Cinnamon: ½ tsp.
- Nutmeg: ¼ tsp.
- Allspice: ¼ tsp.
- Butter (melted): ½ cup
- Pastry: For 1 one-crust pie

For five 9-inch pies
- Apples (thinly sliced): 3 qts. and ½ cup or 6 lb. 4 oz.
- Pot cheese: 5 lbs.
- Bread crumbs: 2½ cups or 10 oz.
- Grated orange rind: 3½ Tbsps. or 1¼ oz.
- Eggs (slightly beaten): 15 or 1 lb. 14 oz.
- Cream (heavy): 5 cups or 2 lbs. 9⅞ oz.
- Sugar: 5 cups or 2 lbs. 8 oz.
- Cinnamon: 2½ tsps. or scant ¼ oz.
- Nutmeg: 1 tsp. or 1/10 oz.
- Allspice: 1 tsp. or 1/10 oz.
- Butter (melted): 2½ cups or 1¼ lb.
- Pastry: For 5 one-crust pies

Steam sliced apples until almost tender. Cool. Combine with pot cheese, bread crumbs, orange rind and eggs. Blend well, adding all the remaining ingredients. Line a pie pan with pastry rolled ⅛-inch thick; turn mixture into pastry-lined pan. Place in a very hot oven (450° F.) and bake 10 minutes; reduce heat to 350° F. and continue baking for 40 minutes. Serve cold with any accompaniment.

(95)   # APPLE POT PIE—DUTCH STYLE

NOTE: This is not a baked pie, but a real Apple Pot Pie, boiled on top of the range, over a low flame. It is very popular in Pennsylvania, Wisconsin, and Missouri.

For one pot pie
- Lard: ½ cup
- Flour: 4 cups
- Salt: ¼ tsp.
- Apples: 6 or 2 lbs.
- Water
- Sugar: to taste
- Cinnamon: 1 tsp.
- Butter: 4 Tbsps.

For five pot pies
- Lard: 2½ cups or 1 lb. 4 oz.
- Flour: 5 qts. or 5 lbs.
- Salt: 1¼ tsps. or $5/24$ oz.
- Apples: 30 or 10 lbs.
- Water
- Sugar: to taste
- Cinnamon: 1⅔ Tbsps. or $5/12$ oz.
- Butter: 1¼ cups or 10 oz.

Make a crust of the lard, flour, and salt, adding enough ice water to moisten and hold together. Roll out like an ordinary pie crust, ⅛-inch thick, and cut into 2-inch squares. Wash, peel, and core apples; cut into eighths. Put alternate layers of apples and dough squares into a kettle, sprinkling each layer of apples generously with sugar, the amount or weight depending on the tartness of apples; add a little cinnamon to each layer. Have crust as top layer, as for deep dish pie; dot with butter; cover and cook over low heat until apples are soft, or about 40 to 45 minutes. Serve with cream.

....

(96)   # APPLE PRUNE PIE
CRISSCROSS PIE

For one 9-inch pie
- Pastry: For 1 one-crust pie
- Apples (thickly sliced): 2¾ cups
- Prunes (cooked, pitted): 1½ cups
- Sugar: 1 cup
- Lemon juice: 1 Tbsp.
- Cinnamon: ½ tsp.
- Nutmeg: ¼ tsp.

For five 9-inch pies
- Pastry: For 5 one-crust pies
- Apples (thickly sliced): scant 3½ qts. or 6 lbs. 14 oz
- Prunes (cooked, pitted): 7½ cups or 1 lb. 10 oz.
- Sugar: 5 cups or 2 lbs. 8 oz.
- Lemon juice: ⅓ cup or 2½ oz.
- Cinnamon: 2½ tsps. or ¼ oz.
- Nutmeg: 1½ tsps. or ⅛ oz.

Line pie pan with pastry rolled to ⅛-inch thick. Fill with alternate layers of apples and prunes, halved; sprinkle with sugar, lemon juice, and cinnamon and nutmeg. Cover with strips of pastry, as indicated for No. 40, For Crisscross Pies; brush with milk and bake 10 minutes in a hot oven (450° F.); reduce heat to 350° F. and continue baking 40 minutes longer. Serve cold or warm with whipped cream topping.

....

(97)   # APPLE RHUBARB PIE
CRISSCROSS PIE

For one 9-inch pie
- Pastry: For 1 crisscross pie
- Butter (creamed): 1 Tbsp.
- Apples (sliced): 2 cups
- Rhubarb (diced): 2 cups
- Sugar: 1½ cups
- Flour: ¼ cup
- Salt: ⅛ tsp.

For five 9-inch pies
- Pastry: For 5 crisscross pies
- Butter: ⅓ cup or 2½ oz.
- Apples (sliced): 2½ qts. or 5 lbs.
- Rhubarb (diced): 2½ qts. or 2 lbs. 13⅗ oz.
- Sugar: 7½ cups or 3 lbs. 12 oz.
- Flour: 1¼ cups or 5 oz.
- Salt: ⅝ tsp.

Line 9-inch pie pan with pastry rolled ⅛-inch thick; spread bottom and sides with creamed butter to prevent sogginess of the crust. Chill. Pare, core and slice apples; wash and dice unpeeled rhubarb. Arrange alternate layers of apples and rhubarb in shell, sprinkling each layer with mixed sugar, flour and salt. Pile the center higher than the sides. Cover top with strips of pastry, as indicated for No. 40, For Crisscross Pies; moistened lightly. Bake 35–40 minutes in a 425° F. oven. Serve cold with whipped cream topping.

(98)
APPLE SOUR CREAM PIE
TWO-CRUST PIE

For one 9-inch pie
- Pastry: For 1 two-crust pie
- Flour: 2 Tbsps.
- Quick-cooking tapioca: 1 Tbsp.
- Apple quarters: 1 #2½ can
- Sour cream: 1 cup
- Sugar (granulated): ½ cup
- Sugar (brown): 1 cup
- Cinnamon: ¾ tsp.

For five 9-inch pies
- Pastry: For 5 two-crust pies
- Flour: ⅝ cup or 2½ oz.
- Quick-cooking tapioca: ⅓ (scant) cup or 2½ oz.
- Apple quarters: 1 #10 can or 6 lbs.
- Sour cream: 5 cups or 2 lb. 9⅞ oz.
- Sugar (granulated): 2½ cups or 1 lb. 4 oz.
- Sugar (brown): 5 cups or 1 lb. 10⅔ oz.
- Cinnamon: 3¾ tsps. or 1 generous ¼ oz.

Line 9-inch pie pan with pastry rolled ⅛-inch thick. Pat mixed flour and tapioca around the sides and bottom. Dip each apple quarter into sour cream, mixed with both granulated and brown sugars and cinnamon; arrange neatly, packing solid in pie shell; pour remaining cream over apple mixture. Cover with top crust, press edges firmly together and trim off surplus pastry, after pressing edge between thumb and forefinger of right hand and forefinger of left hand. Brush top lightly with ice water or milk. Bake 10 minutes in a hot oven (450° F.); reduce heat to 350° F. and continue baking for 35 minutes longer. Serve cold with cheese.

(99)
APRICOT PIE RECIPES
A FEW FACTS ABOUT APRICOTS

Usually apricots are picked when slightly immature in order to reach the market in good condition. The finest quality and best flavor are found only in fruits that have ripened on the tree. Because of their extreme perishability, such fruits are difficult to ship. They are found usually only in markets adjacent to the district in which they are grown.

Apricots are in season the country over during June, July, and August. They are shipped mainly from California, Oregon, and Washington. Well-matured apricots are plump, fairly firm and a uniformly golden-yellowish color; the flesh is juicy. Immature apricots are usually greenish yellow in color, the flesh is firm to hard and by the time they get to market shriveling is evident. Typical apricot flavor is lacking. The fruits that have been bruised or injured deteriorate so quickly that they should be avoided, or used immediately in pies, tarts, and the like. The beginning of decay is usually indicated by softness verging almost to mushiness, and a dull, practically dead appearance. Sometimes a shrunken or shriveled condition is evident. The flavor of such fruit is likely to be somewhat insipid. It is much better to use canned apricots when such case arises, and the pie grade is sufficiently satisfactory for cooking purposes. They are canned halved and pitted; bulk are not peeled because the fruit bruises easily without skin and, therefore, appears spoiled. A small amount of apricots is canned whole-peeled and sliced-peeled. The skin is so tender that peeling is unnecessary.

Dried apricots are among the most inexpensive fruits that can be bought. Most of those on the market have been treated in the drying process with sulphur fumes, which improves the keeping qualities. Large peeled apricots cost more than smaller unpeeled ones. For cooking dried apricots, see No. 24, Dried Fruit Preparation.

....

(100)   ## APRICOT ALMOND CUSTARD PIE—
HOME METHOD
GRAHAM CRACKER CRUST

For one 9-inch pie
- Pastry: 1 baked graham cracker crust No. 55
- Currant jelly: ¼ cup
- Dried cooked apricots (whole unsweetened): 2 cups
- Sugar (granulated): 1¼ cups
- Salt: ¼ tsp.
- Whole eggs (slightly beaten): 3
- Milk (scalded): 1¼ cups
- Vanilla: ½ tsp.
- Almonds, blanched, shredded: ¼ cup

For five 9-inch pies
- Pastry: 5 baked graham cracker crusts
- Currant jelly: 1¼ cups or 15 oz.
- Dried cooked apricots (whole unsweetened): 2½ qts. or 3 lb. 5⅓ oz.
- Sugar (granulated): 6¼ cups or 3⅛ lbs.
- Salt: 1¼ tsps. or 5/24 oz.
- Whole eggs (slightly beaten): 15 or 1⅞ lb.
- Milk (scalded): 6¼ cups or a scant 3 lbs.
- Vanilla: 2½ tsps. or 5/12 oz.
- Almonds, blanched, shredded: 1¼ cups or 3¾ oz.

Spread crust evenly with jelly; arrange apricots over currant jelly. Combine sugar, salt, and eggs; very slowly, while stirring constantly, stir in milk. Place in top of double boiler and cook over hot water, stirring constantly, until mixture thickens and coats spoon. Remove from hot water, add vanilla and almonds and blend thoroughly. As slowly as possible, pour custard mixture over apricots. Bake in a moderate oven (350° F.) for 25 to 30 minutes, or until inserted knife comes out clean. Cool thoroughly before serving with or without plain whipped cream.

NOTE: The same recipes for crust and filling may be used to make other dried-fruit pies. Cooked dried prunes, peaches, pears, apples, etc., even raisins, can be used in the same proportions as the apricots. Date proportion should be 1½ cups and chopped. The dates will float to the top of the pie when the custard is added; however, they will settle to the bottom during baking.

....

(101)
APRICOT BUTTERSCOTCH PIE, CREAM TOPPING
ONE-CRUST PIE

For one 9-inch pie
- Apricots (dried): 2 cups
- Butterscotch Arrowroot pudding: 1 pkg.
- Sugar: ½ cup
- Almond extract: ⅛ tsp.
- Pastry: 1 baked pie shell

For five 9-inch pies
- Apricots (dried): 10 cups or 3 lbs. 5⅓ oz.
- Butterscotch Arrowroot pudding: 5 pkgs.
- Sugar: 2½ cups or 1¼ lbs.
- Almond extract: ⅝ tsp.
- Pastry: 5 baked pie shells

Cook dried apricots as indicated for No. 24, Dried Fruit Preparation. Mix butterscotch with ¾ cup of apricot juice. Bring to a boil, stirring constantly; adding granulated sugar gradually. Drain cooked apricots thoroughly, cut into quarters and stir into butterscotch mixture with the almond extract. Pour while still warm into pre-baked pie shell. Chill and garnish with sweetened whipped cream.

(102)   APRICOT COCONUT CUSTARD PIE DE LUXE
ONE-CRUST PIE

For one 9-inch pie
- Apricots (dried): 1½ cups
- Sugar: ¼ cup
- Flour: ¼ cup
- Salt: ¼ tsp.
- Egg yolks: 4
- Milk: 2 cups scalded
- Coconut: ¾ cup
- Vanilla extract: 1 tsp.
- Pastry: 1 baked pie shell
- Egg whites: 4
- Sugar: ½ cup
- Coconut: ¾ cup

For five 9-inch pies
- Apricots (dried): 7½ cups or 2½ lbs.
- Sugar: 1¼ cups or 10 oz.
- Flour: 1¼ cups or 5 oz.
- Salt: 1¼ tsps. or $5/24$ oz.
- Egg yolks: 20 or 1¼ lbs.
- Milk: 2½ qts. or 5 lbs. scalded
- Coconut: 3¾ cups or 12 oz.
- Vanilla extract: 5 tsps. or $5/6$ oz.
- Pastry: 5 baked pie shells
- Egg whites: 20 or 1 lb. 4 oz.
- Sugar: 2½ cups or 1 lb. 4 oz.
- Coconut: 3¾ cups or 12 oz.

Cook apricots in water, cool and drain. Make a custard with the sugar, flour, salt, egg yolks and milk in the usual way; as soon as thickened, remove from fire and add the first amount of coconut and vanilla extract. Pour half the custard into baked shell. Arrange a layer of apricots over the custard. Cover with the remaining custard and top with the rest of the apricots. Make a meringue of the egg whites and sugar; pile upon the pie; sprinkle with coconut and brown delicately in a slow oven (300° F.). Serve cold.

(103) APRICOT GOLDEN BLOSSOM PIE
ONE-CRUST PIE

For one 9-inch pie
- Cornstarch: 3 Tbsps.
- Flour: 3 Tbsps.
- Milk: 2¼ cups
- Honey (liquid): ½ cup
- Salt: ¼ tsp.
- Egg yolks: 2
- Pastry: 1 baked pie shell
- Egg whites: 2
- Sugar: ¼ cup
- Apricots (cooked, sieved): ¼ cup

For five 9-inch pies
- Cornstarch: 1 scant cup or 5 oz.
- Flour: 1 scant cup or 3¾ oz.
- Milk: 2 qts. and 3¼ cups or 5 lbs. 5 oz.
- Honey (liquid): 2½ cups or 1 lb. 14 oz.
- Salt: 1¼ tsps. or $5/24$ oz.
- Egg yolks: 10 or 10 oz.
- Pastry: 5 baked pie shells
- Egg whites: 10 or 10 oz.
- Sugar: 1¼ cups or 10 oz.
- Apricots (cooked, sieved): 1¼ cups or $4^4/9$ oz.

Mix cornstarch and flour with ¼ cup of cold milk; scald the remainder. Add honey, salt, and slightly cooled scalded milk. Blend well and cook in double boiler over hot water, stirring almost constantly for 15 minutes, or until thick. Beat egg yolks and gradually stir them into the milk mixture; stir rapidly and constantly while pouring. Continue cooking over hot water for 5 minutes, stirring constantly. Cool. Turn mixture into pre-baked pie shell. Make a meringue with egg whites and sugar in the usual way, and when stiff, fold in the sieved, cooked apricots. Spread this meringue over the pie, using a pastry bag, and bake 15–20 minutes in a moderate oven (300°–325° F.). Serve cold.

(104)   # APRICOT WHIP PIE
ONE-CRUST PIE

For one 9-inch pie
- Dried apricots: 1¼ cups
- Water (hot): 1¼ cups
- Cornstarch: ¼ cup (scant)
- Sugar (granulated): ⅔ cup
- Salt: ¼ tsp.
- Egg whites: 4
- Sugar (powdered): ¼ cup
- Pastry: 1 baked pie shell

For five 9-inch pies
- Dried apricots: 6¼ cups or 2 lb. ⅓ oz.
- Water (hot): 6¼ cups, or more, or 3 lb. 2 oz.
- Cornstarch: 1¼ scant cups or 6⅔ oz.
- Sugar (granulated): 3⅓ cups or 1 lb. 9 oz.
- Salt: 1¼ tsps. or 5/24 oz.
- Egg whites: 20 or 1 lb. 4 oz.
- Sugar (powdered): 1¼ cups or 8¾ oz.
- Pastry: 5 baked pie shells

Wash apricots carefully. Place in hot water and soak for 24 hours, having enough water to cover generously. Do not stir. Keep apricots at room temperature. When ready to use, do not cook apricots, but rub with soaking water through a fine sieve, discarding skins. Reserve ¼ cup of cold mixture to dissolve cornstarch, and cook remaining part with sugar (the first ⅔ cup) until beginning to boil; then stir in the dissolved cornstarch and salt. Cook until mixture is clear and thick; then gradually pour hot mixture over stiffly beaten egg whites, to which powdered sugar has been added, beating vigorously and steadily. Turn mixture, while still warm, into pie shell; and when cold, cover with Lemon Meringue Topping, No. 451.

APRICOT PIE

(105)

TWO-CRUST PIE

For one 9-inch pie
- Apricots (dried): 1 generous cup
- Hot water: to cover generously
- Cornstarch: 2 Tbsps.
- Juice (from soaked apricots): ²/₃ cup
- Sugar: ³/₈ cup
- Salt: ¼ tsp.
- Corn syrup: ¼ cup
- Pastry: for 1 two-crust pie

For five 9-inch pies
- Apricots (dried): 5 generous cups or 1 lb. 12¹/₃ oz.
- Hot water: to cover generously
- Cornstarch: 10 Tbsps. or 3¹/₃ oz.
- Juice (from soaked apricots): 3¹/₃ cups or 1 lb. 10²/₃ oz.
- Sugar: 1⁷/₈ cups or 15 oz.
- Salt: 1¼ tsps. or ⁵/₂₄ oz.
- Corn syrup: 1¼ cups or 15 oz.
- Pastry: for 5 two-crust pies

Wash apricots carefully, but gently. Place in hot water and soak for 24 hours. Do not stir; keep at room temperature. When ready to use, do not cook. Drain, reserving water. Dissolve cornstarch in ²/₃ cup of juice and bring to a boil. Let cook until mixture is clear and thick, stirring almost constantly with a wire whisk, not a spoon, to prevent lumping. Add sugar, salt, corn syrup and let this come to a boil once or twice. The mixture will resemble a heavy syrup. Remove at once from heat and pour very hot over well-drained, whole apricots. Blend well, but gently, lest the mixture mashes. The fruit should be entirely coated with syrup. Turn, while hot, into pastry-lined pie pan; cover with top crust in the usual way; prick with a fork and bake 10 minutes in a hot oven (450° F.); then reduce heat to 350° F. and continue baking for 30 minutes. Serve cold with a plain whipped cream topping or with ice cream.

....

APRICOT PINEAPPLE PIE GOURMET— FRENCH METHOD

(106)

MERINGUE-CRUST PIE

Proceed as indicated for Strawberry Pineapple Pie Gourmet No. 362, substituting fresh halved, pitted apricots, brushed lightly with melted currant jelly—that is, glazed apricots.

(107)   BAKED ALASKA ICE CREAM PIE

NOTE: This type of pie is usually made to order. Almost any kind of ice cream may be used. The main point is that the operation should be done rapidly and the serving done immediately after the pie (or pies) comes out of the oven. Almost any kind of pre-baked pie shell (or shells) may be used. These very attractive pies may be made individually, in tart shells.

Fill a cold, pre-baked pastry shell with ice cream, vanilla, chocolate or any other flavor. Make a meringue of 3 eggs (for a 9-inch pie) or one egg (for an individual pie, or tart) in the usual way. Completely cover ice cream, to the outside edges, with meringue, and brown in a hot oven (450° F.). Serve at once.

It is best to place the pie on a wooden plank, when you put it in the oven; wood will not conduct the heat.

You may spread the bottom of pre-baked shell or shells with fresh, canned, or cooked dried fruit, or alternate layers of ice cream, fruit, and ice cream, before covering the pie with a meringue previous to baking; or you may alternate layers of fruit, whipped cream or stiffly beaten egg white, and ice cream, then cover with a meringue and bake as indicated above.

Scooped brioches or sponge or angel cake may also be used as a container for ice cream, or layers of ice cream, fruit, and whipped cream or stiffly beaten egg whites, sweetened to taste and flavored according to kind of ice cream used.

You may also make fancy designs with the beaten egg whites, using a pastry bag, and designing almost any kind of dessert, such as spiral, flowers, etc.

You may use a meringue mixed with ground pistachio nut meats, almonds, pecans, etc. A way to add eye-appeal to these popular pies is to sprinkle a line of cinnamon (ground), line of ground nut brittle, line of ground almonds or pistachio nuts, either diagonally or vertically over the meringue before setting into the oven to bake.

(108)   A FEW FACTS ABOUT BANANAS

Bananas are a fruit available the year round at low cost. They are always picked green and ripened off the tree. When partially ripe, they are yellow with green tips and, at that stage, may be classed as a vegetable, for they must be cooked to be really edible. When the green tip disappears, they may be eaten raw; but they do not yet have their distinctive sweetness and aromatic flavor. When brown flecked, they have reached eating perfection and are so digestible that they are often the first solid food given to infants. Bananas combine well with all smoked meats, and with sausage in particular. Gingerbread with a banana-flavored whipped cream filling is a prize dessert. Or a banana pie with nut and cream filling is another suggestion. The banana broil is another popular version, especially when it is a part of a mixed grill, always a favorite with men.

....

(109)   BANANA CARAMEL CUSTARD PIE
ONE-CRUST PIE

For one 9-inch pie
- Granulated sugar: ½ cup
- Milk (scalded): 2 cups
- Eggs (slightly beaten): 2
- Salt: ¼ tsp.
- Vanilla extract: ¾ tsp.
- Pastry: for 1 one-crust pie
- Bananas (sliced): 2

For five 9-inch pies
- Granulated sugar: 2½ cups or 1¼ lb.
- Milk (scalded): 2½ quarts or 5 lbs.
- Eggs: (slightly beaten): 10 or 1¼ lb.
- Salt: 1¼ tsps. or $5/24$ oz.
- Vanilla extract: 3¾ tsps. or $5/8$ oz.
- Pastry: for 5 one-crust pies
- Bananas (sliced): 10 or 3⅓ lbs.

Caramelize sugar (not too dark) in a saucepan and stir into scalded milk until entirely dissolved. Pour on slightly beaten eggs, add salt and vanilla, and strain into uncooked pie crust. Add the bananas, sliced (you may if desired mash the bananas). Bake 10 minutes in a very hot oven (450° F.); reduce temperature to 325° F. and continue baking 35 minutes longer, or until custard is set when tested with a knife.

(110)   # BANANA CREAM PIE
                            ## ONE-CRUST PIE

NOTE: Bananas should be sliced only when ready to add to the hot filling; this will prevent them from discoloring. You may place half the banana slices in bottom of shell, and the remainder on top of cream, if desired; or fill the pre-baked pastry shell, then arrange the sliced bananas on top; or you may combine the hot cream with the sliced bananas. If a meringue is the topping, let cool a little before placing the meringue on top. If whipped cream is the topping, wait until filling is thoroughly cooled.

For one 9-inch pie
- Milk: 1½ cups
- Granulated sugar: ½ cup
- Salt: ⅓ tsp.
- Pastry flour (sifted): 2¾ Tbsps.
- Cornstarch: 2½ Tbsps.
- Egg yolks: 3
- Butter: 1 Tbsp.
- Vanilla extract: ¾ tsp.
- Egg whites (stiffly beaten): 2
- Sugar (powdered): ¼ cup
- Bananas (sliced thin): 2 medium-sized
- Pastry: 1 baked pie shell

For five 9-inch pies
- Milk: 7½ cups or 3¾ lbs.
- Granulated sugar: 2½ cups or 1¼ lb.
- Salt: 1⅔ tsps or ⁵/₁₈ oz.
- Pastry flour (sifted): scant ⅞ cup or 3 oz.
- Cornstarch: a generous ¾ cup or 4⅙ oz.
- Egg yolks: 15 or scant lb. or 1¼ cups
- Vanilla extract: 3¾ tsps. or ⅝ oz.
- Butter: 5 Tbsps. or 2½ oz.
- Egg whites (stiffly beaten): 10 or 10 oz. or about 1 cup
- Sugar (powdered): 1¼ cups or 8 oz. or ½ lb.
- Bananas (sliced thin): 10 medium-sized
- Pastry: 5 baked pie shells

Bring to a boil combined milk, sugar and salt, stirring occasionally to ensure the melting of the sugar and salt. Combine pastry flour, cornstarch and egg yolks and stir to a paste, adding a little cold milk to ease the mixing; gradually add the mixture to the hot milk-sugar mixture, stirring constantly, until mixture is clear and thick. Remove from the heat and stir in the butter and vanilla extract. Now fold in the stiffly beaten egg whites, to which has been added the powdered sugar. At this point the sliced bananas should be added to the cream. You may crush the bananas, if desired. Immediately turn mixture into the pre-baked pastry shell while hot. Allow to cool before topping with meringue or whipped cream.

(111)
BANANA CREAM PIE—
FARMER METHOD
ONE-CRUST PIE

For one 9-inch pie
- Pastry: 1 baked pastry shell
- Apricot jam
- Bananas: 3, sliced thin
- Heavy cream: 1½ cups, whipped
- Salt: ¼ tsp.
- Apple butter: ⅓ cup
- Shredded coconut: as much as desired

For five 9-inch pies
- Pastry: 5 baked pastry shells
- Apricot jam
- Bananas: 15 or 5 lbs., sliced thin
- Heavy cream: 1¾ qts., whipped or 3¾ lb.
- Salt: 1¼ tsps. or ⁵⁄₂₄ oz.
- Apple butter: 1⅔ cups or 13⅓ oz.
- Shredded coconut: as much as desired

NOTE: You may, if desired, brush the bottom of the cool, pre-baked pastry shell with your favorite jam or jelly, but apricot jam is suggested. Slice a layer of bananas over the jam; add a layer of whipped cream, unsweetened, to which has been added and folded into gently the apple butter, then another layer of banana slices, and top with whipped cream. Sprinkle over as much shredded coconut as desired. Serve very cold.

....

(112)
A FEW FACTS ABOUT BERRIES

All berries, since they are handled in picking and packing, should be rapidly but thoroughly washed no matter how they are to be used. They should have a fresh, clean, bright appearance and be free of dirt and moisture. They should be looked over carefully to remove any foreign matter or spoiled berries. Just before using, put berries into cold water and agitate so that any particles of sand will fall to the bottom of the vessel. With a perforated ladle lift the berries from the top and put into a strainer to drain. If this operation is done rapidly, no loss of the delicious flavor will occur; and if thoroughly drained, moisture will not deteriorate the fruit, if used at once, nor cause soaking of the pie shell.

(112-a)
BLACKBERRY CREAM PIE
ONE-CRUST PIE, PRE-BAKED PIE SHELL

For one 9-inch pie
- Sweetened Condensed milk: 1 15-oz. can or ¾ cup
- Lemon juice: ¼ cup
- Blackberries (fresh): 1 cup
- Pastry: 1 baked pie shell
- Heavy cream (whipped): ½ cup
- Powdered sugar: 2 Tbsps.

For five 9-inch pies
- Sweetened Condensed milk: 5 cans or 8¾ cups or 4 lb. 11 oz.
- Lemon juice: 1¼ cups or 10 oz.
- Blackberries (fresh): 5 cups or 13⅓ oz.
- Pastry: 5 baked pie shells
- Heavy cream (whipped): 2½ cups or 1 lb.
- Powdered sugar: ⅝ cup or 2⁶/₇ oz.

Blend together sweetened condensed milk and lemon juice. Fold in drained, washed blackberries; turn mixture into pre-baked pie shell and cover with the cream which has been whipped and sweetened with powdered sugar. Serve very cold.

---

(113)
BLACKBERRY PIE
TWO-CRUST PIE

For one 9-inch pie
- Cornstarch: 2⅔ Tbsps.
- Sugar (granulated): 1⅛ cups
- Salt: ⅛ tsp.
- Water: ⅔ cup
- Blackberries (fresh): 1 pint
- Pastry: For 1 two-crust pie
- Whipped cream topping

For five 9-inch pies
- Cornstarch: ⅚ cup or 4⁴/₉ oz.
- Sugar (granulated): 5⅝ cups or 4⁴/₉ oz.
- Salt: ⅝ tsp.
- Water: 3⅓ cups or 1 lb. 10⅔ oz.
- Blackberries (fresh): 2½ qts. or 1 lb. 10⅔ oz.
- Pastry: For 5 two-crust pies
- Whipped cream topping

Combine cornstarch, sugar, and salt, and dissolve in ⅓ of the water. Bring remaining water to a boil and pour in cornstarch mixture. Cook one minute. Cool. When cold, beat with rotary egg beater or electric beater until very smooth. Combine with washed and thoroughly drained fresh blackberries. Turn mixture into pastry-lined pie pan; cover with top crust and bake 10 minutes in a hot oven (450° F.); reduce heat to 350° F. and continue baking for 25–30 minutes longer, or until crust is browned. Serve cold with whipped cream.

(114) BLACKBERRY MINCEMEAT PIE
TWO-CRUST PIE

For one 9-inch pie
- Pastry: For 1 two-crust pie
- Blackberries (canned): 1 #2 can
- Mincemeat (prepared): 1 lb.
- Butter: 2 tsps.
- American cheese

For five 9-inch pies
- Pastry: For 5 two-crust pies
- Blackberries (canned): 1 #10 can, less 2 cups
- Mincemeat (prepared): 5 lbs.
- Butter: 3⅓ Tbsps. or 1⅔ oz.
- American cheese

Drain berries and mix with mincemeat; turn mixture into unbaked pastry shell, dot with butter; cover with top crust slashed to let steam escape. Brush with milk or beaten egg and bake 15 minutes in a very hot oven (450° F.); reduce heat to 350° F. and continue baking for 25 minutes, or until crust is brown. Serve with fresh American cheese.

....

(115) BLACKBERRY PINEAPPLE PIE
TWO-CRUST PIE

NOTE: Other berries may be prepared in the same way, using fresh, canned, or frozen berries.

For one 9-inch pie
- Blackberries (fresh): 2 cups
- Pineapple (canned, cubed): 1¼ cups
- Sugar (granulated): ¾ cup
- Flour: 2 Tbsps.
- Salt: ⅛ tsp.
- Lemon juice: 2 tsps.
- Pastry: For 1 two-crust pie

For five 9-inch pies
- Blackberries (fresh): 2 qts. or 1 lb. 10⅔ oz.
- Pineapple (canned, cubed): 6 cups
- Sugar (granulated): 3¾ cups or 1 lb. 14 oz.
- Flour: 10 Tbsps. or 2½ oz.
- Salt: ⅝ tsp.
- Lemon juice: 3⅓ Tbsps. or 1⅔ oz.
- Pastry: For 5 two-crust pies

Pick, wash, stem, and drain berries thoroughly. Mix with drained, cubed pineapple. Combine sugar, flour, and salt, and stir into the mixed fruit, adding lemon juice while stirring. Line pie pan with pastry rolled ⅛-inch thick; brush bottom and side of crust with melted butter. Let cool, then fill with fruit mixture. Cover with top crust, slash top to let steam escape, and bake 10 minutes in a very hot oven (450° F.); reduce to 350° F. and bake 20 to 25 minutes longer. Serve cold with whipped cream topping.

....

(116)

BLACK BOTTOM PIE
ONE-CRUST PIE

For one 9-inch pie
- Sugar (granulated): ¾ cup
- Cornstarch: ¼ cup
- Flour: 2 Tbsps.
- Salt: ¼ tsp.
- Milk (scalded): 2⅔ cups
- Cream (heavy): 2 Tbsps.
- Egg yolks (slightly beaten): 3
- Butter: 2 Tbsps.
- Vanilla extract: 1 tsp.
- Pastry: For 1 one-crust pie
- Chocolate (grated): ½ cup
- Egg whites: 3
- Salt: ⅛ tsp.
- Sugar (powdered): 6 Tbsps.

For five 9-inch pies
- Sugar (granulated): 3¾ cups or 1 lb. 14 oz.
- Cornstarch: 1¼ cups or 6⅔ oz.
- Flour: ⅝ cup or 2½ oz.
- Salt: 1¼ tsps. or 5/24 oz.
- Milk (scalded): 3 qts. plus 1⅓ cups or 6 lbs. 10⅔ oz.
- Cream (heavy): 10 Tbsps. or 5¹⁵/₆₄ oz.
- Egg yolks (slightly beaten): 15 or 15 oz.
- Butter: ⅔ cup or 5 oz.
- Vanilla extract: 1⅔ Tbsps. or ⅚ oz.
- Pastry: For 5 one-crust pies
- Chocolate (grated): 2½ cups or 13 oz.
- Egg whites: 15 or 15 oz.
- Salt: ⅝ tsp.
- Sugar (powdered): 1⅞ cups or 8⁴/₇ oz.

Mix sugar, cornstarch, flour and salt; slowly stir scalded milk into mixture; when smooth, return to double boiler and cook, stirring constantly until smooth and thickened. Pour the cream slowly over beaten egg yolks, mix and gradually add to sugar-cornstarch mixture, stirring constantly. Cook 3 minutes, stirring all the while. Remove from hot water; stir in butter, and when cool, add vanilla extract. Let stand. Place the uncooked pastry shell rolled ⅛-inch thick in a very hot oven (500° F.) and bake until a light brown, or about 10 minutes. Remove at once; while burning hot, sprinkle grated chocolate over the bottom in a generous layer. (Hence the name of Black Bottom Pie, because the bottom of the pie is black and not brown.) When the chocolate has become firm, pour the cool cream filling into the shell.

Beat egg whites and salt ($\frac{1}{8}$ tsp.) until they stand in peaks; gradually add powdered sugar and beat until glossy. Pile the meringue over the filling roughly. Place the pie in a slow oven (300° F.) and bake until meringue is firm and lightly brown, 15–20 minutes. Serve cold.

The return of the pie to the oven will mellow the crust and filling without melting the chocolate which should be absolutely separated from the filling when the pie is cut into wedges.

....

(117)

BLUEBERRY PIE I
TWO-CRUST PIE

For one 9-inch pie
- Pastry: For 1 two-crust pie
- Blueberries: 1 qt. or 3½ cups
- Lemon juice: 1½ Tbsps.
- Lemon rind (grated): 1 Tbsp.
- Sugar (granulated): ¾ cup
- Salt: ¼ tsp.
- Flour: 2 Tbsps.
- Quick-cooking tapioca: 1½ Tbsps.

For five 9-inch pies
- Pastry: For 5 two-crust pies
- Blueberries: 5 qts. or 5 lbs.
- Lemon juice: 7½ Tbsps. or 3¾ oz.
- Lemon rind (grated): 5 Tbsps. or 1$\frac{7}{8}$ oz.
- Sugar (granulated): 3¾ cups or 1 lb. 14 oz.
- Salt: 1¼ tsps. or $\frac{5}{24}$ oz.
- Flour: $\frac{5}{8}$ cup or 2½ oz.
- Quick-cooking tapioca: ½ scant cup or 1$\frac{7}{8}$ oz.

Line pie pan with pastry rolled $\frac{1}{8}$-inch thick; build up rim of crust. Wash and drain berries; add lemon juice and rind, sugar, salt, and flour or quick-cooking tapioca. The tapioca will give a shiny filling which is attractive. Mix well and fill pie shell. Moisten rim of bottom crust and pinch edges together to seal. Slash top crust in several places to allow escape of steam, and bake 10 minutes in a very hot oven (450° F.); reduce heat to 350° F., and continue baking 30 minutes longer. Serve with whipped cream, if desired.

(118)
BLUEBERRY PIE II
ONE-CRUST PIE, PRE-BAKED SHELL

For one 9-inch pie
- Blueberries (fresh): 1 qt. or 3½ cups
- Lemon juice: 1½ Tbsps.
- Lemon rind (grated): 1 Tbsp.
- Sugar (granulated): 1 cup
- Cornstarch: ¼ cup
- Salt: ¼ tsp,
- Pastry: 1 baked pie shell
- Cream cheese: 1 (3 oz.) pkg.
- Cream (heavy): 2 Tbsps.

For five 9-inch pies
- Blueberries (fresh): 5 qts. or 5 lbs.
- Lemon juice: 7½ Tbsps. or 3¾ oz.
- Lemon rind (grated): 5 Tbsps. or 1⅞ oz.
- Sugar (granulated): 5 cups or 2 lbs. 8 oz.
- Cornstarch: 1¼ cups or 6⅔ oz.
- Salt: 1¼ tsps. or ⁵/₂₄ oz.
- Pastry: 5 baked pie shells
- Cream cheese: 5 (3 oz.) pkgs. or 15 oz.
- Cream (heavy): ⅝ cup or 5¹⁵/₆₄ oz.

Pick over and wash berries; drain. Cook in covered saucepan with lemon rind and juice for 5 minutes. Mix sugar, cornstarch, and salt and combine with blueberries; cook for 10 minutes, stirring occasionally. Cool; pour into pre-baked pastry shell. When cold, decorate with cream cheese which has been whipped with cream, using pastry bag.

NOTE: You may substitute 1 cup of seedless raisins for one cup of blueberries for a variation, if desired. If canned, drained blueberries are used, add berries when cornstarch mixture is still warm. You may also proceed as indicated for No. 113, Blackberry Pie, using canned blueberries instead, or you may make a Blueberry Mincemeat Pie, as indicated for No. 114, Blackberry Mincemeat Pie, substituting blueberries for blackberries.

....

(119)
BOSTON CREAM PIE
ONE-CRUST PIE, PRE-BAKED SHELL

NOTE: A real Boston Cream Pie is made from good sponge cake. Cakes are of two classes—those with fat and those without fat. Cakes without fat are called sponge cakes. In them, eggs supply the liquid and serve as a means of adding air for leavening. Angel foods, plain sponge cakes, sunshine cakes all belong to the sponge cake family, and they vary chiefly in the proportion of egg whites and yolks they contain. Because of their special texture, these cakes require more careful mixing and baking than do cakes with fat. In order to get a fine-grained sponge cake, have the eggs at room temperature. The whites will whip up more quickly to a greater volume than they do when they are used immediately from the refrigerator.

Since the air beaten into egg whites leavens this kind of cake, all the mixing is done gently and quickly in order not to lose any of this air. And when the mixing is through, the cake is baked immediately so that the air has no chance to escape before it does its part in making the cake light.

Sponge cakes sometimes stick to pans in which they are baked because they contain too much sugar; or such condition may have been caused by too low a temperature in baking. Another possible reason is that you may have allowed the cake to remain in the pan too long a time after removing from oven. If you use an electric beater, set it at medium speed; third speed if you have a four-speed machine, and second speed if you are using a three-speed machine; beat for 15 to 20 minutes. Never use high speed. When the beater is removed, the whites are glossy, moist and somewhat foamy. Beating the whites beyond this stage will make the cake coarse-grained. At this point, fold in half of the sugar. This addition of the sugar helps to make the egg foam stronger, so that less air is lost during the rest of the mixing. Then fold in the flour, thoroughly mixed with the rest of the sugar (sifted), with a gentle folding motion, if using a wooden spoon. After the flour and sugar are completely folded into the mixture, bake the cake immediately, preferably in a tube pan. The oven should be ready at a temperature of about 325° F. This temperature gives the interior a chance to set before the outside shrinks and becomes tough.

For one 9-inch pie
Shell
- Egg yolks: 6
- Sugar (fine granulated, sifted): 1 cup
- Lemon juice: 2 Tbsps.
- Grated lemon rind: 1 tsp.
- Egg whites: 6
- Pastry flour (sifted): 1 cup
- Salt: ½ tsp.
- Baking powder: ½ tsp.

For five 9-inch pies
Shell
- Egg yolks: 30 or 1 lb. 14 oz.
- Sugar (fine granulated, sifted): 5 cups or 2 lbs. 5½ oz.
- Lemon juice: ⅝ cup or 5 oz.
- Grated lemon rind: 5 tsps. or ⅝ oz.
- Egg whites: 30 or 1 lb. 14 oz.
- Pastry flour (sifted): 5 cups or 1 lb. 4 oz.
- Salt: 2½ tsps. or $5/12$ oz.
- Baking powder: 2½ tsps. or $20/51$ oz.

Beat egg yolks with wire whisk (or electric beater) until thick; gradually add sifted sugar, beating continually. Add lemon juice and grated rind. Whip egg whites until stiff but not dry; fold half the egg whites into egg yolk mixture. Now fold in mixed and sifted flour, salt, and baking powder, alternately with remaining egg whites, and mix lightly. Bake in ungreased 9-inch pie pan in moderately slow oven (325° F.) for one hour. Remove from oven and turn upside down on a cheese cloth lightly sprinkled with powdered or fine granulated sugar; leave there until ready to use or until cold without removing the pie pan. This allows the layer to cool slowly, become very soft and velvety, and keep all of its moisture.

For one 9-inch pie	*For five 9-inch pies*
Filling	*Filling*
• Milk: ⅔ cup plus 1 Tbsp.	• Milk: scant 3⅔ cups or 1 lb. 13⅙ oz.
• Sugar (granulated): ¼ cup	• Sugar (granulated): 1¼ cups or 10 oz.
• Salt: ⅛ tsp.	• Salt: ⅝ tsp.
• Cornstarch: 1 scant Tbsp.	• Cornstarch: 5 Tbsps. or 1⅔ oz.
• Pastry flour: 2 tsps.	• Pastry flour: 3⅓ Tbsps. or ⅚ oz.
• Milk: ¼ cup	• Milk: 1¼ cup or 10 oz.
• Egg yolks: 2	• Egg yolks: 10 or 10 oz.
• Butter: 2 Tbsps.	• Butter: ⅝ cup or 5 oz.
• Vanilla extract: ½ tsp.	• Vanilla extract: 2½ tsps. or ⁵⁄₁₂ oz.
• Whipped cream (unsweetened)	• Whipped cream (unsweetened)

Combine the first amount of milk, sugar, and salt; place in top of double boiler and cook until sugar is dissolved; then add cornstarch and stir until well blended and free from lumps. Cook, stirring constantly, until mixture is thick. Remove from the heat and stir in combined pastry flour, milk, and egg yolks. Return to the hot water and continue cooking until mixture is thick and very smooth. Remove from the heat and stir in butter and vanilla extract. Cool.

Putting cake and filling together: Split cold cake in half lengthwise with a sharp knife, starting at one edge and finishing out at the other. Remove the upper half and place half of the cream filling on the cut side (exposed part) of one layer, spreading evenly to cover layer completely: adjust the other layer carefully, pressing gently; then spread over the remaining filling. Cover the entire top with whipped cream (unsweetened). Chill slightly before serving.

For a de luxe Boston Cream Pie, you may arrange fresh berries, such as raspberries or strawberries, on top of the whipped cream.

BRANDIED APPLE PIE
TWO-CRUST PIE

(120)

For one 9-inch pie
- Rich pastry: For 1 two-crust pie
- Apples (sliced): 4 cups or 1 qt.
- Sugar (brown): ½ cup
- Lemon juice: 1 tsp.
- Brandy: 3 Tbsps.
- Butter (melted): 1 Tbsp.

For five 9-inch pies
- Rich pastry: For 5 two-crust pies
- Apples (sliced): 5 qts. or 10 lbs.
- Sugar (brown): 2½ cups or 13⅓ oz.
- Lemon juice: 5 tsps. or ⅚ oz.
- Brandy: 1 scant cup or 7½ oz.
- Butter (melted): 5 Tbsps. or 2½ oz.

Line a 9-inch pie pan with pastry rolled ⅛-inch thick. Fill with apples; sprinkle over brown sugar alternately with lemon juice and brandy, then the melted butter. Cover with top crust; slash for escaping steam and seal edges with fork or pastry roller. Bake 10 minutes in a very hot oven (450° F.); reduce temperature to 350° F. and continue baking 25 minutes longer. Serve cold or warm with a piece of American cheese.

BRANDIED CUSTARD PIE ROYAL
ONE-CRUST PIE

(121)

For one 9-inch pie
- Pastry: For 1 one-crust pie
- Eggs (whole, beaten): 4
- Sugar (granulated, sifted): ½ cup
- Cream (heavy): ¼ cup
- Brandy: 1 Tbsp.
- Milk (scalded): 1½ cups
- Almonds (shredded): 1½ Tbsps.
- Nutmeg: To taste

For five 9-inch pies
- Pastry: For 5 one-crust pies
- Eggs (whole, beaten): 20 or 2½ lbs.
- Sugar (granulated, sifted): 2½ cups or 1 lb. 4 oz.
- Cream (heavy): 1¼ cups or 10 ¹⁵⁄₃₂ oz.
- Brandy: 5 Tbsps. or 2½ oz. or more
- Milk (scalded): 7½ cups or 3¾ lbs.
- Almonds (shredded): 7½ Tbsps. or 2½ oz.
- Nutmeg: To taste

Line a 9-inch pie pan with pastry rolled ⅛-inch thick. Separate 1 egg and drop the white (unbeaten) in the center; roll around until pastry is coated (this will prevent a soggy crust). Return egg white and yolk to the other eggs for the filling; chill the pastry.

For the filling: Blend the beaten eggs, sugar and cream, and brandy thoroughly. Stir in the scalded milk. Blend well. Pour mixture into chilled unbaked pastry shell and sprinkle with a little nutmeg (optional). Place in a very hot oven (450° F.) and bake 10 minutes; reduce heat to 350° F. and continue baking for 30 minutes longer. Remove from oven, sprinkle with shredded almonds; return to oven to brown the almonds, or about 5 minutes. Serve cold.

....

(122)   # BRANDIED PUMPKIN PIE
ONE-CRUST PIE

For one 9-inch pie
- Rich pastry: For 1 one-crust pie
- Canned pumpkin (sieved): 2¼ cups
- Sugar (brown): ½ cup
- Eggs (whole, well beaten): 2
- Salt: ⅛ tsp.
- Milk (scalded): 1¼ cups
- Molasses: ¼ cup
- Brandy: 3 Tbsps.
- Ginger (powdered): ½ tsp.
- Cinnamon: ¾ tsp.

For five 9-inch pies
- Rich pastry: For 5 one-crust pies
- Canned pumpkin (sieved): 2 qts. plus 3¼ cups or 9 lbs. 2¼ oz.
- Sugar (brown): 2½ cups or 13⅓ oz.
- Eggs (whole, well beaten): 10 or 1 lb. 4 oz.
- Salt: ⅝ tsp.
- Milk (scalded): 1 qt. plus 2¼ cups or 3 lbs. 2 oz.
- Molasses: 1¼ cups or 15 oz.
- Brandy: 1 cup less 1 Tbsp. or 7½ oz.
- Ginger (powdered): 5 tsps. or $5/24$ oz.
- Cinnamon: 3¾ tsps. or $5/16$ oz.

Line a 9-inch pie pan with rich pastry rolled ⅛-inch thick; separate one egg and drop the white (unbeaten) in the center; roll around until pastry is coated to prevent a soggy crust. Return egg white and yolk to the other eggs for the filling. Chill the pastry.

For the filling: Force pumpkin through a sieve and add the sugar and well beaten eggs to which has been added salt; blend well. Combine all the remaining ingredients and mix well. Mix into pumpkin mixture, beating slightly. Pour mixture into unbaked shell and bake 10 minutes in a hot oven (450° F.); reduce heat to 350° F. and continue baking for 35 minutes longer, or until knife inserted in center of pie comes out clean. Serve cold, plain or heaped with sweetened whipped cream.

....

(123) BUTTERMILK LEMON MERINGUE PIE— ENGLISH STYLE
ONE-CRUST PIE, PRE-BAKED SHELL

For one 9-inch pie
- Buttermilk (rich): 2 cups
- Lemon rind (grated): 1 Tbsp.
- Sugar (granulated): 1 cup
- Sugar (brown): ½ cup
- Cornstarch: 2 Tbsps.
- Flour (pastry, sifted): 1 Tbsp.
- Salt: ¼ tsp.
- Egg yolks (slightly beaten): 2
- Lemon juice: ¼ cup
- Egg whites (stiffly beaten): 3
- Salt: a pinch
- Sugar (granulated): 3 Tbsps.
- Almond extract (optional): ½ tsp.
- Rich pastry: 1 baked pie shell

For five 9-inch pies
- Buttermilk (rich): 2½ qts. or 5 lbs.
- Lemon rind (grated): 5 Tbsps. or 1⅞ oz.
- Sugar (granulated): 5 cups or 2½ lbs.
- Sugar (brown): 2½ cups or 1 lb. 1⅞ oz.
- Cornstarch: 10 Tbsps. or ⅝ cup or 3⅓ oz.
- Flour (pastry, sifted): 5 Tbsps. or 1¼ oz.
- Salt: 1¼ tsps. or ⁵⁄₂₄ oz.
- Egg yolks (slightly beaten): 10 or 10 oz.
- Lemon juice: 1¼ cups or 10 oz. or ⅝ lb.
- Egg whites (stiffly beaten): 15 or 15 oz.
- Salt: ¾ tsp. or ⅛ oz.
- Sugar (granulated): scant cup, or 7½ oz.
- Almond extract (optional): 1 scant Tbsp. or ⁵⁄₁₂ oz.
- Pastry: 5 baked pie shells

Place buttermilk, lemon rind, and the cup of granulated sugar in top of double boiler over hot water; bring water to a boil, stirring mixture almost constantly. Mix thoroughly brown sugar, cornstarch, flour, ¼ tsp. salt, slightly beaten egg yolks, and lemon juice (if a tart pie is desired add a little more lemon juice), then add boiling buttermilk mixture, stirring constantly, adding a little of buttermilk at a time to prevent curdling; place mixture over hot water, and cook, stirring constantly until mixture is thick and clear. Remove from the heat and beat rapidly for one minute. Turn mixture into pre-baked pie shell; top with a meringue made with stiffly beaten egg whites, pinch of salt, sugar and almond extract, and bake 15–20 minutes in a moderate oven (325° F.), or until meringue is delicately brown. Serve cold.

(124) BUTTERSCOTCH CREAM PIE
ONE-CRUST PIE, PRE-BAKED SHELL

For one 9-inch pie
- Butter: ¼ cup
- Sugar (dark brown): ⅔ cup
- Milk (cold): 1⅔ cups
- Cornstarch: 2 Tbsps.
- Flour (bread): 2 Tbsps.
- Salt: ½ tsp.
- Egg yolks (beaten): 4
- Vanilla extract: 1 tsp.
- Butter: 1 Tbsp.
- Egg whites (stiffly beaten): 2
- Sugar (granulated): ¼ cup
- Pastry: 1 baked pie shell

For five 9-inch pies
- Butter: 1¼ cups or 10 oz.
- Sugar (dark brown): 3⅓ cups or 1 lb. 1⁷⁄₉ oz.
- Milk (cold): 2 qts. plus ⅓ cup or 4 lb. 2⅔ oz.
- Cornstarch: ⅝ cup or 3⅓ oz.
- Flour (bread): ⅝ cup or 2½ oz.
- Salt: 2½ tsps. or ⁵⁄₁₂ oz.
- Egg yolks (beaten): 20 or 1 lb. 4 oz.
- Vanilla extract: 1⅔ Tbsps. or ⅚ oz.
- Butter: 5 Tbsps. or 2½ oz.
- Egg whites (stiffly beaten): 10 or 10 oz.
- Sugar (granulated): 1¼ cups or 10 oz.
- Pastry: 5 baked pie shells

Melt ¼ cup butter over low heat; add brown sugar all at once and stir until mixture is thoroughly blended and sugar melted (if using thermometer, until mixture reaches 220° F.), stirring constantly. Then add 1⅓ cups of the milk, which has been brought to the scalding point, very slowly to prevent crystalizing or lumping of sugar mixture, and stir constantly with a wooden spoon or wood paddle. When milk has been added, increase heat and bring to a boil, stirring constantly. Place over hot water. Mix cornstarch, remaining ⅓ cup of milk, flour, and salt. Blend thoroughly. Gradually add cornstarch mixture alternately with beaten egg yolks to the boiling butterscotch; stir constantly and vigorously with a wire whisk until thickened. Remove from heat and cool a little; stir in vanilla and remaining butter, then fold in the stiffly beaten egg whites with the remaining sugar. Turn butterscotch cream filling into a pre-baked shell and top with meringue. Bake 15 minutes in a slow oven (300°–325° F.) or until meringue is delicately brown. Serve cold.

....

(125)

BUTTERSCOTCH, PINEAPPLE AND NUT PIE
ONE-CRUST PIE, PRE-BAKED SHELL

For one 9-inch pie
- Sugar (brown): 1 cup
- Flour: 1 Tbsp.
- Salt: ¼ tsp.
- Water or milk (cold): 1 cup
- Egg yolks (beaten): 3
- Butter: 1 Tbsp.
- Pineapple (canned crushed): 1¾ cups
- Vanilla extract: 1 tsp.
- Nut meats (cut fine): ½ cup
- Pastry: 1 baked pie shell
- Honey Meringue Topping: No. 451

For five 9-inch pies
- Sugar (brown): 5 cups or 1 lb. 10⅔ oz.
- Flour: 5 Tbsps. or 1¼ oz.
- Salt: 1¼ tsps. or ⅚ oz.
- Water or milk (cold): 5 cups or 2½ lbs.
- Egg yolks (beaten): 15 or 15 oz.
- Butter: 5 Tbsps. or 2½ oz.
- Pineapple (canned crushed): 2 qts. plus ¾ cup or 6 lb. 9 oz.
- Vanilla extract: 1⅔ Tbsps. or ⅚ oz.
- Nut meats (cut fine): 2½ cups or 11³/₇ oz.
- Pastry: 5 baked pie shells
- Honey Meringue Topping: No. 451

Mix sugar, flour, and salt with cold water (or milk) and eggs. Stir until thick. Remove from the heat and stir in butter, pineapple, vanilla, and nut meats. Blend well. Fill pre-baked pie shell and top with No. 451, Honey Meringue Topping. Bake 15 minutes in a moderately slow oven (325° F.), or until delicately brown. Serve cold.

Variation: Substitute 1¼ cups seedless raisins for pineapple, proceeding exactly as indicated and using the same amount of other ingredients.

....

(126)

BUTTERSCOTCH MERINGUE PECAN PIE—NEW MEXICO METHOD
ONE-CRUST PIE, PRE-BAKED SHELL

For one 9-inch pie
- Flour (pastry, sifted): 5 Tbsps.
- Sugar (brown): ¾ cup
- Butter: 3 Tbsps.
- Milk (rich, scalded): 2 cups
- Egg yolks (well-beaten): 4
- Salt: ¼ tsp.
- Vanilla extract: ¾ tsp.
- Pecans (chopped): ½ cup
- Egg whites (stiffly beaten): 4
- Salt: a pinch
- Lemon juice: 2 tsps.
- Powdered sugar: ½ cup
- Pastry: 1 baked pie shell

For five 9-inch pies
- Flour (pastry, sifted): A scant 1⅝ cups or 6¼ oz.
- Sugar (brown): 3¾ cups or 1 lb. 10⅔ oz.
- Butter: 1 scant cup or 7½ oz.
- Milk (rich, scalded): 2½ qts. or 5 lbs.
- Egg yolks (well-beaten): 20 or 1¼ lb.
- Salt: 1¼ tsps. or ⁵⁄₂₄ oz.
- Vanilla extract: 1 Tbsp. plus ¾ tsp. or ⅝ oz.
- Pecans (chopped): 2½ cups or 10 oz. or ⅝ lb.
- Egg whites (stiffly beaten): 20 or 1¼ lb.
- Salt: ½ tsp. or ¹⁄₁₂ oz.
- Lemon juice: 3⅓ Tbsps. or 1⅔ oz.
- Powdered sugar: 2½ cups or 11³⁄₇ oz.
- Pastry: 5 baked pie shells

Cream flour, sugar and butter thoroughly and put in a warm place to soften butter. Add scalded milk to flour-sugar-butter mixture; stir until well blended and free from lumps. Place mixture over hot water and cook, stirring frequently, until mixture thickens. Add well-beaten egg yolks and salt gradually to milk mixture; cook a few minutes longer, stirring constantly lest mixture curdle. Remove from heat, add vanilla extract and chopped pecans, reserving about 1 tablespoon, and pour into pre-baked shell. Top with a meringue made with stiffly beaten egg whites, salt, lemon juice and powdered sugar. Sprinkle remaining chopped pecans over top and brown lightly in a 325° F. oven for 15–20 minutes, or until meringue is delicately brown. Serve cold.

....

(127) BUTTERSCOTCH PEANUT BUTTER PIE— SOUTHERN METHOD
ONE-CRUST PIE, PRE-BAKED SHELL

For one 9-inch pie
- Brown sugar: 1 cup
- Cornstarch: 3 Tbsps.
- Salt: ¼ tsp.
- Egg yolks (slightly beaten): 2
- Orange juice: ¼ cup
- Milk (scalded): 2 cups
- Peanut butter: 3 Tbsps.
- Butter: 1 Tbsp.
- Rich pastry: 1 baked pie shell
- Whipped cream (unsweetened)

For five 9-inch pies
- Brown sugar: 5 cups or 1 lb. 10⅔ oz.
- Cornstarch: 1 scant cup or 5 oz.
- Salt: 1¼ tsps. or $^5/_{24}$ oz.
- Egg yolks (slightly beaten): 10 or 10 oz.
- Orange juice: 1¼ cups or 10 oz.
- Milk (scalded): 2½ qts. or 5 lbs.
- Peanut butter: 1 scant cup or 7½ oz.
- Butter: 5 Tbsps. or 2½ oz.
- Rich pastry: 5 baked pie shells
- Whipped cream (unsweetened)

Beat together brown sugar, cornstarch, salt, egg yolks, and orange juice. Gradually add scalded milk to cornstarch mixture, stirring briskly. Place mixture in top of double boiler and cook over hot water, stirring constantly until mixture begins to thicken; then add peanut butter and butter, and stir until both are dissolved; let mixture simmer gently for 4 or 5 minutes, stirring almost constantly. Remove from hot water; cool a little and pour into pre-baked pie shell. Cool. When cold, decorate with unsweetened, unflavored whipped cream by forcing through pastry bag with a fancy tube, forming circles by starting from edge of pie top and finishing in center with a large puff of whipped cream. Top may be sprinkled with finely chopped nut meats, such as peanut, pistachio nut (for contrast of color), or any other kind of nut meats desired.

(128)

CARAMEL PECAN PIE
ONE-CRUST PIE, PRE-BAKED SHELL

For one 9-inch pie
- Sugar (brown): 1 cup
- Flour: ¼ cup
- Salt: ½ tsp.
- Milk (hot): 2 cups
- Egg yolks (well beaten): 2
- Butter: 1 Tbsp.
- Pecans (chopped): ¾ cup
- Vanilla extract: 1½ tsps.
- Egg whites (stiffly beaten): 2
- Sugar (granulated): ¼ cup
- Pastry: 1 baked pie shell

For five 9-inch pies
- Sugar (brown): 5 cups or 1 lb. 10⅔ oz.
- Flour: 1¼ cups or 5 oz.
- Salt: 2½ tsps. or ⁵⁄₁₂ oz.
- Milk (hot): 2½ qts. or 5 lbs.
- Egg yolks (well beaten): 10 or 10 oz.
- Butter: 5 Tbsps. or 2½ oz.
- Pecans (chopped): 3¾ cups or 1 lb. 1¹⁄₇ oz.
- Vanilla extract: 2½ Tbsps. or 1¼ oz.
- Egg whites (stiffly beaten): 10 or 10 oz.
- Sugar (granulated): 1¼ cups or 10 oz.
- Pastry: 5 baked pie shells

Mix thoroughly sugar, flour, and salt. Gradually add to the hot milk, stirring until mixture is smooth and thick. Cover and cook over hot water for 15 minutes, stirring frequently. Pour slowly over well-beaten egg yolks, stirring vigorously and constantly. Return to hot water and cook 2 or 3 minutes, stirring occasionally. Remove from hot water and stir in butter. Cool. When cold, stir in pecans and vanilla extract. Turn mixture into a pre-baked pie shell. Cover with the meringue made from the stiffly beaten egg whites and sugar; sprinkle top of the meringue with broken pecan meats and brown in a slow oven (300° F.) for 15–25 minutes. Serve cold.

Variations: Equal parts of seedless raisins and pecans may be used or equal parts of pecan and peanuts (roasted). Topping may be substituted by a Marshmallow Meringue No. 472.

(129)

CARAMEL PECAN RUM PIE—
ILLINOIS METHOD
ONE-CRUST PIE, PRE-BAKED SHELL

For one 9-inch pie
- Sugar (brown): 1 cup
- Cornstarch: 1½ Tbsps.
- Milk (cold): ¼ cup
- Milk (scalded): 1¾ cups
- Salt: ¼ tsp.
- Eggs (whole, slightly beaten): 2
- Almond extract: ⅛ tsp.
- Pecans (chopped): ⅔ cup
- Rum: 2 Tbsps.
- Whipped Cream Topping
- Pecan halves
- Pastry: 1 baked pie shell

For five 9-inch pies
- Sugar (brown): 5 cups or 1¼ qts. or
  1 lb. 10⅔ oz.
- Cornstarch: 7½ Tbsps. or 2½ oz.
- Milk (cold): 1¼ cups or 10 oz.
- Milk (scalded): 2 qts. plus ¾ cup or
  4 lb. 6 oz.
- Salt: 1¼ tsps. or 5/24 oz.
- Eggs (whole, slightly beaten): 10 or
  1¼ lbs.
- Almond extract: ⅝ tsp.
- Pecans (chopped): 3⅓ cups or 13⅓ oz.
- Rum: ⅝ cup or 5 oz.
- Whipped Cream Topping
- Pecan halves
- Pastry: 5 baked pie shells

Caramelize sugar in heavy frying pan over low heat. Mix cornstarch to a smooth paste with cold milk; slowly add hot milk to caramelized sugar, stirring constantly until dissolved. Stir in dissolved cornstarch, and cook over hot water 10 minutes, or until slightly thickened, stirring constantly. Pour hot mixture, to which has been added salt, slowly on beaten whole eggs, mixing thoroughly; add pecans and rum and fill pre-baked pastry shell. Chill thoroughly and top with unsweetened, unflavored whipped cream, forced through a pastry bag with a large fancy tube. Garnish edge of pie with selected pecan halves. Serve very cold.

(130)

CARROT CREAM PIE— MIDDLE WEST METHOD
ONE-CRUST PIE

For one 9-inch pie
- Cooked grated carrots: 1½ cups
- Cinnamon (ground): ½ tsp.
- Nutmeg (ground): ¼ tsp.
- Salt: ½ tsp.
- Egg yolks (slightly beaten): 3
- Sweetened condensed milk: ⅓ cup
- Butter (melted): 3 Tbsps.
- Egg whites (stiffly beaten): 3
- Rich pastry: For 1 one-crust pie

For five 9-inch pies
- Cooked grated carrots: 7½ cups or 3¾ lbs.
- Cinnamon (ground): 2½ tsps. or $5/24$ oz.
- Nutmeg (ground): 1¼ tsps.
- Salt: 2½ tsps. or $5/12$ oz.
- Egg yolks (slightly beaten): 15 or 15 oz.
- Sweetened condensed milk: $1^2/3$ cups or 1¼ lbs.
- Butter (melted): scant cup or 7½ oz.
- Egg whites (stiffly beaten): 15 or 15 oz.
- Rich pastry: For 5 one-crust pies

Combine carrots, spices, salt, and egg yolks; stir in the undiluted, sweetened condensed milk, then the butter. Fold in the stiffly beaten egg whites. Turn filling into unbaked pie crust; bake 10 minutes in a hot oven (450° F.); reduce heat to moderate (350° F.) and continue baking 30 minutes longer. Serve each portion with plain whipped cream.

CARROT CREAM PIE—
PENNSYLVANIA STYLE
ONE-CRUST PIE

(131)

For one 9-inch pie
- Raw carrots (ground): 1½ cups
- Sugar (granulated): ¾ cup
- Whole eggs (well beaten): 3
- Cinnamon (ground): 1 tsp.
- Allspice (ground): 1 tsp.
- Ginger (ground): ⅛ tsp.
- Salt: ¼ tsp.
- Milk (scalded): 1 cup
- Butter (melted): 1½ Tbsps.
- Rich pastry: For 1 one-crust pie
- Whipped cream topping
- Nut meats: ground

For five 9-inch pies
- Raw carrots (ground): 7½ cups or 3¾ lbs.
- Sugar (granulated): 3¾ cups or 1 lb. 14 oz.
- Whole eggs (well beaten): 15 or 1 lb. 14 oz.
- Cinnamon (ground): 1⅔ Tbsps. or ⁵⁄₁₂ oz.
- Allspice (ground): 1⅔ Tbsps. or ⁵⁄₁₂ oz.
- Ginger (ground): ⅝ tsp.
- Salt: 1¼ tsps. or ⁵⁄₂₄ oz.
- Milk (scalded): 5 cups or 1¼ qts. or 2½ lbs.
- Butter (melted): 7½ Tbsps. or 3¾ oz.
- Rich pastry: For 5 one-crust pies
- Whipped cream topping
- Nut meats: ground

Wash or scrub carrots thoroughly; put through food chopper, and cook with salt in as little water as possible; cool; force through a potato ricer 3 or 4 times. Then mix all remaining ingredients in order given, blending thoroughly. Turn filling into an unbaked pastry shell, the bottom of which has been brushed with butter, then sprinkled with very little flour to prevent sogginess. Bake 10 minutes in a hot oven (450° F.); reduce heat to moderate (350° F.) and continue baking 30 minutes longer. When cold, top with sweetened and flavored whipped cream, then dust (optional) with shredded, blanched almonds, or any kind of nut meats, shredded or chopped.

Variations: You may combine equal parts of carrots and drained, canned crushed pineapple instead of carrots only.

You may brush bottom of unbaked pastry with apricot jam, orange marmalade, prune jam, or any desired jam before turning in the filling.

You may use only one cup of carrots and ½ cup of chopped nut meats.

(132)

CHEESE CUSTARD PIE
ONE-CRUST PIE

NOTE: You may add vanilla extract, but the flavor of the cheese will be changed.

For one 9-inch pie
- Sugar (granulated): 1 cup
- Grated cheese: $1/3$ cup
- Salt: ¼ tsp.
- Flour: 2 Tbsps.
- Eggs (whole, well beaten): 1 cup
- Milk (scalded): $1^3/5$ cups
- Pastry: For 1 one-crust pie

For five 9-inch pies
- Sugar (granulated): 5 cups or 2½ lbs.
- Grated cheese: $1^2/3$ cups or $5^1/3$ oz.
- Salt: 1¼ tsps. or $5/24$ oz.
- Flour: $5/8$ cup or 2½ oz.
- Eggs (whole, well beaten): 5 cups or 2½ lbs.
- Milk (scalded): 2 qts. or 4 lbs.
- Pastry: For 5 one-crust pies

Combine sugar, cheese, salt, and flour. Blend well. Add well-beaten eggs and blend thoroughly. Gradually add scalded milk, beating vigorously after each addition. Fill unbaked pie crust and bake 10 minutes in a very hot oven (450° F.); reduce temperature to 325° F. and continue baking 30 to 35 minutes longer. Serve with or without unsweetened whipped cream.

(133)   # COTTAGE CHEESE PINEAPPLE PIE
ONE-CRUST PIE

For one 9-inch pie

- Sugar (granulated): 2/3 cup
- Butter (softened): 2 Tbsps.
- Salt: 1/4 tsp.
- Flour: 5 Tbsps.
- Cottage cheese (sieved): 2 cups
- Eggs (whole, unbeaten): 2
- Milk: 1 1/3 cups
- Evaporated milk: 2 cups
- Vanilla extract: 1 tsp.
- Egg whites, beaten: 2
- Sugar (granulated): 2 Tbsps.

Pineapple Filling

- Crushed, canned pineapple: 1 cup
- Corn syrup: 2 tsps.
- Sugar (granulated): 1/4 cup
- Cornstarch: 2 1/2 tsps.
- Water or pineapple juice: 1 Tbsp.
- Pastry: For 1 one-crust pie

For five 9-inch pies

- Sugar (granulated): 3 1/3 cups or 1 lb. 10 2/3 oz.
- Butter (softened): 10 Tbsps. or 5 oz.
- Salt: 1 1/4 tsps. or 5/24 oz.
- Flour: 1 cup plus 9 Tbsps. or 6 1/4 oz.
- Cottage cheese (sieved): 2 1/2 qts. or 4 lb. 6 oz.
- Eggs (whole, unbeaten): 10 or 1 lb. 4 oz.
- Milk: 6 2/3 cups or 3 lb. 5 1/3 oz.
- Evaporated milk: 2 1/2 qts. or 6 lbs. 2/3 oz.
- Vanilla extract: 5 tsps. or 5/6 oz.
- Egg whites, beaten: 10 or 1 lb. 4 oz.
- Sugar (granulated): 5/8 cup or 5 oz.

Pineapple Filling

- Crushed, canned pineapple: 5 cups or 3 3/4 lbs.
- Corn syrup: 3 1/3 Tbsps. or 2 1/2 oz.
- Sugar (granulated): 1 1/4 cups or 9 7/17 oz.
- Cornstarch: 4 Tbsps. (generous) or 1 1/3 oz.
- Water or pineapple juice: 5 Tbsps. or 2 1/2 oz.
- Pastry: For 5 one-crust pies

For Cheese Filling: Combine the first 2/3-cup granulated sugar, softened butter, and salt; rub—do not cream—together for 1 short minute, or until mixed. To this gradually add flour alternately with sieved cottage cheese, blending well after each addition; beat until mixture is stiff. Gradually add whole, unbeaten eggs one at a time, alternately with combined fresh and evaporated milk (thin cream may be substituted for evaporated milk). Blend thoroughly, adding vanilla extract with the last milk addition. Lastly fold in the stiffly beaten egg whites with remaining 2 Tbsps. sugar for meringue.

For Pineapple Filling: In a saucepan place pineapple (juice and pulp), corn syrup, and sugar; blend well. Bring this to a boil. Dissolve cornstarch in water (or pineapple juice) and add slowly to the boiling pineapple mixture, stirring constantly until thick and clear. Remove from the heat and cool.

Spread pineapple filling on bottom of unbaked pie crust evenly; then pour over the cheese filling, completely filling the pie. Here you may sprinkle over 4 or 5 tablespoons of chopped pecans mixed with equal parts of seeded or seedless raisins or currants. Bake 10 minutes in a very hot oven (450° F.); reduce heat to 350° F. and continue baking 30 to 35 minutes longer. The top should be nicely browned. Serve cold. Individual pies may be prepared in the same way.

....

(134)   **A FEW FACTS ABOUT CHERRIES**

There are many varieties of this fruit, but in general these may be divided into two classes: (a) sweet and (b) sour.

Sweet cherries may be either flesh colored, as the Royal Anne, or very dark red, as the Bing. Sour cherries are usually smaller than sweet cherries, and vary in color, the earlier ones being lighter red and less sour than later varieties. The Duke is a variety of cherry half way between sweet and sour. No matter what the kind, the chief points in their selection are: unbruised skin, fruit with stems left on, freedom from mold and worms and brown spots. Cherries start to decay at the stem and so the fruit should not be separated from the stem. Cherries should be washed carefully, since the trees have to be sprayed frequently and the skins may be contaminated. There are several mechanical devices for removing pits from cherries, the simplest of which is a wire bent like a hairpin.

(134-a)

CHERRY PIE
ONE- OR TWO-CRUST PIE

For one 9-inch pie
- Cherries (frozen, thawed): 2¾ cups
- Juice: ⅔ cup
- Corn syrup: ¼ cup
- Cornstarch: 2⅔ Tbsps.
- Salt: ⅛ tsp.
- Sugar (granulated): 1 cup
- Pastry: For 1 one- or two-crust pie

For five 9-inch pies
- Cherries (frozen, thawed): 1 #10 can or 6 lb. 10 oz.
- Juice: 3⅓ cups or 1 lb. 10⅔ oz.
- Corn syrup: 1¼ cups or 15 oz.
- Cornstarch: ⅚ cup or 13⅓ Tbsps. or 4⁴⁄₉ oz.
- Salt: ⅝ tsp.
- Sugar (granulated): 5 cups or 2 lb. 8 oz.
- Pastry: For 5 one- or two-crust pies

Thaw and drain cherries, reserving juice (there should be ⅔ cup; if not, add sufficient cold water to balance). Place juice, except about 3 Tbsps., in saucepan with corn syrup. Bring to a quick boil. Dissolve cornstarch in reserved juice and add alternately with mixed salt and sugar to boiling syrup, stirring constantly until mixture thickens and becomes clear. Continue boiling for a minute or two. Remove from heat, stir in the cherries, using a wooden spoon or paddle so as not to tear fruit. Cool. When cold, turn into pastry-lined pie pan (either one-crust or two-crust) and bake 10 minutes at 450° F.; reduce heat to 350° F. and continue baking 25 minutes longer. If using meringue for one-crust pie, flavor with a few drops of almond flavoring. Serve cold.

(135) CHERRY PIE—FRENCH METHOD
ONE- OR TWO-CRUST PIE

For one 9-inch pie
- Cherries (fresh, ripe): 1 qt. or 4 cups
- Fine bread crumbs: 3 Tbsps.
- Ground almonds: 2 Tbsps.
- Sugar (granulated): ½ cup
- Egg yolk: 1
- Cream (heavy): 3 Tbsps.
- Salt: ¼ tsp.

For five 9-inch pies
- Cherries (fresh, ripe): 5 qts. or 4 lb. 2⅔ oz.
- Fine bread crumbs: 1 cup (scant) or 4 oz.
- Ground almonds: ⅔ cup (scant) or 5 oz.
- Sugar (granulated): 2½ cups or 1 lb. 4 oz.
- Egg yolks: 5 or 5 oz.
- Cream (heavy): 1 scant cup or 7¹³/₁₆ oz.
- Salt: 1¼ tsps. or ⁵/₂₄ oz.

Wash and pit cherries, reserving liquid that has run out when pitting. Place a thin layer of the special dough given below on pie pan; sprinkle top with bread crumbs mixed with ground almonds. Spread cherries over the crumb and almond mixture evenly. Sprinkle with sugar (a few grains of cinnamon may be mixed with sugar, if desired). Beat egg yolk and salt until light, adding the cream gradually; then beat in the reserved cherry juice and pour over the cherries. Bake in a hot oven (450° F.) for 10 minutes; reduce heat to 350° F. and continue baking for 25 minutes longer, or until browned at bottom. Cover with top crust or meringue (see No. 26) if desired.

For the special dough: (one pie)
- Flour: 1 cup
- Baking powder: ½ tsp.
- Sugar (granulated): ¼ cup
- Salt: ⅛ tsp.
- Shortening: 1 Tbsp.
- Egg (whole): 1

For the special dough: (five pies)
- Flour: 5 cups or 1 lb. 4 oz.
- Baking powder: 2½ tsps.
- Sugar (granulated): 1¼ cup or 10 oz.
- Salt: ⅝ tsp.
- Shortening: 5 Tbsps. or 2½ oz.
- Egg (whole): 5 or 10 oz.

Mix and sift flour, baking powder, sugar and salt twice; work in shortening (preferably butter or lard) alternately with egg. Toss on slightly floured board and roll to scant ¼-inch thick. Fit onto 9-inch pie pan and proceed as indicated above.

(136)

CHERRY MINCEMEAT PIE
ONE-CRUST CRISSCROSS PIE

For one 9-inch pie
- Cherries (fresh or canned, pitted): 1½ cups
- Sugar (fine granulated or confectioners'): ½ cup
- Mincemeat: 1 (9 oz.) pkg.
- Water (or fruit juice): ½ cup
- Salt: ⅛ tsp.
- Egg (whole): 1
- Flour: 3 Tbsps.
- Pastry: For 1 one-crust crisscross pie

For five 9-inch pies
- Cherries (fresh or canned, pitted): 7½ cups or 2 lb. 2²/₇ oz.
- Sugar (fine granulated or confectioners'): 2½ cups or 1 lb. 4 oz.
- Mincemeat: 2 lbs. 13 oz.
- Water (or fruit juice): 2½ cups or 1 lb. 4 oz.
- Salt: ⅝ tsps.
- Egg (whole): 5 or 10 oz.
- Flour: 1 scant cup or 3¾ oz.
- Pastry: For 5 one-crust crisscross pies

Cover cherries with half the sugar and let stand 15 minutes to mellow and absorb all or almost all the sugar, stirring frequently and gently. Break mincemeat into pieces; add cold water or fruit juice and place over low heat, stirring constantly, until all lumps are thoroughly broken up. Bring to a brisk boil and continue boiling for 3 minutes or so, or until mixture is practically dry. Cool. Combine mincemeat and cherries (with juice drawn by sugar) and add all the remaining ingredients. Turn into unbaked pie crust; arrange pastry strips across top in the usual way, moistening edge of pie with cold water. Bake in hot oven (450° F.) for 10 minutes; reduce to 350° F. and continue baking for 25 minutes longer. Serve cold or warm.

(137) CHERRY RHUBARB PIE
TWO-CRUST PIE

For one 9-inch pie
- Pastry: For 1 two-crust pie
- Butter (softened): 2 Tbsps.
- Sugar (granulated): 1½ cups
- Flour: 3½ Tbsps.
- Salt: ⅛ tsp.
- Rhubarb (cut up): 4 cups
- Cherries (sour): 1 cup

For five 9-inch pies
- Pastry: For 5 two-crust pies
- Butter (softened): 10 Tbsps. or 5 oz.
- Sugar (granulated): 7½ cups or 3¾ lbs.
- Flour: 1 cup and 1½ Tbsps. or 4⅜ oz.
- Salt: ⅝ tsp.
- Rhubarb (cut up): 4 qts. or 4 lbs.
- Cherries (sour): 5 cups or 1 lb. 6⁶⁄₇ oz.

Line pie pan with pastry rolled ⅛-inch thick. Do not stretch the crust when fitting, as pastry shrinks during baking. Spread the bottom and sides with 2 tsps. of the softened butter to prevent soaking of crust. Mix sugar, flour and salt together; sprinkle 3 tablespoons of flour mixture over bottom of buttered crust; add half of the sliced rhubarb, then the drained pitted cherries and half the remaining flour mixture; cover with the rest of the rhubarb and sprinkle with the remaining flour mixture; dot with remaining butter. Cover with top crust, make slashes for escape of steam. Moisten the rim with water and press lightly; trim; press edge and rim together with tines of a fork or pastry roller and bake in a hot oven (400° F.) for 40 minutes. Serve warm or cold with a whipped cream topping.

(138) CHERRY CUSTARD PIE
ONE-CRUST PIE

For one 9-inch pie
- Pastry: For 1 one-crust pie
- Eggs (slightly beaten): 2
- Sugar (granulated): ¼ cup
- Salt: ¼ tsp.
- Vanilla extract: ½ tsp.
- Milk (scalded): 1½ cups
- Cherries (canned): 1¼ cups

For five 9-inch pies
- Pastry: For 5 one-crust pies
- Eggs (slightly beaten): 10 or 1 lb. 4 oz.
- Sugar (granulated): 1¼ cups or 10 oz.
- Salt: 1¼ tsps. or ⁵⁄₂₄ oz.
- Vanilla extract: 2½ tsps. or ⁵⁄₁₂ oz.
- Milk (scalded): 7½ cups or 3 lbs. 12 oz.
- Cherries (canned): 6¼ cups or 3 lb. 12 oz.

Line pie pan with pastry rolled ⅛-inch thick and make fluted standing rim. Combine the slightly beaten eggs with sugar and salt, vanilla and milk, and add well-drained, pitted cherries. Blend well and easily. Pour this mixture into pie shell and bake 10 minutes in a hot oven (450° F.) and continue baking for 25–30 minutes longer, or until inserted knife blade comes out clean. Serve cold.

....

(139)

CHERRY CREAM PIE
ONE-CRUST PIE, PRE-BAKED PIE SHELL

For one 9-inch pie
- Milk: 1¼ cups
- Sugar (granulated): ⅔ cup
- Salt: ½ tsp.
- Cornstarch: 2½ Tbsps.
- Pastry flour: 3 Tbsps.
- Milk: ⅜ cup
- Egg (whole): 1
- Vanilla extract: ½ tsp.
- Butter: 1 Tbsp.
- Egg whites (stiffly beaten): 2
- Sugar (granulated): 3 Tbsps.
- Pastry: 1 baked pie shell
- Glazed Cherry Topping: No. 461
- Whipped Cream Topping

For five 9-inch pies
- Milk: 6¼ cups or 3 lbs. 2 oz.
- Sugar (granulated): 3⅓ cups or 1 lb. 10⅔ oz.
- Salt: 2½ tsps. or 5/12 oz.
- Cornstarch: 12½ Tbsps. or 4⅙ oz.
- Pastry flour: 1 cup, less 1 Tbsp. or 3¾ oz.
- Milk: 1⅞ cups or 15 oz.
- Egg (whole): 5 or 10 oz.
- Vanilla extract: 2½ tsps. or 5/12 oz.
- Butter: 5 Tbsps. or 2½ oz.
- Egg whites (stiffly beaten): 10 or 10 oz.
- Sugar (granulated): 1 cup, less 1 Tbsp. or 7½ oz.
- Pastry: 5 baked pie shells
- Glazed Cherry Topping: No. 461
- Whipped Cream Topping

Combine the first amounts of milk, granulated sugar and salt, and stir until sugar is thoroughly dissolved; bring this to a boil. Dissolve cornstarch and pastry flour in remaining milk and stir in the whole egg, blending well. Gradually add cornstarch mixture to boiling milk mixture, a small amount at a time, stirring constantly. Let this boil once or twice; remove at once from the heat, and add vanilla extract and butter. Do not stir. Beat egg whites until stiff, add the remaining sugar and continue beating until sugar is thoroughly incorporated, but mixture not too stiff. Slowly pour cream mixture (still hot) over beaten egg whites, stirring very gently; turn this filling at once into pre-baked shell, filling it about ⅔ full. Let cool. When cold add Glazed Cherry Topping made as indicated for No. 461. Then cover with remaining cream filling. Lastly, pipe a "collar" of unsweetened and unflavored whipped cream around the outer edge. This leaves a bit of the filling exposed to view and presents a most attractive appearance.

(140) CHOCOLATE COCONUT PIE
ONE-CRUST PIE, PRE-BAKED SHELL

For one 9-inch pie

- Chocolate (bitter): 3 squares
- Milk: 2 cups
- Sugar (granulated): ¾ cup
- Flour: 5 Tbsps.
- Salt: ½ tsp.
- Egg yolks (slightly beaten): 2
- Shredded coconut: 1 cup
- Vanilla extract: 1 tsp.
- Pastry: 1 baked pie shell
- Egg whites (stiffly beaten): 2
- Sugar (granulated): ¼ cup

For five 9-inch pies

- Chocolate (bitter): 15 squares or 15 oz.
- Milk: 2½ qts. or 5 lbs.
- Sugar (granulated): 3¾ cups or 1 lb. 14 oz.
- Flour: 1½ cups plus 1 Tbsp. or 6¼ oz.
- Salt: 2½ tsps. or ⁵/₁₂ oz.
- Egg yolks (slightly beaten): 10 or 10 oz.
- Shredded coconut: 5 cups or 1 lb.
- Vanilla extract: 5 tsps. or ⁵/₆ oz.
- Pastry: 5 baked pie shells
- Egg whites (stiffly beaten): 10 or 10 oz.
- Sugar (granulated): 1¼ cups or 10 oz.

Add broken chocolate to milk and heat in double boiler over hot water. When chocolate is melted, beat with rotary egg beater until blended and smooth. Combine sugar, flour and salt and add gradually to chocolate mixture. Cook until mixture is thickened, stirring constantly. When thickened, continue cooking 10 minutes longer, stirring occasionally. Pour small amount of chocolate mixture over slightly beaten egg yolks, stirring briskly and constantly, lest egg yolks cook and curdle. Return to double boiler and cook 2 minutes longer. Remove from hot water; add coconut and vanilla extract. Cool. When cold, turn into pre-baked pie shell, spreading evenly. Make a meringue with egg whites and sugar in the usual way; pile on filling, covering it entirely, and bake 15 minutes in a slow oven (325° F.), or until meringue is delicately brown. Serve cold.

....

(141)   # CHOCOLATE MIX PASTE

NOTE: To save time you may prepare ahead of time and keep on hand in the refrigerator a supply of Chocolate Mix Paste. This will keep fresh for over a month and may be used as needed to finish the number of chocolate pies or tarts or chocolate fillings you may require in a hurry.

This Chocolate Mix Paste is quite heavy, but it must be remembered that it is only the basic foundation of fillings, and should be completed before using by addition of egg white, to lighten it, as well as fresh heavy cream. This paste being mainly used commercially, the writer gives here the recipe for 5 pies:

Ingredients: First Part
- Water: 7 cups or 1¾ qts. or 3½ lbs.
- Sugar (granulated): 3⅛ cups or 1 lb. 8½ oz.
- Cocoa (powder): 1 cup or 4 oz.
- Chocolate (grated): ½ cup or 2⅔ oz.
- Salt: 1 Tbsp. or ½ oz.
- Corn syrup: 1¾ cups or 1 lb. 5 oz.
- Cornstarch: 1¾ cups or 9⅓ oz.

Ingredients: Second Part
- Cold water: 2 cups or 1 pint or 1 lb.
- Egg whites (stiffly beaten): 1 cup or 8 oz.
- Sugar (granulated): 1 cup or 8 oz. or ½ lb.
- Heavy cream: 1 cup or 8 oz. or ½ lb.
- Sugar (granulated): ½ cup or 4 oz.
- Vanilla extract: 1 Tbsp. or ½ oz.
- Whipped cream for topping

Directions: Mix together the first six ingredients and blend thoroughly. Place over high heat and bring to the boiling point, stirring constantly, until mixture boils. Dissolve cornstarch in cold water, and slowly add to boiling mixture, stirring vigorously and constantly, until mixture thickens, using a wire whisk. Let this boil 1–2 minutes, stirring constantly. Remove from the heat and pour into a shallow, dry pan, spreading evenly and smoothly. Immediately cover with waxed or buttered paper to prevent tough skin forming on top, pressing paper so as to touch mix all over. Place in refrigerator until needed.

Completing Filling: Take the required amount of mix and beat until smooth and soft, using a wooden spoon or paddle. If you have an electric beater, set the machine in second speed, adding vanilla as mixture gets smooth. Make a meringue with egg whites and sugar in the usual way (No. 26), and mix it with chocolate mix, alternately with heavy cream, adding a little amount at a time and beating well after each addition. Do not beat too long, lest mixture curdle. The filling is then ready to pour into pre-baked pie shell. Top with sweetened, flavored whipped cream, forced through pastry bag. Serve cold.

Should you wish a smoother, lighter filling, you may add a little more plain heavy cream.

(142) CHOCOLATE BANANA CREAM PIE
ONE-CRUST PIE, PRE-BAKED PIE SHELL

Have ready a Chocolate Mix Paste made as indicated for No. 141 above, and a chilled, pre-baked 9-inch one-crust shell. Slice 3 bananas (1 lb.) in bottom of shell and pour over the completed Chocolate Mix Paste. Arrange banana slices in circle around top of pie and pile whipped sweetened and flavored cream in the center.

(143)

CHOCOLATE CREAM PIE
ONE-CRUST PIE, PRE-BAKED SHELL

For one 9-inch pie
- Milk: 1⅓ cups
- Sugar (granulated): ⅞ cup
- Chocolate (grated squares): 4 squares
- Salt: ½ tsp.
- Milk (hot): ½ cup
- Cornstarch: 2½ Tbsps.
- Pastry flour: 2 Tbsps.
- Whole egg (slightly beaten): 1
- Egg yolks: 2
- Butter: 1 Tbsp.
- Vanilla extract: 1 tsp.
- Pastry: 1 baked pie shell

For five 9-inch pies
- Milk: 6⅔ cups or 3 lbs. 5⅓ oz.
- Sugar (granulated): 1 qt. plus ⅜ cup or 2 lbs. 3 oz.
- Chocolate (grated squares): 1 lb. 4 oz.
- Salt: 2½ tsps. or $5/12$ oz.
- Milk (hot): 2½ cups or 1 lb. 4 oz.
- Cornstarch: ¾ cup plus ½ Tbsp. or 4⅙ oz.
- Pastry flour: 10 Tbsps. or 2½ oz.
- Whole eggs (slightly beaten): 5 or 10 oz.
- Egg yolks: 10 or 10 oz.
- Butter: 5 Tbsps. or 2½ oz.
- Vanilla extract: 1 Tbsp. plus 1 generous tsp. or $5/7$ oz.
- Pastry: 5 baked pie shells

Into a kettle put the first four ingredients and blend well. Bring to a boil, stirring constantly, until mixture is smooth and has boiled up 2 or 3 times. Slowly add the combined hot milk, cornstarch, and pastry flour, and blend thoroughly, stirring constantly until mixture thickens. Let this simmer gently for 5 minutes, stirring constantly. Remove from the heat and beat in slowly combined whole egg and egg yolks, slightly beaten. Return to the heat and cook 2 minutes, beating vigorously with a wire whisk. Remove from the heat, add butter and vanilla and cool. Pour into pre-baked pie shell. Cover with a meringue made in the usual way, and bake 15–20 minutes in moderately slow oven (325°F.), or until meringue is delicately brown. Serve cold.

(144)   # CHOCOLATE CUSTARD PIE
ONE-CRUST PIE

For one 9-inch pie
- Sugar (granulated): 14 Tbsps. or ⅞ cup
- Tapioca flour: 2¼ tsps.
- Salt: ⅛ tsp.
- Cocoa: 6 Tbsps.
- Eggs (whole): 3
- Egg yolk: 1
- Milk (cold): 2 cups
- Butter (melted): ¾ Tbsp.
- Vanilla extract: ¼ tsp.
- Pastry: For 1 one-crust pie

For five 9-inch pies
- Sugar (granulated): 1 qt. plus ⅜ cup or 2 lbs. 3 oz.
- Tapioca flour: 3 Tbsps. plus 2¼ tsp. or 1 scant oz.
- Salt: ⅝ tsp.
- Cocoa: 1⅞ cup or 7½ oz.
- Eggs (whole): 15 or 1 lb. 14 oz.
- Egg yolks: 5 or 5 oz.
- Milk (cold): 2½ qts. or 5 lbs.
- Butter (melted): 3¾ Tbsps. or 1⅞ oz.
- Vanilla extract: 1¼ tsps. or ⅚₄ oz.
- Pastry: For five one-crust pies

Combine and sift together the first four ingredients. Slightly beat whole eggs and egg yolks together and blend with sugar mixture until sugar is dissolved. Slowly add milk, stirring constantly, until mixture is smooth and free from lumps, adding with the last part of milk the vanilla extract. Stir well, but do not beat; or strain through a fine sieve into pastry-lined pie pan which has been brushed with softened butter. Bake 10 minutes in a very hot oven (450° F.); reduce temperature to 325° F. and continue baking 25–30 minutes longer. Serve cold. You may pipe a "collar" of whipped cream around the outer edge, sweetened and flavored with either nutmeg or vanilla extract.

(145)   # CHOCOLATE NUT CREAM PIE
ONE-CRUST PIE

Use pre-baked 9-inch pastry shell and any kind of toasted, cooled nut meats, such as almonds, filberts, pecans, peanuts, walnuts, etc. However, if nuts are mixed with cream filling, an unbaked 9-inch pastry shell should be baked at once, to prevent nut meats from sinking to the bottom of the pie. If a pre-baked 9-inch pastry shell is used, proceed as follows:

Have ready a filling made as indicated for No. 143, Chocolate Cream Pie. Spread ¼ cup of toasted, cooled nut meats in bottom of pre-baked pastry shell; pour over this the filling and sprinkle over another ¼ cup of toasted, cooled nut meats. Serve cold.

On the other hand, if using an unbaked pastry shell, bake the pie 10 minutes in a hot oven (450° F.); reduce temperature to moderate (350° F.) and continue baking 30 minutes longer. You may spread a thin layer of unsweetened whipped cream on top of the nut meats, if desired. Serve cold.

(146)   # CIDER PIE
ONE-CRUST CRISSCROSS PIE

For one 9-inch pie
- Cider: 1⅝ cups
- Sugar (granulated): ½ cup
- Salt: ¼ tsp.
- Pastry flour: ¼ cup
- Cornstarch: 2⅔ Tbsps.
- Whole egg (slightly beaten): 1
- Egg yolk (slightly beaten): 1
- Butter: 1 Tbsp.
- Pastry: For 1 crisscross pie

For five 9-inch pies
- Cider: 2 qts. plus ⅛ cup or 4 lb. 1 oz.
- Sugar (granulated): 2½ cups or 1 lb. 4 oz.
- Salt: 1¼ tsp. or scant ¼ oz.
- Pastry flour: 1¼ cups or 5 oz.
- Cornstarch: 13⅓ Tbsps. or 4⁴⁄₉ oz.
- Whole eggs (slightly beaten): 5 or 10 oz.
- Egg yolks (slightly beaten): 5 or 5 oz.
- Butter: 5 Tbsps. or 2½ oz.
- Pastry: For 5 crisscross pies

Combine 1 cup cold cider, granulated sugar, and salt; stir until sugar is dissolved. Slowly bring mixture to a boil. Combine pastry flour and cornstarch, and dissolve in remaining cold cider; stirring constantly, gradually add this to the hot cider mixture alternately with slightly beaten whole egg and egg yolk, beaten together; let this boil gently, stirring constantly, until mixture thickens. Remove from the heat and stir in the butter. Turn filling into unbaked pastry shell; cover with unbaked pastry, crisscross fashion; brush crisscross strips with cold milk and bake 10 minutes in a hot oven (450° F.); reduce heat to moderate (350° F.) and continue baking 30 minutes longer. Serve cold with plain whipped cream.

....

(147)   **IMPORTANT FACTS
ABOUT CREAM PIES**

Everyone knows that cooked cream pies, eclairs, puffed creams and the like are composed of milk, flour, sugar, and eggs, plus salt and flavoring. In the preparation of the cream, the yolks, which stand a temperature rather high, are sterilized, but the whites are not. The albumin has not coagulated and the microbes, if there are any, are intact.

This action of the ptomaines and leucomaines makes it imperative for the baker, professional or homemaker, to employ only the clarified whites of eggs for cream filling for pastry of any description. Sterilized whites are egg whites which have not been exposed to the air for even the shortest length of time. If there have been yolks or whites left over from some previous baking or operation, they should be used only for those preparations which require baking in the oven.

When making a cooked cream filled by either the old or new method, it is imperative to mix the egg whites completely with the boiling cream so as to ensure smoothness; watch carefully that there are absolutely no lumps which, having been subjected to a temperature insufficient to pasteurize them, will easily decompose and cause trouble and spoilage.

It has been noted that cases of ptomaine poisoning by cooked cream generally occur in summer, seldom during other periods of the year. Consequently, it is wise, when making cream fillings during summer, to substitute whipped cream for egg whites. Also, another important point is not to use alum for the treatment of egg whites to prevent graining. The commercial alum is a double acid sulphate of aluminum and potash which, under the influence of a certain temperature, and sometimes just cold, produces sulphate of copper, which is a well-known energetic vomitive.

(148) **CREAM PIE—MASTER RECIPE**
ONE-CRUST PIE, PRE-BAKED PIE SHELL

For one 9-inch pie
- Milk (cold): 1⅝ cups
- Sugar (granulated): ½ cup
- Salt: ½ tsp.
- Pastry flour: ¼ cup
- Cornstarch: 2⅔ Tbsps.
- Whole egg (slightly beaten): 1
- Egg yolk (slightly beaten): 1
- Vanilla extract (or other kind): ½ tsp.
- Butter: 1 Tbsp.
- Pastry: 1 baked pie shell

For five 9-inch pies
- Milk (cold): 2 qts. plus ⅛ cup or 4 lb. 1 oz.
- Sugar (granulated): 2½ cups or 1 lb. 4 oz.
- Salt: 2½ tsps. or ⁵⁄₁₂ oz.
- Pastry flour: 1¼ cup or 5 oz.
- Cornstarch: 13⅓ Tbsps. or 4⁴⁄₉ oz.
- Whole eggs (slightly beaten): 5 or 10 oz.
- Egg yolks (slightly beaten): 5 or 5 oz.
- Vanilla extract (or other kind): 2½ tsps. or ⁵⁄₁₂ oz.
- Butter: 5 Tbsps. or 2½ oz.
- Pastry: 5 baked pie shells

Combine half the milk with sugar and salt in a saucepan and stir until sugar is dissolved. Place over a low heat and slowly bring mixture to a boil. Sift together pastry flour and cornstarch and dissolve in remaining cold milk. Stirring constantly, gradually add this to the hot sugar-milk mixture, alternately with the slightly beaten whole egg and egg yolk; cook until mixture thickens. Let this boil 3 or 4 minutes, stirring constantly. Remove from the heat; stir in flavoring extract and butter, and immediately transfer cream into a cold container to cool slightly. While still warm, pour into pre-baked one-crust shell.

NOTE: Should you leave mixture to cool in the saucepan in which it has been cooked, the mixture will continue cooking in center, which may cause breaking and separating milk and eggs. It is the water resulting from the breaking which may generate microbes, especially in summer. This filling may be used for puffs, eclairs, etc. You may, if desired, top the filled shell with a meringue, made in the usual way, and bake 15 minutes in a moderate oven (350° F.), or until meringue is delicately brown.

(149)   # COFFEE CUSTARD CREAM PIE—
HOME METHOD
ONE-CRUST PIE

For one 9-inch pie
- Milk: 3 cups
- Thin cream or evaporated milk: 1 cup
- Coffee (ground): ¾ cup
- Whole eggs (slightly beaten): 3
- Sugar (granulated): ¾ cup
- Salt: ¼ tsp.
- Pastry: For 1 one-crust pie
- Heavy cream: 1 cup
- Vanilla extract: ¾ tsp.
- Sugar: 3 Tbsps.

For five 9-inch pies
- Milk: 3¾ qts. or 7½ lbs.
- Thin cream or evaporated milk: 5 cups or 2½ lbs.
- Coffee (ground): 3¾ cups or 15 oz.
- Whole eggs (slightly beaten): 15 or 1⅞ lbs.
- Sugar (granulated): 3¾ cups or 1⅞ lbs.
- Salt: 1¼ tsps. or ⁵/₂₄ oz.
- Pastry: For 5 one-crust pies
- Heavy cream: 5 cups or 1¼ qts. or 2½ lbs.
- Vanilla extract: 1 Tbsp. plus ¾ tsp. or ⅝ oz.
- Sugar: scant cup or 7½ oz.

Scald combined milk and cream or evaporated milk (unsweetened and undiluted) with freshly ground good coffee. Let stand 30 minutes; strain through a fine sieve, then through double cheesecloth. Beat whole fresh eggs slightly; add sugar and salt and blend well. Slowly, while stirring constantly, pour coffee-flavored milk over egg mixture, stirring well while pouring so as to blend thoroughly. Turn custard into unbaked pie shell, the inside of which has been brushed with unbeaten egg white, and bake 10 minutes in a hot oven (450° F.); then at 325° F. for 30 minutes longer. Cool the pie and cover with whipped cream flavored with vanilla and sweetened with sugar, forced through a pastry bag with a fancy tube.

(150)
COTTAGE CHEESE PIE— NEW ENGLAND METHOD
ONE-CRUST PIE

For one 9-inch pie
- Flour (pastry): 2 cups
- Sugar (granulated): ½ cup
- Baking powder: 1 tsp.
- Salt: ½ tsp.
- Shortening: ¼ cup
- Eggs (whole): 2 (slightly beaten)

For five 9-inch pies
- Flour (pastry): 2½ qts. or 2½ lbs.
- Sugar (granulated): 2½ cups or 1 lb. 4 oz.
- Baking powder: 5 tsps. or scant ¾ oz.
- Salt: 2½ tsps. or ⁵/₁₂ oz.
- Shortening: 1¼ cups or 10 oz.
- Eggs (whole): 10 or 1 lb. 4 oz. (slightly beaten)

Sift flour, sugar, and baking powder, and salt together twice; cut in shortening until mixture resembles corn meal; moisten with slightly beaten eggs. Roll dough ¼-inch thick and line a 9-inch pie pan with it. Chill while preparing filling.

Filling
- Cottage cheese (sieved): 3 cups
- Flour (pastry): ¼ cup
- Salt: ¼ tsp.
- Sugar (granulated): ¼ cup
- Honey (liquid): ½ cup
- Lemon rind (grated): 1 Tbsp.
- Heavy cream: ¼ cup
- Egg yolks (beaten): 4
- Egg whites (stiffly beaten): 4

Filling
- Cottage cheese (sieved): 3¾ qts. or 6 lbs. 9 oz.
- Flour (pastry): 1¼ cups or 5 oz.
- Salt: 1¼ tsp. or ⁵/₂₄ oz.
- Sugar (granulated): 1¼ cups or 10 oz.
- Honey (liquid): 2½ cups or 1 lb. 14 oz.
- Lemon rind (grated): 5 Tbsps. or 1⅞ oz.
- Heavy cream: 1¼ cups or 10⅝ oz.
- Egg yolks (beaten): 20 or 1 lb. 4 oz.
- Egg whites (stiffly beaten): 20 or 1¼ lbs.

Force cottage cheese through a fine sieve; add flour, salt, sugar, honey (strained), lemon grating, heavy cream, and beaten egg yolks; beat until very smooth and thoroughly blended; then fold in the stiffly beaten egg whites. Place in pan lined with the special pastry (above) and spread over the following topping:

Topping
- Sugar (granulated): ¼ cup
- Cinnamon: ¾ tsp.
- Nut meats (any kind, chopped): ½ cup

Topping
- Sugar (granulated): 1¼ cups or 10 oz.
- Cinnamon: 3¾ tsps. or $5/16$ oz.
- Nut meats (any kind, chopped): 2½ cups or 13⅓ oz.

Combine the three ingredients and spread over top of filling. Bake in a moderately slow oven (325° F.) for 45 minutes. Serve cold.

....

(151)

COTTAGE CHEESE PIE— PENNSYLVANIA METHOD
ONE-CRUST PIE

For one 9-inch pie
- Cottage cheese: 1 cup
- Flour (pastry): 2½ Tbsps.
- Sugar (granulated): 1 cup
- Salt: ⅓ tsp.
- Vanilla extract: 1 tsp.
- Egg yolks (well beaten): 3
- Milk (scalded, then cooled): 3 cups
- Egg whites (stiffly beaten): 3
- Pastry: For 1 one-crust pie

For five 9-inch pies
- Cottage cheese: 5 cups or 1¼ qts. or $2^3/16$ lbs.
- Flour (pastry): A generous ¾ cup or $3^1/8$ oz.
- Sugar (granulated): 5 cups or 1¼ qts. or 2½ lbs.
- Salt: $1^2/3$ tsps. or $5/18$ oz.
- Vanilla extract: $1^2/3$ Tbsps. or $5/6$ oz.
- Egg yolks (well beaten): 15 or 15 oz.
- Milk (scalded, then cooled): 3¾ qts. or 7½ lbs.
- Egg whites (stiffly beaten): 15 or 15 oz.
- Pastry: For 5 one-crust pies

Put cottage cheese in a mixing bowl and mash. Add flour, sugar, salt, vanilla, and egg yolks, and blend thoroughly. Gradually add milk, stirring well to make a smooth mixture. Lastly fold in stiffly beaten egg whites. Pour mixture into unbaked pastry shell, bake 10 minutes in a hot oven (450° F.); reduce heat to 300° F. and bake for 35 minutes longer. Serve cold. Maple syrup may be poured over each piece.

(152)

CRANBERRY PIE
ONE-CRUST PIE, PRE-BAKED SHELL

For one 9-inch pie
- Canned cranberries (drained): 1 #2½ can
- Cranberry juice and water: 1⅓ cups
- Salt: ⅛ tsp.
- Cinnamon (optional): ⅛ tsp.
- Cornstarch: 2 Tbsps.
- Sugar (granulated): 1 cup
- Pastry: 1 baked pie shell

For five 9-inch pies
- Canned cranberries (drained): 1 #10 can or 6 lbs. 7 oz.
- Cranberry juice: 6⅔ cups or 3 lbs. 5⅓ oz.
- Salt: ⅝ tsp.
- Cinnamon (optional): ⅝ tsp.
- Cornstarch: 10 Tbsps. or 3⅓ oz.
- Sugar (granulated): 5 cups or 2⅔ lbs.
- Pastry: 5 baked pie shells

Drain cranberries, reserving juice. There should be ⅓ of a cup (if not, add enough cold water to balance the amount). Place juice in a saucepan, reserving 2 Tbsps. to dissolve the salt, cinnamon (optional), and cornstarch, and bring to a boil. When boiling, gradually stir in the cornstarch mixture, and stir constantly until mixture is thick; allow to boil 2 or 3 minutes, stirring frequently, until clear and thick. Add sugar and continue cooking 2 minutes longer, stirring frequently. Remove from the heat; add drained berries and stir, using a wooden spoon, to blend thoroughly. Cool before turning into pre-baked 9-inch pastry shell. Serve plain or topped with whipped cream.

....

(153)

CRANBERRY APRICOT PIE
ONE-CRUST PIE

Spread ½-cup dried, cooked, and sweetened apricots on a 9-inch pre-baked pie crust before turning in cranberry mix made as in No. 152, topped with a meringue made of 2 egg whites, stiffly beaten, then sweetened with ¼-cup sugar, and place another ½-cup of cooked, sweetened dried apricots on top of meringue; then sprinkle (optional) with ½-cup of shredded coconut. Do not bake. Serve as is, or substitute whipped cream for meringue and arrange cooked dried apricots neatly on top.

(154)
CRANBERRY ORANGE PIE
ONE-CRUST PIE

For one 9-inch pie
- Fresh cranberries (ground): 4 cups
- Orange juice: ¾ cup
- Orange rind (grated): 1 tsp.
- Sugar (granulated): 2 cups
- Butter (melted): 1 Tbsp.
- Quick-cooking tapioca: 2½ Tbsps.
- Salt: ½ tsp.
- Pastry: For 1 one-crust pie
- Frozen Cream Whipped Topping: No. 459

For five 9-inch pies
- Fresh cranberries (ground): 5 qts. or 4 lbs.
- Orange juice: 3¾ cups or 1 lb. 14 oz.
- Orange rind (grated): 1⅔ Tbsps. or ⅝ oz.
- Sugar (granulated): 2½ qts. or 5 lbs.
- Butter (melted): 5 Tbsps. or 2½ oz.
- Quick-cooking tapioca: ¾ cup, plus 1 Tbsp. or 3⅛ oz.
- Salt: 2½ tsps. or ⁵⁄₁₂ oz.
- Pastry: For 5 one-crust pies
- Frozen Cream Whipped Topping: No. 459

Grind or chop fresh cranberries after washing rapidly; add orange juice, orange rind, sugar, melted butter, tapioca, and salt. Mix thoroughly. Line a 9-inch pie pan with pastry rolled ⅛-inch thick and roll 1 egg white over bottom and sides; turn out excess egg white. This prevents a soggy crust. Turn mixture into shell and bake 10 minutes in a very hot oven (450° F.); reduce temperature to moderate (350° F.) and bake 25–30 minutes longer. Serve warm, topped with Frozen Cream Whipped Topping made as indicated for No. 459.

(155)   CRANBERRY NUT MERINGUE PIE
ONE-CRUST PIE, PRE-BAKED SHELL

For one 9-inch pie
- Sugar (granulated): 1½ cups
- Cornstarch: 1 Tbsp.
- Water: 1½ cups
- Fresh cranberries: 3 cups
- Butter: 2 Tbsps.
- Salt: ⅛ tsp.
- Walnut meats (broken): ½ cup
- Pastry: 1 baked pie shell
- Egg whites: 3
- Brown sugar: 3 Tbsps.

For five 9-inch pies
- Sugar (granulated): 7½ cups or 3¾ lbs.
- Cornstarch: 5 Tbsps. or 1⅔ oz.
- Water: 1 qt. plus 3½ cups or 3¾ lbs.
- Fresh cranberries: 3¾ qts. or 3 lbs.
- Butter: 10 Tbsps. or 5 oz.
- Salt: ⅝ tsp.
- Walnut meats (broken): 2½ cups or 13⅓ oz.
- Pastry: 5 baked pie shells
- Egg whites: 15 or 15 oz.
- Brown sugar: 1 cup, less 1 Tbsp. or 5 oz.

Blend sugar and cornstarch; add water, stir well and bring to a boil. Quickly wash and drain berries; add to sugar-water mixture and cook as slowly as possible until cranberries pop open. Then add butter, salt, and nut meats, and set aside to cool. *Do not stir.* When cold, turn filling into pre-baked 9-inch pie shell. Make a meringue with egg whites and brown sugar in the usual way. Pile meringue on filling; or force meringue through pastry bag with a large tube, and pipe a "collar" of the meringue around the outer edge. This will show cranberries and walnut meats poking up in the center, surrounded by a "collar" of toasted meringue. Bake in a slow oven (325° F.) for 20 minutes, or until delicate brown. Serve cold.

(156)
CRANBERRY CUSTARD PIE
ONE-CRUST PIE

For one 9-inch pie
- Fresh cranberries: 4 cups
- Sugar (granulated): 1¼ cups
- Corn syrup (white): ½ cup
- Salt: ½ tsp.
- Cinnamon: ⅛ tsp.
- Pastry: For 1 one-crust pie
- Eggs (whole): 3
- Sugar (granulated): ¼ cup
- Salt: ¼ tsp.
- Nutmeg (ground): ⅛ tsp.
- Milk: 1¼ cups
- Pecans (ground): ½ cup

For five 9-inch pies
- Fresh cranberries: 5 qts. or 4 lbs.
- Sugar (granulated): 6¼ cups or 3 lbs. 2 oz.
- Corn syrup (white): 2½ cups or 1lb. 14 oz.
- Salt: 1¼ tsps. or $5/24$ oz.
- Cinnamon: ⅝ tsp.
- Pastry: For 5 one-crust pies
- Eggs (whole): 15 or 1 lb. 14 oz.
- Sugar (granulated): 1¼ cups or 10 oz.
- Salt: 1¼ tsps. or $5/25$ oz.
- Nutmeg (ground): ⅝ tsp.
- Milk: 6¼ cups or 3 lb. 2 oz.
- Pecans (ground): 2½ cups or $11^3/7$ oz.

Put cranberries through food chopper, using fine blade. Combine with 1¼-cups of sugar, corn syrup, salt and cinnamon. Cook until sugar dissolves, or about 3 minutes, stirring occasionally. Spread mixture over bottom of unbaked 9-inch pastry shell. Make a custard mixture by beating eggs slightly, combining with ¼-cup sugar, nutmeg, salt and milk. Strain over the ground berry mixture in the shell and bake 10 minutes in a hot oven (450° F.); reduce temperature to 325°–350° F. and continue baking 40 minutes longer, adding ground nut meats over the top of pie the last 10 minutes. Serve cold.

(157)

CRANBERRY MOLASSES PIE— SOUTHERN METHOD
ONE-CRUST CRISSCROSS PIE

For one 9-inch pie

- Cranberries (cooked): 1 qt.
- Sugar (brown): ¾ cup
- Sugar (granulated): ¾ cup
- Baking soda: ½ tsp.
- Salt: ½ tsp.
- Molasses: 1 cup
- Nutmeg (ground): ¼ tsp.
- Cinnamon (ground): ½ tsp.
- Cloves (ground): ¼ tsp.
- Butter: 1 Tbsp.
- Pastry: For 1 crisscross pie

For five 9-inch pies

- Cranberries (cooked): 5 qts. or 5 lbs.
- Sugar (brown): 3¾ cups or 1 lb. 4 oz.
- Sugar (granulated): 3¾ cups or 1 lb. 14 oz.
- Baking soda: 2½ tsps. or $5/16$ oz.
- Salt: 2½ tsps. or $5/12$ oz.
- Molasses: 5 cups or 1¼ qts. or 3¾ lbs.
- Nutmeg (ground): 1¼ tsps.
- Cinnamon (ground): 2½ tsps. or $5/24$ oz.
- Cloves (ground): 1¼ tsps.
- Butter: 5 Tbsps. or 2½ oz.
- Pastry: For 5 crisscross pies

Combine all ingredients in order given and cook very slowly for 10 minutes. Cool. Fill pastry-lined 9-inch pie pan, arrange pastry strips crisscross fashion on top of filling in the usual way. Brush with cold milk, and bake 10 minutes in a hot oven (450° F.); reduce temperature to moderate (350° F.) and continue baking 30 minutes longer. Serve cold.

(158)

CRANBERRY RAISIN FRUIT MERINGUE PIE
ONE-CRUST PIE

For one 9-inch pie
- Cranberries (raw): 1½ cups
- Raisins (seedless): 1 cup
- Sugar (granulated): 1½ cups
- Flour (pastry): 1½ Tbsps.
- Salt: ¼ tsp.
- Orange juice: ½ cup
- Vanilla extract: 1 tsp.
- Pastry: For 1 one-crust pie

Meringue Topping
- Egg whites (stiffly beaten): 3
- Salt: ⅛ tsp.
- Sugar (granulated): 3 Tbsps.
- Sugar (brown): 3 Tbsps.
- Candied mixed fruits (chopped): ¼ cup

For five 9-inch pies
- Cranberries (raw): 7½ cups or 1½ lbs.
- Raisins (seedless): 5 cups or 1 lb. 10⅔ oz.
- Sugar (granulated): 7½ cups or 3¾ lbs.
- Flour (pastry): 7½ Tbsps. or 1⅞ oz.
- Salt: 1¼ tsps. or ⁵/₂₄ oz.
- Orange juice: 2½ cups or 1¼ lbs.
- Vanilla extract: 1⅔ Tbsps. or 5 tsps. or ⅚ oz.
- Pastry: For 5 one-crust pies

Meringue Topping
- Egg whites (stiffly beaten): 15 or 15 oz.
- Salt: ⅝ tsp.
- Sugar (granulated): 1 cup or 7½ oz.
- Sugar (brown): 1 cup or 6⅔ oz.
- Candied mixed fruits (chopped): 1¼ cups or 10 oz.

Wash, pick, drain raw cranberries. Do not chop. Rinse raisins quickly in lukewarm water and drain. Blend granulated sugar, flour, and salt; stir in orange juice mixed with vanilla extract. Combine fruits and sugar-flour mixture thoroughly. Brush bottom of 9-inch pastry-lined pie pan with butter, turn filling into it, and bake 10 minutes in a hot oven (450° F.); reduce heat to moderate (350° F.) and continue baking 25 minutes longer. Top with a meringue made with the ingredients listed; return pie to moderate oven (325° F.) and bake for 15 minutes, or until meringue is delicately brown and firm. Serve cold.

(159) CRANBERRY ZWIEBACK CREAM PIE— WISCONSIN METHOD
ONE-CRUST PIE, PRE-BAKED PIE SHELL

For one 9-inch pie
- Sugar (granulated): 2 cups
- Water (cold): 2 cups or enough to barely cover the berries
- Cranberries: 2 qts.
- Salt: ¼ tsp.
- Cloves (ground): ¼ tsp.
- Cinnamon (ground): ¼ tsp.
- Nutmeg (ground): $^1/_8$ tsp.
- Heavy cream: 2 cups
- Vanilla extract: ¼ tsp.
- Zwieback (crushed): 6 slices
- Pre-baked pastry: 1 zwieback pie shell

For five 9-inch pies
- Sugar (granulated): 10 cups or 5 lbs.
- Water (cold): 2½ qts. or enough to barely cover the berries or 5 lbs. (about)
- Cranberries: 10 qts. or 10 lbs.
- Salt: 1¼ tsps. or $^5/_{24}$ oz.
- Cloves (ground): 1¼ tsps.
- Cinnamon (ground): 1¼ tsps.
- Nutmeg (ground): $^5/_8$ tsp.
- Heavy cream: 2½ qts. or 5 lbs.
- Vanilla extract: 1¼ tsps. or $^5/_{24}$ oz.
- Zwieback (crushed): 30 slices
- Pre-baked pastry: 5 zwieback pie shells

Boil sugar and water together about 8 minutes. Carefully place whole cranberries, which have been washed and drained, in syrup; add salt, cloves, cinnamon, and nutmeg, and simmer slowly for 8 minutes, or until tender but not mushy. Remove whole berries with a skimmer, reserving syrup for other uses. Cool. Whip heavy cream and fold in vanilla extract. Place a layer of cooked cranberries in zwieback shell, then whipped cream, and sprinkle with zwieback crumbs. Make several layers, ending with crumbs on top. Serve thoroughly chilled.

Variations: (1) Sprinkle coarsely ground nut meats over top. (2) For each pie, fold ½-cup chopped nut meats into whipped cream. (3) Fold ¼-cup of cold, cooked dried apricots, strained, into the whipped cream. (4) Use macaroon crumbs, cake crumbs, ladyfinger crumbs, etc., instead of zwieback crumbs, reducing amount of sugar according to sweetness of crumbs.

(160) CRANBERRY WHITE RAISIN CREAM PIE— HOME METHOD
ONE-CRUST PIE

For one 9-inch pie
- Graham crackers: 15
- Butter (melted): ½ cup
- Cinnamon (ground): ½ tsp.
- Salt: ¼ tsp.
- Milk (iced): 2 Tbsps.
- Cranberries (raw): 3 cups
- Sugar (granulated): ½ cup
- Sugar (brown): ½ cup
- Heavy cream (unwhipped): 1 cup
- Flour (pastry): 3 Tbsps.
- Heavy cream (whipped): 1 cup

For five 9-inch pies
- Graham crackers: 75 or 7½ cups
- Butter (melted): 2½ cups or 1¼ lbs.
- Cinnamon (ground): 2½ tsps. or $5/24$ oz.
- Salt: 1¼ tsps. or $5/24$ oz.
- Milk (iced): 10 Tbsps. or $5/8$ cup or 5 oz.
- Cranberries (raw): 15 cups or 5 lbs.
- Sugar (granulated): 2½ cups or 1¼ lbs.
- Sugar (brown): 2½ cups or 1 lb. $1 7/9$ oz.
- Heavy cream (unwhipped): 5 cups or 1¼ qts. or 2½ lbs.
- Flour (pastry): 15 Tbsps. or scant cup or 3¾ oz.
- Heavy cream (whipped): 5 cups or 2½ lbs.

Roll graham crackers finely; mix with melted butter to which has been added cinnamon and salt, then blend with iced milk. Press around sides and bottom of buttered 9-inch pie tin. Prick each cranberry and combine with all the remaining ingredients in order given. Pour filling into prepared graham cracker crust and bake 25–30 minutes in a 425° F. oven, or until berries are tender. Cool and spoon whipped cream (unsweetened, unflavored) over top of pie. Serve cold.

(161)   # CREAM CHEESE CUSTARD PIE—
HOME METHOD
ONE-CRUST PIE

For one 9-inch pie
- Cream cheese: 2 (3 oz.) pkgs.
- Evaporated milk (or thin cream): ¾ cup
- Sugar (granulated): ⅔ cup
- Pastry flour: 1½ Tbsps.
- Salt: ¼ tsp.
- Orange rind (grated): 1 Tbsp.
- Egg yolks (slightly beaten): 3
- Nutmeg (ground): ¼ tsp.
- Egg whites (stiffly beaten): 3
- Pastry: For 1 one-crust pie
- Ginger Meringue Topping No. 451

For five 9-inch pies
- Cream cheese: 10 (3 oz.) pkgs. or 1 lb. 14 oz.
- Evaporated milk (or thin cream): 3¾ cups or a generous 2 lbs.
- Sugar (granulated): 3⅓ cups or 1 lb. 10⅔ oz.
- Pastry flour: 7½ Tbsps. or 1⅞ oz.
- Salt: 1¼ tsps. or ⁵/₂₄ oz.
- Orange rind (grated): 5 Tbsps. or 1⅞ oz.
- Egg yolks (slightly beaten): 15 or 15 oz.
- Nutmeg (ground): 1¼ tsps. or ⁵/₂₄ oz.
- Egg whites (stiffly beaten): 15 or 15 oz.
- Pastry: For 5 one-crust pies
- Ginger Meringue Topping No. 451

Blend cream cheese with undiluted evaporated milk or thin cream; then force through a sieve. Mix sugar, flour, salt, and grated orange rind together; to this add slightly beaten egg yolks and nutmeg. Combine cheese mixture with sugar-flour mixture and blend thoroughly. Now fold in the stiffly beaten egg whites. Turn into pastry-lined pie pan and bake 10 minutes in a hot oven (450° F.); reduce heat to moderate (350° F.) and continue baking 25–30 minutes longer. Cool a little and top with Ginger Meringue Topping No. 451; bake 15 minutes longer, or until meringue is delicately brown. Serve cold.

NOTE: You may, if desired, spread a thin layer of your favorite jam, jelly, or marmalade in bottom of unbaked pastry shell before pouring in filling.

(162) CREAM CHEESE STRAWBERRY JAM PIE— HOME METHOD
ONE-CRUST PIE, PRE-BAKED PIE SHELL

For one 9-inch pie
- Cream cheese: 2 (3 oz.) pkgs.
- Salt: ¼ tsp.
- Heavy cream: Enough to moisten
- Heavy cream (whipped): 2 cups
- Sugar (granulated): 1 cup
- Strawberry jam: 1½ cups
- Almond extract: ¼ tsp.
- Pastry: 1 pre-baked pie shell
- Fresh strawberries

For five 9-inch pies
- Cream cheese: 10 pkgs. or 1 lb. 14 oz.
- Salt: 1¼ tsps. or ⁵/₂₄ oz.
- Heavy cream: Enough to moisten
- Heavy cream (whipped): 2½ qts. or 5 lbs.
- Sugar (granulated): 5 cups or 1¼ qts. or 2½ lbs.
- Strawberry jam: 7½ cups or 4 lbs. 11 oz.
- Almond extract: 1¼ tsps. or ⁵/₂₄ oz.
- Pastry: 5 pre-baked pie shells
- Fresh strawberries

Blend cheese and salt with enough heavy cream to moisten. Force mixture through a sieve. Fold in heavy cream to which has been added sugar, strawberry jam and almond extract. Blend well and force through a pastry bag with a large tube into pre-baked pie shell, making circles. Garnish the edges of the pie with fresh (or thawed frozen) strawberries. Serve very cold.

CREAM CHEESE PIE
ONE-CRUST PIE

(163)

For one 9-inch pie
- Cream cheese: 1 lb. (about 5 pkgs.)
- Salt: 1/3 tsp.
- Lemon rind (grated): 2 tsps.
- Egg yolks (slightly beaten): 6
- Heavy cream (unwhipped): 1 cup
- Nutmeg: a few grains
- Almond extract: A few drops
- Sugar (granulated): 1 cup
- Egg whites (stiffly beaten): 6
- Pastry: 1 half-baked pie shell

For five 9-inch pies
- Cream cheese: 5 lbs. (about 25 pkgs.)
- Salt: 1²/₃ tsps. or ⁵/₁₈ oz.
- Lemon rind (grated): 3¹/₃ Tbsps. or 1¼ oz.
- Egg yolks (slightly beaten): 30 or 1⁷/₈ lbs.
- Heavy cream (unwhipped): 5 cups or 2½ lbs.
- Nutmeg: ½ tsp. or 1/24 oz.
- Almond extract: ½ tsp. or 1/12 oz.
- Sugar (granulated): 5 cups or 2½ lbs.
- Egg whites (stiffly beaten): 30 or 1⁷/₈ lbs.
- Pastry: 5 half-baked pie shells

Combine cream cheese, salt, lemon gratings, and force through a sieve, gradually adding the egg yolks mixed with heavy cream, nutmeg, almond extract, and sugar. Stir in the stiffly beaten egg whites gradually. Turn filling into half-baked pastry shell, the bottom and sides of which have been brushed with softened butter. Bake in a moderate oven (350° F.) for 35–40 minutes, or until filling is delicately brown and firm. Serve very cold.

....

(164) CRÈME BRÛLÉ PIE—FRENCH METHOD
ONE-CRUST PIE, PRE-BAKED PIE SHELL

NOTE: You may line pre-baked, cooled pastry shell with a thin layer or film of either apricot puree, guava jelly, cranberry jelly, currant jelly, orange marmalade or any kind of jam, marmalade or sieved fruit pulp desired, before pouring the burnt cream into the pre-baked pastry shell. Or you may use a meringue shell, if desired. In Paris, this is called a Flan Brûlé, and is served with fruit preserves.

For one 9-inch pie
- Heavy cream: 2 cups
- Brown sugar: 6 Tbsps.
- Egg yolks (well beaten): 5
- Salt: ¼ tsp.
- Almond extract: ¼ tsp.
- Rich pastry: 1 pre-baked pie shell

For five 9-inch pies
- Heavy cream: 2½ qts. or 5 lbs.
- Brown sugar: 1⅞ cups or 11⅑ oz.
- Egg yolks (well beaten): 25 or 1 lb. 9 oz.
- Salt: 1¼ tsps. or ⁵⁄₂₄ oz.
- Almond extract: 1¼ tsps. or ⁵⁄₂₄ oz.
- Rich pastry: 5 pre-baked pie shells

Scald the cream and 3 tablespoons of the brown sugar in a double boiler, but do not allow to boil. Combine ½-cup of hot cream mixture with egg yolks, salt, and almond extract. Return this mixture to double boiler and cook until mixture thickens slightly, stirring constantly. Do not over-cook lest mixture curdle. When mixture coats the spoon, remove at once from hot water, allow to cool slightly, and turn into pre-baked rich pie shell. Cool, then chill in refrigerator. When well chilled, sprinkle with remaining sugar (you may, if desired, use shaved maple sugar instead of brown sugar). Just before serving, place pie under broiler until sugar is caramelized, watching carefully so sugar does not scorch. Cool again before serving.

Variations: (1) Spread bottom of pre-baked pastry shell with a coat of almost any kind of jam, jelly, or marmalade. Honey, also, may be used. (2) Mix ½-cup of finely chopped nut meats (almonds, pistachio, etc.) into the cream before turning into the pie shell.

....

(165)   CURDS PIE—ENGLISH METHOD
ONE-CRUST PIE

For one 9-inch pie
- Curds or dry pot cheese: 1 cup
- Whole eggs (well beaten): 3
- Currants (cleaned): ½ cup
- Lemon juice: 2 Tbsps.
- Salt: ¼ tsp.
- Lemon rind (grated): 1 Tbsp.
- Pastry: For 1 one-crust pie

For five 9-inch pies
- Curds or dry pot cheese: 5 generous cups or 1¼ qts.
- Whole eggs (well beaten): 15 or 1⅞ lbs.
- Currants (cleaned): 2½ cups or 13⅓ oz.
- Lemon juice: ⅝ cup or 5 oz.
- Salt: 1¼ tsps. or ⁵⁄₂₄ oz.
- Lemon rind (grated): 5 Tbsps. or 1⅞ oz.
- Pastry: For 5 one-crust pies

Beat curds smooth and add all remaining ingredients. Add a little milk if mixture seems too dry and turn into pastry-lined pie pan. Bake for 1 hour and 15 minutes in a slow oven (325° F.). Serve cold with ginger preserves.

....

(166) CURRANT TAPIOCA MERINGUE PIE— HOME METHOD
ONE-CRUST PIE, PRE-BAKED PIE SHELL

For one 9-inch pie
- Fresh currants: 1 qt.
- Sugar (granulated): 1 cup
- Quick-cooking tapioca: 3 Tbsps.
- Water: 3 Tbsps.
- Lemon juice: 1 Tbsp.
- Salt: ¼ tsp.
- Pastry: 1 pre-baked pie shell

For five 9-inch pies
- Fresh currants: 5 qts. or 6 lb. 10⅔ oz.
- Sugar (granulated): 5 cups or 1¼ qts. or 2½ lbs.
- Quick-cooking tapioca: 1 scant cup or 3¾ oz.
- Water: 1 scant cup or 7½ oz.
- Lemon juice: 5 Tbsps. or 2½ oz.
- Salt: 1¼ tsps. or $5/24$ oz.
- Pastry: 5 pre-baked pie shells

Wash, stem, pick, and sponge fresh currants. Combine with sugar, tapioca, water, lemon juice, and salt; cook for about 15 minutes, or until tapioca is transparent. Cool. Pour mixture into cold pre-baked rich pie crust. Cover with a meringue made in the usual way, having center a little higher than edges. Bake in a moderately slow oven (325° F.) 15–20 minutes, or until meringue is firm and delicately brown. Serve cold.

Variations: (1) Use either a nut pastry, oatmeal pastry, potato pastry, or vanilla wafer pastry, if desired. (2) Spread bottom of pre-baked pastry shell with orange marmalade, or any favorite jelly. (3) If a crunchy pie is desired, add ½-cup of chopped nut meats (any kind) to the mixture before pouring it into the pre-baked pastry shell. (4) Use half fresh currants and half fresh or frozen raspberries, strawberries, or blackberries.

(167) A FEW POINTS ABOUT CUSTARD PIES

A custard pie which is curdled is a heart scald, a thin custard pie a disappointment. At a point between the two is the perfect custard, smoothly thickened, creamy, and delicate. True custard pies are thickened by *eggs alone* which act as a binder, leavener, thickener, stabilizer, and give texture as well as flavor. The temperature at which eggs coagulate is almost unbelievably low, and since we are accustomed to watching food bubble as it cooks, custard trouble is apt to happen now and then. Disastrous results follow too much heat. After the pie has been baked in a hot oven (450° F.) for 10 minutes to set the crust, the temperature should be lowered to 325° F. and the baking continued for 30 minutes longer.

The correct proportions are, of course, essential in order to make the perfect custard pie as well as the so-popular cup custard. Custards usually whey or separate because they are cooked at too high a temperature. Soft custards may curdle when they are cooked for too long a time or are not stirred constantly. Milk that is a little sour may cause curdling of a custard, too.

For the sake of economy, certain bakers substitute tapioca flour or some kind of starch as part of eggs as stabilizers, but this gives less fineness, smoothness, and flavor in the finished product. As a rule, the ratio of eggs to milk in custard pies is 3 whole eggs for each pint of fresh milk, or equal parts of fresh milk and coffee cream, if a richer custard is desired. Four eggs for each pint of fresh milk, or half fresh milk and coffee cream, gives the traditional rich custard pie with its smooth, mellow flavor and satisfying body. The whole eggs should be slightly beaten (so as not to incorporate too many air bubbles in the mixture); combine with the milk and other indicated ingredients, and pour into an unbaked shell, which has been brushed with egg white to prevent soaking and dusted with nutmeg. Immediately set into the hot oven. A very important point is to allow the brushed unbaked shell to dry before pouring in the custard mixture.

A true chocolate custard pie, while pleasant in flavor, is not pleasing in texture. The fat in the chocolate prevents a smooth jellying or coagulating of the custard mixture during cooking. It is wiser to make a cornstarch chocolate custard, the cornstarch doing much to bind the fat of the chocolate with the milk.

A good custard pie filling resembles a good fruit jelly in that it is tender and quivery, yet keeps its angles when cut and does not "weep" on standing. Furthermore, it has a delicate golden-brown surface entirely free from the heavy, dark-brown layer sometimes observed on this type of pie.

If the temperature of the oven is not reduced after the crust has set, the filling will be tough and have a tendency to "weep"; whereas if it is too low, the filling will soak into the crust unless the latter has been baked before the filling is added. Since, then, it is extremely difficult to find the temperature suitable for baking both filling and crust at the same time, it is highly desirable to bake the crust separately. When this is done, the temperature of the oven can be regulated to that required by the filling, without danger of a soaked crust.

Cool custard pies on cake rack to prevent lower crust from steaming after pies are baked. If no cake rack is available, set pie or pies on something so air may circulate underneath.

An absolutely foolproof method to prevent soggy crust is as follows: Take 2 pie pans of identical size. In one bake a pastry shell. Butter the second pie pan and bake the custard filling in that. When the custard and the baked pie shell are both thoroughly cooled, slip the custard filling into the cold baked pie shell just before serving.

....

(168) CUSTARD PIE—MASTER RECIPE
ONE-CRUST PIE

For one 9-inch pie

- Unbaked pastry: For 1 one-crust pie
- Egg white (unbeaten): 1
- Sugar (granulated): 7/8 cup
- Tapioca flour: 1½ tsp.
- Salt: ¼ tsp.
- Eggs (whole): 3
- Milk (fresh): 2 cups
- Butter (melted): 1 Tbsp.
- Vanilla extract: ¾ to 1 tsp.
- Nutmeg: ¼ tsp.

For five 9-inch pies

- Unbaked pastry: For 5 one-crust pies
- Egg white (unbeaten): 5 or 5 oz.
- Sugar (granulated): 4⅜ cups or 2 lb. 3 oz.
- Tapioca flour: 2½ Tbsps. or ⅝ oz.
- Salt: 1¼ tsps. or 5/24 oz.
- Eggs (whole): 15 or 1 lb. 14 oz.
- Milk (fresh): 2½ qts. or 5 lbs.
- Butter (melted): 5 Tbsps. or 2½ oz.
- Vanilla extract: 4½ tsps. or ¾ oz.
- Nutmeg: 1¼ tsps.

Line pie pan with pastry rolled ⅛-inch thick; roll in it the egg white, spreading it all over bottom and sides. Chill crust. Combine sugar, tapioca flour and salt; slightly beat whole eggs; then blend with sugar-tapioca-salt mixture. Stir in the fresh milk combined with melted butter gradually, stirring gently and constantly until mixture is thoroughly blended. Sprinkle chilled pie shell with nutmeg and strain filling into it through a fine sieve. Bake 10 minutes in a very hot oven (450° F.); reduce temperature to 325° F., and continue baking 30 minutes longer. Remove from oven and cool. The custard will stiffen while cooling.

(169) CUSTARD PIE—FRENCH METHOD
ONE-CRUST PIE

For one 9-inch pie
- Egg yolks: 3
- Flour (pastry): 1 Tbsp. or ¼ oz.
- Sugar (granulated): 3 Tbsps.
- Salt: ¼ tsp.
- Nutmeg: ⅛ tsp.
- Vanilla extract: ½ tsp.
- Almond extract: ¼ tsp.
- Egg whites (stiffly beaten): 3
- Fresh milk: 1½ cups
- Coffee cream (or evaporated milk): ½ cup
- Puff paste (No. 42): For 1 one-crust pie

For five 9-inch pies
- Egg yolks: 15 or 15 oz.
- Flour (pastry): 5 Tbsps. or 1¼ oz.
- Sugar (granulated): 1 cup, less 1 Tbsp. or 7½ oz.
- Salt: 1¼ tsps. or $5/24$ oz.
- Nutmeg: ⅝ tsp.
- Vanilla extract: 2½ tsps. or $5/12$ oz.
- Almond extract: 1¼ tsps. or $5/24$ oz.
- Egg whites (stiffly beaten): 15 or 15 oz.
- Fresh milk: 7½ cups or 3¾ lbs.
- Coffee cream (or evaporated milk): 2½ cups or 1¼ lbs.
- Puff paste (No. 42): For 5 one-crust pies

Beat egg yolks to a cream. Stir in flour mixed with sugar (this separates the particles of flour and there will be no lumps). Add salt, nutmeg, and flavoring extracts. Blend thoroughly, using a wire whisk. Then stir in the stiffly beaten egg whites, and last, combined fresh milk and coffee cream (or evaporated milk), scalded and somewhat cooled. Strain mixture into a puff paste pie shell and bake 10 minutes in a hot oven (450° F.); then reduce temperature to 325° F. and continue baking 30 minutes longer. Remove immediately from the oven and cool on a pastry rack to allow air to circulate underneath.

....

(170) COCONUT CUSTARD PIE
ONE-CRUST PIE

Into Recipe No. 168, Custard Pie—Master Recipe, stir 1 cup of long-thread shredded coconut. Turn into pastry-lined 9-inch pie pan and bake as indicated.

(171)

COFFEE CUSTARD PIE
ONE-CRUST PIE

In Master Recipe No. 168, Custard Pie—Master Recipe, substitute 1 cup of double-strength cold coffee for 1 cup of fresh milk. Proceed as directed for baking. Serve cold.

....

(172)

CHOCOLATE CUSTARD PIE
ONE-CRUST PIE

To Recipe No. 168, Custard Pie—Master Recipe, add 3 Tbsps. of cocoa when combining sugar, tapioca, and salt. Then proceed as indicated for mixing and baking. Serve cold.

....

(173)

CARAMEL CUSTARD PIE
ONE-CRUST PIE

For one 9-inch pie
- Sugar (granulated): ½ cup
- Milk (scalded): 2 cups
- Whole eggs (slightly beaten): 3
- Sugar (granulated): ⅓ cup
- Salt: ¼ tsp.
- Flour (pastry): 1 Tbsp.
- Nutmeg (ground): ⅛ tsp.
- Pastry: 1 unbaked Bread Crumb Crust, No. 51

For five 9-inch pies
- Sugar (granulated): 2½ cups or 1¼ lbs.
- Milk (scalded): 2½ qts. or 5 lbs.
- Whole eggs (slightly beaten): 15 or 1 lb. 14 oz.
- Sugar (granulated): 1⅔ cups or 13⅓ oz.
- Salt: 1¼ tsps. or ⁵⁄₂₄ oz.
- Flour (pastry): 5 Tbsps. or 1¼ oz.
- Nutmeg (ground): ⅝ tsp.
- Pastry: 5 unbaked Bread Crumb Crusts, No. 51

Caramelize the ½ cup of sugar by stirring it in a saucepan over moderate heat until it is melted and light brown. Gradually pour this syrup into the scalded milk and heat until the caramel is dissolved. Beat eggs slightly; add remaining granulated sugar combined with salt, flour, and nutmeg; stir until thoroughly blended. Cook until slightly thickened. Pour filling into unbaked Bread Crumb Crust (No. 51), the bottom and sides of which have been brushed with slightly beaten egg white, then sprinkled very lightly with flour. Bake 20 minutes in a 375° F. oven. Serve cold.

....

(174)
CHEESE CUSTARD PIE
ONE-CRUST PIE

For one 9-inch pie
- Sugar (granulated): 1 cup
- Cheese (grated): ¾ cup
- Tapioca flour: 1 tsp.
- Whole eggs (slightly beaten): 1 cup
- Salt: ½ tsp.
- Milk: 2 cups
- Vanilla extract (optional): ½ tsp.
- Unbaked pastry: For 1 one-crust pie

For five 9-inch pies
- Sugar (granulated): 5 cups or 2½ lbs.
- Cheese (grated): 3¾ cups
- Tapioca flour: 5 tsps. or $5/12$ oz.
- Whole eggs (slightly beaten): 5 cups or 2½ lbs.
- Salt: 2½ tsps. or $5/12$ oz.
- Milk: 2½ qts. or 5 lbs.
- Vanilla extract (optional): 2½ tsps. or $5/12$ oz.
- Unbaked pastry: For 5 one-crust pies

Combine sugar, cheese and tapioca flour and blend thoroughly. Gradually beat in the eggs alternately with salted milk and vanilla extract, beating constantly after each addition; blend thoroughly.

Turn this mixture into unbaked one-crust pie shell and bake 10 minutes in a very hot oven (450° F.); reduce to 350° F. and continue baking 30 minutes longer. Serve cold.

(175)
MINCEMEAT CUSTARD PIE
ONE-CRUST PIE

Have ready Recipe No. 168, Custard Pie—Master Recipe and proceed as follows: Line a 9-inch pie pan with pastry rolled ⅛-inch thick. Spread in bottom 2 cups of homemade mincemeat and very gently strain prepared custard recipe over the mincemeat. Be sure to pour mixture very slowly, so as not to disturb the mincemeat. Bake as indicated for Custard Pie—Master Recipe. Serve cold.

NOTE: You may omit vanilla extract and substitute 1½ tablespoons or more of either rum, brandy or apple brandy, if desired.

(176)
FRUIT CUSTARD PIE
ONE-CRUST PIE

For one 9-inch pie
- Custard filling (Recipe No. 168)
- Pastry: For 1 one-crust pie
- Canned fruit (any kind): 1 cup
- Juice from the fruit: ¼ cup
- Sugar (granulated): 3 Tbsps.
- Cornstarch: 1 Tbsp.
- Salt: ⅛ tsp.

For five 9-inch pies
- Custard filling (Recipe No. 168)
- Pastry: For 5 one-crust pies
- Canned fruit (any kind): 5 cups or 4 lb. 6 oz.
- Juice from the fruit: 1¼ cups or 10 oz.
- Sugar (granulated): ⅞ cup or 7½ oz.
- Cornstarch: 5 Tbsps. or 1⅔ oz.
- Salt: ⅝ tsp.

Have ready Recipe No. 168, Custard Pie—Master Recipe. Line a 9-inch pie pan with pastry rolled ⅛-inch thick with the following mixture: Drain canned fruit. Combine sugar and cornstarch and dissolve mixture in ¼ cup of the juice. Place over a high heat and bring to a boil. Let this boil until clear, or about 3 minutes, stirring constantly. Remove from the heat, stir in salt and drained fruit. Cool. When cold, spread in bottom of unbaked shell; strain over the custard recipe, as gently as possible, so as not to disturb fruit mixture, which should remain at bottom of pie. Bake 10 minutes in a very hot oven (450° F.); reduce temperature to 325° F. and continue baking 30 minutes longer. Serve cold.

(177)
DATE CUSTARD PIE
ONE-CRUST PIE, PRE-BAKED PIE SHELL

For one 9-inch pie
- Sugar (granulated): ⅔ cup
- Flour (pastry): ½ cup
- Cinnamon: ⅛ tsp.
- Nutmeg: ⅛ tsp.
- Cloves: ⅛ tsp.
- Salt: ½ tsp.
- Milk (scalded): 2 cups
- Egg yolks (slightly beaten): 3
- Butter: 2 Tbsps.
- Vanilla extract: 1 tsp.
- Dates (pitted, halved): 1 cup
- Egg whites: 3
- Sugar (granulated): ⅓ cup
- Pastry: 1 pre-baked pie shell

For five 9-inch pies
- Sugar (granulated): 3⅓ cups or 1 lb. 10⅔ oz.
- Flour (pastry): 2½ cups or 10 oz.
- Cinnamon: ⅝ tsp.
- Nutmeg: ⅝ tsp.
- Cloves: ⅝ tsp.
- Salt: 2½ tsps. or ⁵⁄₁₂ oz.
- Milk (scalded): 2½ qts. or 5 lbs.
- Egg yolks (slightly beaten): 15 or 15 oz.
- Butter: 10 Tbsps. or 5 oz.
- Vanilla extract: 1½ Tbsps. or ⅚ oz.
- Dates (pitted, halved): 5 cups or 2 lbs.
- Egg whites: 15 or 15 oz.
- Sugar (granulated): 1⅔ cup or 13⅓ oz.
- Pastry: 5 pre-baked pie shells

Combine and blend well sugar, flour, spices and salt. Gradually stir this into scalded, cooled milk. Cook over hot water 10 minutes, or until mixture begins to thicken, stirring constantly. Remove from hot water and slowly add slightly beaten egg yolks, stirring constantly; cook 3 minutes, stirring constantly. Remove from heat, add butter and vanilla. Cool. Have ready a pre-baked pastry shell. Line bottom with halved, pitted dates, and strain cold custard slowly over the dates. Cover with meringue made with stiffly beaten egg whites and remaining sugar and bake in a moderately slow oven (325° F.) for 15 minutes, or until meringue is delicately brown. Serve cold.

(178)
PRUNE CUSTARD PIE
ONE-CRUST PIE

For one 9-inch pie

- Prunes (cooked, diced): 2 cups
- Pastry: For 1 one-crust pie
- Sugar (granulated): 7/8 cup
- Egg yolks (beaten until light): 2
- Nutmeg: ½ tsp.
- Salt: ¼ tsp.
- Heavy cream (unwhipped): 1 cup
- Egg whites (stiffly beaten): 2
- Honey Meringue Topping No. 451

For five 9-inch pies

- Prunes (cooked, diced): 2½ qts or 2 lb. 3⁵/₉ oz.
- Pastry: For 5 one-crust pies
- Sugar (granulated): 4⅜ cups or 2 lb. 3 oz.
- Egg yolks (beaten until light): 10 or 10 oz.
- Nutmeg: 2½ tsps. or ⁵/₂₄ oz.
- Salt: 1¼ tsps. or ⁵/₂₄ oz.
- Heavy cream (unwhipped): 5 cups or 2 lb. 8 oz.
- Egg whites (stiffly beaten): 10 or 10 oz.
- Honey Meringue Topping No. 451

Remove pits from cooked prunes and dice. Arrange evenly over bottom of unbaked 9-inch one-crust pie shell. Add sugar to beaten egg yolks. Stir nutmeg and salt into heavy cream and combine with egg yolks. Gently fold in the stiffly beaten egg whites, and spoon over the prunes. Bake 10 minutes in a very hot oven (450° F.); reduce temperature to 325° F. and continue baking for 30 minutes. Top pie with Honey Meringue Topping No. 451; return to moderately slow oven (325° F.) and bake for 15 minutes, or until meringue is delicately brown. Serve cold.

(179) **PECAN CUSTARD PIE**
ONE-CRUST PIE

For one 9-inch pie
- Whole eggs: 3
- Sugar (granulated): ½ cup
- Corn syrup (dark): 1 cup
- Butter (melted): 2 Tbsps.
- Salt: ½ tsp.
- Vanilla extract: 1 tsp.
  or
- Rum, brandy or apple brandy: 3 Tbsps.
- Pastry: For 1 one-crust pie
- Pecans (broken, not chopped): 1 cup

For five 9-inch pies
- Whole eggs: 15 or 1 lb. 14 oz.
- Sugar (granulated): 2½ cups or 1 lb. 4 oz.
- Corn syrup (dark): 5 cups or 3¾ lbs.
- Butter (melted): ⅝ cup or 5 oz.
- Salt: 2½ tsps. or $5/12$ oz.
- Vanilla extract: 1½ Tbsps. or $5/6$ oz.
  or
- Rum, brandy or apple brandy: ⅞ cup or 7½ oz.
- Pastry: For 5 one-crust pies
- Pecans (broken, not chopped): 5 cups or 1 lb. $6^{6}/_{7}$ oz.

Beat eggs slightly, just enough to break them; then beat them with the sugar, until sugar is dissolved, adding the corn syrup gradually, a small amount at a time. Melt butter with salt and blend with mixture. Add vanilla or rum. Have ready a 9-inch pie pan lined with pastry rolled ⅛-inch thick; brush bottom of shell with butter and sprinkle lightly with pastry flour. Over the flour spread broken pecan meats, and gently pour over the custard mixture as evenly as possible. Bake 10 minutes in a very hot oven (450° F.); reduce temperature to 325° F. and bake 30 minutes longer. Serve cold.

NOTE: This pie may be flavored with either vanilla, brandy, rum, or apple brandy if desired. It may be varied by spreading in bottom of unbaked shell 8-oz. of homemade mincemeat or fruit (canned), or any one of the ingredients used in custard pie variations, if desired, and served for special holiday menu. It may also be covered with a meringue and baked 15 minutes longer, or until meringue is delicately brown.

SPICED RHUBARB CUSTARD PIE
ONE-CRUST PIE

(180)

For one 9-inch pie

- Egg (whole): 1
- Egg yolks: 2
- Sugar (granulated): ¾ cup
- Salt: ¼ tsp.
- Light cream (or evaporated milk): 1⅔ cups
- Rhubarb (small pieces): 1⅓ cups
- Nutmeg: ⅛ tsp.
- Cloves: ⅛ tsp.
- Cinnamon: ⅛ tsp.
- Vanilla extract: ½ tsp.
- Semi-Puff Paste, No. 66: For 1 one-crust pie
- Marshmallow Topping No. 470

For five 9-inch pies

- Eggs (whole): 5 or 10 oz.
- Egg yolks: 10 or 10 oz.
- Sugar (granulated): 3¾ cups or 1 lb. 14 oz.
- Salt: 1¼ tsps. or $5/24$ oz.
- Light cream (or evaporated milk): 2 qts. and ⅓ cup or 4 lb. 2⅔ oz.
- Rhubarb (small pieces): 6⅔ cups or 1 lb. 14 $^{10}/_{21}$ oz.
- Nutmeg: ⅝ tsp.
- Cloves: ⅝ tsp.
- Cinnamon: ⅝ tsp.
- Vanilla extract: 2½ tsps. or $5/24$ oz.
- Semi-Puff Paste, No. 66: For 5 one-crust pies
- Marshmallow Topping No. 470

Combine whole egg and egg yolks with sugar and salt, and beat until sugar is dissolved. Gradually add cream alternately with rhubarb, spices, and vanilla extract, mixing thoroughly. Blend well. Turn mixture into unbaked Crunchy Semi-Puff Paste shell, which has been brushed with unbeaten egg white, then dried, and bake 10 minutes in a hot oven (450° F.); reduce temperature to 325° F. and continue baking for 30 minutes longer. Top with Marshmallow Topping and bake about 5 minutes more, or until marshmallow topping is brown. Serve cold.

(181)   SOUTHERN CUSTARD PIE
ONE-CRUST PIE

For one 9-inch pie
- Custard filling (No. 168)
- Alabama Pastry No. 50: 1
- Plain boiled rice (cold): ½ cup
- Cooked dry apricots (sieved): ½ cup

For five 9-inch pies
- Custard filling (No. 168)
- Alabama Pastry No. 50: 5
- Plain boiled rice (cold): 2½ cups or 13⅓ oz.
- Cooked dry apricots (sieved): 2½ cups or 8⁸⁄₉ oz.

Have ready a No. 168, Custard Pie. Also have ready pie pan lined with Alabama, or Hot Water Pastry No. 50. Combine cold boiled rice and cold, sieved apricots and spread in bottom of pie shell. Over this strain the custard recipe and bake 10 minutes in a hot oven (450° F.); reduce temperature to moderately slow (325° F.), and continue baking 25–30 minutes longer. Cool. When cold, cover with sweetened, walnut-flavored whipped cream, forced through a pastry bag with a fancy tube. Serve very cold.

....

(182)   CUSTARD PIE—DANISH METHOD
ONE-CRUST PIE

For one 9-inch pie
- Pastry: 1 zwieback pie crust, No. 67
- Egg yolks (slightly beaten): 4
- Cornstarch: 2 Tbsps.
- Salt: ¼ tsp.
- Milk (scalded): 2 cups
- Egg whites (stiffly beaten): 4
- Salt: ⅛ tsp.
- Sugar (granulated): ½ cup
- Zwieback crumbs (fine): ½ cup

For five 9-inch pies
- Pastry: 5 zwieback pie crusts, No. 67
- Egg yolks (slightly beaten): 20 or 1¼ lbs.
- Cornstarch: 10 Tbsps. or ⅝ cup or 3⅓ oz.
- Salt: 1¼ tsps. or ⁵⁄₂₄ oz.
- Milk (scalded): 2½ qts or 5 lbs.
- Egg whites (stiffly beaten): 20 or 1¼ lbs.
- Salt: ⅝ tsp.
- Sugar (granulated): 2½ cups or 1¼ lbs.
- Zwieback crumbs (fine): 2½ cups or 10 oz. or ⅝ lb.

Prepare zwieback pastry and line bottom and sides of a 9-inch square shallow pan as evenly as possible. Bake in moderate oven (350° F.) about 10 minutes. Cool. Beat egg yolks slightly and blend them with cornstarch and salt until they form a smooth paste. Scald milk and add gradually to the egg yolk paste, stirring constantly until smooth and free from any lumps. Return mixture to top of double boiler and cook, stirring constantly, over hot water until thickened and spoon leaves streak when drawn through the custard. Cool and pour into the cooled zwieback pastry shell. Beat egg whites until stiff, add combined salt and sugar and continue beating until sugar is all absorbed and egg whites are smooth and hold their peaks. Using a pastry bag with a fancy tube, spread wave-like over the custard; sprinkle evenly with fine zwieback crumbs. Bake 15–20 minutes in a moderately slow oven (325° F.), or until top is delicately browned. Serve cold, cut into squares.

....

(183)   # CUSTARD PIE—DUTCH METHOD
ONE-CRUST PIE

For one 9-inch pie
- Whole eggs (slightly beaten): 3
- Brown sugar: 1 cup
- Flour (pastry): 1 tsp.
- Salt: ¼ tsp.
- Milk (scalded): 2 cups
- Pastry: For 1 one-crust pie
- Cinnamon: ½ tsp.

For five 9-inch pies
- Whole eggs (slightly beaten): 15 or 1⅞ lb.
- Brown sugar: 5 cups or 1¼ qts. or 1 lb. 10⅔ oz.
- Flour (pastry): 1⅔ Tbsps. or ⁵/₁₂ oz.
- Salt: 1¼ tsps. or ⁵/₂₄ oz.
- Milk (scalded): 2½ qts. or 5 lbs.
- Pastry: For 5 one-crust pies
- Cinnamon: 2½ tsps. or ⁵/₂₄ oz.

Beat eggs slightly; add combined brown sugar, flour, and salt, and beat well. When mixture is thoroughly blended, gradually stir in the scalded milk. Strain mixture into unbaked 9-inch pastry shell; sprinkle with cinnamon, and bake 10 minutes in a hot oven (450° F.); reduce temperature to 325° F. and continue baking 30 minutes longer. Serve cold.

(184)

JAM CUSTARD PIE—
OLD-FASHIONED METHOD
ONE-CRUST PIE

For one 9-inch pie
- Sugar (granulated): ¼ cup
- Sugar (brown): ¼ cup
- Salt: ¼ tsp.
- Nutmeg (ground): ¼ tsp.
- Whole eggs (slightly beaten): 3
- Milk (scalded): 2 cups
- Vanilla extract: ½ tsp.
- Pastry: For 1 one-crust pie
- Jam or preserve (any kind)
- Whipped cream (unsweetened)

For five 9-inch pies
- Sugar (granulated): 1¼ cups or 10 oz.
- Sugar (brown): 1¼ cups or 6⅔ oz.
- Salt: 1¼ tsps. or 5/24 oz.
- Nutmeg (ground): 1¼ tsps. or 5/24 oz.
- Whole eggs (slightly beaten): 15 or 1⅞ lbs.
- Milk (scalded): 2½ qts. or 5 lbs.
- Vanilla extract: 2½ tsps. or 5/12 oz.
- Pastry: For 5 one-crust pies
- Jam or preserve (any kind)
- Whipped cream (unsweetened)

Combine sugars, salt, and nutmeg, and blend thoroughly with slightly beaten eggs. To scalded milk add vanilla extract and gradually add to egg-sugar mixture, beating well while pouring. Strain through a fine sieve into unbaked pastry shell and bake 10 minutes in a hot oven (450° F.); reduce temperature to 325° F. and continue baking 30 minutes longer. Remove from oven, let cool until just slightly warm, spread jam or preserve over top; when cold, top with unsweetened whipped cream. Serve warm or cold.

(185) LEMON CUSTARD PIE—HOME METHOD
ONE-CRUST PIE

For one 9-inch pie
- Butter (melted): 2 tsps.
- Zwieback (crushed): 6 slices
- Egg yolks (well beaten): 3
- Condensed milk (sweetened): ½ can
- Lemon juice: 3 Tbsps.
- Egg whites (stiffly beaten): 3
- Salt: ¼ tsp.
- Lemon rind (grated): 1 Tbsp.

For five 9-inch pies
- Butter (melted): 3⅓ Tbsps. or 1⅔ oz.
- Zwieback (crushed): 30 slices
- Egg yolks (well beaten): 15 or 1⅞ lb.
- Condensed milk (sweetened): 2½ cans or 2 lbs. ³/₁₆ oz.
- Lemon juice: 1 scant cup or 7½ oz.
- Egg whites (stiffly beaten): 15 or 15 oz.
- Salt: 1¼ tsps. or ⁵/₂₄ oz.
- Lemon rind (grated): 5 Tbsps. or 1⅞ oz.

Spread butter evenly in a 9-inch pie pan. Crush zwieback on board with rolling pin. Spread half the zwieback crumbs over bottom of buttered pie pan. Beat egg yolks until lemon-colored and thick. Add sweetened condensed milk, mixed with lemon juice, and beat thoroughly. Beat egg whites until stiff, then add salt and grated lemon rind, and beat until egg whites hold their peaks but are not too dry. Fold egg-white mixture into egg-yolk mixture and strain over zwieback crumbs in pie pan. Sprinkle remaining crumbs over top and bake in a hot oven (450° F.) for 10 minutes; reduce heat to 325° F. and continue baking 30 minutes longer, or until knife inserted in center comes out clean. Serve cold with a side dish of your favorite preserves.

(186)

PEACH CUSTARD PIE— FRENCH METHOD
ONE-CRUST PIE

NOTE: This delicious French pie does not require baking or cooking, and may be prepared on demand or requirement.

For one 9-inch pie
- Ground nut meats (any kind): 1 cup
- Shredded coconut: 1 cup
- Butter (melted): ¼ cup
- Salt: ⅛ tsp.
- Nutmeg: ¼ tsp.
- Sugar (granulated): ¾ cup
- Peaches: 3 large ones
- Lemon juice: 2 Tbsps.
- Heavy sour cream (chilled): 1 cup
- Egg yolks (well beaten): 2
- Vanilla extract: ½ tsp.
- Almond extract: ½ tsp.
- Sugar (powdered): ¼ cup
- Salt: ⅛ tsp.
- Heavy cream (whipped): 1 cup

For five 9-inch pies
- Ground nut meats (any kind): 5 cups or 1¼ lbs.
- Shredded coconut: 5 cups or 1¼ qts. or 1 lb.
- Butter (melted): 1¼ cups or 10 oz. or ⅝ lb.
- Salt: ⅝ tsp.
- Nutmeg: 1¼ tsps.
- Sugar (granulated): 3¾ cups or 1⅞ lbs.
- Peaches: 15 large ones
- Lemon juice: ⅝ cup or 5 oz.
- Heavy sour cream (chilled): 5 cups or 1¼ qts. or 2½ lbs.
- Egg yolks (well beaten): 10 or 10 oz.
- Vanilla extract: 2½ tsps. or ⁵⁄₁₂ oz.
- Almond extract: 2½ tsps. or ⁵⁄₁₂ oz.
- Sugar (powdered): 1¼ cups or 8 oz. or ½ lb.
- Salt: ⅝ tsp.
- Heavy cream (whipped): 5 cups or 1¼ qts. or 2½ lbs.

Combine nut meats, coconut, butter, salt, and nutmeg. Mix thoroughly and spread on bottom and sides of a 9-inch pie pan. Chill thoroughly. Add sugar to sliced peaches, which may be fresh, brandied, or frozen; and sprinkle with 1 tablespoon of lemon juice. Fill the well-chilled crust with sliced peaches. Combine sour cream, egg yolks, vanilla and almond extracts, remaining lemon juice, 2 tablespoons of the powdered sugar, and the salt; after blending thoroughly, spread over sliced peaches. Add remaining powdered sugar to whipped cream and spread over all. Serve very cold.

(187)

DATE MINCEMEAT PIE
TWO-CRUST PIE

For one 9-inch pie
- Mincemeat (dry, packaged): 1 (9 oz.) pkg.
- Dates (pitted, chopped): 1 cup
- Water: 1½ cups
- Apples (tart, coarsely chopped): ¼ cup
- Pastry: For 1 two-crust pie

For five 9-inch pies
- Mincemeat (dry, packaged): 2 lb. 13 oz.
- Dates (pitted, chopped): 5 cups or 2 lbs.
- Water: 7½ cups or 3¾ lbs.
- Apples (tart, coarsely chopped): 1¼ cups or 10 oz.
- Pastry: For 5 two-crust pies

Break mincemeat into pieces. Add chopped dates and water. Place over heat and stir until lumps are thoroughly broken up. Bring to a brisk boil and continue boiling for one minute. Allow to cool; then stir in the coarsely chopped tart apples. Line 9-inch pie pan with pastry rolled ⅛-inch thick and fill with mincemeat mixture. Cover with top crust in the usual way, making several slits in the top pastry to allow steam to escape. Bake 10 minutes in a very hot oven (450° F.); reduce temperature to 350° F. and continue baking for 30 minutes longer. Serve warm with rum hard sauce.

(188)   # DATE PECAN PIE
ONE-CRUST PIE

For one 9-inch pie
- Corn syrup: 1 cup
- Sugar (granulated): 3 Tbsps.
- Flour (sifted): 3 Tbsps.
- Salt: ½ tsp.
- Cinnamon: ½ tsp.
- Butter (melted): 2 Tbsps.
- Vanilla extract: ½ tsp.
- Egg yolks (well beaten): 2
- Egg whites (stiffly beaten): 2
- Pecan meats (broken): 1 cup
- Dates (chopped): 1 cup
- Pastry: For 1 one-crust pie
- Meringue topping: optional

For five 9-inch pies
- Corn syrup: 5 cups or 3¾ lbs.
- Sugar (granulated): ⅞ cup or 7½ oz.
- Flour (sifted): ⅞ cup or 3¾ oz.
- Salt: 2½ tsps. or $5/24$ oz.
- Cinnamon: 2½ tsps. or $5/24$ oz.
- Butter (melted): 10 Tbsps. or 5 oz.
- Vanilla extract: 2½ tsps. or $5/12$ oz.
- Egg yolks (well beaten): 10 or 10 oz.
- Egg whites (stiffly beaten): 10 or 10 oz.
- Pecan meats (broken): 5 cups or 1 lb. 9oz.
- Dates (pitted, chopped): 5 cups or 2 lbs.
- Pastry: For 5 one-crust pies
- Meringue topping: optional

Mix corn syrup with sugar, flour, salt, cinnamon, butter and vanilla extract. Combine with well-beaten egg yolks, then fold in stiffly beaten egg whites, alternately with combined pecan meats (broken, not chopped) and dates. Turn mixture into pastry-lined pie pan and bake 10 minutes in a very hot oven (450° F.); reduce temperature to 350° F. and continue baking 30–35 minutes longer. You may, if desired, top pie with a meringue and bake 15 minutes longer in a moderately slow oven (325° F.), or until meringue is delicately brown. Serve cold.

(189) # DATE PIE—NEW ENGLAND METHOD
TWO-CRUST PIE

For one 9-inch pie
- Water: 1½ cups
- Tapioca (quick cooking): 1½ Tbsps.
- Sugar (dark brown): 2 Tbsps.
- Salt: ¼ tsp.
- Dates (pitted, quartered): 2 cups
- Butter: 2½ Tbsps.
- Lemon juice: 3 Tbsps.
- Pastry: For 1 two-crust pie

For five 9-inch pies
- Water: 7½ cups or 3¾ lbs.
- Tapioca (quick cooking): 7½ Tbsps. or 1⅞ oz.
- Sugar (dark brown): 10 Tbsps. or 3⅓ oz.
- Salt: 1¼ tsps. or ⁵⁄₂₄ oz.
- Dates (pitted and quartered): 2½ qts. or 4 lbs.
- Butter: 12½ Tbsps. or 6¼ oz.
- Lemon juice: ⅞ cup or 7½ oz.
- Pastry: For 5 two-crust pies

Bring water to a boil over direct heat. Combine tapioca, sugar, salt, and dates and add to briskly boiling water; boil 1 minute, stirring once from bottom of saucepan. Remove from the heat and add butter and lemon juice. Cool. Turn mixture into pastry-lined pie pan; fold edge back to form standing rim. Cover with top crust, make slits in it to permit escape of steam, and flute rim with fingers. Bake 10 minutes in a very hot oven (450° F.); reduce temperature to 350° F. and continue baking 30 minutes longer. Serve cold with whipped cream sweetened and flavored to taste.

NOTE: The lemon juice will slightly sour the mixture, thus giving it the semblance of having used sour cream, a flavor which combines well with dates.

....

(190) # DEEP DISH PIES

There are so many varities of deep dish pies that a full listing would require a complete volume. The crust of the deep dish pie—as that of the cobbler, its first cousin—should be soft enough so that it may spread over the filling, but not soft enough to pour. A rather deep dish should be used, since sugar and fruit when cooked together are likely to boil high. While a deep dish pie or cobbler furnishes its own juice or sauce, you may serve it with cream, plain or whipped, sweetened and flavored or not, or a hard sauce. In very few cases, deep dish pie is served cold; but cobbler is always served hot—as hot as possible.

For topping, use recipe for one-crust pastry (No. 38), or you may use sweetened biscuit mix. Fill buttered deep dish with any one of the fruit recipes indicated in this book for one 9-inch pie; add a small amount of water, milk, light cream, or fruit juice, if fruit seems dry. Cover with top crust, fitting it into position over filling as you would for a two-crust pie, and fasten it on the sides of the dish (you may use custard dish for individual deep dish pies). Make slits on top of crust to allow escape of steam and bake as you would an ordinary 9-inch pie. For individual deep dish pies, bake the same length of time, that is 10 minutes, in a very hot oven (450° F.), then 25–30 minutes in a 350° F. oven.

You may allow baked pies to cool a little, then lift up the, crust very carefully and cover the fruit filling with cream which has been whipped; replace the crust and serve at once. A 9-inch deep dish pie usually yields 6 servings.

....

(191) EGGNOG LEMON MERINGUE PIE— SOUTHERN METHOD
ONE-CRUST PIE, PRE-BAKED PIE SHELL

For one 9-inch pie
- Egg yolks (slightly beaten): 6
- Lemon juice: 1/3 cup
- Lemon rind (grated): 2½ Tbsps.
- Sugar (granulated): 1 cup
- Salt: ¼ tsp.
- Water (cold): 2 Tbsps.
- Egg whites: 6
- Baking powder: 1/8 tsp.
- Sugar (granulated): ¼ cup
- Pastry: 1 baked Alabama Pastry shell, No. 50

For five 9-inch pies
- Egg yolks (slightly beaten): 2½ doz. or 1⅞ lbs.
- Lemon juice: 1⅔ cups or 13⅓ oz.
- Lemon rind (grated): generous ¾ cup or 4½ oz.
- Sugar (granulated): 5 cups or 2½ lbs.
- Salt: 1¼ tsps. or 5/24 oz.
- Water (cold): 10 Tbsps. or 5 oz.
- Egg whites: 30 or 1⅞ lbs.
- Baking powder: 5/8 tsp.
- Sugar (granulated): 1¼ cups or 10 oz.
- Pastry: 5 baked Alabama Pastry shells, No. 50

Beat egg yolks until thick and lemon-colored. Add lemon juice and rind, sugar, and salt, and beat until thoroughly blended. Cook this mixture over hot water until very thick, stirring constantly. Now add cold water to egg whites and beat until stiff but not dry. Combine baking powder and remaining sugar, and add to beaten egg white mixture and beat until stiff. Fold hot lemon mixture into half the egg-white meringue; fill baked pastry shell and cover with remaining meringue. Sprinkle lightly with sugar and bake 15 minutes in a moderately slow oven (325° F.), or until meringue is delicately brown. Serve cold.

Variations: (1) Omit lemon juice and rind and use fruit juice, such as orange, pineapple, cherry, or any other kind, and stir in 2 tablespoons of grated sweet chocolate. Then proceed as directed above. (2) Stir into the mixture, just before turning it into the pre-baked pastry shell, ¾ cup of shredded, toasted, cooled coconut. More eggnog pies will be found in Chiffon Pies section.

....

(192)   # ELDERBERRY PIE—HOME METHOD
TWO-CRUST PIE

For one 9-inch pie
- Flour (pastry): 2 Tbsps.
- Sugar (fine granulated): ¾ cup
- Elderberries (fresh or canned): 3¼ cups
- Salt: ½ tsp.
- Lemon rind (grated): ½ tsp.
- Nutmeg (ground): ⅛ tsp.
- Sour cream: 1 cup
- Pastry: For 1 two-crust pie
- Butter: 1 Tbsp.

For five 9-inch pies
- Flour (pastry): 10 Tbsps. or 2½ oz.
- Sugar (fine granulated): 3¾ cups or 1 lb. 14 oz.
- Elderberries (fresh or canned): 4 qts. plus ¼ cup or 4 lb. 1 oz.
- Salt: 2½ tsps. or ⁵/₁₂ oz.
- Lemon rind (grated): 2½ tsps. or ⁵/₁₆ oz.
- Nutmeg (ground): ⅝ tsp.
- Sour cream: 5 cups or 2½ lbs.
- Pastry: For 5 two-crust pies
- Butter: 5 Tbsps. or 2½ oz.

Combine flour and sugar, sift once and mix with cleaned, stemmed elderberries, if using fresh ones. If canned elderberries are used, drain well. Let stand 15 minutes, then drain again. Combine flour-sugar mixture with fruit. Add salt, lemon grating, and ground nutmeg to sour cream, and combine with elderberry mixture. Turn filling into unbaked 9-inch pastry lined pie plate, which has been brushed with a little melted butter; dot with butter; cover with top crust in the usual way, making several slits for escape of steam; brush top crust with a little sour cream, milk, or butter. You may, if desired, use a crisscross topping instead of a plain crust. Bake 10 minutes in a hot oven (450° F.); reduce temperature to 325° F. and continue baking 30 minutes longer. Serve cold.

....

(193)   # ENGLISH TOFFEE PIE
ONE-CRUST PIE, PRE-BAKED PIE SHELL

For one 9-inch pie
- Flour (sifted): ¼ cup
- Salt: ½ tsp.
- Sugar (granulated): ½ cup
- Milk: 2 cups
- Rum toffee candy: 1 cup
- Whole eggs (slightly beaten): 3
- Marshmallows (quartered): 12
- Vanilla extract: ½ tsp.
- Pastry: 1 baked pie shell

For five 9-inch pies
- Flour (sifted): 1¼ cups or 5 oz.
- Salt: 2½ tsps. or 5/12 oz.
- Sugar (granulated): 2½ cups or 1 lb. 4 oz.
- Milk: 2½ qts. or 5 lbs.
- Rum toffee candy: 5 cups or 2 lb. 3 oz.
- Whole eggs (slightly beaten): 15 or 1⅞ lbs.
- Marshmallows (quartered): 60 or 1 lb.
- Vanilla extract: 2½ tsps. or ⁵/₁₂ oz.
- Pastry: 5 baked pie shells

Sift together flour, salt, and sugar and place in top of double boiler over hot water. Gradually add milk, stirring constantly until mixture begins to thicken. Stir in the toffee candy cut into small pieces with wet scissors. Blend thoroughly. Beat whole eggs slightly and gradually add to first mixture alternately with marshmallows; stir constantly from the bottom of the pan; cook until mixture is thick and smooth. Cool before turning mixture into pre-baked pastry shell. Cover with whipped cream, and sprinkle over a little chopped toffee. Serve well-chilled.

(194)   # FRENCH CREAM PIE
                  ## ONE-CRUST PIE, PRE-BAKED PIE SHELL

For one 9-inch pie

- Pastry: 1 baked Puff Paste Pie Shell No. 41
- Pastry: 1 8-inch Puff Paste round
- Flour (pastry): 5 Tbsps.
- Salt: ¼ tsp.
- Sugar (granulated): ¾ cup
- Whole egg: 1
- Egg yolks: 2
- Milk: 2 cups
- Vanilla extract: 1 tsp.
- Heavy Cream (whipped): 1 cup
- Chopped nut meats (any kind): ⅓ cup
- Chopped maraschino cherries: 3 Tbsps.

For five 9-inch pies

- Pastry: 5 baked Puff Paste Pie Shells No. 41
- Pastry: 5 8-inch Puff Paste rounds
- Flour (pastry): 1 cup 9 Tbsps. or 6¼ oz.
- Salt: 1¼ tsps.
- Sugar (granulated): 3¾ cups or 1 lb. 14 oz.
- Whole eggs: 5 or 10 oz.
- Egg yolks: 10 or 10 oz.
- Milk: 2½ qts. or 5 lbs.
- Vanilla extract: 1⅔ Tbsps. or ⅚ oz.
- Heavy cream (whipped): 5 cups or 2 lbs. 9⅞ oz.
- Chopped nut meats (any kind): 1⅔ cup or 6⅔ oz.
- Chopped maraschino cherries: scant cup or 15 oz.

Bake a 9-inch pie shell, also an 8-inch pastry round, just a round of pastry which will fit into the baked pastry shell. Cool. Mix and sift flour, sugar, and salt. Slightly beat combined whole egg and egg yolks, and stir into cold fresh milk. Combine with flour-sugar-salt mixture and blend until smooth; strain through a sieve. Cook slowly over hot water until mixture thickens, stirring constantly. Remove from hot water; stir in vanilla; cool. When cold, turn a small layer of the custard in bottom of pre-baked, cooled pie shell; over the custard turn a thin layer of the whipped cream, then arrange the pre-baked pastry round over whipped cream. Repeat with a layer of custard, then a layer of whipped cream. Sprinkle top with chopped, toasted, cooled nut meats, mixed with drained red or green maraschino cherries. Serve very cold.

NOTE: Do not prepare many in advance, as mixture does not keep more than three or four days.

(195)   FRIED INDIVIDUAL FRUIT PIES—
TEXAS METHOD
ONE-CRUST PIE, PRE-BAKED PIE SHELL

NOTE: Any kind of dried fruit may be used, such as apples, pears, peaches, prunes, raisins, etc. Frying time depends on size of individual pies, but these very popular fried pies should be brown on both sides, and thoroughly drained before being served sizzling hot.

For 5 individual pies
- Flour (pastry): 2 cups
- Baking powder: 1 tsp.
- Shortening (any kind): 1¼ Tbsps.
- Salt: ¼ tsp.
- Cinnamon: ¼ tsp.
- Water (iced): enough to make dough
- Apricots (dried): 1 pound
- Sugar (granulated): 1 cup
- Nutmeg: ⅛ tsp.
- Almond extract: ¼ tsp.
- Salt: ¼ tsp.

For 25 individual pies
- Flour (pastry): 2½ qts. or 2½ lbs.
- Baking powder: 1⅔ Tbsps. or ⅝ oz.
- Shortening (any kind): 6¼ Tbsps. or 3⅛ oz.
- Salt: 1¼ tsp. or ⁵⁄₂₄ oz.
- Cinnamon: 1¼ tsps.
- Water (iced): enough to make dough
- Apricots (dried): 5 lbs.
- Sugar (granulated): 5 cups or 1¼ qts. or 2½ lbs.
- Nutmeg: ⅝ tsp.
- Almond extract: 1¼ tsps. or ⁵⁄₂₄ oz.
- Salt: 1¼ tsps. or ⁵⁄₂₄ oz.

To make the crust proceed as for any ordinary pie crust and roll out ⅛-inch thick. Cut into circles the size of an ordinary individual pie. Put one tablespoon of the following in the center of each circle. Cook apricots as indicated for No. 24, Dried Fruit Preparation, adding sugar mixed with nutmeg. When done, mash and force through a sieve; then add almond extract and salt. Fold circle in middle and press wet edges firmly together. Fry in deep hot fat until brown on both sides. Serve hot with a hard sauce.

(196) FROSTED MARASCHINO PIE
ONE-CRUST PIE, PRE-BAKED PIE SHELL

For one 9-inch pie
- Sugar (granulated): 1 cup
- Cornstarch: ½ cup
- Salt: ¼ tsp.
- Boiling water: 2 cups
- Butter: 1 tsp.
- Maraschino cherries (coarsely chopped): 6 oz. or 2 3-oz. bottles
- Lemon juice: 2 Tbsps.
- Red vegetable coloring (or green): 1 tsp.
- Pastry: 1 baked pie shell
- Sugar (granulated): 1 cup
- Corn syrup (white): 1 tsp.
- Water: ½ cup
- Egg whites (beaten stiffly): 2
- Vanilla extract: ½ tsp.

For five 9-inch pies
- Sugar (granulated): 5 cups or 2½ lbs.
- Cornstarch: 2½ cups or 13⅓ oz.
- Salt: 1¼ tsps. or ⁵/₂₄ oz.
- Boiling water: 2½ qts. or 5 lbs.
- Butter: 1½ Tbsps. or ¾ oz.
- Maraschino cherries (coarsely chopped): 1 lb. 14 oz.
- Lemon juice: 10 Tbsps. or 5 oz.
- Red vegetable coloring (or green): 1½ Tbsps.
- Pastry: 5 baked pie shells
- Sugar (granulated): 5 cups or 2½ lbs.
- Corn syrup (white): 1⅔ Tbsps. or 1¼ oz.
- Water: 2½ cups or 1 lb. 4 oz.
- Egg whites (beaten stiffly): 10 or 10 oz.
- Vanilla extract: 2½ tsps. or ⁵/₁₂ oz.

Sift sugar, cornstarch, and salt together; stir in boiling water, and cook over hot water until mixture is thickened, stirring constantly; simmer 2 minutes longer, stirring frequently. Remove from hot water, stir in butter and maraschino cherries, coarsely chopped and thoroughly drained; add maraschino juice mixed with lemon juice and coloring. Blend well. Cool. When cold, pour into pre-baked 9-inch pastry shell and cover with boiled frosting made as follows:

Add sugar, corn syrup and salt to water and cook over direct heat to 244° F., until it spins a thread an inch long. Pour in a thin stream into stiffly beaten egg whites, continuing to beat vigorously, until cold. Add vanilla extract and spread over the cold pie filling. Decorate the top with cocktail cherries and pieces cut from green gumdrops or angelica to resemble leaves.

(197)   **FROZEN APRICOT PIE**
            A 9-INCH ONE-CRUST PIE

NOTE: In making the frozen pies given here, the kind of pre-baked pie shell depends on personal preference and on the filling. The following crusts are suggested: Vanilla Wafer Pie Crust, Nut Pastry, Zwieback Pie Crust, Puff Paste shell and Semi-Puff Paste shell. You may use also a thin sponge cake round instead of the pastry as a base for the frozen pies.

For one 9-inch pie
- Dried apricots (cooked, sieved): $^4/_5$ cup
- Sugar (granulated): $^2/_5$ cup
- Whole eggs: 2
- Salt: $^1/_8$ tsp.
- Almond extract: $^1/_8$ tsp.
- Granulated gelatin: $^1/_2$ tsp.
- Cold water: 2 tsps.
- Brandy, rum or apple brandy: $1^1/_2$ Tbsps.
- Heavy cream (whipped): $1^3/_4$ cups
- Powdered sugar: $^1/_2$ cup
- Pastry: 1 baked Rich Pastry shell No. 70 or Semi-Sweet Crust No. 63

For five 9-inch pies
- Dried apricots (cooked, sieved): 1 qt. or 14 oz.
- Sugar (granulated): 2 cups or 1 lb.
- Whole eggs: 10 or 1 lb. 4 oz.
- Salt: $^5/_8$ tsp.
- Almond extract: $^5/_8$ tsp.
- Granulated gelatin: $2^1/_2$ tsps. or $^5/_{24}$ oz.
- Cold water: $3^1/_3$ Tbsps. or $1^2/_3$ oz.
- Brandy, rum or apple brandy: $7^1/_2$ Tbsps. or $3^3/_4$ oz.
- Heavy cream (whipped): 2 qts. and $^3/_4$ cup or 4 lbs. $9^9/_{32}$ oz.
- Powdered sugar: $2^1/_2$ cups or $11^3/_7$ oz.
- Pastry: 5 baked Rich Pastry shells No. 70 or Semi-Sweet Crusts No. 63

Cook dried apricots as indicated for No. 24, Dried Fruit Preparation, and force through a fine sieve. Chill thoroughly. Beat whole eggs with salt and granulated sugar in double boiler over hot water, beating until mixture just begins to thicken and is very light. Immediately remove from hot water and beat mixture with a wire whisk—not a spoon—until cold and thoroughly blended and fluffy, adding meanwhile the chilled, cooked, sieved dried apricots. You may, if desired, add a drop of red coloring. Now beat in the almond extract, alternately with gelatin which has been soaked in 2 teaspoons of cold water, then dissolved over hot water, and mixed with either rum, brandy or apple brandy. Lastly fold in the whipped heavy cream sweetened with powdered sugar. Turn mixture into pre-baked pastry shell or into 9-inch pie pan, the bottom of which has been lined with a thin sheet of sponge cake. Make fancy design over the top, using a clean, wet spatula, and place in refrigerator freezing compartment over-night, or at least 6 hours. Serve very cold and keep in refrigerator constantly when not serving. These pies do not keep long.

(198)   # FROZEN CHOCOLATE PIE
ONE-CRUST PIE, PRE-BAKED PIE SHELL
OR SPONGE CAKE ROUND

For one 9-inch pie

- Whole eggs: 2
- Sugar (granulated): $2/5$ cup
- Salt: $1/8$ tsp.
- Brandy, rum or apple brandy: 1½ Tbsps. or ¾ oz.
- Chocolate (melted): $2/5$ cup
- Granulated gelatin: ½ tsp.
- Cold water: 1 Tbsp.
- Heavy cream: 1¾ cups
- Sugar (powdered): ½ cup
- Chocolate (sweet, shaved): ¼ cup
- Pastry: Either 1 baked pie shell or sponge cake round

For five 9-inch pies

- Whole eggs: 10 or 1 lb. 4 oz.
- Sugar (granulated): 2 cups or 1 lb.
- Salt: $5/8$ tsp.
- Brandy, rum or apple brandy: 7½ Tbsps. or 3¾ oz.
- Chocolate (melted): 2 cups or 1 lb.
- Granulated gelatin: 2½ tsps. or $5/24$ oz.
- Cold water: 5 Tbsps. or 2½ oz.
- Heavy cream: 2 qts. and ¾ cup or 4 lbs. $9^9/32$ oz.
- Sugar (powdered): 2½ cups or $11^3/7$ oz.
- Chocolate (sweet, shaved): 1¼ cups or $6^2/3$ oz.
- Pastry: Either 5 baked pie shells or sponge cake rounds

Beat whole eggs with sugar and salt; cook over hot water until just beginning to thicken. Remove from hot water and beat, using wire whisk or electric mixer at medium speed, until mixture is cold. Stir in either brandy, rum, or apple brandy, alternately with melted chocolate mixed with gelatin, which has been soaked in cold water, then dissolved over hot water. Whip cream, sweetened with powdered sugar; gently fold into egg-chocolate mixture. Turn mixture into either pre-baked pastry shell or over thin round of sponge cake placed in a pie pan. Smooth evenly, or make fancy design, using a spatula; sprinkle with sweet, shaved chocolate. Set in freezing compartment of refrigerator to freeze over-night or at least 6 hours. Serve very cold.

(199) FROZEN EGGNOG LEMON PIE
ONE-CRUST PIE, PRE-BAKED PIE SHELL
OR SPONGE CAKE ROUND

For one 9-inch pie
- Whole eggs: 2
- Sugar (granulated): ⅖ cup
- Salt: ⅛ tsp.
- Lemon juice (strained): 1½ Tbsps.
- Granulated gelatin: ½ tsp.
- Cold water: 1 Tbsp.
- Brandy, rum or apple brandy: 1½ Tbsps.
- Heavy cream (whipped): 1¾ cup
- Sugar (powdered): ½ cup
- Nutmeg: ¾ tsp.
- Pastry: 1 baked sponge cake round or rich pie shell

For five 9-inch pies
- Whole eggs: 10 or 1 lb. 4 oz.
- Sugar (granulated): 2 cups or 1 lb.
- Salt: ⅝ tsp.
- Lemon juice (strained): 7½ Tbsps. or 3¾ oz.
- Granulated gelatin: 2½ tsps. or ⁵⁄₂₄ oz.
- Cold water: 4½ Tbsps. or 2¼ oz.
- Brandy, rum or apple brandy: 7½ Tbsps. or 3¾ oz.
- Heavy cream (whipped): 8¾ cups or 4 lb. 8½ oz.
- Sugar (powdered): 2½ cups or 11½ oz.
- Nutmeg: 3¾ tsps. or ⁵⁄₁₆ oz.
- Pastry: 5 baked sponge cake rounds or rich pie shells

Beat whole eggs with sugar and salt until smooth and light; blend in strained lemon juice and cook over hot water until mixture just begins to thicken slightly, stirring constantly (about 15 minutes). Immediately remove from hot water and beat mixture until cold, either with rotary egg beater or electric beater set at second speed. Stir in granulated gelatin which has been soaked in the cold water, then dissolved over hot water, alternately with brandy, rum, or apple brandy. Now fold in the whipped cream sweetened with powdered sugar and flavored with nutmeg. Place on pre-baked, 9-inch sponge round or turn into pre-baked pastry shell. Dust lightly with nutmeg after smoothing mixture or making fancy design with wet spatula and place in freezing compartment of refrigerator overnight or at least 6 hours.

(200)   # FROZEN LEMON PIE
ONE-CRUST PIE, PRE-BAKED PIE SHELL
OR SPONGE CAKE ROUND

For one 9-inch pie
- Lemon rind (grated): 2 Tbsps.
- Sugar (granulated): 1 Tbsp.
- Water: ⅕ cup
- Whole eggs (beaten): 2
- Sugar (granulated): ⅖ cup
- Salt: ⅛ tsp,
- Lemon juice (strained):¼ cup
- Brandy, rum or apple brandy: 1½ Tbsps.
- Granulated gelatin: ½ tsp.
- Heavy cream (whipped): 1¾ cups
- Sugar (powdered): ½ cup
- Pastry: 1 baked sponge cake round or rich pie shell

For five 9-inch pies
- Lemon rind (grated): 10 Tbsps. or 1¼ oz.
- Sugar (granulated): 5 Tbsps. or 2½ oz.
- Water: 1 cup or 8 oz.
- Whole eggs (beaten): 10 or 1 lb. 4 oz.
- Sugar (granulated): 2 cups or 1 lb.
- Salt: ⅝ tsp.
- Lemon juice (strained): 1¼ cups or 10 oz.
- Brandy, rum or apple brandy: 7½ Tbsps. or 3¾ oz.
- Granulated gelatin: 2½ tsps or ⁵⁄₂₄ oz.
- Heavy cream (whipped): 2 qts. plus ¾ cup or 4 lbs. 8½ oz.
- Sugar (powdered): 2½ cups or 11½ oz.
- Pastry: 5 baked sponge cake rounds or rich pie shells

Combine the first three ingredients in a saucepan, and stir over heat until sugar is dissolved. Then boil down to make a thick syrup, or until there are 2 tablespoons left in saucepan. Strain while hot; cool. Combine eggs, sugar, salt, lemon juice and cooled lemon syrup in top of double boiler and cook, stirring constantly, until mixture just begins to thicken and is light. Remove from hot water and beat with wire whisk or egg beater, or electric mixer placed at medium speed, until mixture is cold and fluffy. This takes about 15 minutes. Add brandy, or rum, or apple brandy alternately with gelatin soaked in cold water, then dissolved over hot water. Blend thoroughly. Lastly fold in the whipped cream sweetened with powdered sugar. Turn mixture into 9-inch pie pan lined with baked thin sponge cake round or fill 9-inch pre-baked pastry shell. Smooth evenly or make fancy designs with wet spatula. Place in freezing compartment of refrigerator until thoroughly chilled and partially frozen (about 5 or 6 hours).

A crust made of 1 cup of crushed corn flakes, ⅓ cup melted butter, and 3 tablespoons powdered sugar may be used, but the above indicated shells are much finer. To save time, you may freeze, or half-freeze, filling, then fill pre-baked pastry shell with mixture when ready to serve.

(201)

FROZEN MOCHA PIE
ONE-CRUST PIE, PRE-BAKED PIE SHELL
OR SPONGE CAKE ROUND

For one 9-inch pie
- Roasted coffee beans: ¾ cup
- Powdered sugar: ¼ cup
- Evaporated milk (scalded): 1 (14½ oz.) can
- Salt: ¼ tsp.
- Vanilla extract: $^1/_8$ tsp.

For five 9-inch pies
- Roasted coffee beans: 3¾ cups or 15 oz.
- Powdered sugar: 1¼ cups or ½ lb.
- Evaporated milk (scalded): 5 cans or 4 lbs 8½ oz.
- Salt: 1¼ tsps. or $^5/_{24}$ oz.
- Vanilla extract: $^5/_8$ tsp.

Spread whole coffee beans in bottom of a lightly buttered heavy skillet and sprinkle with powdered sugar. Place over a low heat and stir constantly until powdered sugar is caramelized and beans are entirely coated. Very slowly pour in the scalded evaporated milk (or light cream), stirring constantly; do not allow to boil. Pour mixture into mixing bowl, cover with a dry clean towel, then with a lid. Place over cracked ice for 20 minutes; when cold, strain through double cheesecloth or fine muslin. Add salt and vanilla extract. Meanwhile prepare the following ingredients:

For one 9-inch pie
- Whole eggs: 2
- Sugar (granulated): $^2/_5$ cup
- Coffee extract (above mixture): $^1/_5$ cup
- Salt: $^1/_8$ tsp.
- Brandy, rum or apple brandy: 1½ Tbsps.
- Granulated gelatin: ½ tsp.
- Water (cold): 1 Tbsp.
- Heavy cream: 1¾ cups
- Sugar (powdered): ½ cup
- Nutmeg: $^1/_8$ tsp.
- Pastry: 1 baked sponge cake round or Puff Paste pie shell, Nos. 41 & 42

For five 9-inch pies
- Whole eggs: 10 or 1 lb. 4 oz.
- Sugar (granulated): 2 cups or 1 lb.
- Coffee extract (above mixture): 1 cup or 8 oz.
- Salt: $^5/_8$ tsp.
- Brandy, rum or apple brandy: 7½ Tbsps. or 3¾ oz.
- Granulated gelatin: 2½ tsps. or $^5/_{24}$ oz.
- Water (cold): 5 Tbsps. or 2½ oz.
- Heavy cream: 8¾ cups or 4 lbs. 8½ oz.
- Sugar (powdered): 2½ cups or 11½ oz.
- Nutmeg: $^5/_8$ tsp.
- Pastry: 5 baked sponge cake rounds or Puff Paste pie shells, Nos. 41 & 42

Beat eggs, sugar, and coffee extract and salt thoroughly. Strain into top of double boiler and cook over hot water until mixture begins to thicken, stirring constantly. Remove at once from hot water and place over cracked ice; beat mixture with a wire whisk, an egg beater, or electric beater set at medium speed, until mixture is cold—about 15 minutes. Stir in the brandy, rum, or apple brandy alternately with the gelatin which has been soaked in cold water and dissolved over hot water. Whip cream, add powdered sugar and nutmeg, and fold into first mixture. Fill pie pan lined with baked thin sponge cake round or Puff Paste shell and place in freezing compartment of refrigerator for 6 hours or overnight.

....

(202)   **FROZEN ORANGE PIE**
            ONE-CRUST PIE, PRE-BAKED PIE SHELL
               OR SPONGE CAKE ROUND

Use your favorite pre-baked pastry shell or sponge cake round. Proceed as indicated for No. 200, Frozen Lemon Pie, substituting grated orange rind and orange juice for grated lemon rind and lemon juice.

(203)

FROZEN PEACH PIE
ONE-CRUST PIE, PRE-BAKED PIE SHELL
OR SPONGE CAKE ROUND

For one 9-inch pie

- Peaches (fresh or frozen): 6 large ones
- Sugar (granulated): 2 tsps.
- Whole eggs: 2
- Sugar (granulated): ²⁄₅ cup
- Almond extract (bitter): 1 drop
- Red vegetable coloring: 1 drop
- Brandy, rum or apple brandy: 1½ Tbsps.
- Granulated gelatin: ½ tsp.
- Water (cold): 1 Tbsp.
- Heavy cream: 1¾ cups
- Sugar (powdered): ½ cup
- Pastry: 1 baked pie shell or sponge cake round

For five 9-inch pies

- Peaches (fresh or frozen): 30 large ones
- Sugar (granulated): 3⅓ Tbsps. or 1⅔ oz.
- Whole eggs: 10 or 1 lb. 4 oz.
- Sugar (granulated): 2 cups or 1 lb.
- Almond extract (bitter): 5 drops
- Red vegetable coloring: 5 drops
- Brandy, rum or apple brandy: 7½ Tbsps. or 3¾ oz.
- Granulated gelatin: 2½ tsps. or ⁵⁄₂₄ oz.
- Water (cold): 5 Tbsps. or 2½ oz.
- Heavy cream: 2 qts. plus ¾ cup or 4 lbs. and 8½ oz.
- Sugar (powdered): 2½ cups or 11½ oz.
- Pastry: 5 baked pie shells or sponge cake rounds

Peel peaches, split in half, remove stones and force through a sieve. Spread in bottom of shallow pan and sprinkle with the first 2 teaspoons granulated sugar. Let stand in refrigerator until well-chilled, or overnight. Beat eggs with second amount of granulated sugar (²⁄₅ cup) until light and cook in top of double boiler over hot water, until mixture just begins to thicken. Remove at once from the hot water and beat mixture with wire whisk, egg beater, or electric beater, set at medium speed, until cold, or about 15 minutes. Combine this with peach mixture, almond extract, coloring, rum or apple brandy, and gelatin soaked in cold water and dissolved over hot water. Whip heavy cream sweetened with powdered sugar and fold into mixture. Turn mixture into pre-baked pastry shell, or over pie pan; line with thin slice of sponge cake and place in freezing compartment of refrigerator; let freeze slightly, then fill pastry shell, or pie plate lined with thin slice of sponge cake round. Decorate with sliced peaches around edge of pie. Serve well-chilled.

(204)
FROZEN PUMPKIN PIE
ONE-CRUST PIE, PRE-BAKED PIE SHELL
OR SPONGE CAKE ROUND

For one 9-inch pie
- Pumpkin (fresh cooked): 1½ cups
- Sugar (granulated): ⅔ cup
- Whole egg (beaten): 1
- Egg yolk (beaten): 1
- Salt: ¼ tsp.
- Ginger (ground): ⅛ tsp.
- Cinnamon: ⅛ tsp.
- Nutmeg: ⅛ tsp.
- Brandy, rum or apple brandy: 1½ Tbsps.
- Heavy cream (whipped): 1 cup
- Milk: 1 cup
- Pastry: For 1 one-crust pie

For five 9-inch pies
- Pumpkin (fresh cooked): 7½ cups or 6 lbs. 1½ oz.
- Sugar (granulated): 3⅓ cups or 1 lb. 10⅔ oz.
- Whole eggs (beaten): 5 or 10 oz.
- Egg yolk (beaten): 5 or 5 oz.
- Salt: 1¼ tsps or ⁵⁄₂₄ oz.
- Ginger (ground): ⅝ tsp.
- Cinnamon: ⅝ tsp.
- Nutmeg: ⅝ tsp.
- Brandy, rum or apple brandy: 7½ Tbsps. or 3¾ oz.
- Heavy cream (whipped): 5 cups or 2 lbs. 9⅞ oz.
- Milk: 5 cups or 2 lbs. 8 oz.
- Pastry: For 5 one-crust pies

Wash a whole pumpkin. Do not peel, but cut in small pieces. Cook until dry and brown without burning, stirring occasionally. Force through a fine sieve, discarding the coarse parts remaining in the sieve. Cool. When cold, combine with all the remaining ingredients in order named, blending thoroughly, and turn into an unbaked pastry shell. Bake in a slow oven (300° F.) for 1¼ to 1½ hours. Cool, then place the cold baked pie in freezing compartment of refrigerator to remain overnight or at least 6 hours. Top with either whipped cream, ice cream, one or several flavors, and serve ice cold.

(205)
FROZEN RASPBERRY PIE
ONE-CRUST PIE, PRE-BAKED PIE SHELL
OR SPONGE CAKE ROUND

For one 9-inch pie
- Raspberries (fresh or frozen): ⅘ cup
- Sugar (granulated): 2 tsps.
- Whole eggs: 2
- Sugar (granulated): ⅖ cup
- Granulated gelatin: ½ tsp.
- Water (cold): 1 Tbsp.
- Lemon juice: ⅗ Tbsp. or ³/₁₀ oz.
- Red vegetable coloring: 1 drop
- Brandy, rum or apple brandy: 1½ Tbsps.
- Heavy cream: 1¾ cups
- Sugar (powdered): ½ cup
- Pastry: 1 baked pie shell or sponge cake round

For five 9-inch pies
- Raspberries (fresh or frozen): 4 cups or 1 lb. 2¾ oz.
- Sugar (granulated): 3⅓ Tbsps. or 1⅔ oz.
- Whole eggs: 10 or 1 lb. 4 oz.
- Sugar (granulated): 2 cups or 1 lb.
- Granulated gelatin: 2½ tsps. or ⁵/₂₄ oz.
- Water (cold): 5 scant Tbsps. or 2¼ oz.
- Lemon juice: 3 Tbsps. or 1½ oz.
- Red vegetable coloring: 4 or 5 drops
- Brandy, rum or apple brandy: 7½ Tbsps. or 3¾ oz.
- Heavy cream: 8¾ cups or 4 lbs. 8½ oz.
- Sugar (powdered): 2½ cups or 11½ oz.
- Pastry: 5 baked pie shells or sponge cake rounds

Press raspberries through a coarse sieve. Sprinkle with the first amount of granulated sugar and place in refrigerator to chill about 4 hours. Beat whole eggs with ⅖ cup granulated sugar until thoroughly blended. Cook over hot water until mixture just begins to thicken, stirring constantly. Remove at once from hot water, and beat with wire whisk, egg beater, or electric beater set to medium speed, until mixture is cold, about 15–20 minutes. Soak gelatin in cold water and dissolve over hot water. Combine gelatin, raspberry pulp, lemon juice, red vegetable coloring (optional) and brandy, rum or apple brandy, and blend with cold egg-sugar mixture. Whip heavy cream, sweeten with powdered sugar and fold into mixture. Pour into pre-baked pastry shell or on sponge cake round in a pie pan and place in freezing compartment of refrigerator overnight, or at least 6 hours.

(206)   **FROZEN STRAWBERRY PIE**
                ONE-CRUST PIE, PRE-BAKED PIE SHELL
                    OR SPONGE CAKE ROUND

Proceed as indicated for No. 205, Frozen Raspberry Pie, substituting fresh or frozen strawberries for raspberries.

NOTE: Dates, figs, seedless raisins and, in fact, all the dried fruits may be prepared in this way. The dried fruit should be cooked, as indicated for No. 24, Dried Fruit Preparation, drained and forced through a sieve while hot. Use the same amount of weight as you would for raspberries or strawberries. You may reserve a few whole—or halved, if large—raspberries or strawberries for garnish when serving, if desired.

(207)   # FROZEN TUTTI FRUTTI PIE
ONE-CRUST PIE, PRE-BAKED PIE SHELL
OR SPONGE CAKE ROUND

For one 9-inch pie
- Whole eggs: 2
- Egg yolk: 1
- Sugar (granulated): ⅖ cup
- Granulated gelatin: ½ tsp.
- Water (cold): 1 Tbsp.
- Candied cherries (chopped): ¾ cup
- Candied pineapple (chopped): ¾ cup
- Angelica (chopped): ½ tsp.
- Raisins (seedless, chopped): ½ cup
- Almonds (chopped, toasted): ¼ cup
- Pistachio nuts (chopped): ¼ cup
- Brandy, rum or apple brandy: 1½ Tbsps.
- Heavy cream: 1¾ cups
- Sugar (powdered): ½ cup
- Pastry: 1 baked pie shell or sponge cake round

For five 9-inch pies
- Whole eggs: 10 or 1 lb. 4 oz.
- Egg yolk: 5 or 5 oz.
- Sugar (granulated): 2 cups or 1 lb.
- Granulated gelatin: 2½ tsps. or ⁵⁄₂₄ oz.
- Water (cold): 5 scant Tbsps. or 2¼ oz.
- Candied cherries (chopped): 4 cups or 1 lb. 2¾ oz.
- Candied pineapple (chopped): 4 cups or 1 lb. 2¾ oz.
- Angelica (chopped): 2½ tsps.
- Raisins (seedless, chopped): 1¼ cups or 7 oz.
- Almonds (chopped, toasted): 1¼ cups or 7 oz.
- Pistachio nuts (chopped): 1¼ cups or 7 oz.
- Brandy, rum or apple brandy: 7½ Tbsps. or 3¾ oz.
- Heavy cream: 8¾ cups or 4 lb. 8½ oz.
- Sugar (powdered): 2½ cups or 11½ oz.
- Pastry: 5 baked pie shells or sponge cake rounds

Beat whole eggs and egg yolks with granulated sugar until sugar is thoroughly dissolved. Cook in top of double boiler over hot water for 15 minutes, or until mixture just begins to thicken. Remove at once from hot water and beat with a wire whisk, rotary egg beater or electric beater, set at medium speed, until cold. Soak gelatin in cold water, then dissolve over hot water and stir into egg-sugar mixture. Combine candied fruit and nuts with brandy, rum or apple brandy and stir into mixture. Whip heavy cream, sweeten with powdered sugar and fold into mixture. Turn into either pre-baked pastry shell or over a thin slice of sponge cake placed in bottom of a 9-inch pie pan and place in freezing compartment of refrigerator to freeze for at least 8 hours, or overnight. When ready to serve, sprinkle over the following topping:

For one 9-inch pie
- Candied cherries (chopped): 1 Tbsp.
- Almonds (toasted, chopped): 1 Tbsp.
- Pistachio nuts (chopped): 1 Tbsp.
- Angelica (chopped): 1 Tbsp.

For five 9-inch pies
- Candied cherries (chopped): 5 Tbsps or $1\frac{7}{8}$ oz.
- Almonds (toasted, chopped): 5 Tbsps. or $1\frac{2}{3}$ oz.
- Pistachio nuts (chopped): 5 Tbsps or $1\frac{2}{3}$ oz.
- Angelica (chopped): 5 Tbsps. or $1\frac{7}{8}$ oz.

Combine all the above ingredients, and sprinkle over the pie or pies.

....

(208)

FRUIT SALAD PIE
ONE-CRUST PIE, PRE-BAKED PIE SHELL

For one 9-inch pie
- Mixed fruits (canned): 1 (#2½) can
- Granulated gelatin: 1 Tbsp.
- Canned fruit juice: 1 cup
- Salt: $\frac{1}{8}$ tsp.
- Heavy cream (whipped): 1 cup
- Sugar (powdered): 3 Tbsps.
- Ginger: $\frac{1}{8}$ tsp.
- Pastry: 1 baked pie shell

For five 9-inch pies
- Mixed fruits (canned): 1 (#10) can or 6 lbs. 14 oz.
- Granulated gelatin: 5 Tbsps. or 1¼ oz.
- Canned fruit juice: 5 cups or 2½ lbs.
- Salt: $\frac{5}{8}$ tsps.
- Heavy cream (whipped): 5 cups or 2 lbs. $9\frac{7}{8}$ oz.
- Sugar (powdered): $\frac{7}{8}$ cup or $4\frac{2}{7}$ oz.
- Ginger: $\frac{5}{8}$ tsp.
- Pastry: 5 baked pie shells

Drain the fruit, reserving juice, and cut up any large pieces of fruit. Soak gelatin in fruit juice from the can and heat gently over hot water until gelatin has dissolved. Cool. When beginning to thicken, add fruit and salt and blend thoroughly, but gently, so as not to break and mash fruit. Fold in the whipped cream, sweetened and flavored with sugar and ginger (other flavoring may be substituted, if desired) and chill in freezing compartment of refrigerator. When cold, put in pre-baked, 9-inch pie shell and pipe a "collar" of whipped cream around the outer edge, and garnish with a few well-drained maraschino red cherries.

(209)

GOOSEBERRY PIE I—
WISCONSIN METHOD
TWO-CRUST PIE

For one 9-inch pie
- Gooseberries: 3½ cups
- Tapioca (quick cooking): 2 Tbsps.
- Sugar (granulated): 1½ cups
- Salt: ¼ tsp.
- Orange rind (grated): 1 tsp.
- Unbaked pastry: For 1 two-crust pie
- Butter (melted): 2 Tbsps.

For five 9-inch pies
- Gooseberries: 4 qts. plus 1½ cups or 6 lbs. 9 oz.
- Tapioca (quick cooking): ⅝ cup or 2½ oz.
- Sugar (granulated): 7½ cups or 3¾ lbs.
- Salt: 1¼ tsps. or ⁵⁄₂₄ oz.
- Orange rind (grated): 1⅔ Tbsps. or ⅝ oz.
- Unbaked pastry: For 5 two-crust pies
- Butter (melted): ⅝ cup or 5 oz.

If using fresh gooseberries, remove stem and blossom ends, wash quickly in cold water and cut the large ones into halves. Add tapioca, sugar, salt and orange rind and let stand 15–20 minutes. Line 9-inch pie plate with pastry rolled ⅛-inch thick and brush bottom and sides with slightly beaten egg whites; sprinkle lightly with flour. Fill with gooseberry mixture, sprinkle with melted butter and cover with top crust, making a few slits in it for escape of steam. Bake 10 minutes in a hot oven (450° F.); reduce heat to 350° F. and bake 30 minutes longer. Serve cold. If served warm, serve with hard sauce.

NOTE: Should you desire to substitute cornstarch for quick-cooking tapioca, use 3 tablespoons of cornstarch. You may also steam the berries for 8 or ten minutes, or until berries just begin to soften; then allow to cool slightly before combining with remaining ingredients.

(210)

GOOSEBERRY PIE II
ONE-CRUST CRISSCROSS PIE

For one 9-inch pie
- Gooseberries (fresh or canned): 3½ cups
- Sugar (granulated): 1½ cups
- Cinnamon: ¾ tsp.
- Cloves (ground): ½ tsp.
- Water or juice: ½ cup
- Flour (pastry): 2 Tbsps.
- Salt: ⅛ tsp.
- Nutmeg (ground): ⅛ tsp.
- Butter (melted): 2 Tbsps.
- Pastry: For 1 crisscross pie
- Marshmallows: as many as required

For five 9-inch pies
- Gooseberries (fresh or canned): 4 qts. plus 1½ cups or 6 lbs. 9 oz.
- Sugar (granulated): 7½ cups or 3¾ lbs.
- Cinnamon: 3¾ tsps. or ⁵/₁₆ oz.
- Cloves (ground): 2½ tsps. or ⁵/₂₄ oz.
- Water or juice: 2½ cups or 1 lb. 4 oz.
- Flour (pastry): 10 Tbsps. or 2½ oz.
- Salt: ⅝ tsp.
- Nutmeg (ground): ⅝ tsp.
- Butter (melted): 10 Tbsps. or 5 oz.
- Pastry: For 5 crisscross pies
- Marshmallows: as many as required

Cook together the gooseberries (stemmed at both ends), sugar, cinnamon, cloves and water (or juice, if using canned fruit) until berries are tender, or about 10 minutes; cool. Add flour, salt and nutmeg and sprinkle with butter. Line 9-inch pie plate with pastry rolled ⅛-inch thick and pour in the filling. Crisscross in the usual way and bake in a hot oven (400° F.) for 25–30 minutes, or until nicely browned on the top. When pastry is almost brown, remove the pie from oven and place a marshmallow between each square of the crisscross work; return to oven to finish browning. Serve cold.

....

(211)

A FEW FACTS ABOUT GRAPES

Almost any kind of grape, seeded or seedless, may be used for pie-making. However, popularity of the Concord grape has made it a favorite fruit for pies.

It is a blue-skinned grape with a green pulp. Horticulturists term it a slip-skin because the skin readily slips off the pulp. The Concord is the grape used for preserving. Jams, jellies, conserves, grape juice, and many desserts are made from it.

The Concords—there are several species—are high in iron content, particularly the skin, which should be used whenever possible. But it must be remembered that each variety has its own special quota of vitamins and minerals.

One of the grapes that is rapidly gaining popularity and on the market practically all year is the small seedless, yellow-green Thompson. California sends in heavy shipments of this variety, and during the winter months Chile and the Argentine keep the markets well supplied. This grape is green when under-ripe, but is sweet and has a golden tint when ripe. It is widely used for pies and especially tarts. It is used also in cooking to replace the Malaga and Tokay grapes, which are also very popular. The green Malagas—there are several varieties—and the tawny Tokays (several varieties) are much used in fancy pastries. But they have to be seeded. Both Malagas and Tokays are of firm flesh, while Concord and Delaware grapes are of the soft-flesh variety and do not keep very well.

When buying grapes for pies or other purposes, choose bunches which are compact, of well-formed grapes, with no soft or moldy fruit. If grapes fall from the stems, it is an indication that they are over-ripe or frost-bitten. Avoid them.

....

(212)

GRAPE PIE I
TWO-CRUST PIE

For one 9-inch pie
- Water: ³/₈ cup
- Sugar (granulated): ½ cup
- Salt: ⅛ tsp.
- Tapioca flour: 1¼ Tbsps.
- Water: 1 Tbsp.
- Yellow vegetable coloring: 1 drop
- Pineapple juice: 2 tsps.
- Concord grapes (stemmed, seeded, washed): ¾ lb.
- Pastry: For 1 two-crust pie

For five 9-inch pies
- Water: 1⅞ cups or 15 oz.
- Sugar (granulated): 2½ cups or 1 lb. 4 oz.
- Salt: ⅝ tsp.
- Tapioca flour: 6¼ Tbsps. or 1⁹/₁₆ oz.
- Water: 5 Tbsps. or 2½ oz.
- Yellow vegetable coloring: 4 or 5 drops
- Pineapple juice: 3⅓ Tbsps. or 1⅔ oz.
- Concord grapes (stemmed, seeded, washed): 3¾ lbs.
- Pastry: For 5 two-crust pies

Combine the ⅜ cup water, sugar and salt in saucepan and stir until sugar is dissolved. Bring this to a boil. Dissolve tapioca flour in the remaining tablespoon of water, add the yellow vegetable coloring (it may be omitted) gradually to the boiling syrup, stirring constantly with a wire whisk until mixture thickens. Let this boil 3 minutes longer, stirring almost constantly to prevent scorching. Remove from the heat and add pineapple juice and washed, stemmed, and seeded grapes Turn mixture into a 9-inch pastry-lined pie pan; cover with top crust, making several slits to permit escape of steam, and bake 10 minutes in a very hot oven (450° F.); then reduce temperature to 350° F. and continue baking 25–30 minutes longer.

....

(213) GRAPE PIE II—MIDDLE WEST METHOD
ONE-CRUST CRISSCROSS PIE

For one 9-inch pie
- Concord grapes: 7 cups
- Cornstarch: 3 Tbsps.
- Cold water: 2 Tbsps.
- Sugar (granulated): 1½ cups
- Salt: ¾ tsp.
- Orange rind (grated): 1 Tbsp.
- Unbaked pastry: For 1 crisscross pie

For five 9-inch pies
- Concord grapes: 8¾ qts.
- Cornstarch: scant 1 cup or 5 oz.
- Cold water: 10 Tbsps. or 5 oz.
- Sugar (granulated): 7½ cups or 3¾ lbs.
- Salt: 3¾ tsps. or ⅝ oz.
- Orange rind (grated): 5 Tbsps. or 1⅞ oz.
- Unbaked pastry: For 5 crisscross pies

Wash and stem grapes before measuring. Slip skins from pulp and reserve. Heat pulp to the boiling point and boil for 5 minutes. Force through a sieve to remove seeds. Dissolve cornstarch in cold water, and stir into the hot grape mixture, alternately with sugar, salt, and orange rind. Let this boil once, then stir in the grape pulp alternately with grape skins, and allow to cook, stirring constantly until mixture is thickened. Pour into 9-inch pastry-lined pie pan; top with strips of pastry, crisscross fashion, and bake 10 minutes in a very hot oven (450° F.); reduce temperature to 350° F. and bake for 25–30 minutes longer. Serve cold.

(214)
GRAPE PIE III—
OLD-FASHIONED DEEP DISH METHOD
ONE-CRUST PIE

For 4 individual pies
- Concord grapes (stemmed, washed and seeded): 4 cups
- White seedless grapes (whole): 2 cups
- Sugar (granulated): 1 cup
- Nutmeg: ¼ tsp.
- Orange rind (grated): 2 tsps.
- Salt: ⅛ tsp.
- Unbaked pastry: For 4 one-crust individual pies

For 20 individual pies
- Concord grapes (stemmed, washed and seeded): 5 qts.
- White seedless grapes (whole): 2½ qts.
- Sugar (granulated): 5 cups or 2½ lbs.
- Nutmeg: 1¼ tsps.
- Orange rind (grated): 3⅓ Tbsps. or 1¼ oz.
- Salt: ⅝ tsp.
- Unbaked pastry: For 20 one-crust individual pies

Stem, wash, seed Concord grapes before measuring and cook in a very small amount of water (to barely cover) until soft; then force through coarse strainer. There should be 1 pint of purée. Combine puréed grapes and stemmed, seedless, whole white grapes, sugar, nutmeg, orange rind and salt and bring this to a boil, stirring gently and occasionally. Transfer mixture into well-buttered individual deep pie dishes, dividing mixture equally; then top with a rich top crust, letting crust extend over edge of dishes; make several slits in each crust to permit escape of steam and bake 20 minutes in a moderate oven (375° F.). Serve warm with hard sauce, preferably lemon or orange.

(215)

GRAPE SOUFFLÉ PIE—
CALIFORNIA METHOD
ONE-CRUST PIE, PRE-BAKED PASTRY SHELL

For one 9-inch pie
- Water: ⁵/₆ cup
- Butter: 1½ Tbsps.
- Sugar (granulated): 6 Tbsps.
- Salt: ¼ tsp.
- Corn syrup (light): 1 Tbsp.
- Cornstarch: ¼ cup
- Water (cold): ¼ cup
- Egg whites (stiffly beaten): 2
- Sugar (powdered): ¼ cup
- Lemon rind (grated): 1 tsp.
- Pastry: 1 baked Puff Paste Pastry shell No. 42
- Thompson seedless grapes (weighed after being stemmed): ¾ lb.
- Water: ²/₅ cup
- Tapioca flour: 1¹/₅ Tbsps.
- Water (cold): 1 Tbsp.
- Sugar (granulated): ½ cup
- Salt: A few grains

For five 9-inch pies
- Water: 4¹/₆ cups or 2 lb. 1¹/₃ oz.
- Butter: 7½ Tbsps. or 3¾ oz.
- Sugar (granulated): 1⁷/₈ cups or 15 oz.
- Salt: 1¼ tsps. or ⁵/₂₄ oz.
- Corn syrup (light): 5 Tbsps. or 3¾ oz.
- Cornstarch: 1¼ cups or 6²/₃ oz.
- Water (cold): 1¼ cups or 10 oz.
- Egg whites (stiffly beaten): 10 or 10 oz.
- Sugar (powdered): 1¼ cups or 5⁵/₇ oz.
- Lemon rind (grated): 5 tsps. or ⁵/₈ oz.
- Pastry: 5 baked Puff Paste Pastry shells No. 42
- Thompson seedless grapes (weighed after being stemmed): 3¾ lbs.
- Water: 2 cups or 1 pt. or 1 lb.
- Sugar (granulated): 2½ cups or 1 lb. 4 oz.
- Tapioca flour: ³/₈ cup or 1½ oz.
- Water (cold): 5 Tbsps. or 2½ oz.
- Salt: ¼ tsp. or ¹/₂₄ oz.

Combine ⁵/₆ cup of water, butter, granulated sugar, salt, and corn syrup in a saucepan and stir until mixture is thoroughly combined and sugar dissolved. Place over high heat and bring to a boil. Dissolve cornstarch in ¼ cup of cold water and gradually add to the boiling syrup, stirring constantly until mixture thickens. Remove from the heat and beat until cool, using either wire whisk, rotary egg beater, or electric beater set at medium speed. When mixture is cooled, fold in the stiffly beaten egg whites, sweetened with powdered sugar and flavored with lemon rind. Spread this mixture into pre-baked Puff Paste Pastry shell evenly, filling it half full. Set aside while preparing Grape Topping as follows:

Stem, wash, dry, and weigh seedless Thompson grapes. There should be ¾ lb. for each pie. Combine ⅖ cup of water and ½ cup granulated sugar and stir until sugar is dissolved; bring to a boil over direct heat. Dissolve tapioca flour in remaining cold water (pineapple juice may be substituted) with salt, and gradually add to the boiling syrup, stirring constantly until mixture is thickened and clear. Remove from heat and stir in the well-drained, dried grapes. Cool to lukewarm and spread over the soufflé filling in pre-baked puff paste shell. Force a ring of whipped cream, sweetened and flavored to taste, around the outer edge through pastry tube and decorate with uniform seedless Thompson grapes. Serve very cold.

(216)   GRAPE JUICE CREAM PIE— SOUTHERN METHOD
ONE-CRUST PIE, PRE-BAKED PASTRY SHELL

For one 9-inch pie
- Milk: 1 cup
- Sugar (granulated): 1 cup
- Cornstarch: 2 Tbsps.
- Milk (cold): 2 Tbsps.
- Salt: ¼ tsp.
- Egg yolks: 3
- Grape juice: 1 cup
- Thompson grapes (stemmed and washed): ¾ cup
- Pastry: 1 baked Alabama Pastry shell No. 50
- Egg whites (stiffly beaten): 3
- Sugar (powdered): 3 Tbsps.

For five 9-inch pies
- Milk: 5 cups or 2½ lbs.
- Sugar (granulated): 5 cups or 2½ lbs.
- Cornstarch: 10 Tbsps. or 3⅓ oz.
- Milk (cold): 10 Tbsps. or 5 oz.
- Salt: 1¼ tsps. or 5/24 oz.
- Egg yolks: 15 or 15 oz.
- Grape juice: 5 cups or 2½ lbs.
- Thompson grapes (stemmed and washed): 3¾ cups
- Pastry: 5 baked Alabama Pastry shells No. 50
- Egg whites (stiffly beaten): 15 or 15 oz.
- Sugar (powdered): 1 cup or 4²/₇ oz.

Combine milk and granulated sugar and stir until sugar is dissolved. Place over direct heat and bring to a boil, stirring occasionally. Dissolve cornstarch in remaining milk and beat with egg yolks until thoroughly blended. Add gradually to boiling milk-sugar mixture, stirring constantly from bottom of pan until mixture thickens. Now stir in combined grape juice and Thompson grapes; remove from the heat. Cool; when cold, turn into pre-baked 9-inch Alabama pastry shell and pile on top a meringue made with egg whites and powdered sugar. Bake 15–20 minutes in a moderately slow oven (325° F.), or until meringue is delicately brown. Serve cold.

....

(217)

WHITE GRAPE PIE— CALIFORNIA METHOD
ONE-CRUST PIE, PRE-BAKED PASTRY SHELL

NOTE: If using early Thompson grapes, the amount of sugar should be raised, as these grapes are not so sweet as those picked late, or at the end of the grape season.

For one 9-inch pie
- White seedless Thompson grapes (washed and stemmed): 2½ cups
- Orange juice: ½ cup
- Lemon juice: ¼ cup
- Sugar (granulated): ½ cup
- Cornstarch: 1 Tbsp.
- Orange juice: 2 Tbsps.
- Nutmeg (ground): ¼ tsp.
- Pastry: 1 baked pie shell
- Heavy cream (whipped): ½ cup

For five 9-inch pies
- White seedless Thompson grapes (washed and stemmed): 3 qts. plus ½ cup
- Orange juice: 2½ cups or 1¼ lbs.
- Lemon juice: 1½ cups or 10 oz. or ⅝ lb.
- Sugar (granulated): 2½ cups or 1¼ lbs.
- Cornstarch: 5 Tbsps. or ⅔ oz.
- Orange Juice: ⅝ cup or 5 oz.
- Nutmeg (ground): 1¼ tsps.
- Pastry: 5 baked pie shells
- Heavy cream (whipped): 2½ cups or 1¼ lbs.

Place stemmed, washed, drained grapes in a saucepan with ½ cup of orange juice; simmer until tender, or about 20 minutes. Add lemon juice and sugar. Mix cornstarch with the remaining orange juice and add to grapes with nutmeg. Allow this to simmer for 5 minutes, or until thickened, stirring constantly. Cool. When cold, pour into pastry shell and spread whipped cream over the top, using a pastry bag.

....

(218) # MAPLE CUSTARD RAISIN PIE— WISCONSIN METHOD
ONE-CRUST PIE, PRE-BAKED PASTRY SHELL

For one 9-inch pie
- Butter: 1½ Tbsps.
- Flour (pastry): 2 Tbsps.
- Salt: ¼ tsp.
- Lemon rind (grated): 1 tsp.
- Egg yolks (slightly beaten): 2
- Maple syrup: 1 cup
- Water (cold): ½ cup
- Raisins (seedless): ½ cup
- Pastry: 1 baked pie shell
- Heavy cream (whipped): 1 cup

For five 9-inch pies
- Butter: 7½ Tbsps. or 3¾ oz.
- Flour (pastry): 10 Tbsps. or ⅝ cup or 2½ oz.
- Salt: 1¼ tsps. or 5/24 oz.
- Lemon rind (grated): 5 tsps. or ⅝ oz.
- Egg yolks (slightly beaten): 10 or 10 oz.
- Maple syrup: 5 cups or 1¼ qts. or 3¾ lbs.
- Water (cold): 2½ cups or 1¼ lbs.
- Raisins (seedless): 2½ cups or 13⅓ oz.
- Pastry: 5 baked pie shells
- Heavy cream (whipped): 5 cups or 2½ lbs.

Cream butter with flour and salt until fluffy; add lemon rind mixed with slightly beaten egg yolks. Blend thoroughly. Combine maple syrup and cold water and stir into the creamed butter mixture, blending thoroughly. Lastly stir in the washed, parboiled seedless raisins and turn mixture into top of double boiler. Cook until mixture forms a thick custard. Cool a little, then turn into pre-baked 9-inch pastry shell. Allow to cool thoroughly, then top with unsweetened, unflavored whipped cream, forced through pastry bag with a small fancy tube. Serve very cold.

(219) MAPLE PECAN CHESS PIE— MAINE METHOD
ONE-CRUST PIE

For one 9-inch pie
- Butter: 2 Tbsps.
- Maple sugar: 1 cup
- Eggs (well beaten): 2
- Flour (pastry): 2 Tbsps.
- Salt: ⅛ tsp.
- Maple syrup: 1 cup
- Pecans (coarsely broken): 1½ cups
- Pastry: For 1 one-crust pie
- Whipped cream topping

For five 9-inch pies
- Butter: 10 Tbsps. or 5 oz.
- Maple sugar: 5 cups or 1 lb. 10⅔ oz.
- Eggs (well beaten): 10 or 1 lb. 4 oz.
- Flour (pastry): 10 Tbsps. or 2½ oz.
- Salt: ⅝ tsp.
- Maple syrup: 5 cups or 3¾ lbs.
- Pecans (coarsely broken): 7½ cups or 2 lbs. 2²⁄₇ oz.
- Pastry: For 5 one-crust pies
- Whipped cream topping

Cream butter and sugar. Add well-beaten eggs alternately with combined flour and salt. Blend thoroughly, then add maple syrup and mix well. Lastly stir in the broken (coarsely) pecans. Turn mixture into unbaked 9-inch one-crust shell and bake 30 minutes in a moderate oven (350° F.). When cold, top with whipped cream, sweetened and flavored to taste.

....

(220) MAPLE MERINGUE CREAM PIE— VERMONT METHOD
ONE-CRUST PIE, PRE-BAKED PASTRY SHELL

For one 9-inch pie
- Butter (melted): 2 Tbsps.
- Flour (pastry): ½ cup
- Sugar (brown): ⅔ cup
- Salt: ¼ tsp.
- Milk: 2 cups
- Egg yolks (beaten): 2
- Maple flavoring extract: 1 tsp.
- Pastry: 1 baked pie shell

For five 9-inch pies
- Butter (melted): 10 Tbsps. or 5 oz.
- Flour (pastry): 2½ cups or 10 oz.
- Sugar (brown): 3⅓ cups or 1 lb. 1⁷⁄₉ oz.
- Salt: 1¼ tsps. or ⁵⁄₂₄ oz.
- Milk: 2½ qts. or 5 lbs.
- Egg yolks (beaten): 10 or 10 oz.
- Maple flavoring extract: 1⅔ Tbsps. or ⅚ oz.
- Pastry: 5 baked pie shells

Melt butter; stir in the flour all at once; gradually stir in sugar and salt; gradually add the milk mixed with beaten egg yolks, stirring constantly. Cook over hot water until thick and smooth, stirring constantly. Remove from hot water; add the maple flavoring extract, and when cold turn into pre-baked 9-inch one-crust pastry shell. Top with a meringue made in the usual way (No. 26), and bake 15 minutes in a moderately slow oven (325° F.), or until meringue is lightly browned. Serve cold.

....

(221)   # MAPLE NUT CREAM PIE—
HOME METHOD
ONE-CRUST PIE, PRE-BAKED PASTRY SHELL

Proceed as indicated for No. 124, Butterscotch Cream Pie I, substituting maple sugar for brown (dark) sugar; add, while folding in the stiffly beaten egg whites, ½ cup toasted chopped pecans or any other kind of nuts desired. After topping the filled pre-baked 9-inch pastry shell with a meringue (No. 26), sprinkle with chopped, toasted, cooled pecans or any other kind of nut. If using a whipped cream topping, then sprinkle topping with nuts.

(222)
MAPLE SUGAR PIE—
NEW ENGLAND METHOD
ONE-CRUST PIE, PRE-BAKED PASTRY SHELL

For one 9-inch pie
- Maple sugar (shaved): 1 cup
- Cornstarch: 3 Tbsps.
- Whole eggs (slightly beaten): 3
- Milk (lukewarm): 2 cups
- Salt: ¼ tsp.
- Butter: 1 Tbsp.
- Pastry: 1 baked pie shell
- Heavy cream (whipped): 1 cup
- Sugar (powdered): ¼ cup
- Vanilla extract: ½ tsp.

For five 9-inch pies
- Maple sugar (shaved): 5 cups or 3¾ lbs.
- Cornstarch: 1 scant cup or 5 oz.
- Whole eggs (slightly beaten): 15 or 1 lb. 14 oz.
- Milk (lukewarm): 2½ qts. or 5 lbs.
- Salt: 1¼ tsps. or $5/24$ oz.
- Butter: 5 Tbsps. or 2½ oz.
- Pastry: 5 baked pie shells
- Heavy cream (whipped): 5 cups or 2½ lbs.
- Sugar (powdered): 1¼ cups or $5^{5}/_{7}$ oz.
- Vanilla extract: 2½ tsps. or $5/12$ oz.

Combine soft maple sugar and cornstarch in top of double boiler. To the slightly beaten whole fresh eggs add lukewarm milk and blend thoroughly. Pour this over the maple sugar mixture and salt, and cook until thick and smooth, stirring constantly. Remove from hot water and stir in butter. Cool. When cold, turn filling into pre-baked 9-inch pastry shell, then chill thoroughly. Before serving, spread whipped cream, sweetened with powdered sugar and flavored with vanilla extract, over top of pie. Serve cold.

(223)   # GREEN TOMATO MINCEMEAT—
SOUTHERN METHOD
FILLING FOR TEN 9-INCH PIES

- Green tomatoes: 3 lbs.
- Corned beef: 3 lbs.
- Apples (greenings): 3 lbs.
- Sugar (dark brown): 2 lbs.
- Raisins (seeded): 1 lb.
- Raisins (seedless): 1 lb.
- Salt: 1 Tbsp. (or more to taste)
- Kidney suet: 1 cup
- Vinegar (cider): 1¼ cups or 10 oz.
- Cinnamon (ground): 2 Tbsps. or ½ oz.
- Cloves (ground): 2 tsps. or ⅙ oz.
- Nutmeg (ground): 1 Tbsp. or ¼ oz.
- Lemon rind (grated): 1½ Tbsps. or 9/16 oz.
- Orange rind (grated): 2 Tbsps. or ¾ oz.
- Citron: ½ cup or 3 oz.
- Dry white wine: ¼ cup or 2 oz.

Wash tomatoes carefully, dry and chop fine. Drain thoroughly and discard the liquid. Cover with cold water and boil for five minutes, counting time when actual boiling starts. Have cooked, drained and coarsely ground corned beef ready. Put apples through food chopper, unpeeled, but carefully washed and dried. Combine green tomato mixture, beef mixture and apples in a large kettle and add all the remaining ingredients; cover with broth from the corned beef and simmer very gently for at least 1½ hours. Remove from the heat, and while hot, fill hot sterilized jars. Seal carefully; when cold, store in a cool, dry place.

NOTE: You may, just before sealing, add 1 tablespoon of good brandy to each jar. This will enhance the flavor of the mincemeat and will keep indefinitely.

(224)   # MINCEMEAT I—MASTER RECIPE

Appropriate for pies, tarts, turnovers, muffins, filling for cookies,
steamed puddings, cakes, etc.

For one 9-inch pie

- Beef (boiled, lean, chopped): 3 Tbsps. or 1$\frac{3}{5}$ oz.
- Beef suet (kidney, chopped): 3 Tbsps. or 1$\frac{3}{5}$ oz.
- Apples (raw, pared, chopped): 1½ cups or ¾ lb.
- Currants (seeded, chopped): 3 Tbsps. or 1$\frac{3}{5}$ oz.
- Raisins (seedless, chopped): 3 Tbsps. or 3$\frac{1}{5}$ oz.
- Salt: ½ tsp.
- Candied orange peel (chopped): 1 Tbsp. or $\frac{8}{15}$ oz.
- Candied lemon peel (chopped): 1 Tbsp. or $\frac{8}{15}$ oz.
- Candied citron (chopped): 1 Tbsp. or $\frac{8}{15}$ oz.
- Sugar (brown): 1 cup or 5$\frac{1}{3}$ oz.
- Cinnamon: 4/5 tsp. or $\frac{1}{15}$ oz.
- Nutmeg: $\frac{2}{5}$ tsp.
- Ginger: $\frac{1}{5}$ tsp.
- Cloves (ground): $\frac{1}{10}$ tsp.
- Cider: 1 cup or 8 oz.

For five 9-inch pies

- Beef (boiled, lean, chopped): ½ lb.
- Beef suet (kidney, chopped): ½ lb.
- Apples (raw, pared, chopped): 3¾ lbs.
- Currants (seeded, chopped): ½ lb.
- Raisins (seedless, chopped): 1 lb.
- Salt: 1 Tbsp. or ½ oz.
- Candied orange peel (chopped): 2$\frac{2}{3}$ oz.
- Candied lemon peel (chopped): 2$\frac{2}{3}$ oz.
- Candied citron (chopped): 2$\frac{2}{3}$ oz.
- Sugar (brown): 5 cups or 1 lb. 10$\frac{2}{3}$ oz.
- Cinnamon: 3 Tbsps. or $\frac{1}{3}$ oz.
- Nutmeg: 1$\frac{1}{3}$ Tbsps.
- Ginger: 1 tsp. or $\frac{1}{6}$ oz.
- Cloves (ground): ½ tsp. or $\frac{1}{24}$ oz.
- Cider: 5 cups or 2 lbs. 8 oz.

Combine the ingredients in order named in a kettle and allow to simmer very gently for 2 long hours, stirring occasionally; (place a pad under the kettle to prevent scorching). Cool. Turn into hot sterilized jars; seal. Place in a dry, cool place. This will keep six months.

The grated rind of two medium-sized lemons can be added to mixture before simmering. Brandy may be added before cooking, but the flavor will evaporate. Wait until baked, then push a small syringe filled with brandy, or equal parts of brandy and sherry, into the slits of the pie and force the brandy or brandy mixture into the pie. Mince pies with a lattice (crisscross) are easier to flavor. If using a crisscross pie, here are some helpful suggestions for ways of improving still further the old-time favorite pie. Besides, the pie (or pies) will look more attractive and certainly thrill your most critical guest when you drop a spoonful of crushed pineapple in alternate squares of the crisscross and top each with a bit of maraschino cherry. Pineapple and mincemeat have a certain affinity. Another attractive topping for a single crust mince pie is a topping of pineapple tidbits sprinkled lightly with brown sugar and slipped under a broiler long enough to slightly melt the sugar.

(225)
MINCEMEAT II—
NEW ENGLAND METHOD

For one 9-inch pie
- Beef (raw, lean): 3 Tbsps. or 1³/₅ oz.
- Water: enough to cover meat
- Salt: ½ tsp.
- Apples: ¾ lb. or 12 oz.
- Sugar (brown): 1 cup or 5¹/₃ oz.
- Raisins (seedless, chopped): 3 Tbsps. or 3¹/₅ oz.
- Currants (seeded, chopped): 3 Tbsps. or 1³/₅ oz.
- Citron (chopped): ½ oz.
- Lemon juice: 2 Tbsps. or 1 oz.
- Lemon rind (grated): 1 Tbsp. or ³/₈ oz.
- Orange juice: 2 Tbsps. or 1 oz.
- Orange rind (grated): 1 Tbsp. or ³/₈ oz.
- Stock (from boiled meat): ½ cup
- Mace: ²/₅ tsp.
- Nutmeg: ²/₅ tsp.
- Cinnamon: ⁴/₅ tsp.
- Cloves: ¹/₁₀ tsp.
- Almonds (toasted, chopped): ¼ cup

For five 9-inch pies
- Beef (raw, lean): ½ lb.
- Water: enough to cover meat
- Salt: 2½ tsps. or ⁵/₁₂ oz.
- Apples: 3¾ lbs.
- Sugar (brown): 5 cups or 1 lb. 10²/₃ oz.
- Raisins (seedless, chopped): 1 lb.
- Currants (seeded, chopped): ½ lb.
- Citron (chopped): 2½ oz.
- Lemon juice: 10 Tbsps. or 5 oz.
- Lemon rind (grated): 5 Tbsps. or 1⁷/₈ oz.
- Orange juice: 10 Tbsps. or 5 oz.
- Orange rind (grated): 5 Tbsps. or 1⁷/₈ oz.
- Stock (from boiled meat): 2½ cups or 1 lb. 4 oz.
- Mace: 2 tsps. or ¹/₆ oz.
- Nutmeg: 2 tsps. or ¹/₆ oz.
- Cinnamon: 4 tsps. or ¹/₃ oz.
- Cloves: ½ tsp. or ¹/₂₄ oz.
- Almonds (toasted, chopped): 1¼ cups or 6²/₃ oz.

NOTE: This recipe may be used as indicated for No. 224, Mincemeat I. Liquid may be grape juice, wine, canned fruit juice or water. It should be ripened before using for at least one month. This will keep several months.

Cover meat with water; add salt and simmer until tender. Cool in water in which it has been cooked. Chop meat fine. Pare, core and chop apples, and combine with meat. Add all the remaining ingredients and simmer slowly for two hours, placing a pad under the kettle to prevent scorching; stir occasionally. Cool. Pack in hot sterilized jars or stone crock. Seal. Ripen before using.

You may add ¼ cup brandy when turning mixture into fruit jars or crock, or proceed as indicated for No. 224, Mincemeat I, that is, using a syringe and forcing brandy, or equal parts of brandy and sherry wine, into each pie before baking.

(226) MINCEMEAT III—FRENCH METHOD

For one 9-inch pie

- Beef (raw, lean): 1½ oz.
- Veal kidney suet (chopped): 1½ oz.
- Water: enough to barely cover meat
- Salt: ½ tsp.
- Apples (pared, cored, chopped): 1 cup
- Raisins (seedless, white, chopped): 3 oz.
- Sugar (granulated): 2 Tbsps.
- Dried apricots: ½ cup
- Sugar (granulated): ¼ cup
- Pineapple (canned, crushed): ½ cup
- Candied citron (chopped): ½ oz.
- Candied orange peel (chopped): ½ oz.
- Candied lemon peel (chopped): ½ oz.
- Honey (strained): 2 Tbsps.
- Lemon juice: 2 Tbsps.
- White wine: ½ cup
- Mace: $3/5$ tsp.
- Nutmeg: $2/5$ tsp.
- Cinnamon: $4/5$ tsp.
- Allspice: $2/5$ tsp.
- Cloves: $1/5$ oz.
- Almonds (toasted, chopped): ¼ cup

For five 9-inch pies

- Beef (raw, lean): 7½ oz.
- Veal kidney suet (chopped): 7½ oz.
- Water: enough to barely cover meat
- Salt: 2½ tsps. or $5/12$ oz.
- Apples (pared, cored, chopped): 5 cups or 2½ lbs.
- Raisins (seedless, white, chopped): 15 oz.
- Sugar (granulated): 10 Tbsps. or 5 oz.
- Dried apricots: 2½ cups or $13 1/3$ oz.
- Sugar (granulated): 1¼ cups or 10 oz.
- Pineapple (canned, crushed): 2½ cups or $1 7/8$ lbs.
- Candied citron (chopped): 2½ oz.
- Candied orange peel (chopped): 2½ oz.
- Candied lemon peel (chopped): 2½ oz.
- Honey (strained): 10 Tbsps. or 7½ oz.
- Lemon juice: 10 Tbsps. or 5 oz.
- White wine: 2½ cups or 1 lb. 4 oz.
- Mace: 1 Tbsp. or ¼ oz.
- Nutmeg: 2 tsps. or $1/6$ oz.
- Cinnamon: $1 1/3$ Tbsps. or $1/3$ oz.
- Allspice: 2 tsps. or $1/6$ oz.
- Cloves: 1 oz.
- Almonds (toasted, chopped): 1¼ cups or $6 2/3$ oz.
- Sugar (granulated): 10 Tbsps. or 5 oz.

NOTE: This recipe may be used as indicated for No. 224, Mincemeat I. It is called "Jubile d'Or Mincemeat," and is a favorite of the Hotel Continental, Paris, France.

Cover meat with water; add salt and simmer until tender, about 30 minutes. Cool in water in which it has been cooked. Chop meat fine and combine with chopped veal kidney suet and apples. Add the remaining ingredients and simmer gently for 2 hours, placing a pad under the kettle to prevent scorching; stir occasionally. The mixture will be almost dry. Cool. Pack in hot, sterilized fruit jars or stone crock; seal, and do not use before 3 weeks.

....

(227)   # MINCEMEAT PIE
TWO-CRUST PIE

Line 9-inch pie plate with Cheese Pie Crust, No. 52, rolled ⅛-inch thick. Fill with 2 lbs. of mincemeat. Cover with top crust; press edges together with a fork or a pastry wheel, slash the upper crust with one long incision and four short ones and bake 10 minutes in a very hot oven (450° F.); then reduce temperature to 350° F. and continue baking for 25–30 minutes longer. While the crust is still hot and still rises above the filling slightly, insert a small funnel into the large incision, and pour 3 Tbsps. of brandy, or equal parts of brandy and sherry, into the pie. The liquid will spread over the filling immediately. Return your pie (or pies) to the oven and let it stand 3 or 4 minutes. Remove. Keep warm. Serve with American Cheese.

(228)   # MINCEMEAT APPLE CRUMB PIE—
PENNSYLVANIA METHOD
ONE-CRUST PIE

For one 9-inch pie
- All-purpose flour (sifted): 2 cups
- Salt: 1/3 tsp.
- Lard: 1/2 cup
- Water (iced): 1/4 cup
- Olive oil: 1 tsp.
- Mincemeat: 1 lb.
- Apples (tart, pared, sliced): 2 1/4 cups
- Sugar (granulated): 1/3 cup
- Flour (sifted): 1/2 cup
- Salt: 1/8 tsp.
- Sugar (granulated): 1/3 cup
- Butter (chilled): 1/4 cup

For five 9-inch pies
- All-purpose flour (sifted): 2 1/2 qts. or 2 1/2 lbs.
- Salt: 1 2/3 tsps. or 5/18 oz.
- Lard: 2 1/2 cups or 1 1/4 lbs.
- Water (iced): 1 1/4 cups (about) or 10 oz.
- Olive oil: 5 tsps. or 1 2/3 Tbsps. or 5/6 oz.
- Mincemeat: 5 lbs.
- Apples (tart, pared, sliced): 11 1/4 cups or 3 lbs. 2 oz.
- Sugar (granulated): 1 2/3 cups or 13 1/3 oz.
- Flour (sifted): 2 1/2 cups or 10 oz.
- Salt: 5/8 tsp.
- Sugar (granulated): 1 2/3 cups or 13 1/3 oz.
- Butter (chilled): 1 1/4 cups or 10 oz.

Mix in bowl the sifted all-purpose flour and salt; cut in thoroughly chilled lard, with 2 knives or a pastry blender. When flour and lard particles are about size of navy beans, gradually add the iced water blended with olive oil. Mix just enough to make a smooth dough. Chill for an hour. Divide dough in half; place one half on slightly floured board, pat pastry lightly, then roll 1/8-inch thick and a little larger than 9-inch pie pan. Fold sheet of pastry in half and place in ungreased pie pan; then unfold and press lightly to fit pan; trim edges. Keep in a cold place for 15–20 minutes.

Spread mincemeat over bottom of pastry. Combine tart sliced apples with granulated sugar. (If apples are very tart, more sugar will be required.) Blend well and arrange apple mixture over mincemeat.

Sift remaining flour, salt and sugar, then work in the thoroughly chilled butter, so as to make a crumby mixture. Sprinkle these crumbs over the apples and bake 10 minutes in a hot oven (450° F.); reduce temperature to moderate (370° F.), and continue baking 30 minutes longer. Serve warm, with or without your favorite hard sauce.

(229)
MINCEMEAT CUSTARD PIE— HOME METHOD
ONE-CRUST PIE

For one 9-inch pie
- Pastry: For 1 one-crust pie
- Mincemeat (well-drained): 1¾ cups
- Flour (pastry): 2 Tbsps.
- Sugar (brown): ¾ cup
- Salt: ⅛ tsp.
- Butter: 3 Tbsps.
- Egg yolks (slightly beaten): 2
- Milk (cold): 1 cup
- Ginger (ground): ⅛ tsp.
- Lemon juice: 3 Tbsps.
- Lemon rind (grated): 2 Tbsps.
- Egg whites (stiffly beaten): 2

For five 9-inch pies
- Pastry: For 5 one-crust pies
- Mincemeat (well-drained): 8¾ cups or 4⅜ lbs.
- Flour (pastry): ⅝ cup or 2½ oz.
- Sugar (brown): 3¾ cups or 1 lb. 10⅔ oz.
- Salt: ⅝ tsp.
- Butter: scant 1 cup or 7½ oz.
- Egg yolks (slightly beaten): 10 or 10 oz.
- Milk (cold): 5 cups or 1¼ qts. or 2½ lbs.
- Ginger (ground): ⅝ tsp.
- Lemon juice: scant cup or 7½ oz.
- Lemon rind (grated): 10 Tbsps. or 3¾ oz.
- Egg whites (stiffly beaten): 10 or 10 oz.

Brush unbaked 9-inch pastry shell with unbeaten egg white; when egg white is dry, spread in the prepared mincemeat. Put aside. Combine and sift flour, brown sugar and salt, and blend with butter. Add egg yolks, milk, ginger, lemon juice and lemon rind, which have been mixed together, and beat with rotary beater until smooth. Lastly fold in the stiffly beaten egg whites. Pour this custard over mincemeat and bake 10 minutes in a hot oven (450° F.); reduce temperature to 325° F. and continue baking 45 minutes longer, or until custard is firm. Serve lukewarm or cold.

(230) MINCEMEAT MERINGUE CUSTARD— MISSISSIPPI METHOD
ONE-CRUST PIE, PRE-BAKED PIE SHELL

For one 9-inch pie
- Cornstarch: 2 Tbsps.
- Sugar (granulated): 2 Tbsps.
- Salt: ¼ tsp.
- Milk (scalded): 1½ cups
- Egg yolks (slightly beaten): 3
- Mincemeat: ½ cup or 4 oz.
- Pastry: 1 baked pie shell
- Egg whites (stiffly beaten): 3
- Salt: ⅛ tsp.
- Sugar (granulated): 6 Tbsps.
- Orange gratings: 1 tsp.

For five 9-inch pies
- Cornstarch: ⅝ cup or 3⅓ oz.
- Sugar (granulated): ⅝ cup or 5 oz.
- Salt: 1¼ tsps. or $5/24$ oz.
- Milk (scalded): 7½ cups or 3¾ lbs.
- Egg yolks (slightly beaten): 15 or 15 oz.
- Mincemeat: 2½ cups or 1¼ lbs.
- Pastry: 5 baked pie shells
- Egg whites (stiffly beaten): 15 or 15 oz.
- Salt: ⅝ tsp.
- Sugar (granulated): 1⅞ cups or 15 oz.
- Orange gratings: 1⅔ Tbsps. or ⅝ oz.

Combine cornstarch, sugar, and salt in top of double boiler; gradually add, while stirring constantly from bottom of pan, scalded milk. Cook in top of double boiler, stirring constantly until slightly thickened. Beat egg yolks slightly, add mincemeat, mix thoroughly, and add to custard, stirring frequently; continue cooking about 10 minutes, or until the consistency of soft custard. Turn into buttered pre-baked 9-inch pastry shell; let cool a little, then top with a meringue made of stiffly beaten egg whites, salt, sugar, and orange rind. Bake 15 minutes in a slow oven (325° F.), or until meringue is delicately brown. Serve hot.

(231)
MINCEMEAT RHUBARB PIE—
HOME METHOD
ONE-CRUST CRISSCROSS PIE

For one 9-inch pie
- Mincemeat (your favorite): ¾ lb.
- Rhubarb (fresh, diced): 2½ cups
- Sugar (granulated): ½ cup
- Flour (pastry): 1 Tbsp.
- Whole egg (well beaten): 1
- Pastry: For 1 crisscross pie

For five 9-inch pies
- Mincemeat (your favorite): 3¾ lbs.
- Rhubarb (fresh, diced): 3 qts. plus ½ cup or 3 lbs. 2 oz.
- Sugar (granulated): 2½ cups or 1¼ lbs.
- Flour (pastry): 5 Tbsps. or 1¼ oz.
- Whole eggs (well beaten): 5 or 10 oz.
- Pastry: For 5 crisscross pies

Combine all the ingredients in order named and turn into a 9-inch pie pan lined with pastry rolled ⅛-inch thick. Arrange crisscross of pastry strips (lattice fashion) across top. Moisten edge of pastry and finish with narrow strips of pastry around the edge of pie. Bake in a hot oven (450° F.) for 10 minutes; reduce temperature to 350° F. and continue baking 30 minutes longer. Serve warm.

(232) MOCK MINCE PIE—HOME METHOD
TWO-CRUST PIE

For one 9-inch pie
- Seedless raisins: 1½ cups
- Apples (diced): 1½ cups
- Cranberries (raw, chopped): 1½ cups
- Cider (hard): 1½ cups
- Sugar (brown): ½ cup
- Vinegar (cider): 1 Tbsp.
- Butter: ¼ cup
- Flour (pastry): 2 Tbsps.
- Cinnamon (ground): ½ tsp.
- Nutmeg (ground): ½ tsp.
- Cloves (ground): ¼ tsp.
- Candied orange peel (minced): 2 Tbsps.
- Pastry: For 1 two-crust pie

For five 9-inch pies
- Seedless raisins: 7½ cups or 2½ lbs.
- Apples (diced): 7½ cups or 3¾ lbs.
- Cranberries (raw, chopped): 7½ cups or 1½ lbs.
- Cider (hard): 7½ cups or 3¾ lbs.
- Sugar (brown): 2½ cups or 13⅓ oz.
- Vinegar (cider): 5 Tbsps. or 2½ oz.
- Butter: 1¼ cups or 10 oz.
- Flour (pastry): ⅝ cup or 2½ oz.
- Cinnamon (ground): 2½ tsps. or $5/24$ oz.
- Nutmeg (ground): 2½ tsps. or $5/12$ oz.
- Cloves (ground): 1¼ tsps.
- Candied orange peel (minced): ⅝ cup or 3¾ oz.
- Pastry: For 5 two-crust pies

Wash and drain raisins. Combine the remaining ingredients and let simmer gently for 15 minutes. Add raisins, simmer 5 minutes longer, and cool. Turn filling into 9-inch pie pan lined with pastry rolled ⅛-inch thick; cover with top crust in the usual way, making a few slits for escape of steam, and bake 10 minutes in a hot oven (450° F.); reduce temperature to 350° F. and continue baking 30 minutes longer. Serve warm with your favorite hard sauce or a piece of American cheese.

(233)   A FEW FACTS ABOUT MOLASSES

Today molasses is used principally for flavoring rather than sweetening. Nothing can substitute for its rich, mellow flavor. But in using molasses as a flavoring, remember it has sweetening power. In cookery a cupful of high-grade molasses furnishes about the same sweetening contained in three-quarters of a cup of granulated sugar. When substituting molasses for sugar take into account that a cupful of molasses carries about 12½ fluid ounces of liquid into the recipe or formula, and compensation should be made, especially in baking recipes, by decreasing the water, milk, or other indicated liquid ingredients, accordingly.

In baking, the baking soda serves the purpose of neutralizing the acid in the molasses, thereby providing the leavening gas. This action is similar to the effect obtained by using sour cream or buttermilk with baking soda. It aerates and raises cakes and controls the spread and spring of cookies. Molasses is one of the energy-giving foods—rich in iron and calcium, it helps build good teeth and strong bones.

Molasses calls for a touch of spice, a liberal amount of butter, raisins and a few nuts. That is the reason molasses recipes are always used to prepare the way for richer and heavier food.

(234)   MOLASSES FLUFFY PIE—
NEW ENGLAND METHOD
ONE-CRUST PIE

For one 9-inch pie
- Whole eggs (well beaten): 3
- Salt: ¼ tsp.
- Molasses: 3 cups
- Sugar (granulated): 1 cup
- Nutmeg (ground): ½ tsp.
- Butter (melted): 1 Tbsp.
- Lemon juice: 2 Tbsps.
- Pastry: For 1 one-crust pie

For five 9-inch pies
- Whole eggs (well beaten): 15 or 1⅞ lbs.
- Salt: 1¼ tsps. or ⁵/₂₄ oz.
- Molasses: 3¾ qts. or 11¼ lbs.
- Sugar (granulated): 5 cups or 1¼ qts. or 2½ lbs.
- Nutmeg (ground): 2½ tsps. or ⁵/₂₄ oz.
- Butter (melted): 5 Tbsps. or 2½ oz.
- Lemon juice: 10 Tbsps. or ⁵/₈ cup or 5 oz.
- Pastry: For 5 one-crust pies

Combine all the ingredients and beat until thoroughly blended. Turn mixture into unbaked 9-inch pastry shell and bake 10 minutes in a hot oven (450° F.); reduce temperature to 350° F. and continue baking 30 minutes longer, or until knife inserted in center comes out clean. Serve cold with or without whipped cream.

....

(235)

MOLASSES CRUMB PIE
ONE-CRUST PIE

For one 9-inch pie
- Flour (sifted): 7/8 cup
- Sugar (granulated): 1/3 cup
- Salt: 1/4 tsp.
- Cinnamon (ground): 1/4 tsp.
- Cloves (ground): 1/4 tsp.
- Allspice (ground): 1/4 tsp.
- Butter: 1 Tbsp.
- Pastry: For 1 one-crust pie
- Baking soda: 1/2 tsp.
- Molasses (dark): 1/2 cup
- Water (boiling): 1/2 cup

For five 9-inch pies
- Flour (sifted): 1 qt. plus 3/8 cup or 1 lb. and 1 1/2 oz.
- Sugar (granulated): 1 2/3 cups or 13 1/3 oz.
- Salt: 1 1/4 tsps. or 5/24 oz.
- Cinnamon (ground): 1 1/4 tsps.
- Cloves (ground): 1 1/4 tsps.
- Allspice (ground): 1 1/4 tsps.
- Butter: 5 Tbsps. or 2 1/2 oz.
- Pastry: For 5 one-crust pies
- Baking soda: 2 1/2 tsps. or 5/16 oz.
- Molasses (dark): 2 1/2 cups or 1 7/8 lbs.
- Water (boiling): 2 1/2 cups or 1 1/4 lbs.

Mix and sift flour, sugar, salt, and spices into a bowl; add the butter; mix thoroughly with the hands (the mixture is called *crumbs*). Sprinkle half the crumbs in the bottom of pastry-lined 9-inch pie pan, built up with a fluted rim. Add the soda to the boiling water and stir into the dark molasses until a bubbling mixture results, then pour into the crumbs in the pastry shell. Sprinkle with the remaining crumbs, pressing them into the molasses mixture. Bake in a hot oven (450° F.) for 10 minutes; then reduce temperature to 350° F. and continue baking 25–30 minutes longer, or until the crust is brown and the filling almost firm. Serve warm with or without plain or whipped cream.

(236)

MOLASSES PEANUT PIE—
ARKANSAS METHOD
ONE-CRUST PIE

For one 9-inch pie
- Sugar (granulated): 1 cup
- Flour (pastry): 1 Tbsp.
- Molasses: 1 cup
- Butter (melted): 3 Tbsps.
- Whole eggs (unbeaten): 3
- Salt: ¼ tsp.
- Nutmeg (ground): ½ tsp.
- Cinnamon (ground): ½ tsp.
- Peanuts (salted, coarsely chopped): 1 cup
- Pastry: For 1 one-crust pie

For five 9-inch pies
- Sugar (granulated): 5 cups or 2½ lbs.
- Flour (pastry): 5 Tbsps. or 1¼ oz.
- Molasses: 5 cups or 3¾ lbs.
- Butter (melted): scant cup or 7½ oz.
- Whole eggs (unbeaten): 15 or 1 lb. 14 oz.
- Salt: 1¼ tsps. or ⁵⁄₂₄ oz.
- Nutmeg (ground): 2½ tsps. or ⁵⁄₂₄ oz.
- Cinnamon (ground): 2½ tsps. or ⁵⁄₂₄ oz.
- Peanuts (salted, coarsely chopped): 5 cups or 1 lb. 10⅔ oz.
- Pastry: For 5 one-crust pies

Combine sugar and flour and add to the molasses with melted butter; blend thoroughly. Beat whole eggs, one at a time, into the mixture, beating briskly after each addition; with the last egg add the salt and spices (if peanuts are too salty, omit salt). Lastly stir in the coarsely chopped salted peanuts. Turn mixture into unbaked 9-inch pastry shell which has been brushed with slightly beaten egg white or sprinkled with a very little flour. Bake 10 minutes in a hot oven (450° F.); reduce temperature to 350° F. and continue baking 30 minutes longer. Serve cold with or without whipped cream topping.

(237) MOLASSES PIE—COUNTRY STYLE
ONE-CRUST CRISSCROSS PIE

For one 9-inch pie
- Pastry: For 1 crisscross pie
- Bread crumbs (sieved): 1 cup
- Raisins (seedless): 1 cup
- Molasses: 1 cup
- Sugar (brown): 6 Tbsps.
- Lemon rind (grated): 1 Tbsp.
- Flour (sifted): 3 Tbsps.
- Cinnamon (ground): 2 tsps.
- Shortening: 2 Tbsps.
- Sugar (brown): ¼ cup
- Flour (pastry): 6 Tbsps.
- Salt: ⅛ tsp.

For five 9-inch pies
- Pastry: For 5 crisscross pies
- Bread crumbs (sieved): 5 cups or 1 lb. 4 oz.
- Raisins (seedless): 5 cups or 1 lb. 10⅔ oz.
- Molasses: 5 cups or 3¾ lbs.
- Sugar (brown): 1⅞ cups or 10 oz.
- Lemon rind (grated): 5 Tbsps. or 1⅞ oz.
- Flour (sifted): scant 1 cup or 3¾ oz.
- Cinnamon (ground): 3⅓ Tbsps. or ⅚ oz.
- Shortening: ⅝ cup or 5 oz.
- Sugar (brown): 1¼ cups or 6⅔ oz.
- Flour (pastry): 1⅞ cups or 7½ oz.
- Salt: ⅝ tsp.

Line 9-inch pie pan with pastry rolled ⅛-inch thick; over this spread sieved bread crumbs, then the seedless raisins, carefully washed and drained. Into the molasses put the 6 tablespoons of brown sugar, lemon rind, 3 tablespoons of flour and cinnamon, thoroughly blended, and carefully pour this over the bread crumbs and raisins. In another mixing bowl, mix shortening, remaining brown sugar, flour and salt. Mix this well with finger tips and sprinkle over the filling in the pie; cover with crisscross pastry strips in the usual way; brush strips with water or milk and bake 40–45 minutes in a moderately slow oven (325° F.). Serve cold.

Variation: Add ½ cup chopped nut meats when combining the molasses with brown sugar, lemon rind, flour, cinnamon, and salt.

(238)

MOLASSES SHOO-FLY PIE—
PENNSYLVANIA METHOD
ONE-CRUST PIE

For one 9-inch pie
- Flour (pastry): ¾ cup
- Nutmeg: ⅛ tsp.
- Ginger: ⅛ tsp.
- Cloves: ⅛ tsp.
- Salt: ¼ tsp.
- Cinnamon: ½ tsp.
- Sugar (brown): ½ cup
- Shortening: 2 Tbsps.
- Baking soda: 1½ tsp.
- Molasses: ½ cup
- Water (boiling): ¾ cup
- Egg yolk (well beaten): 1
- Pastry: For 1 one-crust pie

For five 9-inch pies
- Flour (pastry): 3¾ cups or 15 oz.
- Nutmeg: ⅝ tsp.
- Ginger: ⅝ tsp.
- Cloves: ⅝ tsp.
- Salt: 1¼ tsps. or 5/24 oz.
- Cinnamon: 2½ tsps. or 5/24 oz.
- Sugar (brown): 2½ cups or 13⅓ oz.
- Shortening: 10 Tbsps. or 5 oz.
- Baking soda: 2½ Tbsps. or 5/16 oz. or scant ounce
- Molasses: 2½ cups or 1 lb. 14 oz.
- Water (boiling): 3¾ cups or 1 lb. 14 oz.
- Egg yolks (well beaten): 5 or 5 oz.
- Pastry: For 5 one-crust pies

Combine flour, nutmeg, ginger, cloves, salt, cinnamon, and brown sugar. Blend well. Cut in shortening (preferably lard). Add soda and molasses to boiling water; add beaten egg yolk and stir well to blend thoroughly. Line 9-inch pie pan with pastry rolled ⅛-inch thick. Make alternate layers of flour-spice-sugar mixture and molasses mixture, having on top a layer of flour-spice-sugar mixture. Bake 10 minutes in a very hot oven (450° F.); reduce temperature to 350° F. and continue baking 30 minutes longer, or until filling is firm. Serve cold, with or without American cheese.

(239)   # MOLASSES WALNUT CHESS PIE
ONE-CRUST PIE

For one 9-inch pie
- Molasses: ½ cup
- Whole eggs (well beaten): 2
- Sugar (dark brown): 1 cup
- Flour (pastry): 1 Tbsp.
- Salt: ⅛ tsp.
- Milk (cold): 2 Tbsps.
- Vanilla extract: scant 1 tsp.
- Black walnuts (coarsely chopped): ¾ cup
- Pastry: For 1 one-crust pie

For five 9-inch pies
- Molasses: 2½ cups or 1 lb. 14 oz.
- Whole eggs (well beaten): 10 or 1 lb. 4 oz.
- Sugar (dark brown): 5 cups or 1 lb. 10⅔ oz.
- Flour (pastry): 5 Tbsps. or 1¼ oz.
- Salt: ⅝ tsp.
- Milk (cold): 10 Tbsps. or 5 oz.
- Vanilla extract: 1½ Tbsps. or ¾ oz.
- Black walnuts (coarsely chopped): 3¾ cups or 15 oz.
- Pastry: For 5 one-crust pies

Combine all the ingredients in order named, adding nuts last. Pour into unbaked 9-inch one-crust pastry shell, which has been brushed with melted butter, then lightly sprinkled with flour. Bake 40 minutes in a moderate oven (350° F.), or until all the filling is firm with the exception of a small spot in the center. Serve with whipped cream.

(240) NEW ENGLAND MERINGUE CHESS PIE
ONE-CRUST PIE

For one 9-inch pie

- Butter (creamed): ½ cup
- Sugar (brown): 1 cup
- Whole egg: 1
- Egg yolks (well beaten): 3
- Walnuts (coarsely chopped): ½ cup
- Raisins (seedless, chopped): ½ cup
- Salt: ¼ tsp.
- Pastry: For 1 one-crust pie
- Meringue Topping (No. 26)

For five 9-inch pies

- Butter (creamed): 2½ cups or 1 lb. 4 oz.
- Sugar (brown): 5 cups or 1 lb. 10⅔ oz.
- Whole eggs: 5 or 10 oz.
- Egg yolks (well beaten): 15 or 15 oz.
- Walnuts (coarsely chopped): 2½ cups or 10 oz.
- Raisins (seedless, chopped): 2½ cups or 13⅓ oz.
- Salt: 1¼ tsps. or ⁵⁄₂₄ oz.
- Pastry: For 5 one-crust pies
- Meringue Topping (No. 26)

Cream butter and brown sugar. Beat together the whole egg and egg yolks and blend with creamed butter-sugar mixture; then fold in combined coarsely chopped walnuts, chopped seedless raisins and salt. Turn mixture into 9-inch unbaked pastry shell, the bottom and sides of which have been brushed with unbeaten egg white, and bake 30–35 minutes in a moderate oven (350° F.). Top with a meringue, made in the usual way, and bake 15 minutes longer in a moderately slow oven (325° F.), or until meringue is delicately brown. Serve warm or cold.

(241)   OLD-FASHIONED VINEGAR PIE— VIRGINIA METHOD
ONE-CRUST PIE, PRE-BAKED PIE SHELL

For one 9-inch pie
- Flour (sifted): ¼ cup
- Sugar (granulated): 1 cup
- Water: 1 cup
- Egg yolks: 3
- Salt: ⅛ tsp.
- Butter: 1 Tbsp.
- Lemon extract: ¼ tsp.
- Vinegar: 3 Tbsps.
- Pastry: 1 baked pie shell
- Meringue Topping No. 26

For five 9-inch pies
- Flour (sifted): 1¼ cups or 5 oz.
- Sugar (granulated): 5 cups or 2½ lbs.
- Water: 5 cups or 2½ lbs.
- Egg yolks: 15 or 15 oz.
- Salt: ⅝ tsp.
- Butter: 5 Tbsps. or 2½ oz.
- Lemon extract: 1¼ tsps. or ⁵⁄₂₄ oz.
- Vinegar: 1 cup or 7½ oz.
- Pastry: 5 baked pie shells
- Meringue Topping No. 26

Mix flour with half the sugar. Add water gradually and cook in top of double boiler for 15 minutes, or until thickened, stirring constantly. Combine remaining sugar with egg yolks and salt and beat until sugar is dissolved. Add the flour-sugar mixture (hot) to egg yolk mixture gradually, beating vigorously until mixture is thoroughly blended. Return to double boiler, and cook over hot water 3 minutes longer, or until mixture is thick and smooth. Add butter, flavoring, and vinegar; blend well and cool. Pour into 9-inch pre-baked pastry shell; top with meringue, made in the usual way, and bake 15 minutes in a moderately slow oven (325° F.), or until meringue is delicately brown. Serve hot.

....

(242)   A FEW FACTS ABOUT ORANGES

Most of us are familiar with the use of baking soda and some acid ingredient, such as chocolate, molasses, or brown sugar, acting as a leavening agent. Orange juice is mildly acid and when used in certain recipes in which baking soda is an ingredient, it can form the entire source of liquid. Because of the mildness of the acidity in orange juice, ¾ cup is required to react with ½ teaspoonful of baking soda for leavening, which, as a general rule, can be used with 2 cups of flour. Furthermore, the delightful yellow crumb and the rich brown crust developed when using orange juice is very pleasing and appealing.

The flavor of orange juice is delicate; the aroma refreshing. Some of this is lost while the baked products are hot, but is regained on cooling. Grated orange rind, on the other hand, has a very pleasing aroma while hot or cold.

A point to be remembered by the baker is this: When orange juice is used as a liquid in recipes, without taking into consideration the need for a neutralizing agent (baking soda), the resulting baked products have a coarse, damp crumb and a pale crust unevenly browned. This applies for cakes, pies, muffins, bread, etc.

It is also recommended not to strain orange juice. To do so means that only the water soluble material of the orange is used, and there is a good deal of nutrient value, notably vitamins A and C and iron, in the suspended particles of pulp which are discarded.

To segment an orange, cut a thick layer off the top and one off the bottom of the orange, and then cut off sections of peel from sides, cutting deep enough to remove all white membrane and to leave fruit exposed. With sharp knife cut each section separately.

When you buy oranges, do not buy them with your eyes but with your hands—by feel! Lift them, see if they are heavy with juice; that's the test. For economy you want your oranges thin-skinned, free from useless pulp, and heavy with juice—and remember, the more juice, the more vitamins.

(243)
ORANGE BOSTON PIE
TWO-CRUST PIE

NOTE: See Boston Cream Pie (No. 119) for the crust, which should be a good sponge cake.

For one 9-inch pie
- Sugar (granulated): ⅓ cup
- Cornstarch: 1 Tbsp.
- Salt: ⅛ tsp.
- Milk: ⅔ cup
- Whole egg (slightly beaten): 1
- Egg yolk (slightly beaten): 1
- Butter: 1 Tbsp.
- Orange juice: ½ cup
- Orange rind (grated): 1 tsp.
- Pastry: 2 baked sponge cake layers
- Heavy cream (whipped): ¾ cup

For five 9-inch pies
- Sugar (granulated): 1⅔ cups or 13⅓ oz.
- Cornstarch: 5 Tbsps. or 1⅔ oz.
- Salt: ⅝ tsp.
- Milk: 3⅓ cups or 1 lb. 10⅔ oz.
- Whole eggs (slightly beaten): 5 or 10 oz.
- Egg yolks (slightly beaten): 5 or 5 oz.
- Butter: 5 Tbsps. or 2½ oz.
- Orange juice: 2½ cups or 1 lb. 4 oz.
- Orange rind (grated): 1⅔ Tbsps. or ⅝ oz.
- Pastry: 10 baked sponge cake layers
- Heavy cream (whipped): 3¾ cups or scant 2 lbs.

Mix sugar, cornstarch and salt. Add milk, combined with slightly beaten whole egg and egg yolk, and blend thoroughly. Cook over hot water until mixture thickens, stirring contantly. When mixture is thick and smooth, remove from hot water and stir in the butter. Then add orange juice and rind and stir until blended. Return to hot water and allow to simmer gently for 4 or 5 minutes, stirring occasionally. Cool, then pour over one sponge cake layer, placed in bottom of a 9-inch pie pan; cover with remaining sponge cake layer and top with whipped cream, forced through a pastry bag, making fancy designs. Arrange in center of the top a pinwheel made of orange sections, free from seeds and membrane. Serve cold. You may omit whipped cream, and sprinkle top layer with powdered sugar, if desired.

(244) ORANGE COCONUT MERINGUE PIE
ONE-CRUST PIE, PRE-BAKED PIE SHELL

For one 9-inch pie

- Egg yolks (slightly beaten): 3
- Orange juice: ½ cup
- Lemon juice: 1½ Tbsps.
- Orange rind (grated): 1 Tbsp.
- Sugar (granulated): 1 cup
- Salt: ¼ tsp.
- Butter: 1 Tbsp.
- Hot water: 1½ cups
- Cornstarch: 3 Tbsps.
- Coconut (shredded): ½ cup
- Pastry: 1 baked pie shell
- Egg whites (beaten stiffly): 3
- Salt: a few grains
- Sugar: ¾ cup
- Lemon juice: 1 tsp.
- Coconut (shredded): ⅓ cup

For five 9-inch pies

- Egg yolks (slightly beaten): 15 or 15 oz.
- Orange juice: 2½ cups or 1 lb. 4 oz.
- Lemon juice: 7½ Tbsps. or 3¾ oz.
- Orange rind (grated): 5 Tbsps. or 1⅞ oz.
- Sugar (granulated): 5 cups or 2½ lbs.
- Salt: 1¼ tsps. or 5/24 oz.
- Butter: 5 Tbsps. or 2½ oz.
- Hot water: 7½ cups or 3¾ lbs.
- Cornstarch: scant cup or 5 oz.
- Coconut (shredded): 2½ cups or 8 oz. or ½ lb.
- Pastry: 5 baked pie shells
- Egg whites (beaten stiffly): 15 or 15 oz.
- Salt: ¼ tsp. or 1/24 oz.
- Sugar: 3¾ cups or 1 lb. 14 oz.
- Lemon juice: 1½ Tbsps. or ¾ oz.
- Coconut (shredded): 1⅔ cups or 5⅓ oz.

Beat egg yolks slightly, then add orange juice, 1½ Tbsps. lemon juice and orange rind and blend thoroughly. Gradually beat in first amount of sugar. Combine salt, butter, and hot water; stir in the cornstarch, which has been dissolved in a little cold water, and stir into the first mixture, blending well. Cook over hot water until mixture thickens, stirring constantly. Remove from hot water. Cool. When cool, not cold, gently stir in first amount of coconut. Turn mixture into pre-baked 9-inch pastry shell and top with meringue made with stiffly beaten egg whites, salt, remaining sugar and remaining lemon juice. Sprinkle with remaining coconut and bake in a moderately slow oven (325° F.) 15 minutes, or until meringue is delicately brown. Serve cold.

(245)   ORANGE CREAM MERINGUE PIE
ONE-CRUST PIE, PRE-BAKED PIE SHELL

For one 9-inch pie
- Orange sections: 1 cup
- Condensed milk: 1 15-oz. can or 1¾ cups
- Lemon juice: 2 Tbsps.
- Orange juice: ¼ cup
- Salt: ⅛ tsp.
- Pastry: 1 baked pie shell
- Meringue or whipped cream topping No. 26

For five 9-inch pies
- Orange sections: 5 cups or 2½ lbs.
- Condensed milk: 5 15-oz. cans or 8¾ cups or 4 lb. 11 oz.
- Lemon juice: 10 Tbsps. or 5 oz.
- Orange juice: 1¼ cups or 10 oz.
- Salt: ⅝ tsp.
- Pastry: 5 baked pie shells
- Meringue or whipped cream topping No. 26

Prepare orange sections by first paring whole fruit, cutting sections entirely free from center membrane, then cutting each section again in half. Blend condensed milk with lemon and orange juice, salt, and orange sections. Chill well. Pour into pre-baked 9-inch pastry shell. Cover with meringue made in the usual way, and brown lightly in a moderately slow oven (325° F.) for 15 minutes, or cover with sweetened whipped cream. Serve cold.

....

(246)   ORANGE MARMALADE CUSTARD PIE
ONE-CRUST PIE

For one 9-inch pie
- Pastry: For 1 one-crust pie
- Whole eggs (slightly beaten): 2
- Egg yolks (slightly beaten): 2
- Sugar (granulated): ½ cup
- Salt: ⅛ tsp.
- Orange rind (grated): 1 Tbsp.
- Orange marmalade: ¼ cup
- Milk (hot): 2 cups

For five 9-inch pies
- Pastry: For 5 one-crust pies
- Whole eggs (slightly beaten): 10 or 1 lb. 4 oz.
- Egg yolks (slightly beaten): 10 or 10 oz.
- Sugar (granulated): 2½ cups or 1 lb. 4 oz.
- Salt: ⅝ tsp.
- Orange rind (grated): 5 Tbsps. or 1⅞ oz.
- Orange marmalade: 1¼ cups or 15 oz.
- Milk (hot): 2½ qts. or 5 lbs.

Brush unbaked pastry shell lightly with unbeaten egg white. Place in refrigerator to dry and to chill pastry thoroughly. Combine lightly beaten whole eggs and yolks with sugar, salt, orange rind and marmalade. Gradually add hot milk, stirring until mixture is well-blended. Pour into the unbaked, chilled shell and bake 10 minutes in a very hot oven (450° F.); reduce temperature to 325° F. and continue baking for 30 to 35 minutes longer, or until custard is firm. Serve cold.

....

(247)   # ORANGE PIE—FLORIDA STYLE
ONE-CRUST PIE

For one 9-inch pie
- Flour (sifted): 1½ cups
- Sugar (granulated, fine): 1 Tbsp.
- Salt: ⅓ tsp.
- Orange rind (grated): 1 tsp.
- Shortening (any kind): ½ cup
- Orange juice (ice cold): ¼ cup (about)

For five 9-inch pies
- Flour (sifted): 7½ cups or 1⅞ lbs.
- Sugar (granulated, fine): 5 Tbsps. or 2½ oz.
- Salt: 1⅔ tsps. or ⁵⁄₁₈ oz.
- Orange rind (grated): 1⅔ Tbsps. or ⅝ oz.
- Shortening (any kind): 2½ cups or 1¼ lbs.
- Orange juice (ice cold): 1¼ cups (about 10 oz.)

Mix sifted flour with sugar and salt, and sift once more; add orange rind and blend thoroughly. Cut in the shortening coarsely. Gradually add cold orange juice—enough to bind dough together. Roll pastry ⅛-inch thick and line 9-inch pie pan. Bake in a hot oven (450° F.) for about 15 minutes. Cool.

Filling
- Sugar (granulated): 1 cup
- Cornstarch: 5 Tbsps.
- Salt: ¼ tsp.
- Orange peel (shredded): 1 Tbsp.
- Orange juice: 2 cups
- Egg yolks (slightly beaten): 3
- Butter: 1 Tbsp.
- Lemon juice: 2 Tbsps.

Filling
- Sugar (granulated): 5 cups or 2½ lbs.
- Cornstarch: 1 cup plus 9 Tbsps. or 8⅓ oz.
- Salt: 1¼ tsps. or ⁵⁄₂₄ oz.
- Orange peel (shredded): 5 Tbsps. or 1⅞ oz.
- Orange juice: 2½ qts. or 5 lbs.
- Egg yolks (slightly beaten): 15 or 15 oz.
- Butter: 5 Tbsps. or 2½ oz.
- Lemon juice: ⅝ cup or 5 oz.

Mix sugar, cornstarch, salt, and orange peel thoroughly; stir in orange juice, and cook in top of double boiler until mixture is thickened, stirring frequently. Strain into another double boiler top and gradually add slightly beaten egg yolks, stirring briskly. Return to the heat, and cook over hot water, stirring constantly from bottom of pan, for 2 or 3 minutes. Remove from the hot water and stir in the butter alternately with lemon juice. Cool and pour into pre-baked 9-inch pastry shell. Top with a meringue made as follows:

Meringue Topping
- Egg whites (stiffly beaten): 3
- Sugar (granulated): 3 Tbsps.
- Sugar (brown): 3 Tbsps.
- Salt: ⅛ tsp.
- Orange extract: ⅛ tsp.
- Almond extract: ⅛ tsp.
- Orange sections

Meringue Topping
- Egg whites (stiffly beaten): 15 or 15 oz.
- Sugar (granulated): 15 Tbsps. or 7½-oz.
- Sugar (brown): 15 Tbsps. or 5 oz.
- Salt: ⅝ tsp.
- Orange extract: ⅝ tsp.
- Almond extract: ⅝ tsp.
- Orange sections

To the stiffly beaten egg whites add combined remaining ingredients and beat until meringue holds its peaks. Spoon wavelike over the filling and bake 10 minutes in a moderately slow oven (325° F.). Open the door of oven and press, pinwheel-fashion, sections of orange into meringue; sprinkle orange sections with granulated sugar mixed with a little ground cinnamon; continue baking about 8 to 10 minutes, or until meringue is delicately brown and orange sections glazed. Serve cold.

(248) ORANGE RAISIN PIE—TEXAS METHOD
TWO-CRUST PIE

For one 9-inch pie
- Pastry: For 1 two-crust pie
- Raisins (seedless): 2 cups
- Sugar (granulated): ½ cup
- Cornstarch: 2 Tbsps.
- Salt: ½ tsp.
- Water (boiling): 2 cups
- Butter: 1 Tbsp.
- Orange rind (grated): 1 Tbsp.
- Orange juice: 3 Tbsps.
- Lemon juice: 1 Tbsp.
- Orange-flavored whipped cream

For five 9-inch pies
- Pastry: For 5 two-crust pies
- Raisins (seedless): 2½ qts. or 3 lbs. 5⅓ oz.
- Sugar (granulated): 2½ cups or 1¼ lbs.
- Cornstarch: 10 Tbsps. or ⅝ cup or 3⅓ oz.
- Salt: 2½ tsps. or 5/12 oz.
- Water (boiling): 2½ qts. or 5 lbs.
- Butter: 5 Tbsps. or 2½ oz.
- Orange rind (grated): 5 Tbsps. or 1⅞ oz.
- Orange juice: scant cup or 7½ oz.
- Lemon juice: 5 Tbsps. or 2½ oz.
- Orange-flavored whipped cream

Line 9-inch pie pan with pastry rolled ⅛-inch thick; spread slightly beaten egg white or soft butter over bottom and sides to keep the crust from soaking. Parboil seedless raisins and drain. Mix sugar, cornstarch, and salt in saucepan, and stir in boiling water. Add drained seedless raisins and bring to a boil over low heat. Let boil gently for 5 minutes, stirring almost constantly. Remove from the heat; stir in butter, orange rind, orange and lemon juice. Turn mixture into prepared pastry shell; cover with top crust in the usual way (strips or crisscross pastry may be used), brush with milk after making a few slits for escape of steam, and bake 10 minutes in a hot oven (450° F.); reduce temperature to 350° F. and continue baking 25–30 minutes longer, or until top is delicately brown. Serve cold with orange-flavored whipped cream.

(249) ORANGE SPICY PUMPKIN CREAM PIE— HOME METHOD
ONE-CRUST PIE

For one 9-inch pie
- Butter: 2 Tbsps.
- Milk (rich, scalded): 1²/₃ cups
- Sugar (brown, well-packed): ¾ cup
- Salt: ¼ tsp.
- Cinnamon (ground): 1 tsp.
- Ginger (ground): ½ tsp.
- Allspice (ground): ¹/₈ tsp.
- Orange rind (grated): 1½ Tbsps.
- Whole eggs (slightly beaten): 3
- Pumpkin (cooked, sieved or canned): 1 cup
- Pastry: For 1 one-crust pie
- Heavy cream (whipped): 1 cup
- Orange juice (strained): 1 Tbsp.
- Cinnamon (ground): ¹/₁₆ tsp.
- Salt: A few grains

For five 9-inch pies
- Butter: 10 Tbsps. or ⁵/₈ cup or 5 oz.
- Milk (rich, scalded): 8¹/₃ cups or 4 lbs. 2 oz.
- Sugar (brown, well-packed): 3¾ cups or 1 lb. 4 oz.
- Salt: 1¼ tsps. or ⁵/₂₄ oz.
- Cinnamon (ground): 1²/₃ Tbsps. or ⁵/₁₂ oz.
- Ginger (ground): 2½ tsps. or ⁵/₂₄ oz.
- Allspice (ground): ⁵/₈ tsp.
- Orange rind (grated): 7½ Tbsps. or scant 2⁷/₈ oz.
- Whole eggs (slightly beaten): 15
- Pumpkin (cooked, sieved or canned): 5 cups or 1¼ qts. or 3¾ lbs.
- Pastry: For 5 one-crust pies
- Heavy cream (whipped): 5 cups or 2½ lbs.
- Orange juice (strained): 5 Tbsps. or 2½ oz.
- Cinnamon (ground): ⁵/₁₆ tsp.
- Salt: A few grains

Add butter to scalded milk; cool slightly. Mix sugar, salt, spices and orange rind in a bowl; stir in the slightly beaten whole eggs. Whip pumpkin smooth and add to sugar-spice mixture in bowl. Slowly, stirring constantly, add the scalded milk. Turn mixture into 9-inch unbaked pastry-lined pie pan and bake 10 minutes in a hot oven (450° F.); reduce temperature to 350° F. and continue baking 35 minutes longer, or until mixture is firm like a custard. When cold top with whipped cream to which have been added orange juice, cinnamon, and a few grains of salt. Serve cold.

(250) A FEW FACTS ABOUT PEACHES

Brillat-Savarin, the gourmet philosopher, in attempting to analyze the sensation of taste, uses the peach as an example. "He who eats the peach is first agreeably struck by the odor which emanates from it; he puts it in his mouth and feels the sensation of freshness and of sourness which induces him to continue. But it is only at the moment when he swallows it that the perfume is revealed to him. This completes the sensation which a peach ought to produce. Finally it is only when it has been swallowed that the taster says to himself, "How delicious!"

General appearance, firmness of the flesh, freedom from blemishes, and a fresh tone, all are looked for as signs of sound, ripe fruit. The blush alone is not a true sign of maturity. For long-distance shipment, the fruit is picked slightly green; it ripens quickly at the market. If picked too green, however, peaches will not ripen, though they may change color and acquire the tint of ripeness. They will be slightly wrinkled near the stem end and they will lack flavor. The peach ripens so quickly that in two or three days it will advance from an immature stage to one which is too far advanced for shipping. Early peaches are the white-fleshed varieties, while the late varieties have yellow flesh.

Fresh peaches are usually peeled, sliced, and served with sugar and cream. With some varieties the skin may be removed easily, but with others it is necessary to plunge them into boiling water for a few seconds, then into cold, in order to loosen the skins. They should be peeled and served at once. When it is necessary to prepare them in large quantity, they may be peeled and kept in milk, heavy fruit juice or in a solution of ascorbic acid, and then sliced as needed. One pound of peaches, or about 4 to 6, yields 2 to 2½ cups of slices, or about 3 to 4 portions. A bushel of peaches averages 15 quarts when canned.

Peach shortcake is almost as good as that made with strawberries. If peaches are used in cobblers, be sure that at least one stone is cooked with the fruit for the special tang it gives to the flavor. This is also good practice when you make peach marmalade or can the halved fruit. For spicing or brandying, the fruit is generally left whole.

(251)   # PEACH AND BLACKBERRY PIE— WISCONSIN METHOD
TWO-CRUST PIE

For one 9-inch pie
- Flour (sifted): 2 cups
- Salt: ½ tsp.
- Cream cheese: 2 (3-oz.) pkgs.
- Shortening: ½ cup
- Ice water: about 6 Tbsps.
- Quick-cooking tapioca: 1½ Tbsps.
- Sugar (granulated): ⅔ cup
- Salt: ⅛ tsp.
- Orange rind (grated): 1 tsp.
- Peaches (fresh, sliced): 2 cups
- Blackberries (fresh): 2 cups

For five 9-inch pies
- Flour (sifted): 2½ qts. or 2½ lbs.
- Salt: 2½ tsps. or ⁵⁄₁₂ oz.
- Cream cheese: 1 lb. 14 oz. or 10 3-oz. pkgs.
- Shortening: 2½ cups or 1 lb. 4 oz.
- Ice water: about 1⅞ cups
- Quick-cooking tapioca: 7½ Tbsps. or 1⅞ oz.
- Sugar (granulated): 3⅓ cups or 1 lb. 10⅔ oz.
- Salt: ⅝ tsp.
- Orange rind (grated): 1⅔ Tbsps. or ⅝ oz.
- Peaches (fresh, sliced): 2½ qts. or 5 lbs. ⅔ oz.
- Blackberries (fresh): 2½ qts. or 1 lb. 10⅔ oz.

Mix and sift flour and salt. Cut in cream cheese, alternately with shortening. Add enough ice water to hold ingredients and roll out in the usual way for a 9-inch two-crust pastry. Chill in refrigerator while preparing filling, as follows: Mix quick-cooking tapioca, sugar, salt, and orange rind thoroughly. Sprinkle ⅓ of this mixture on 9-inch pastry-lined pie pan. Combine fruits with remaining tapioca-sugar mixture, and fill pie shell. Adjust pastry crust in the usual way, making a few slits for escape of steam, and bake 35–40 minutes in a hot oven (425° F.). Serve cold with or without whipped cream topping.

(252) **PEACH CREAM PIE—FRENCH METHOD**
ONE-CRUST PIE, PRE-BAKED PIE SHELL

For one 9-inch pie

- Sugar (granulated): ½ cup
- Salt: ⅛ tsp.
- Cornstarch: 2⅔ Tbsps.
- Flour (pastry): 2 Tbsps.
- Egg yolks (slightly beaten): 2
- Milk (cold): 10 Tbsps.
- Milk (hot): 1 cup
- Butter: 1 Tbsp.
- Egg whites (stiffly beaten): 2
- Sugar (granulated): 2 Tbsps.
- Vanilla extract: ½ tsp.
- Sliced fresh peaches
- Pastry: 1 baked pie shell

For five 9-inch pies

- Sugar (granulated): 2½ cups or 1¼ lbs.
- Salt: ⅝ tsp.
- Cornstarch: ⅞ cup or 4⁴⁄₉ oz.
- Flour (pastry): ⅝ cup or 2½ oz.
- Egg yolks (slightly beaten): 10 or 10 oz.
- Milk (cold): 3⅛ cups or 1 lb. 9 oz.
- Milk (hot): 5 cups or 2½ lbs.
- Butter: 5 Tbsps. or 2½ oz.
- Egg whites (stiffly beaten): 10 or 10 oz.
- Sugar (granulated): ⅝ cup or 5 oz.
- Vanilla extract: 2½ tsps. or ⁵⁄₁₂ oz.
- Sliced fresh peaches
- Pastry: 5 baked pie shells

Combine first amount of granulated sugar with salt, cornstarch and flour and sift once. Add slightly beaten egg yolks, which have been mixed with the cold milk. Beat well until smooth, and strain to remove any possible lumps. Gradually stir in the hot milk, beating vigorously until thoroughly blended. Turn mixture into top of double boiler and cook over hot water until mixture thickens and is very smooth. Allow to simmer gently for 3 or 4 minutes, stirring frequently. Remove from hot water and add butter bit by bit. Do not stir; allow butter to melt by itself. When melted, stir gently, cool, and stir in the stiffly beaten egg whites sweetened with sugar and flavored with vanilla extract. Turn mixture into cold pre-baked 9-inch pastry shell which has been lined with fresh, peeled, sliced, juicy peaches, and pipe a "collar" of whipped cream around the edge, leaving center exposed to view. Serve very cold.

(253) PEACH WHIPPED CREAM PIE— FRENCH METHOD
ONE-CRUST PIE, MERINGUE SHELL

NOTE: For a very special occasion make this "Peach Whipped Cream Pie" with its crisp meringue crust. Make the meringue, bake it and put it aside until it is ready to be used. Fill the meringue shell with fresh, peeled, sliced, juicy peaches; cover with a fluffy meringue and bake it for 3 or 4 minutes in a hot oven (400° F.) or until delicately brown. Meringue shells will keep indefinitely, when kept in a dry, cool place, and may be used for almost any kind of fresh or canned fruits, single or in combination. You may make individual or large meringue shells.

For one 9-inch pie
- Egg whites (stiffly beaten): 3
- Salt: ¼ tsp.
- Cream of tartar: ¼ tsp.
- Sugar (powdered or fine granulated): 1 cup
- Vinegar: 1 tsp.
- Water (cold): 1 tsp.
- Vanilla extract: ½ tsp.
- Almond extract: ½ tsp.
- Sliced fresh peaches
- Sweetened whipped cream

For five 9-inch pies
- Egg whites (stiffly beaten): 15 or 15 oz.
- Salt: 1¼ tsps. or $5/24$ oz.
- Cream of tartar: 1¼ tsps. or $5/24$ oz.
- Sugar (powdered or fine granulated): 5 cups or 1 lb. 6⁶/₇ oz.
- Vinegar: 1²/₃ Tbsps. or ⁵/₆ oz.
- Water (cold): 1½ Tbsps. or ¾ oz.
- Vanilla extract: 2½ tsps. or ⁵/₁₂ oz.
- Almond extract: 2½ tsps. or ⁵/₁₂ oz.
- Sliced fresh peaches
- Sweetened whipped cream

Combine egg whites with salt and cream of tartar and beat to a stiff foam. Add sugar to the beaten eggs, 1 tablespoon at a time, alternately with combined vinegar, cold water, and flavoring extracts; beat after each addition until sugar is well blended, before adding another amount of both mixtures. Continue to beat after all of them have been added until the fluff will hold in mounds. Butter the bottom of a heavy 9-inch pie pan; cover with heavy buttered paper and spread the meringue mixture in the pan, pulling it up the sides to make a rim. Bake in a 250° F. oven for about ¾ to 1 hour, or until done. Loosen from the pie pan while the meringue is still warm, but not hot, and allow to cool. Just before serving, fill the meringue shell with sliced fresh peaches, mixed with sweetened, unflavored whipped cream. (The sliced peaches should be sprinkled lightly with sugar 30 minutes before putting in the shell, to extract the liquid.) Cover with some of this meringue, or an ordinary meringue made in the usual way (No. 26). Place the pie pan on a heavy board and bake in a very hot oven (450° F.) for 3 minutes, or until the meringue is delicately brown. Remove from the oven and serve at once, while still hot.

(254)

PEACH WHIPPED CREAM PIE—
AMERICAN METHOD
ONE-CRUST PIE, PRE-BAKED PIE SHELL

For one 9-inch pie
- Peaches (canned): 1 #2½ can
- Peach juice (from fruit): ¾ cup
- Corn syrup (white): 2 Tbsps.
- Cornstarch: 2 Tbsps.
- Sugar (granulated): ⅞ cup
- Salt: ¼ tsp.
- Lemon rind (grated): ¼ tsp.
- Almond extract: ⅛ tsp.
- Pastry: 1 baked pie shell

For five 9-inch pies
- Peaches (canned): 1 #10 can or 6 lb. 10 oz.
- Peach juice (from fruit): 3¾ cups or 1 lb. 14 oz.
- Corn syrup (white): 10 Tbsps. or 7½ oz.
- Cornstarch: 10 Tbsps. or 3⅓ oz.
- Sugar (granulated): 4⅜ cups or 2 lbs. 3 oz.
- Salt: 1¼ tsps. or $5/24$ oz.
- Lemon rind (grated): 1¼ tsps.
- Almond extract: ⅝ tsp.
- Pastry: 5 baked pie shells

Drain the fruit, reserving juice. There should be ¾ cup; if not, add enough cold water to make the required amount. Combine the liquid with corn syrup, cornstarch, sugar, salt, and lemon rind. Blend thoroughly. Place over medium heat and cook, stirring constantly, until mixture thickens; cook slowly 3 minutes longer, stirring frequently. Remove from the heat, cool a little and add almond extract. When slightly cooled, add the drained, canned peaches. Blend well, but gently, so as not to break the peach slices. Turn mixture into a pre-baked 9-inch pastry shell. Allow to cool thoroughly, then top with whipped cream. Decorate the edge of the pie with peach slices. Serve cold.

(255)

PEACH CUSTARD PIE—
CALIFORNIA METHOD
ONE-CRUST PIE

For one 9-inch pie

- Egg yolks (slightly beaten): 2
- Sugar (granulated): 1 cup
- Butter (melted): 1 Tbsp.
- Cornstarch: 2 Tbsps.
- Water (or peach juice, depending on how juicy the peaches are): 2 Tbsps.
- Pastry: For 1 one-crust pie
- Peaches (sliced, fresh): 1 cup
- Meringue topping (optional): No. 26

For five 9-inch pies

- Egg yolks (slightly beaten): 10 or 10 oz.
- Sugar (granulated): 5 cups or 2½ lbs.
- Butter (melted): 5 Tbsps. or 2½ oz.
- Cornstarch: 10 Tbsps. or 3⅓ oz.
- Water (or peach juice, depending on how juicy the peaches are): 10 Tbsps. or 5 oz.
- Pastry: For 5 one-crust pies
- Peaches (sliced, fresh): 5 cups
- Meringue topping (optional): No. 26

Combine all the first five ingredients in the usual method when making custard pie. Line a 9-inch unbaked pastry shell with the fresh, sliced peaches; pour over the custard preparation and bake 10 minutes in a very hot oven (450° F.); reduce temperature to 325° F. and continue baking for 30 minutes longer. Remove at once, place pie on a wire pastry rack, being sure air is circulating underneath, lest the custard keeps on cooking and turns watery. Top or not with a meringue, made in the usual way, place in a moderately slow oven (325° F.) and bake 15 minutes, or until meringue is delicately brown. Serve cold.

NOTE: Canned peaches may be used; in such case, omit water or peach juice, as the peach slices are sufficiently juicy to keep enough moisture during baking process.

(256)
PEACH PIE À LA MODE
TWO-CRUST PIE

For one 9-inch pie
- Peaches (canned, drained): 1 #2½ can
- Peach juice: ¾ cup
- Cornstarch: 2½ Tbsps.
- Sugar (granulated): ⅞ cup
- Salt: ½ tsp.
- Nutmeg: A few grains
- Pastry: For 1 two-crust pie

For five 9-inch pies
- Peaches (canned, drained): 1 #10 can or 6 lbs. 8 oz.
- Peach juice: 3¾ cups or 1 lb. 14 oz.
- Cornstarch: 12½ Tbsps. or 4⅙ oz.
- Sugar (granulated): 4⅜ cups or 2 lbs. 3 oz.
- Salt: 2½ tsps. or 5/12 oz.
- Nutmeg: ⅝ tsp.
- Pastry: For 5 two-crust pies

Drain peaches, reserving juice. There should be ¾ cup; if not, add enough cold water to make the difference. Place over direct heat and bring to a boil. Combine cornstarch with sugar, salt, and nutmeg and dissolve with a little of the cold fruit juice reserved for that. Slowly stir cornstarch mixture into the boiling juice, stirring constantly, until mixture is smooth and thick. Then let cook gently for 2 minutes; stir constantly to prevent scorching (you may place mixture over hot water to eliminate this danger). Remove from the heat and pour hot over the peaches, mixing gently. Cool. When cold, turn mixture into a 9-inch pie pan lined with pastry rolled ⅛-inch thick; cover with top crust in the usual way, prick top crust with the tines of a fork or sharp knife, brush with milk and bake 10 minutes in a very hot oven (450° F.); reduce temperature to (350° F.) and continue baking 25 minutes longer. Serve cold, topped with a small scoop of any kind of ice cream.

(257) PEACH PIE DE LUXE—FRENCH METHOD
TWO-CRUST PIE

For one 9-inch pie
- Flour (pastry): 2 Tbsps.
- Sugar (fine granulated): 1 cup
- Salt: ⅛ tsp.
- Nutmeg: ⅛ tsp.
- Shredded almonds: 2 Tbsps.
- Pastry: For 1 two-crust pie
- Peaches (fresh, sliced): 2 lbs.
- Butter: 1 Tbsp.

For five 9-inch pies
- Flour (pastry): 10 Tbsps. or 2½ oz.
- Sugar (fine granulated): 5 cups or 2½ lbs.
- Salt: ⅝ tsp.
- Nutmeg: ⅝ tsp.
- Shredded almonds: 10 Tbsps. or 2⁶/₇ oz.
- Pastry: For 5 two-crust pies
- Peaches (fresh, sliced): 10 lbs.
- Butter: 5 Tbsps. or 2½ oz.

Combine pastry flour, sugar, salt and nutmeg and sift once. Add shredded almonds and mix well. Sprinkle half of this mixture in bottom of unbaked 9-inch pastry shell; add the fresh peaches, peeled and sliced, over the sugar mixture; top peaches with remaining sugar mixture and dot with butter; cover with top crust; prick open designs with the end of a fork or sharp knife; brush with milk and bake 10 minutes in a very hot oven (450° F.); reduce temperature to 350° F. and continue baking for 25 minutes longer. Serve cold, topped with whipped cream, or à la mode.

NOTE: Sugar amount may be raised or diminished, according to sweetness or sourness of fruit. Do not peel and slice fruit until ready to fill the bottom, unbaked shell. Moisture is furnished by the juice of the fruit.

(258)   # PEACH PIE—ALASKA METHOD
ONE-CRUST PIE, PRE-BAKED PIE SHELL

For one 9-inch pie
- Egg whites (stiffly beaten): 4
- Sugar (granulated): ¾ cup
- Salt: ⅛ tsp.
- Pastry: 1 baked pie shell, chilled
- Sugar (granulated): ¼ cup
- Peaches (fresh or canned, sliced and thoroughly drained): 3 cups
- Peach ice cream: 1 pint

For five 9-inch pies
- Egg whites (stiffly beaten): 20 or 1 lb. 4 oz.
- Sugar (granulated): 3¾ cups or 1 lb. 14 oz.
- Salt: ⅝ tsp.
- Pastry: 5 baked pie shells, chilled
- Sugar (granulated): 1¼ cups or 10 oz.
- Peaches (fresh or canned, sliced and thoroughly drained): 3¾ qts. or 7½ lbs.
- Peach ice cream: 2½ qts. or 5 lbs.

Beat egg whites until stiff; gradually add the ¾ cup of granulated sugar and salt, beating until sugar is dissolved. Have ready a pre-baked 9-inch one-crust pastry shell; sprinkle in bottom half of the remaining granulated sugar, arrange prepared peaches over the sugar, and sprinkle with remaining ¼ cup of granulated sugar (more sugar may be required, according to sweetness of fruit). When ready to serve, and not before, cover sliced peaches with very solidly frozen peach ice cream; cover the entire surface of the pie top with the stiff meringue (No. 26). Bake in a very hot oven (450° F.) for a few minutes, or until meringue is delicately brown. Serve at once.

(259)   PEACH PIE—NORWEGIAN METHOD
ONE-CRUST PIE, PRE-BAKED PIE SHELL

For one 9-inch pie

- Peaches (canned, juice and fruit): 1 #2½ can
- Sugar (brown): ¾ cup
- Butter (melted): 1 Tbsp.
- Cornstarch: 1½ Tbsps.
- Salt: ¼ tsp.
- Water (cold): 2 Tbsps. or 1 oz.
- Walnut meats (finely chopped): 1½ Tbsps. or ⅜ oz.
- Maple flavoring: ½ tsp. or ¹/₁₂ oz.
- Pastry: 1 baked pie shell, chilled
- Heavy cream (whipped): 1 cup

For five 9-inch pies

- Peaches (canned, juice and fruit): 1 #10 can or 6 lbs. 8 oz.
- Sugar (brown): 3¾ cups or 1 lb. 4 oz.
- Butter (melted): 5 Tbsps. or 2½ oz.
- Cornstarch: 7½ Tbsps. or 2½ oz.
- Salt: 1¼ tsps. or ⁵/₂₄ oz.
- Water (cold): 10 Tbsps. or 5 oz.
- Walnut meats (finely chopped): 7½ Tbsps. or 1⅞ oz.
- Maple flavoring: 2½ tsps. or ⁵/₁₂ oz.
- Pastry: 5 baked pie shells, chilled
- Heavy cream (whipped): 5 cups or 2 lbs. 9⅞ oz.

Empty the canned peaches, juice and fruit, into saucepan; add sugar and butter; stir gently, so as not to break fruit slices, until sugar is dissolved. Heat to the boiling point and add cornstarch mixed to a smooth paste with salt and cold water. Cook, stirring very gently from the bottom of the saucepan, until mixture thickens. Remove from the heat, add walnut meats and maple flavoring. Cool. Turn mixture into a cold, pre-baked pastry shell and top with whipped cream, sweetened to taste and flavored with maple flavoring. Serve cold.

....

(260)   A FEW FACTS ABOUT PEARS

Raw pears combine well with other fruits in cups and salads. Like Cousin Susie, they are interesting in a mild way and may be trusted to get along well with their more tart relatives, and pears served with cheese make a good dessert. Pears have insufficient pectin for jellies, but make delicious preserves.

The perfect pear for eating is soft but not mushy. At the base of the stem it yields readily to a slight pressure of the fingers. And if it's a Bartlett, it's a deep straw yellow in color. Pears to avoid are those that are wilted or shriveled, because these lack flavor and are of generally poor quality. Another pear fault sometimes seen is "limb-rub"—which the fruit gets when it is developing on the tree. This usually is a rough, discolored area on the surface of the fruit. Underneath the flesh may be hard and woody. These parts should be removed when making pie. When preparing a large amount of pears for pies, put the pared fruit into a solution of 2 Tbsps. each of salt and vinegar to a gallon of water; this will prevent discoloration that otherwise would set in rapidly.

Pears having a distinct, but rather mild and bland, flavor will blend with foods that are distinctly flavored. They also make splendid carriers for flavors that are sharp and perhaps a bit acrid.

Clapp pear, which is somewhat like the Bartlett in appearance, is an excellent cooking pear. So is the Seckel pear, small, dumpy and reddish russet with a delicious spicy tang when cooked. In some localities the Kieffer, a golden-brown, red-cheeked Bartlett hybrid, is the popular cooking and baking pear. Anjou and Winter Nelis are other favorite cooking pears.

....

(261)   ## PEAR MINCEMEAT PIE
           ### ONE-CRUST CRISSCROSS PIE

For one 9-inch pie
- Mincemeat (packaged): 1 (9-oz.) package
- Pear juice and water: 1½ cups
- Sugar (granulated or brown): 3 Tbsps.
- Pastry: For 1 crisscross pie
- Pears (Bartlett or Kieffer): 6 halves

For five 9-inch pies
- Mincemeat (packaged): 5 (9-oz.) packages or 2 lbs. 13 oz.
- Pear juice and water: 7½ cups or 3¾ lbs.
- Sugar (granulated or brown): 1 scant cup or 7½ oz. or 5 oz.
- Pastry: For 5 crisscross pies
- Pears (Bartlett or Kieffer): 30 halves or 4 lbs. 1 oz.

NOTE: If using packaged commercial mincemeat, it is advisable to add both suet and apple to enrich the product. Both ingredients are instrumental in preventing mincemeat from drying out too rapidly during the baking process. The amount to be added depends on the dryness of the product, and you will note a great improvement in the texture of pies made either entirely of mincemeat or part of it with other fruit.

Break mincemeat into pieces. Add pear juice (adding enough water to complete the amount if necessary) and sugar. Place over direct heat and stir gently until all lumps are thoroughly broken up. Bring to a brisk boil; continue boiling for 1 minute. Allow to cool. Line 9-inch pie pan with pastry rolled ⅛-inch thick and arrange canned pear halves in bottom of pie (you may quarter the pears, if desired). Gently pour the prepared mincemeat over the fruit and arrange crisscross strips on top; or for effect, proceed as follows: Start the strips of pastry in the center and carry them to the outer edge, twisting them slightly for a curled effect. Moisten and fasten at the edges with four-leaf clovers, or any other designs cut from unbaked pastry with tiny cookie cutter or other fancy cutter. Bake in a very hot oven (450° F.) for 10 minutes, reduce temperature to 350° F. and continue baking for 30 minutes longer. Serve warm with or without brandy hard sauce.

....

(262)   # PEAR PIE—FRENCH METHOD
ONE-CRUST PIE, PRE-BAKED PIE SHELL

For one 9-inch pie
- Flour (pastry): ⅓ cup
- Sugar (granulated): ⅔ cup
- Salt: ⅛ tsp.
- Milk (scalded): 2 cups
- Butter: 2 tsps.
- Egg yolks (slightly beaten): 3
- Vanilla extract: ¾ tsp.
- Almond extract: 3 drops
- Pastry: 1 baked pie shell
- Bartlett pears (canned, drained): 6 to 8 or 1 (#2½) can
- Meringue or whipped cream topping

For five 9-inch pies
- Flour (pastry): 1⅔ cups or 6⅔ oz.
- Sugar (granulated): 3⅓ cups or 1 lb. 10⅔ oz.
- Salt: ⅝ tsp.
- Milk (scalded): 2½ qts. or 5 lbs.
- Butter: 3⅓ Tbsps. or 1⅔ oz.
- Egg yolks (slightly beaten): 15 or 15 oz.
- Vanilla extract: 3¾ tsps. or ⅝ oz.
- Almond extract: ¼ tsp.
- Pastry: 5 baked pie shells
- Bartlett pears (canned, drained): 1 (#10) can or 6 lbs. 10 oz.
- Meringue or whipped cream topping

Combine flour, sugar, and salt in double boiler; add scalded milk slowly, stirring well. Cook over hot water, stirring almost constantly, until mixture is thick and smooth (about 15 minutes). Add butter and beaten egg yolks, stirring briskly. Continue cooking until mixture is thick and smooth. Cool. Add combined flavorings, and turn into pre-baked pastry shell; arrange well-drained canned pear halves, rounded end toward rim of pastry, pressing lightly so that surface of pear is flush with filling. Fill hollows of pears with whole or chopped cherries, chopped preserved ginger, or any kind of jam, etc. Top with meringue, and bake 15 minutes in a 325° F. oven; or top with whipped cream, sweetened and flavored to taste; or simply fill space between pears and in center with whipped cream, sweetened and flavored to taste, using pastry bag with star tube. Serve very cold.

(263) PEAR CRUMB PIE—SOUTHERN METHOD
ONE-CRUST PIE

For one 9-inch pie
- Pears (Bartlett): 1 #2½ can
- Pastry: For 1 one-crust pie
- Sugar (granulated): ¼ cup
- Cornstarch: 1 Tbsp.
- Lemon gratings: 1 tsp.
- Pear juice: ¾ cup
- Sugar (brown, light): ¾ cup
- Flour (pastry): ½ cup
- Cinnamon (ground): ½ tsp.
- Ginger (ground): ½ tsp.
- Mace (ground): ¼ tsp.
- Nutmeg (ground): ¼ tsp.
- Butter (softened): ¼ cup

For five 9-inch pies
- Pears (Bartlett): 1 #10 can or 6 lbs. 12 oz.
- Pastry: For 5 one-crust pies
- Sugar (granulated): 1¼ cups or 10 oz.
- Cornstarch: 5 Tbsps. or 1⅔ oz.
- Lemon gratings: 1½ Tbsps. or ⅝ oz.
- Pear juice: 3¾ cups or 1 lb. 14 oz.
- Sugar (brown, light): 3¾ cups or 1 lb. 4 oz.
- Flour (pastry): 2½ cups or 10 oz.
- Cinnamon (ground): 2½ tsps. or 5/24 oz.
- Ginger (ground): 2½ tsps. or 5/24 oz.
- Mace (ground): 1¼ tsps. or ⅛ oz.
- Nutmeg (ground): 1¼ tsps. or ⅛ oz.
- Butter (softened): 1¼ cups or 10 oz.

Drain pears, reserving the juice. There should be ¾ cup; if not, add water to make the correct amount. Cut the pears in quarters and arrange neatly in unbaked pastry shell, which has been brushed with melted butter and chilled. Mix together granulated sugar, cornstarch, lemon gratings and juice, and spread over the pears. Now mix together the remaining ingredients thoroughly and stir well with a fork until mixture is of crumb consistency; sprinkle crumbs over the pears and bake 10 minutes in a very hot oven (450° F.); reduce temperature to 350° F. and continue baking 30 minutes longer, or until crumbs are nicely brown. Cool. Serve very cold with whipped cream.

....

(264)   PEAR PIE—HOME METHOD
TWO-CRUST PIE

For one 9-inch pie
- Unbaked pastry: For 1 one-crust pie
- Pears (fresh, peeled, sliced): 4 cups
- Sugar (granulated): ½ cup
- Cinnamon (ground): 1 tsp.
- Cloves (ground): ¼ tsp.
- Nutmeg (ground): ⅛ tsp.
- Salt: ¼ tsp.
- Cornstarch: 1½ tsp.
- Butter: 2 Tbsps.

For five 9-inch pies
- Unbaked pastry: For 5 one-crust pies
- Pears (fresh, peeled, sliced): 5 qts. or 10 to 12 lbs.
- Sugar (granulated): 2½ cups or 1 lb. 4 oz.
- Cinnamon (ground): 1⅔ Tbsps. or 5/12 oz.
- Cloves (ground): 1¼ tsps.
- Nutmeg (ground): ⅝ tsp.
- Salt: 1 tsp. or 5/24 oz.
- Cornstarch: 2½ Tbsps. or ⅚ oz.
- Butter: 10 Tbsps. or 5 oz.

Line 9-inch pie pan with pastry rolled ⅛-inch thick; spread softened butter over bottom and sides to prevent soaking of the crust. Fill generously with prepared pears. Mix sugar, spices, salt, and cornstarch, and sprinkle over the fruit; then dot with butter. Moisten the edges of the lower crust; cover with top crust, pressing the edges together with the tines of a fork; cut 3 or 4 slits in the top crust. Bake 10 minutes in a very hot oven (450° F.); reduce temperature to 350° F. and continue baking for 30–35 minutes, time depending on quality of fruit. Serve warm or cold with a slice of soft, yellow American cheese.

Variations: (1) Omit one cup of prepared pears, and add 1 cup of seedless raisins, which have been parboiled and thoroughly drained. (2) Substitute 1 cup of pitted, halved dates for 1 cup pears. (3) Substitute 1 cup, peeled, stoned, sliced fresh peaches for 1 cup pears. (4) Substitute 1 cup broken nut meats for 1 cup pears. (5) Substitute 1 cup, coarsely chopped, parboiled figs or dried apricots for 1 cup pears. (6) Line bottom of unbaked crust with cooked, sieved, stoned prunes, or apricots. (7) Line bottom of unbaked crust with orange marmalade.

....

(265)   # PECAN PIE—TEXAS METHOD
ONE-CRUST PIE, PARTIALLY BAKED PIE SHELL

For one 9-inch pie
- Butter: ½ cup
- Sugar (granulated): ½ cup
- Corn syrup (light): ½ cup
- Maple syrup: ½ cup
- Whole eggs (well beaten): 3
- Salt: ¼ tsp.
- Pecans (broken): 1¼ cups
- Vanilla extract: ¾ tsp.
- Pastry: 1 partially baked pie shell

For five 9-inch pies
- Butter: 2½ cups or 1 lb. 4 oz.
- Sugar (granulated): 2½ cups or 1 lb. 4 oz.
- Corn syrup (light): 2½ cups or 1 lb. 14 oz.
- Maple syrup: 2½ cups or 1 lb. 14 oz.
- Whole eggs (well beaten): 15 or 1 lb. 14 oz.
- Salt: 1¼ tsps. or $5/24$ oz.
- Pecans (broken): 6¼ cups or 1 lb. $12^4/_7$ oz.
- Vanilla extract: 3¾ tsps. or $5/8$ oz.
- Pastry: 5 partially baked pie shells

Cream butter; add sugar and continue creaming while adding combined syrups. Blend thoroughly. Then beat in the well-beaten whole eggs. Lastly add salt, broken pecans and vanilla extract. Pour mixture into the partially baked pastry shell and bake in a moderate oven (350° F.) for 20 minutes, or until knife comes out clean when inserted in center. Serve cold with or without whipped cream.

(266) PECAN PIE—SOUTHERN METHOD
ONE-CRUST PIE

For one 9-inch pie
- Flour (pastry): ¼ cup or 1 oz.
- Sugar (granulated or brown): 2½ Tbsps.
- Corn syrup (light): 2 cups
- Salt: 1 tsp.
- Whole eggs (beaten): 4
- Butter (melted): 2 Tbsps.
- Vanilla extract: 1 tsp.
- Rich pastry: For 1 one-crust pie
- Pecan halves (skinned): 1 cup

For five 9-inch pies
- Flour (pastry): 1¼ cups or 5 oz.
- Sugar (granulated or brown): 12½ Tbsps. or 6¼ oz. or 4⅙ oz.
- Corn syrup (light): 2½ qts. or 7½ lbs.
- Salt: 1½ Tbsps. or ¾ oz.
- Whole eggs (beaten): 20 or 2½ lbs.
- Butter (melted): 10 Tbsps. or 5 oz.
- Vanilla extract: 1½ Tbsps. or ¾ oz.
- Rich pastry: For 5 one-crust pies
- Pecan halves (skinned): 5 cups or 1 lb. 6⁶/₇ oz.

Combine flour, sugar (brown or granulated; the brown will add a caramelized flavor), corn syrup, and salt. Blend thoroughly; gradually add beaten eggs alternately with melted butter, and lastly the vanilla extract. Fill unbaked 9-inch pie shell two-thirds full and then arrange pecan halves over the filling close to one another, pressing in gently. Place in a moderately slow oven (325° F.) and bake for 35 minutes. Serve cold.

Variations: (1) To mixture, before turning it into unbaked shell, add ¾ cup of shredded coconut. (2) Add ¾ cup of seedless, parboiled, well drained raisins. (3) Add ¾ cup of halved, pitted dates. (4) Add ¾ cup of pitted, coarsely chopped raw prunes. (5) Add ¾ cup of dried apricots, parboiled and coarsely chopped.

PERSIMMON MERINGUE PIE
ONE-CRUST PIE, PRE-BAKED PIE SHELL

(267)

For one 9-inch pie
- Persimmons (ripe): 8
- Water (cold): 1 cup
- Salt: ⅛ tsp.
- Sugar (granulated): ¾ cup
- Flour (pastry): 1 tsp.
- Egg yolks (slightly beaten): 2
- Milk: ½ cup
- Butter: 1 Tbsp.
- Cinnamon (ground): ⅛ tsp.
- Mace (ground): ⅛ tsp.
- Raisins (seedless, washed, drained): ½ cup or 2⅔ oz.
- Pastry: 1 baked pie shell
- Ginger Meringue Topping, No. 451

For five 9-inch pies
- Persimmons (ripe): 40 or 6¼ lbs.
- Water (cold): 1¼ qts. or 2½ lbs.
- Salt: ⅝ tsp.
- Sugar (granulated): 3¾ cups or 1 lb. 14 oz.
- Flour (pastry): 1⅔ Tbsps. or 5/12 oz.
- Egg yolks (slightly beaten): 10 or 10 oz.
- Milk: 2½ cups or 1 lb. 4 oz.
- Butter: 5 Tbsps. or 2½ oz.
- Cinnamon (ground): ⅝ tsp.
- Mace (ground): ⅝ tsp.
- Raisins (seedless, washed, drained): 2½ cups or 13⅓ oz.
- Pastry: 5 baked pie shells
- Ginger Meringue Topping, No. 451

Remove seeds from each persimmon; put the fruit in a saucepan with water and salt and cook until soft, or about 20 minutes. Sieve the fruit into double boiler; add sugar, mixed with pastry flour; blend well. Stir in the slightly beaten egg yolks mixed with milk, butter, spices, and raisins. Blend well. Cook over hot water until thickened, about 15 minutes, stirring constantly. Pour mixture into pre-baked 9-inch pastry shell; top with Ginger Meringue Topping, and bake 15 minutes in a moderately slow oven (325° F.), or until delicately brown. Serve cold.

(268) PERSIMMON PIE—CALIFORNIA METHOD
ONE-CRUST PIE

For one 9-inch pie
- Egg yolks (well beaten): 2
- Milk (rich): 3 Tbsps.
- Sugar (granulated): ¾ cup
- Flour (pastry): ½ cup
- Baking soda: 1 tsp.
- Salt: ½ tsp.
- Persimmons (ripe, sieved): 1 cup
- Lemon rind (grated): ½ tsp.
- Corn flakes (rolled fine, sieved): 1 cup
- Pastry: For 1 one-crust pie

For five 9-inch pies
- Egg yolks (well beaten): 10 or 10 oz.
- Milk (rich): ⅞ cup or 7½ oz.
- Sugar (granulated): 3¾ cups or 1 lb. 14 oz.
- Flour (pastry): 2½ cups or 10 oz.
- Baking soda: 1⅔ Tbsps. or ⅝ oz.
- Salt: 2½ tsps. or 1/12 oz.
- Persimmons (ripe, sieved): 5 cups or 6¼ lbs.
- Lemon rind (grated): 2½ tsps. or ⅘ oz.
- Corn flakes (rolled fine, sieved): 5 cups or 1 lb. 4 oz.
- Pastry: For 5 one-crust pies

To the well beaten egg yolks add milk and blend well; then add combined sugar, flour and baking soda sifted once together, stirring until well blended. Stir in salt, persimmons and lemon rind alternately with the rolled and sieved corn flakes, mixing thoroughly. Turn mixture into unbaked 9-inch pastry shell, which has been brushed on bottom and sides with slightly beaten egg white and thoroughly chilled, and bake 10 minutes in a very hot oven (450° F.); reduce temperature to 350° F. and continue baking 35 minutes longer, or until center is firm. Serve lukewarm with a wedge of young American cheese. This pie may be topped with Boiled Meringue, made as indicated for recipe No. 451, Boiled Meringue Topping, arranging the small individual meringues so as to serve one with every serving.

(269)   A FEW FACTS ABOUT PINEAPPLE

Size has little to do with the flavor of pineapple, but shape is of some importance. The stocky square-shouldered variety is more economical to buy than its lean, elongated fellow. When fully ripe the fruit has a golden yellow exterior, is firm but not hard to the touch, and exudes a pungent "piny" odor. If too green, it will not ripen well, even after a few days in a sunny place. If too ripe, it will have a soft, slightly decayed spot at its base. The fruit is ripe enough when a slight pull will lift out a spike. The spike's end will be yellow or white and sweet and tender to the taste. If the fruit weighs about two pounds, the buyer can count on having four cups of grated pineapple or about two and a half cups of cubes. With this formula he can estimate pretty closely for his requirements.

A good method for paring this tropical fruit is as follows: with scissors trim off the tops of the spikes. Then holding the pineapple in the left hand by the remaining leaves, with a sharp knife begin paring at the other end, removing all the skin and digging out "eyes" with the point of the knife. Skin and eyes should never be eaten, because they make the mouth sore. The hard core is discarded in slicing and grating. In tropical countries, a favorite way of serving is to dig into the whole fruit, around each eye, cutting a cone-shaped wedge, which is left in the pineapple. This leaves the fruit solid, with easily removed sections which may be pulled out and dipped in powdered sugar.

....

(270)   PINEAPPLE BOSTON CREAM PIE
ONE-CRUST OR LAYER PIE
SPONGE BATTER

For one 9-inch pie
- Whole eggs: 2
- Sugar (granulated): ½ cup
- Salt: 1/8 tsp.
- Flour (cake): ½ cup plus 1 1/3 Tbsp.
- Baking powder: 1/16 tsp.
- Milk (warm): 2 Tbsps.

For five 9-inch pies
- Whole eggs: 10 or 1 lb. 4 oz.
- Sugar (granulated): 2½ cups or 1 lb. 4 oz.
- Salt: 5/8 tsp.
- Flour (cake): 2½ cups (generous) or 11 2/3 oz.
- Baking powder: 5/16 tsp.
- Milk (warm): 5/8 cup or 5 oz.

Using rotary egg beater or electric machine, beat whole eggs, sugar, and salt until light, or about 15 minutes. Mix together and sift twice cake flour and baking powder and add to beaten egg-sugar-salt mixture, folding in gently and easily. Then add warm (not boiling) milk and mix thoroughly, but easily. Turn batter into greased and floured 9-inch layer cake pan and bake 12 to 14 minutes in a hot oven (400° F.). Remove from oven, turn cake upside down on cheesecloth slightly sprinkled with granulated sugar, and let cool. When cold, split layer in two, using a good sharp knife.

Filling

- Pineapple (crushed): ½ (#2 can)
- Sugar (granulated): ½ cup
- Salt: ⅛ tsp.
- Lemon rind (grated): ⅔ tsp.
- Cornstarch: 2 Tbsps.
- Pineapple juice (canned): 2⅔ Tbsps.
- Egg whites (stiffly beaten): ⅓ cup
- Sugar (granulated): ¼ cup
- Heavy cream (whipped)

Filling

- Pineapple (crushed): 2 lbs. 11⅓ oz.
- Sugar (granulated): 2½ cups or 1 lb. ⅔ oz.
- Salt: ⅝ tsp.
- Lemon rind (grated): 3⅓ tsps. or ⁵⁄₁₂ oz.
- Cornstarch: ⅝ cup or 10 Tbsps. or 3⅓ oz.
- Pineapple juice (canned): ⅞ cup or 13⅓ Tbsps. or 6⅔ oz.
- Egg whites (stiffly beaten): 1⅔ cups 13⅓ egg whites or 13⅓ oz.
- Sugar (granulated): 1¼ cups or 6⅔ oz.
- Heavy cream (whipped)

In a saucepan place pineapple, sugar, salt, and lemon rind; blend well and place over direct heat. Bring to a boil, stirring occasionally. Dissolve cornstarch in canned pineapple juice and gradually add to pineapple-sugar-salt mixture, stirring constantly until thick and clear. Remove from the heat and add stiffly beaten egg whites, sweetened with remaining sugar; then slowly fold into the hot crushed pineapple mixture, using a wire whisk. The filling is then ready to place on sponge layer cakes. Spread it evenly, while still hot, between the two layers. Adjust the top layer on top of the filling and allow to cool. When cold, pipe a neat "collar" of whipped cream around the outer edge of the top layer of the sponge cake, using a pastry bag with a star tube. This border should be quite heavy. Place in refrigerator while preparing the third and last operation as follows:

Glazed Pineapple Topping
- Pineapple tidbits: 1/3 cup
- Sugar (granulated): 1/2 cup
- Salt: 1/8 tsp.
- Lemon rind (grated): 2/3 tsp.
- Tapioca flour: 1 1/3 Tbsps.
- Cornstarch: 1 1/2 tsps.
- Pineapple juice (canned): 2 2/3 Tbsps.)

Glazed Pineapple Topping
- Pineapple tidbits: 1 2/3 cups or 1 lb. 4 oz.
- Sugar (granulated): 2 1/2 (scant) cups or 1 lb. 4 oz.
- Salt: 5/8 tsp.
- Lemon rind (grated): 3 1/3 tsps. or 5/12 oz.
- Tapioca flour: 6 2/3 Tbsps. or 1 2/3 oz.
- Cornstarch: 2 1/2 Tbsps. or 5/6 oz.
- Pineapple juice (canned): 5/6 cup or 13 1/3 Tbsps. or 6 2/3 oz.

Combine pineapple tidbits with sugar, salt, and lemon rind. Blend well, but gently. Bring this to a boil, stirring occasionally; then thicken by gradually adding combined tapioca flour and cornstarch dissolved in canned pineapple juice, stirring constantly, until mixture is thick and clear. Cool. Pour in center of top crust, filling the space left by the whipped cream. Be sure to cover the exposed part of the cake. Serve thoroughly chilled.

(271)

PINEAPPLE CHEESE PIE— HOME METHOD
ONE-CRUST PIE

For one 9-inch pie

- Graham cracker crumbs (sieved): Approximately 13 crackers
- Butter (softened): ¼ cup
- Salt: ⅛ tsp.
- Sugar (granulated): 3 Tbsps.
- Cottage cheese (drained, sieved): 1¼ cups
- Salt: ¼ tsp.
- Sugar (granulated): ½ cup
- Whole eggs (well beaten): 2
- Pineapple (canned, crushed, drained): ¾ cup
- Evaporated milk: ½ cup
- Water (cold): ¼ cup
- Vanilla extract: 1 tsp.

For five 9-inch pies

- Graham cracker crumbs (sieved): 5 cups or approximately 65 crackers or 1 lb. 1½ oz.
- Butter (softened): 1¼ cups or 10 oz.
- Salt: ⅝ tsp.
- Sugar (granulated): 1 scant cup or 7½ oz.
- Cottage cheese (drained, sieved): 6¼ cups or 2 lbs. 11¾ oz.
- Salt: 1¼ tsps. or 5/24 oz.
- Sugar (granulated): 2½ cups or 1 lb. 4 oz.
- Whole eggs (well beaten): 10 or 1 lb. 4 oz.
- Pineapple, (canned, crushed, drained): 3¾ cups or 2 lbs. 13 oz.
- Evaporated milk: 2½ cups or 1½ lbs.
- Water (cold): 1¼ cups or 10 oz.
- Vanilla extract: 1½ Tbsps. or ¾ oz.

Reserve 3 tablespoons graham cracker crumbs, blending remainder with softened butter, ⅛ teaspoon salt and the 3 tablespoons granulated sugar. Press mixture firmly against bottom and sides of generously buttered 9-inch pie pan. Thoroughly mix cottage cheese and remaining ingredients. Turn filling into crumb-lined pie pan; sprinkle reserved cracker crumbs over top of filling and bake 10 minutes in a very hot oven (450° F.); reduce temperature to 350° and continue baking 15 minutes longer, or until top is firm and custard-like. Cool. When cold, pipe a "collar" of whipped cream around outer edge of pie and decorate with sections of pineapple. Serve very cold.

(272)
PINEAPPLE CREAM PIE— HOME METHOD
ONE-CRUST PIE, PRE-BAKED PIE SHELL

For one 9-inch pie
- Milk (fresh): 1⁵⁄₈ cups
- Sugar (granulated): ½ cup
- Salt: ¼ tsp.
- Cornstarch: ¼ cup
- Egg yolks (slightly beaten): 3
- Milk (fresh): ³⁄₈ cup
- Vanilla extract: ½ tsp.
- Butter: 1 Tbsp.
- Pastry: 1 baked pie shell
- Pineapple (canned, crushed): 1¼ cups
- Sugar (granulated): ½ cup
- Salt: ⅛ tsp.
- Cornstarch: 2½ tsps.
- Tapioca flour: 2½ tsps.
- Water: ¼ cup

For five 9-inch pies
- Milk (fresh): 2 qts. plus ⅛ cup or 4 lbs. 1 oz.
- Sugar (granulated): 2½ cups or 1 lb. 4 oz.
- Salt: 1¼ tsps. or ⁵⁄₂₄ oz.
- Cornstarch: 1¼ cups or 6⅔ oz.
- Egg yolks (slightly beaten): 15 or 15 oz.
- Milk (fresh): 1⅞ cups or 15 oz.
- Vanilla extract: 2½ tsps. or ⁵⁄₁₂ oz.
- Butter: 5 Tbsps. or 2½ oz.
- Pastry: 5 baked pie shells
- Pineapple (canned, crushed): 6¼ cups or 4 lbs. 11 oz.
- Sugar (granulated): 2½ cups or 1 lb. 4 oz.
- Salt: ⅝ tsp.
- Cornstarch: 4 Tbsps. plus ½ tsp. or 1⁷⁄₁₈ oz.
- Tapioca flour: 4 Tbsps. plus ½ tsp. or 1¹⁄₂₄ oz.
- Water: 1¼ cups or 10 oz.

Combine the 1⁵⁄₈ cups milk, the ½ cup sugar, and ¼ tsp. salt, and stir until sugar is dissolved. Bring to a boil. Combine cornstarch, egg yolks, and remaining milk, and mix to a paste. Gradually stir this paste into boiling milk mixture, stirring constantly. Allow this to continue boiling a few minutes, stirring frequently. Remove from the heat and stir in vanilla, alternately with butter. Cool, cover with waxed paper well pressed on the surface of the cream filling to prevent the air from coming into contact with the cream filling; this will prevent a film forming upon the surface. When thoroughly cold, remove the waxed paper and stir the filling; then fill pre-baked 9-inch pastry shell two-thirds full. Set aside, and prepare the pineapple topping as follows:

Mix pineapple, remaining sugar and salt in a saucepan. Stir until sugar is thoroughly dissolved, then bring to a boil. Thicken with a paste of cornstarch, tapioca flour, and water, adding the paste gradually and stirring constantly; cook until clear and thick. Remove from the heat, allow to cool to lukewarm, then cover the entire surface of the cream filling with mixture. Cool before piping a "collar" of whipped cream around the outer edge, then a crisscross garnishing of whipped cream across the pineapple topping; leave small squares of the pineapple topping exposed to view. Serve very cold.

....

(273)   PINEAPPLE COCONUT CUSTARD PIE
ONE-CRUST PIE, PRE-BAKED PIE SHELL

For one 9-inch pie
- Egg yolks: 2
- Milk (fresh): 1 cup
- Salt: ½ tsp.
- Flour (pastry): 3 Tbsps.
- Sugar (granulated): ½ cup
- Butter: 2 Tbsps.
- Coconut (shredded): ½ cup
- Pineapple juice (canned): 2 Tbsps.
- Lemon juice: 1 Tbsp.
- Pastry: 1 baked pie shell
- Pineapple (crushed, drained): 1¼ cups
- Powdered sugar: ½ cup
- Meringue Topping No. 26

For five 9-inch pies
- Egg yolks: 10 or 10 oz.
- Milk (fresh): 5 cups or 2½ lbs.
- Salt: 2½ tsps. or $5/12$ oz.
- Flour (pastry): 1 scant cup or 3¾ oz.
- Sugar (granulated): 2½ cups or 1 lb. 4 oz.
- Butter: ⅝ cup or 5 oz.
- Coconut (shredded): 2½ cups or ½ lb.
- Pineapple juice (canned): ⅝ cup or 5 oz.
- Lemon juice: 5 Tbsps. or 2½ oz.
- Pastry: 5 baked pie shells
- Pineapple (crushed, drained): 6¼ cups or 4 lbs. 11 oz.
- Powdered sugar: 2½ cups or $11^3/7$ oz.
- Meringue Topping No. 26

Beat egg yolks thoroughly. Add milk and beat again. Sift salt, flour, and granulated sugar together. Add to milk and egg mixture; mix and stir in butter and shredded coconut. Cook in top of double boiler until thick, stirring almost constantly. Remove from hot water and stir in pineapple juice and lemon juice. Turn mixture into 9-inch pre-baked pastry shell, cover with thoroughly drained pineapple and sprinkle with powdered sugar. Cover with a Plain Meringue, made as indicated for No. 26. Serve cold.

(274)
PINEAPPLE PIE—
OLD-FASHIONED METHOD
TWO-CRUST PIE

For one 9-inch pie
- Pineapple (crushed or tidbits): 3 cups or 1 #2½ can
- Sugar (granulated): ⅞ cup
- Corn syrup (light): ⅙ cup
- Salt: ¼ tsp.
- Cornstarch: 3 Tbsps.
- Water: ¼ cup
- Sugar (granulated): ½ cup
- Pastry: For 1 two-crust pie

For five 9-inch pies
- Pineapple (crushed or tidbits): 3¾ qts. or 1 #10 can or 6 lbs. 12 oz.
- Sugar (granulated): 4⅜ cups or 2 lbs. 3oz.
- Corn syrup (light): ⅚ cup or 10 oz.
- Salt: 1¼ tsps. or ⁵⁄₂₄ oz.
- Cornstarch: 1 scant cup or 5 oz.
- Water: 1¼ cups or 10 oz.
- Sugar (granulated): 2½ cups or 1 lb. 4 oz.
- Pastry: For 5 two-crust pies

Combine pineapple, first amount of granulated sugar, corn syrup, and salt; mix well. Bring to a boil, then thicken with paste of cornstarch, water and sugar, added gradually to the boiling mixture; stir constantly until thick and smooth. Boil again once or twice, remove from the heat, transfer into another container to cool thoroughly before turning into a 9-inch pie pan lined with pastry rolled ⅛-inch thick. Cover with top crust in the usual way; brush the top crust with melted butter, after making a few slits to allow the steam to escape. Bake 10 minutes in a very hot oven (450° F.); reduce temperature to 350° F. and continue baking for 25 minutes longer. Serve cold, plain, or à la mode.

(275)   PINEAPPLE MARSHMALLOW PIE DE LUXE
ONE-CRUST PIE, PRE-BAKED PIE SHELL

NOTE: This pie should be made 24 hours in advance to mellow and ripen, without adding the whipped cream-pineapple mixture, which should be folded in just before serving. Should a tart taste be desired, you may add one tablespoon of cider vinegar to the fruit juices before mixing.

For one 9-inch pie
- Pineapple juice (canned): 1½ cups
- Orange juice: ½ cup
- Flour (pastry): 5 Tbsps.
- Sugar (granulated): ⅔ cup
- Salt: ¼ tsp.
- Egg yolks (slightly beaten): 2
- Marshmallows (cut up): 30
- Heavy cream (whipped): 1 cup
- Salt: ⅛ tsp.
- Pineapple (canned, crushed, drained): 1½ cups
- Pastry: 1 baked pie shell
- Whipped cream
- Maraschino cherries (green or red)

For five 9-inch pies
- Pineapple juice (canned): 7½ cups or 3¾ lbs.
- Orange juice: 2½ cups or 1¼ lbs.
- Flour (pastry): 1½ cups or 6¼ oz.
- Sugar (granulated): 3⅓ cups or 1 lb. 10⅔ oz.
- Salt: 1¼ tsps. or ⁵⁄₂₄ oz.
- Egg yolks (slightly beaten): 10 or 10 oz.
- Marshmallows (cut up): 150 or 2½ lbs.
- Heavy cream (whipped): 5 cups or 2½ lbs.
- Salt: ⅝ tsp.
- Pineapple (canned, crushed, drained): 7½ cups or 5 lbs. 10 oz.
- Pastry: 5 baked pie shells
- Whipped cream
- Maraschino cherries (green or red)

Heat pineapple juice and orange juice, reserving ½ cup. Mix reserved juice, flour, sugar, and salt; pour into the hot mixed juice slowly, stirring constantly until smooth and free from lumps. Bring this to a boil and let cook a few minutes. Beat egg yolks and add a little of the hot fruit-flour mixture, stirring briskly; add to hot mixture, stirring vigorously. Remove from heat and cool to lukewarm; then stir in the cut up marshmallows. Set in refrigerator to ripen and mellow overnight. When ready to serve, fold in the whipped cream alternately with the pineapple. Pour into pre-baked 9-inch pastry shell and decorate with rosettes of plain whipped cream and green or red, well-drained maraschino cherries, cut in fancy shapes (rose, crescent, etc.).

(276)   PINEAPPLE PIE—FRENCH METHOD
ONE-CRUST PIE

For one 9-inch pie
- Butter: ½ cup
- Sugar (granulated): 1 cup
- Egg yolks (well beaten): 5
- Pineapple (canned, crushed): ½ #2 can or 1 cup
- Salt: ¼ tsp.
- Heavy cream (whipped): 1 cup
- Unbaked pastry: 1 Lemon Juice and Egg pie Shell, No. 56
- Egg whites (stiffly beaten): 5
- Powdered sugar: ¼ cup
- Almond extract: ¼ tsp.
- Marshmallows (halved): 2

For five 9-inch pies
- Butter: 2½ cups or 1 lb. 4 oz.
- Sugar (granulated): 5 cups or 2½ lbs.
- Egg yolks (well beaten): 25 or 1 lb. 9 oz.
- Pineapple (canned, crushed): ½ #10 can
- Salt: 1¼ tsps. or $5/24$ oz.
- Heavy cream (whipped): 5 cups or 2 lbs. $9\frac{7}{8}$ oz.
- Unbaked pastry: 5 Lemon Juice and Egg pie Shells, No. 56
- Egg whites (stiffly beaten): 25
- Powdered sugar: 1¼ cups
- Almond extract: 1¼ tsps. or $5/24$ oz.
- Marshmallows (halved): 10 or 3¼ oz.

Cream together butter and sugar; add well beaten egg yolks alternately with thoroughly drained (almost dry) crushed pineapple and salt. Blend well. Lastly, fold in the whipped cream, alternately with 3 stiffly beaten egg whites. Turn this mixture into 9-inch unbaked Lemon Juice and Egg Pie Crust, made as indicated for No. 56, and bake 10 minutes in a very hot oven (450° F.); reduce temperature to 350° F. and continue baking for 25 minutes longer. With the two remaining egg whites, make a meringue in the usual way (No. 26) sweetened with powdered sugar and flavored with almond extract; pipe a narrow "collar," using a star tube, around outer edge of pie; place marshmallow halves, tinted yellow, in center; return to 300° F. oven and bake 12 long minutes. Serve cold.

(277)

PINEAPPLE RHUBARB PIE—
HOME METHOD
TWO-CRUST PIE

For one 9-inch pie
- Rhubarb (fresh, diced): 3 cups
- Pineapple (canned, crushed): 1 cup
- Sugar (granulated): 1 cup
- Lemon rind (grated): 1 tsp.
- Orange rind (grated): 1 tsp.
- Tapioca (quick-cooking): 2 Tbsps.
- Salt: ¼ tsp.
- Pastry: For 1 one-crust pie
- Lemon juice: 2 Tbsps.
- Butter: 1 Tbsp.

For five 9-inch pies
- Rhubarb (fresh, diced): 3¾ qts. or 3¾ lbs.
- Pineapple (canned, crushed): 5 cups or 3¾ lbs.
- Sugar (granulated): 5 cups or 2½ lbs.
- Lemon rind (grated): $1^2/_3$ Tbsps. or $^5/_8$ oz.
- Orange rind (grated): $1^2/_3$ Tbsps. or $^5/_8$ oz.
- Tapioca (quick-cooking): $^5/_8$ cup or 2½ oz.
- Salt: 1¼ tsps. or $^5/_{24}$ oz.
- Pastry: For 5 one-crust pies
- Lemon juice: $^5/_8$ cup or 5 oz.
- Butter: 5 Tbsps. or 2½ oz.

To the diced rhubarb add crushed pineapple, sugar, grated lemon and orange rinds, tapioca, and salt. Blend well. Place in 9-inch pie pan lined with pastry rolled ⅛-inch thick; then sprinkle lemon juice over. Cover with top crust in the usual way and bake 10 minutes in a very hot oven (450° F.); reduce temperature to 350° F. and continue baking 30 minutes longer. Serve cold.

PINEAPPLE SOUFFLÉ PIE
ONE-CRUST PIE, PRE-BAKED PIE SHELL

For one 9-inch pie
- Pineapple (canned, crushed): 1 #2½ can or 2½ cups
- Sugar (granulated): 1 cup
- Egg whites (stiffly beaten): 3
- Sugar (granulated): 1 cup
- Salt: ¼ tsp
- Almond extract: ⅛ tsp.
- Pastry: 1 baked pie shell

For five 9-inch pies
- Pineapple (canned, crushed): 1 #10 can
- Sugar (granulated): 5 cups or 2½ lbs.
- Egg whites (stiffly beaten): 15 or 15 oz.
- Sugar (granulated): 5 cups or 2½ lbs.
- Salt: 1¼ tsps. or $5/24$ oz.
- Almond extract: ⅝ tsp.
- Pastry: 5 baked pie shells

Cook drained pineapple, juice and fruit, and the first cup of sugar for 5 minutes, over low heat, stirring frequently. Cool. Drain off excess juice. Beat egg whites (an electric mixer increases the volume of the soufflé) until they stand in peaks; add remaining sugar, salt, and almond extract, and beat until glossy (sugar should be added gradually). Then very slowly add the drained pineapple and beat for 5 minutes with rotary egg beater or electric mixer. Turn filling into pre-baked 9-inch pastry shell or 8 individual ones, as evenly as possible; swirl the top and bake exactly 4 minutes in a hot oven (400° F.). Cool at room temperature. Top with sweetened, flavored whipped cream forced through a pastry bag with a fancy tube. You may place upon each portion a tablespoon of well drained, canned crushed pineapple, or a teaspoon of chopped candied pineapple, or of preserved pineapple. For a variation, you may add to the mixture, before turning it into the pre-baked pastry shell, ½ cup of chopped nut meats (any kind) or ½ cup of long thread toasted and cooled coconut.

(279)

PINEAPPLE SPONGE PIE—
HOME METHOD
ONE-CRUST PIE

For one 9-inch pie
Filling
- Pineapple (crushed and syrup): 1 (#2) can
- Sugar (granulated): ½ cup
- Salt: ½ tsp.
- Cornstarch: ¼ cup
- Water (cold): ¼ cup
- Pastry: For 1 one-crust pie

For five 9-inch pies
Filling
- Pineapple (crushed and syrup): 5 (#2) cans or 6 lbs. 4 oz.
- Sugar (granulated): 2½ cups or 1 lb. 4 oz.
- Salt: 2½ tsps. or $5/12$ oz.
- Cornstarch: 1¼ cups or $6^2/3$ oz.
- Water (cold): 1¼ cups or 10 oz.
- Pastry: For 5 one-crust pies

Combine pineapple and syrup with sugar and salt; bring to boiling point over direct heat; gradually add the cornstarch dissolved in cold water, stirring constantly until thick and clear; remove from the heat and pour the entire contents into a shallow container, so as to cool rapidly. When cold, pour into 9-inch unbaked pastry shell and let stand while preparing the topping as follows:

Topping
- Butter: 1 Tbsp.
- Sugar (granulated): 1 cup
- Egg yolks (slightly beaten): 2
- Milk (cold): 2 tsps.
- Salt: ½ tsp.
- Lemon rind (grated): 1 tsp.
- Lemon juice: 1 tsp.
- Flour (sifted): 3 Tbsps.
- Milk (cold): ½ cup
- Egg whites (stiffly beaten): 2

Topping
- Butter : 5 Tbsps. or 2½ oz.
- Sugar (granulated): 4¾ cups or 2 lbs. 3 oz.
- Egg yolks (slightly beaten): 10 or 10 oz.
- Milk (cold): $3^1/3$ Tbsps. or $1^2/3$ oz.
- Salt: 2½ tsps. or $5/12$ oz.
- Lemon rind (grated): $1^2/3$ Tbsps. or $5/8$ oz.
- Lemon juice: $1^2/3$ tsps. or $5/6$ oz.
- Flour (sifted): 1 scant cup or 3¾ oz.
- Milk (cold): 2½ cups or 1 lb. 4 oz.
- Egg whites (stiffly beaten): 10 or 10 oz.

Cream butter and sugar until lemon-colored. Gradually blend in the slightly beaten egg yolks, alternately with combined 2 teaspoons milk, salt, lemon rind and juice and blend well. Gradually add the flour and remaining milk, which have been mixed to a smooth paste, stirring and beating at the same time with a wire whisk until mixture is thoroughly blended and smooth. Lastly fold in as gently as possible the stiffly beaten egg whites. Spread this uncooked topping evenly over the pineapple filling in the shell and bake 10 minutes in a very hot oven (450° F.); reduce temperature to 350° F., and continue baking for 30–35 minutes longer, or until the sponge topping has reached custard consistency. Serve cold.

....

(280)   A FEW FACTS ABOUT PLUMS

All the colors of the spectrum are to be found among the many varieties of plums which we find in market during the season. Some are well-known, but the majority are local varieties. They vary in shape from small round to oval, or peach-shaped, and the color may be green, red, purple, blue, or nearly black. Some of the better known varieties are Greengage, a small greenish-yellow, sweet fruit, used fresh, preserved or in delicious tarts and fancy pastries; Damson, which is small, oval, blue-black, too tart to be eaten raw but excellent for pies and preserves; Italian prune, a purplish-black, oval fruit, used for drying; Lombard, a medium to large juicy fruit, with reddish-purple skin and sweet flavor, may be used fresh or dried.

If skins are unbroken, plums may be kept in storage for a month or longer. However, it is better to use them as soon as they are ripe, because the flavor deteriorates rapidly after that time. They should be kept in a cool, dry place.

(281)

PLUM MINCEMEAT PIE—
WASHINGTON METHOD
TWO-CRUST PIE

For one 9-inch pie
- Mincemeat (packaged or homemade): 9 oz.
- Plum juice: 1½ cups
- Plums (canned, juice and fruit): 1 #2 can
- Pastry: For 1 two-crust pie
- Salt: ⅛ tsp.

For five 9-inch pies
- Mincemeat (packaged or homemade): 2 lbs. 13 oz.
- Plum juice: 7½ cups or 3¾ lbs.
- Plums (canned, juice and fruit): 1 #10 can
- Pastry: For 5 two-crust pies
- Salt: ⅝ tsp.

If using homemade mincemeat, use as is. If using packaged mincemeat, proceed as follows: Break mincemeat into small pieces. Add plum juice and enough cold water to make the exact amount or weight; place over heat and stir until all lumps are thoroughly broken up. Bring to a brisk boil; continue boiling for one minute. Cool. Line 9-inch pie pan with pastry rolled ⅛-inch thick and spread mincemeat in bottom of shell. Cut canned plums in halves, remove pits and arrange evenly over mincemeat quite close together; sprinkle salt over plums (spices may be added if commercial mincemeat is not sufficiently spiced to taste); cover with top crust in the usual way, pressing edges firmly together. Trim off surplus pastry; bake 35 minutes in a hot oven (400° F.). Serve warm, with brandy hard sauce.

....

(282)

PLUM PIE I
ONE-CRUST CRISSCROSS PIE

For one 9-inch pie
- Plums (fresh, quartered, pitted): 1½ lbs.
- Water (cold): ⅔ cup
- Sugar (granulated): 1½ cups
- Salt: ½ tsp.
- Cornstarch: 2 Tbsps.
- Water (cold): 2½ Tbsps.
- Pastry: For 1 crisscross pie

For five 9-inch pies
- Plums (fresh, quartered, pitted): 7½ lbs.
- Water (cold): 3⅓ cups or 1 lb. 10⅔ oz.
- Sugar (granulated): 7½ cups or 3¾ lbs.
- Salt: 2½ tsps. or ⁵⁄₁₂ oz.
- Cornstarch: 10 Tbsps. or 3⅓ oz.
- Water (cold): 12½ Tbsps. or 6¼ oz.
- Pastry: For 5 crisscross pies

Prepare plums. Combine ⅔ cup water, sugar and salt and stir until sugar is thoroughly dissolved. Bring mixture to a boil, and allow to boil 3 or 4 minutes without stirring. Dissolve cornstarch with remaining cold water, then gradually add to rapidly boiling syrup, stirring constantly; boil mixture until clear and thick. Now add prepared plums carefully, so as not to stop the boiling process, and continue cooking until clear again, or about 3 minutes. Line a 9-inch pie pan with pastry rolled ⅛-inch thick; brush bottom and sides with unbeaten egg white and let dry. When fruit mixture is cold, turn into pie shell; cover with crisscross pastry in the usual way; brush strips of pastry with butter and bake 10 minutes in a very hot oven (450° F.); reduce temperature to 350° F. and continue baking for 25–30 minutes longer, or until crisscross pastry is delicately brown. Serve cold.

NOTE: This recipe also applies to canned plums, using the fruit juice instead of cold water. Add the thoroughly drained fruit immediately after the syrup is removed from the fire. Allow mixture to cool thoroughly before turning into unbaked pastry shell.

....

(283)   # PLUM PIE II—SOUTHERN METHOD
ONE-CRUST PIE

For one 9-inch pie
- Pastry: For 1 one-crust pie
- Butter: ¾ cup
- Sugar (brown): 1 cup
- Egg yolks (well beaten): 4
- Vanilla extract: 1 tsp.
- Egg whites (stiffly beaten): 4
- Salt: ½ tsp.
- Damson plums (pitted, halved): 1 cup

For five 9-inch pies
- Pastry: For 5 one-crust pies
- Butter: 3¾ cups or 1 lb. 14 oz.
- Sugar (brown): 5 cups or 1 lb. 10⅔ oz.
- Egg yolks (well beaten): 20 or 1 lb. 4 oz.
- Vanilla extract: 1⅔ Tbsps. or ⅚ oz.
- Egg whites (stiffly beaten): 20 or 1 lb. 4 oz.
- Salt: 2½ tsps. or ⁵⁄₁₂ oz.
- Damson plums (pitted, halved): 5 cups

Cream butter and brown sugar until mustard colored; gradually add well-beaten egg yolks, stirring in the vanilla extract with the last addition. Blend thoroughly, then add stiffly beaten egg whites with the salt. Lastly fold in the well-drained, halved, pitted plums (canned plums may be used, if desired). Turn mixture into 9-inch unbaked pastry shell and bake 10 minutes in a very hot oven (450° F.); reduce temperature to 350° F. and continue baking for 30 minutes longer. Serve cold with a "collar" of whipped cream around the edges.

....

(284)   ## PLUM CUSTARD MERINGUE PIE I
ONE-CRUST PIE, PRE-BAKED PIE SHELL

For one 9-inch pie
- Milk (scalded): 2 cups
- Flour (pastry): 3 Tbsps.
- Sugar (fine granulated): ¾ cup
- Salt: ¼ tsp.
- Egg yolks (well beaten): 3
- Greengage plums (pitted): 1½ cups
- Meringue of 3 egg whites for topping (No. 26)
- Pastry: 1 baked rich pie shell (No. 70)

For five 9-inch pies
- Milk (scalded): 2½ qts. or 5 lbs.
- Flour (pastry): 1 scant cup or 3¾ oz.
- Sugar (fine granulated): 3¾ cups or 1⅞ lbs.
- Salt: 1¼ tsps. or ⁵/₂₄ oz.
- Egg yolks (well beaten): 15 or 15 oz.
- Greengage plums (pitted): 7½ cups or 3 lbs. 2 oz.
- Meringue of 15 egg whites for topping (No. 26)
- Pastry: 5 baked rich pie shells (No. 70)

Pour scalded milk over the pastry flour sifted with sugar and salt, stirring constantly. Strain into top of double boiler and cook until thick, stirring constantly. Add well-beaten egg yolks, blended with a little of the hot milk-flour mixture, and cook until smooth and thick, stirring constantly from the bottom of the pan. Cool custard. Line bottom of pre-baked pastry shell with raw, pitted, drained greengage plums. Pour over the custard mixture and cover with the meringue, forced through a pastry bag with a small fancy tube, and form circles starting from the edges of the pie and finishing in the center. Place in moderately slow oven (325° F.) and bake until delicately tinted. Cool and serve with whipped cream, if desired.

(285) # PLUM CUSTARD MERINGUE PIE II
ONE-CRUST PIE, PRE-BAKED PIE SHELL

For one 9-inch pie

Crust
- Nut meats (any kind, ground): 1 cup
- Shredded coconut: 1 cup
- Salt: ⅛ tsp.
- Butter (melted): ¼ cup

Filling
- Heavy cream (scalded): 2 cups
- Sugar (brown): ¾ cup
- Salt: ¼ tsp.
- Nutmeg: ¼ tsp.
- Egg yolks (slightly beaten): 4
- Egg whites (stiffly beaten): 4
- Vanilla extract: ¼ tsp.
- Greengage plums (pitted): 2 cups

For five 9-inch pies

Crust
- Nut meats (any kind, ground): 5 cups or 1¼ lbs.
- Shredded coconut: 5 cups or 1 lb.
- Salt: ⅝ tsp.
- Butter (melted): 1¼ cups or 10 oz.

Filling
- Heavy cream (scalded): 2½ qts. or 5 lbs.
- Sugar (brown): 3¾ cups or 1 lb. 4 oz.
- Salt: 1¼ tsps. or ⁵⁄₂₄ oz.
- Nutmeg: 1¼ tsps.
- Egg yolks (slightly beaten): 20 or 1¼ lbs.
- Egg whites (stiffly beaten): 20 or 1¼ lbs.
- Vanilla extract: 1¼ tsps. or ⁵⁄₂₄ oz.
- Greengage plums (pitted): 2½ qts. or about 5 lbs.

Thoroughly mix nut meats, coconut, first amount of salt and melted butter and line bottom and sides of buttered pie pan with mixture, pressing down firmly; place in refrigerator to chill.

To the scalded cream, add brown sugar, salt and nutmeg and stir until sugar is well and thoroughly dissolved. Gradually pour the hot cream mixture over egg yolks, stirring briskly. Fold in the stiffly beaten egg whites flavored with vanilla extract. Cook mixture over hot water until thick, stirring constantly. Allow to cool. Arrange the washed, pitted and carefully drained greengage plums in bottom of prepared, chilled pastry shell and gently pour over the sponge custard. Top each pie with a meringue made of 2 egg whites, sugar and flavoring extract to taste, and bake 15 minutes in a very moderate oven (325° F.), or until meringue is delicately brown.

POTATO CUSTARD PIE—
SOUTHERN METHOD
ONE-CRUST PIE

(286)

For one 9-inch pie
- Potato (medium-sized, white): 1
- Butter: 2 Tbsps.
- Sugar (granulated): ¾ cup
- Egg yolks (slightly beaten): 2
- Milk (scalded, cooled): ½ cup
- Lemon rind (grated): 1 tsp.
- Lemon juice: 1 Tbsp.
- Salt: ¼ tsp.
- Egg whites (stiffly beaten): 2
- Almond extract (optional): a few drops
- Pastry: For 1 one-crust pie

For five 9-inch pies
- Potato (medium-sized, white): 5
- Butter: ⅝ cup or 5 oz.
- Sugar (granulated): 3¾ cups or 1 lb. 14 oz.
- Egg yolks (slightly beaten): 10 or 10 oz.
- Milk (scalded, cooled): 2½ cups or 1¼ lbs.
- Lemon rind (grated): 1⅔ Tbsps. or ⅝ oz.
- Lemon juice: 5 Tbsps. or 2½ oz.
- Salt: 1¼ tsps. or ⁵⁄₂₄ oz.
- Egg whites (stiffly beaten): 10 or 10 oz.
- Almond extract (optional): ½ tsp.
- Pastry: For 5 one-crust pies

Boil the potato, peel, rice, then mash well, adding alternately the butter and sugar. Let this cool; gradually add beaten egg yolks alternately with combined milk, lemon rind and juice, and salt, beating briskly. Mix together well, then fold in the stiffly beaten egg whites, flavored with a few drops of almond extract. Turn filling into 9-inch pie pan lined with pastry rolled ⅛-inch thick and bake 10 minutes in a hot oven (450° F.); reduce temperature to 350° F. and continue baking 25–30 minutes longer. Serve cold with a side dish of your favorite preserve.

(287) POT CHEESE (COTTAGE CHEESE) PIE I
ONE-CRUST PIE

For one 9-inch pie
- Cottage cheese (sieved): 1½ cups
- Butter (melted): ¼ cup
- Sugar (granulated): ½ cup
- Salt: ¼ tsp.
- Flour (pastry): 1 Tbsp.
- Grated lemon rind: 2 Tbsps.
- Egg yolks (unbeaten): 2
- Raisins (seedless, parboiled): ½ cup
- Nut meats (any kind, chopped): ½ cup
- Pastry: For 1 one-crust pie

For five 9-inch pies
- Cottage cheese (sieved): 7½ cups or 3¾ lbs.
- Butter (melted): 1¼ cups or 10 oz.
- Sugar (granulated): 2½ cups or 1¼ lbs.
- Salt: 1¼ tsps. or $5/24$ oz.
- Flour (pastry): 5 Tbsps. or 1¼ oz.
- Grated lemon rind: 10 Tbsps. or ⅝ cup or 3¾ oz.
- Egg yolks (unbeaten): 10 or 10 oz.
- Raisins (seedless, parboiled): 2½ cups or 13⅓ oz.
- Nut meats (any kind, chopped): 2½ cups or 10 oz.
- Pastry: For 5 one-crust pies

Combine ingredients in the order given, mix thoroughly and pour mixture into an unbaked 9-inch pie shell. Bake in a hot oven (450° F.) for 10 minutes; reduce temperature to 350° F. and continue baking about 30 minutes longer, or until filling is firm. Serve very cold, each portion topped with plain whipped cream. You may top with a meringue, if desired.

....

(288) POT CHEESE (COTTAGE CHEESE) PIE II
ONE-CRUST PIE

Proceed as indicated for Pot Cheese Pie I, No. 287, substituting ½ cup of parboiled dried apricots for raisins. You may top with a meringue, if desired.

(289) POT CHEESE (COTTAGE CHEESE) PIE III
ONE-CRUST PIE

Proceed as indicated for Pot Cheese Pie I, No. 287, substituting drained, canned shredded pineapple for raisins. You may top with a meringue, if desired. A ginger meringue combines perfectly with pot cheese and pineapple.

(290) POT CHEESE (COTTAGE CHEESE) PIE IV
ONE-CRUST PIE

Proceed as indicated for Pot Cheese Pie I, No. 287, spreading a layer of canned applesauce in bottom of unbaked 9-inch pie shell before turning in the pot cheese mixture. Top with a layer of sweetened, flavored whipped cream.

NOTE: Fresh fruits, such as cherries and currants, may be substituted for raisins. Down South, a very popular method of serving pot cheese pie (cottage cheese) is to serve a side dish of fresh raspberries, strawberries, etc. with the cheese. These berries should be thoroughly chilled.

(291) POT CHEESE (COTTAGE CHEESE) PIE V
ONE-CRUST PIE

For one 9-inch pie
- Pot cheese (drained, sieved): 1 cup
- Heavy cream (unwhipped): 1 cup
- Egg yolks (well beaten): 5
- Sugar (granulated): ½ cup
- Butter (melted): ¼ cup
- Salt: ¼ tsp.
- Nutmeg (ground): ¼ tsp.
- Egg whites (stiffly beaten): 5
- Vanilla extract: ¼ tsp.
- Pastry: For 1 one-crust pie

For five 9-inch pies
- Pot cheese (drained, sieved): 5 cups or 3 lbs. 2 oz.
- Heavy cream (unwhipped): 5 cups or 2 lbs. 9⅞ oz.
- Egg yolks (well beaten): 25 or 1 lb. 9 oz.
- Sugar (granulated): 2½ cups or 1 lb. 4 oz.
- Butter (melted): 1¼ cups or 10 oz.
- Salt: 1¼ tsps. or ⁵/₂₄ oz.
- Nutmeg (ground): 1¼ oz.
- Egg whites (stiffly beaten): 25 or 1 lb. 9 oz.
- Vanilla extract: 1¼ tsps.
- Pastry: For 5 one-crust pies

Force pot cheese through a fine sieve; stir in heavy cream, alternately with well-beaten egg yolks and sugar; while stirring, add the melted butter, salt, and nutmeg. Lastly fold in the stiffly beaten egg whites, which may or may not be flavored with a little vanilla extract. Turn mixture into a 9-inch pie pan lined with pastry rolled ⅛-inch thick and bake 35–40 minutes in a hot oven (425° F.). Serve cold.

....

(292)   A FEW FACTS ABOUT PRUNES

One of the first things which the average cook must do is to cast aside his ideas that dried fruits, and dried prunes in particular, must be soaked overnight or for several hours. Nothing is further from the truth. The newer pack, as explained in No. 24, Dried Fruit Preparation, are so tenderized in the process of manufacture that any long soaking is out, and this holds for apricots, peaches, and pears as well.

All prunes are plums, but not all plums are prunes. A prune is a plum which can be dried without the removal of the pit and without fermenting; the result is a fleshy pulp with a high degree of sweetness. Tenderized prunes are the result of a new and finer product. The fruit is plump, extra juicy, tender and good in every way. No soaking but quick cooking (no cooking at all, when eaten as is) are the rules.

The best temperature to store prunes is at 40°–50° F. If prunes are stored in a place where the temperature is too low, the texture of the fruit is changed and some of the flavor is lost. On the other hand, they should never be kept near steam pipes, because the fruit may lose both flavor and color.

....

(293)   PRUNE ANGEL WALNUT PIE— HOME METHOD
ONE-CRUST PIE, PRE-BAKED PIE SHELL

For one 9-inch pie
- Prunes (cooked): 2 cups
- Sugar (granulated): ¼ cup
- Walnut meats (chopped): ½ cup
- Egg whites (stiffly beaten): 2
- Cream of tartar: ⅛ tsp.
- Salt: ¼ tsp.
- Sugar: ¼ cup
- Pastry: 1 baked pie shell
- Mixed candied fruits (chopped): ¼ cup
- Salt: ⅛ tsp.
- Heavy cream (whipped): 1 cup

For five 9-inch pies
- Prunes (cooked): 10 cups or 2½ lbs.
- Sugar (granulated): 1¼ cups or 10 oz.
- Walnut meats (chopped): 2½ cups or 10 oz.
- Egg whites (stiffly beaten): 10 or 10 oz.
- Cream of tartar: ⅝ tsp.
- Salt: 1¼ tsps. or ⁵⁄₂₄ oz.
- Sugar: 1¼ cups or 10 oz.
- Pastry: 5 baked pie shells
- Mixed candied fruits (chopped): 1¼ cups or 10 oz.
- Salt: ⅝ tsp.
- Heavy cream (whipped): 5 cups or 2½ lbs.

Remove pits from well-drained, cooked prunes; force pulp through a sieve, or cut into small pieces, and combine with sugar and walnut meats. Whip egg whites until foamy; add cream of tartar, salt and sugar and beat until stiff but not dry. Lightly fold in the prune mixture and pile filling into cold, pre-baked 9-in. pastry shell. Bake about 20 minutes (400° F.), or until filling is firm in center. Cool. When cold, top with Whipped Cream Candied Fruit Topping, made by adding chopped mixed candied fruits and salt to whipped cream, or top with a meringue, made in the usual way, (No. 26); then bake in a moderately slow oven (325° F.) for 15 minutes, or until meringue is brown. Serve cold.

....

(294)
PRUNE BUTTERSCOTCH ORANGE NUT PIE—HOME METHOD
ONE-CRUST PIE, PRE-BAKED PIE SHELL

For one 9-inch pie
- Prunes (cooked): 2 cups or ½ lb.
- Large oranges (peeled, diced): 2
- Sugar (brown): 1 cup or 5⅓ oz.
- Nut meats (any kind, coarsely chopped): ¼ cup
- Prune juice: 1 cup
- Cornstarch: 2 Tbsps.
- Salt: ¼ tsp.
- Pastry: 1 baked pie shell
- Heavy cream (whipped): 1 cup

For five 9-inch pies
- Prunes (cooked): 2½ qts. or 2½ lbs.
- Large oranges (peeled, diced): 10 or about 5 lbs.
- Sugar (brown): 5 cups or 1 lb. 10⅔ oz.
- Nut meats (any kind, coarsely chopped): 1¼ cups or 5 oz.
- Prune juice: 5 cups or 2½ lbs.
- Cornstarch: ⅝ cup or 3⅓ oz.
- Salt: 1¼ tsps. or 5/24 oz.
- Pastry: 5 baked pie shells
- Heavy cream (whipped): 5 cups or 2½ lbs.

Drain cold, cooked prunes, reserving juice (there should be one cup). Cut prunes into halves and discard pits. Mix in top of double boiler with diced oranges, brown sugar, and coarsely chopped nut meats. Blend the prune juice, cornstarch and salt and add to prune mixture, blending well. Cook mixture until thickened, stirring almost constantly from the bottom of pan. Remove from heat and cool. When cold, pour filling into pre-baked 9-inch pastry shell as evenly as possible. Cover with whipped cream (unsweetened and unflavored), using a pastry bag with a fancy tube, and garnish (optional) the edges of the pie with sections of orange, free from seeds and white filaments. Serve thoroughly chilled.

(295)

PRUNE CIDER PIE
ONE-CRUST PIE, PRE-BAKED PIE SHELL

For one 9-inch pie
- Prune juice: ½ cup
- Cider (sweet): 1½ cups
- Sugar (granulated): ½ cup
- Salt: ½ tsp.
- Nutmeg: ¼ tsp.
- Cinnamon: ¼ tsp.
- Lemon juice: 2 Tbsps.
- Butter: 1½ Tbsps.
- Cornstarch: 3 Tbsps.
- Water (cold): 3 Tbsps.
- Egg yolk (slightly beaten): 1
- Pastry: For 1 one-crust pie

For five 9-inch pies
- Prune juice: 2½ cups or 1 lb.
- Cider (sweet): 7½ cups or 3¾ lbs.
- Sugar (granulated): 2½ cups or 1 lb. 4 oz.
- Salt: 2½ tsps. or ⁵⁄₁₂ oz.
- Nutmeg: 1¼ tsps.
- Cinnamon: 1¼ tsps.
- Lemon juice: ⅝ cup or 5 oz.
- Butter: 7½ Tbsps. or 3¾ oz.
- Cornstarch: scant cup or 5 oz.
- Water (cold): 15 Tbsps. or scant cup
- Egg yolks (slightly beaten): 5 or 5 oz.
- Pastry: For 5 one-crust pies

Combine prune juice, cider, sugar, salt, spices and lemon juice, and bring to a boil; add butter and boil once more. Dissolve cornstarch in cold water and combine with slightly beaten egg yolk. Gradually add cornstarch mixture to the boiling mixture; stir constantly until mixture is thick and clear; let come to a brisk boil; remove from the heat and stir in quartered prunes. Cool slightly and pour filling into unbaked pastry shell; cover with lattice strips of pastry in the usual way, brush strips with milk and bake 10 minutes in a hot oven (425° F.); reduce temperature and continue baking 20 minutes longer. Serve cold with whipped cream.

(296) PRUNE JUICE APPLE MERINGUE PIE
ONE-CRUST PIE, PRE-BAKED PIE SHELL

For one 9-inch pie
- Prune juice (bottled): 2 cups
- Cinnamon (ground): ¼ tsp.
- Sugar (granulated): 1 cup
- Cornstarch: 2 Tbsps.
- Flour (pastry): ⅜ cup
- Egg yolks (well beaten): 3
- Salt: ¼ tsp.
- Lemon juice: 2 Tbsps.
- Egg white (stiffly beaten): 1
- Pastry: 1 baked pie shell
- Apple Meringue Topping, No. 451

For five 9-inch pies
- Prune juice (bottled): 2½ qts. or 5 lbs.
- Cinnamon (ground): 1¼ tsps.
- Sugar (granulated): 5 cups or 2½ lbs.
- Cornstarch: ⅝ cup or 3⅓ oz.
- Flour (pastry): 1⅞ cups or 7½ oz.
- Egg yolks (well beaten): 15 or 15 oz.
- Salt: 1¼ tsps. or 5/24 oz.
- Lemon juice: ⅝ cup or 5 oz.
- Egg whites (stiffly beaten): 5 or 5 oz.
- Pastry: 5 baked pie shells
- Apple Meringue Topping, No. 451

Heat prune juice and cinnamon in top of a double boiler over hot water. Combine sugar, cornstarch, and flour and add the hot prune juice, stirring constantly. Return mixture and cook 10 minutes, stirring constantly until mixture is thick and clear. Gradually pour hot mixture over well-beaten egg yolks, stirring rapidly and constantly. Place again over hot water and cook 5 minutes, stirring constantly. Remove from hot water and add salt and lemon juice. Cool. When cold, fold in the stiffly beaten egg white. Pour into 9-inch pre-baked pie shell and top with the meringue topping. Bake in a moderately slow oven (325° F.) for 15–20 minutes. Serve cold.

(297)   PRUNE MOLASSES CREAM PIE
ONE-CRUST CRISSCROSS PIE

For one 9-inch pie
- Prunes: ½ lb. or 1 cup
- Prune juice: ½ cup
- Sugar (granulated): ¼ cup
- Molasses: ¾ cup
- Egg yolks (slightly beaten): 4
- Butter (softened): ¼ cup
- Salt: ¼ tsp.
- Orange marmalade: ¼ cup
- Pastry: For 1 crisscross pie

For five 9-inch pies
- Prunes: 2½ lbs. or 5 cups
- Prune juice: 2½ cups or 1 lb. 4 oz.
- Sugar (granulated): 1¼ cups or 10 oz.
- Molasses: 3¾ cups or 2 lbs. 13 oz.
- Egg yolks (slightly beaten): 20 or 1 lb. 4 oz.
- Butter (softened): 1¼ cups or 10 oz.
- Salt: 1¼ tsps. or ⁵⁄₂₄ oz.
- Orange marmalade: 1¼ cups or 15 oz.
- Pastry: For 5 crisscross pies

Wash prunes and cook as indicated for No. 24, Dried Fruit Preparation. Cool. Combine juice from prunes, sugar, molasses, and egg yolks. Cut cooked, cooled prunes into bits, removing stones, and mix with butter, salt, and marmalade, then with egg yolk mixture. Turn into pastry-lined pie pan and top with narrow strips of pastry as for crisscross pie. Bake in hot oven (450° F.) 10 minutes; reduce temperature to 350° F. and continue baking 30 minutes longer. Serve cold.

(298)

PRUNE NUT CREAM PIE—
SOUTHERN METHOD
ONE-CRUST PIE, PRE-BAKED PIE SHELL

For one 9-inch pie
- Sugar (granulated): ½ cup
- Flour (pastry): ¼ cup
- Milk: ¾ cup
- Egg yolks (slightly beaten): 2
- Prune pulp (cooked, diced): 1¼ cups
- Maraschino cherries (chopped, drained): ¼ cup
- Citron (chopped): ¼ cup
- Pecans (chopped): ¼ cup or 1¹/₇ oz.
- Salt: ⅛ tsp.
- Butter: 1½ Tbsps.
- Pastry: 1 baked pie shell
- Chocolate Whipped Cream Topping, No. 458

For five 9-inch pies
- Sugar (granulated): 2½ cups or 1 lb. 4 oz.
- Flour (pastry): 1¼ cups or 5 oz.
- Milk: 3¾ cups or 1 lb. 14 oz.
- Egg yolks (slightly beaten): 10 or 10 oz.
- Prune pulp (cooked, diced): 6¼ cups or 3 lbs. 2 oz.
- Maraschino cherries (chopped, drained): 1¼ cups or 10 oz.
- Citron (chopped): 1¼ cups or 5 oz.
- Pecans (chopped): 1¼ cups or 5⁵/₇ oz.
- Salt: ⅝ tsp.
- Butter: 7½ Tbsps. or 3¾ oz.
- Pastry: 5 baked pie shells
- Chocolate Whipped Cream Topping, No. 458

Mix sugar and flour together. Combine milk, slightly beaten egg yolks, prune pulp, chopped maraschino cherries, citron, and pecans, and blend thoroughly. Then blend with sugar-flour mixture. Cook over hot water until thick, stirring constantly from bottom of pan. Add salt and butter. Cool. When cold, pour mixture into pre-baked 9-inch pastry shell and top with Chocolate Whipped Cream Topping, No. 458. Serve very cold.

(299) PRUNE PIE I—ALABAMA METHOD
TWO-CRUST PIE

For one 9-inch pie
- Prunes (pitted): 1¼ cups
- Water: 2 cups
- Sugar (brown): ¼ cup
- Sugar (granulated): ¼ cup
- Corn syrup (dark): 1 Tbsp.
- Salt: ⅛ tsp.
- Cornstarch: 1 Tbsp.
- Pineapple juice (canned): 2 tsp.
- Lemon juice: 1 Tbsp.
- Pastry: For 1 two-crust pie

For five 9-inch pies
- Prunes (pitted): 6¼ cups or 2½ lbs.
- Water: 2½ qts. or 5 lbs.
- Sugar (brown): 1¼ cups or 6⅔ oz.
- Sugar (granulated): 1¼ cups or 10 oz.
- Corn syrup (dark): 5 Tbsps. or 3¾ oz.
- Salt: ⅝ tsp.
- Cornstarch: 5 Tbsps. or 1⅔ oz.
- Pineapple juice (canned): 2½ Tbsps. or 1⅔ oz.
- Lemon juice: 5 Tbsps. or 2½ oz.
- Pastry: For 5 two-crust pies

Wash prunes and add to combined water, brown and granulated sugars, corn syrup, and salt. Cook very slowly for 50 minutes. Combine cornstarch, pineapple juice, and lemon juice, and blend to a smooth paste. Bring the prune mixture to a brisk boil and gradually add the cornstarch mixture, stirring gently but thoroughly, until mixture thickens and liquid is clear. Decrease heat and allow to cook 2 minutes longer. Remove from the heat; transfer mixture into a shallow container and allow to cool. When cold, turn mixture into a 9-inch pastry-lined pie pan; cover with top crust in the usual way, making a few slits in top for escape of steam; brush with melted butter. Bake 10 minutes in a very hot oven (450° F.); reduce temperature to 350° F. and continue baking 30 minutes longer. Serve cold.

(300)   # PRUNE PIE II—HOME METHOD
TWO-CRUST PIE

For one 9-inch pie
- Prunes (canned, pitted): 1 #2 can or 2½ cups
- Sugar (brown): ½ cup
- Corn syrup (dark): 1 Tbsp.
- Salt: ¼ tsp.
- Cinnamon: ⅛ tsp.
- Clove (ground): ⅛ tsp.
- Cornstarch: 2½ Tbsps.
- Lemon juice: 1 Tbsp.
- Pineapple juice (canned): 2 Tbsps.
- Pastry: For 1 two-crust pie

For five 9-inch pies
- Prunes (canned, pitted): 1 #10 can or 6 lbs. 14 oz.
- Sugar (brown): 2½ cups or 13⅓ oz.
- Corn syrup (dark): 5 Tbsps. or 3¾ oz.
- Salt: 1¼ tsps. or ⁵⁄₂₄ oz.
- Cinnamon: ⅝ tsp.
- Clove (ground): ⅝ tsp.
- Cornstarch: 12½ Tbsps. or 4 1/6 oz.
- Lemon juice: 5 Tbsps. or 2½ oz.
- Pineapple juice (canned): ⅝ cup or 5 oz.
- Pastry: For 5 two-crust pies

Empty can of pitted prunes, juice and fruit, into saucepan; add brown sugar, corn syrup, salt and spices. Bring this to a boil; then thicken with combined cornstarch, lemon juice and pineapple juice, adding it very slowly, while mixture is gently boiling, so as not to mash the fruit. Stir gently from the bottom of the saucepan until mixture thickens and is clear. Allow this to boil 1 minute; remove from the heat. Transfer to a shallow container to cool quickly; when cold, turn it into 9-inch pie pan lined with pastry rolled ⅛-inch thick; cover with top crust in the usual way, make a few slits for escape of steam and bake 10 minutes in a very hot oven (450° F.); reduce temperature to 350° F. and continue baking for 30 minutes. Serve cold.

(301) PRUNE PIE III—FRENCH METHOD
ONE-CRUST PIE

For one 9-inch pie

- Prunes (cooked, pitted, diced): 2 cups
- Pastry: For 1 one-crust pie
- Heavy cream (unwhipped): 1 cup
- Egg yolks (slightly beaten): 2
- Sugar (granulated): ½ cup
- Salt: ⅛ tsp.
- Nutmeg (ground): ⅛ tsp.
- Almond extract: ⅛ tsp.
- Chocolate Meringue, No. 451

For five 9-inch pies

- Prunes (cooked, pitted, diced): 2½ qts. or 3 lbs. 2 oz.
- Pastry: For 5 one-crust pies
- Heavy cream (unwhipped): 5 cups or 2 lbs. 9⅞ oz.
- Egg yolks (slightly beaten): 10 or 10 oz.
- Sugar (granulated): 2½ cups or 1 lb. 4 oz.
- Salt: ⅝ tsp.
- Nutmeg (ground): ⅝ tsp.
- Almond extract: ⅝ tsp.
- Chocolate Meringue, No. 451

Arrange diced prunes evenly in bottom of a 9-inch pie pan lined with pastry rolled ⅛-inch thick. Flute the edge of the pastry. Combine all the remaining ingredients in order given, blending well; spoon this mixture very gently over the prunes. Bake 15 minutes in a hot oven (400° F.); reduce temperature to 325° F. and continue baking 30 minutes longer. Remove from the oven; then, using a pastry bag, force Chocolate Meringue, made as indicated for No. 451, over the entire surface of the pie; return to oven and continue baking 15 minutes longer, or until meringue is glossy, puffy, and brown. Serve cold.

(302) PRUNE WHIP PIE—HOME METHOD
ONE-CRUST PIE, PRE-BAKED PASTRY SHELL

For one 9-inch pie
- Prunes (canned): 1 cup
- Sugar (brown): ¼ cup
- Sugar (granulated): 3 Tbsps.
- Salt: ½ tsp.
- Butter: 2 tsps.
- Corn syrup (dark): ¼ cup
- Cinnamon (ground): ⅛ tsp.
- Nutmeg (ground): ⅛ tsp.
- Clove (ground): ⅛ tsp.
- Cornstarch: 3 Tbsps.
- Milk: ¼ cup
- Lemon juice: 1 tsp.
- Vanilla extract: ¼ tsp.
- Egg whites (stiffly beaten): 2
- Pastry: 1 baked pie shell

For five 9-inch pies
- Prunes (canned): 1 #5 can, less 8 oz. or 5 cups or 3 lbs. 4½ oz.
- Sugar (brown): 1¼ cups or 6⅔ oz.
- Sugar (granulated): 1 cup or 7½ oz.
- Salt: 2½ tsps. or ⁵⁄₁₂ oz.
- Butter: 3⅓ Tbsps. or 1⅔ oz.
- Corn syrup (dark): 1¼ cups or 15 oz.
- Cinnamon (ground): ⅝ tsp.
- Nutmeg (ground): ⅝ tsp.
- Clove (ground): ⅝ tsp.
- Cornstarch: 15 Tbsps. or 5 oz.
- Milk: 1¼ cups or 10 oz.
- Lemon juice: 1⅔ Tbsps. or ¾ oz.
- Vanilla extract: 1¼ tsps. or ⁵⁄₂₄ oz.
- Egg whites (stiffly beaten): 10 or 10 oz.
- Pastry: 5 baked pie shells

Place the pitted whole prunes in saucepan with brown and granulated sugar, salt, butter, corn syrup, and spices. Bring mixture to a boil, stirring frequently from the bottom of the pan with a wooden spoon. Reduce heat and allow to simmer for 2 or 3 minutes over very low heat, stirring once or twice. Combine cornstarch and milk, and slowly add to mixture, stirring gently but constantly. Cook slowly until mixture is thick and clear, stirring almost constantly. Remove from heat, cool a little and stir in the lemon juice and vanilla extract. When cold, fold in stiffly beaten egg whites. Turn filling into pre-baked 9-inch pastry shell, and top with whipped cream. A plain meringue may be placed over the filling; bake in a slow oven (325° F.) for 15 minutes, or until meringue is delicately brown. Serve very cold.

(303)   ## A FEW FACTS ABOUT PUMPKIN

The brilliant orange Sweet Sugar or New England pie pumpkin and the lighter yellow Winter Luxury are among the tastiest varieties for pies; the Connecticut Field and the ten Big Cheese types run them a close second. Contrary to James Whitcomb Riley's poetical fancy, none of these is actually improved "when the frost is on the punkin'." Frost does not bring out the flavor of the big gourd, as was popularly supposed, and it does injure its keeping qualities. But sound, ripe pumpkins will keep for a year or more and retain their intrinsic flavor if they are stored in a cool dry place, separated one from the other, and wiped off occasionally with a dry cloth.

When shopping for pumpkins or squash or when choosing those from the home-grown crop, select the ones that feel heavy for their size, have a hard rind, and do not appear damp or watersoaked. Light-weight pumpkins or those with soft rinds are usually immature.

Here are a few pointers about baking pumpkin pies. Never force the dough of crust, or it will stretch and then shrink on baking. If it will not roll easily, it is sticking. The crust will not soak if care is taken to use as little liquid as possible when making a dough of the flour-fat mixture. This is called a "dry crust." It requires very little chilling, maybe 15 minutes, and rolls very easily. If you are unable to handle a "dry crust"—and it does require some skill—use instead of water a beaten egg mixed with 2 tablespoons of lemon juice to wet the pastry. Chill and then roll. This type of crust browns very well and is tender but not flaky; and when rolled thin it does not soak.

Many pumpkin pies are spoiled as the result of over-baking, in which case the filling turns watery and pulls away from the sides of the shells after becoming cold. The time to remove a pumpkin pie from the oven is before it puffs completely over the center.

The color of the surface filling depends a little on the type of oven heat in your range. If you have an oven that is hotter on the top than on the bottom shelf, then the pie will have a skin of brown on its surface. It will even rise a bit in ridges and when cold will set in that shape. In the heat-controlled, insulated ovens of the modern ranges, this will not happen. The filling will set gradually and evenly and will bake to a spice-brown, slightly shiny surface, with no skin to speak of.

If half the sugar is beaten with the eggs, and then the rest of the ingredients are well mixed and added to the mixture, the result will be a dull-surface pumpkin pie. When put in the pie shell, the foam will still ride on top and will brown during baking. This causes a crinkled, slightly crispy skin to form on top of the pie, making a pleasant texture contrast when eaten. The filling does not set as firmly, but is lighter and spongier.

Another method of erasing the plain surface is to float a few tablespoons of cream on top of the pie filling after it is in the pastry shell. This will brown and swell during the baking process and crinkle on cooling, giving an uneven wavelike appearance to the filling. The appearance is much improved by browning under the broiler a minute after baking.

To get a spotty brown appearance on the top of a pumpkin pie bake your pie as usual. Take the pie from oven, "drip" a tablespoon or two of milk very gently on the surface then slip the pie under the broiler for about two minutes. To have the pumpkin pie entirely covered with a brown crust, carefully pour ¼ cup milk over the top of an unbaked, filled pie. The milk does not mix with the filling, but remains on top, forming a firm brown crust during the baking process.

A glass, enamel, or a darkened tin pie pan bakes the best and least soggy undercrusts for pumpkin and custard pies.

NOTE: As a pumpkin pie variation, try black walnut meats, coarsely chopped in the filling. Another way to improve your pumpkin pie is to beat the egg whites separately and fold into your filling just before you fill the shell, or shells. In making a pumpkin pie de luxe use honey to sweeten and ginger root (minced fine) for flavoring. Candied ginger can be used and rich cream, or a tablespoon of brandy or brandy flavoring to each pie. Or, when using pre-baked pastry shell, use a bread crumb crust, or cheese pastry, gingersnap pie crust, graham cracker pie crust, vanilla wafer pie crust, or zwieback pie crust.

One of the most annoying problems is to eliminate the moisture from the pumpkin itself. To reduce moisture after the fresh pumpkin is sieved or strained, or the canned pumpkin is taken from the can, place in a heavy frying pan which has been well oiled or greased. Stew down slowly over low heat, stirring often. Do this until every bit of moisture is out of the pumpkin and it turns dark in color. The quantity diminishes by about one-half, but it is all pumpkin and will absorb milk or cream in place of the missing water. The result will be worth the hour-and-a-half of extra time. Here is how to obtain a pumpkin pie with the full flavor of pumpkin.

(304) PUMPKIN PIE—COUNTRY METHOD
ONE-CRUST PIE

For one 9-inch pie
- Pumpkin (canned): 2 cups
- Butter: 1 Tbsp.
- Whole eggs (well beaten): 4
- Sugar (granulated): ¾ cup (more or less)
- Salt: ¼ tsp.
- Cinnamon (ground): 1 tsp.
- Ginger (ground): ½ tsp.
- Cloves (ground): 1 tsp.
- Flaky pastry: For 1 one-crust pie

For five 9-inch pies
- Pumpkin (canned): 2½ qts. or 8 lbs. 2 oz.
- Butter: 5 Tbsps. or 2½ oz.
- Whole eggs (well beaten): 20 or 2½ lbs.
- Sugar (granulated): 3¾ cups (more or less) or 1⅞ lbs.
- Salt: 1¼ tsps. or ⁵/₂₄ oz.
- Cinnamon (ground): 1⅔ Tbsps. or ⁵/₁₂ oz.
- Ginger (ground): 2½ tsps. or ⁵/₂₄ oz.
- Cloves (ground): 1⅔ Tbsps. or ⁵/₁₂ oz.
- Flaky pastry: For 5 one-crust pies

Stew contents of one can pumpkin until dry enough to stick together. Add butter and blend thoroughly. Add well-beaten eggs. Blend well. Combine sugar, salt, cinnamon, ginger, and cloves and stir into pumpkin mixture. Turn filling into unbaked 9-inch rich flaky pastry shell as evenly as possible. Bake in a hot oven (450° F.) for 15–20 minutes; reduce temperature to 300° F. and continue baking 25 minutes longer, or until filling puffs up in the middle. Serve cold with or without plain whipped cream.

(305)

FRIED PUMPKIN PIES—
MEXICAN METHOD

For 15 little pies

Crust

- Whole wheat flour: 2 Tbsps.
- Corn meal: 1 Tbsp.
- Flour (pastry): ¾ cup
- Cinnamon (ground): ¼ tsp.
- Nutmeg (ground): ¼ tsp.
- Sugar (granulated): ¼ tsp.
- Baking powder: ¼ tsp.
- Salt: ¼ tsp.
- Butter (sweet): 3 Tbsps.
- Egg yolk (well beaten): 1
- Water (hot): 2½ Tbsps.

For 75 little pies

Crust

- Whole wheat flour: ⅝ cup or 2½ oz.
- Corn meal: 5 Tbsps. or 1¼ oz.
- Flour (pastry): 3¾ cups or 15 oz.
- Cinnamon (ground): 1¼ tsps.
- Nutmeg (ground): 1¼ tsps.
- Sugar (granulated): 1¼ tsps. or $5/24$ oz.
- Baking powder: 1¼ tsps.
- Salt: 1¼ tsps. or $5/24$ oz.
- Butter (sweet): 1 cup or 7½ oz.
- Egg yolks (well beaten): 5 or 5 oz.
- Water (hot): 12½ Tbsps. or ¾ cup or 6¼ oz.

Sift all the dry ingredients together. Blend with the butter as for pie crust, add egg yolk, beaten with hot water. Blend well and cool mixture in refrigerator.

Filling

- Cornstarch: 2 tsps.
- Cold water: 2 tsps.
- Pumpkin (cooked or canned): ¾ cup
- Milk (cold): ½ cup
- Salt: ¼ tsp.
- Honey (strained): 2 Tbsps.
- Molasses (dark): 2 Tbsps.
- Butter: 1 Tbsp.
- Anise seeds (crushed): ½ tsp.
- Egg yolks (well beaten): 2
- Vanilla extract: 2 tsps.

Filling

- Cornstarch: 3⅓ Tbsps. or 1⅑ oz.
- Cold water: 3⅓ Tbsps. or 1⅔ oz.
- Pumpkin (cooked or canned): 3¾ cups or 2 lbs. 13 oz.
- Milk (cold): 2½ cups or 1¼ lbs.
- Salt: 1¼ tsps. or $5/24$ oz.
- Honey (strained): ⅝ cup or 7½ oz.
- Molasses (dark): ⅝ cup or 7½ oz.
- Butter: 5 Tbsps. or 2½ oz.
- Anise seeds (crushed): 2½ tsps.
- Egg yolks (well beaten): 10 or 10 oz.
- Vanilla extract: 3⅓ Tbsps. or 1⅔ oz.

NOTE: These little fried pumpkin pies are very popular in Mexico, Texas, Arizona, and in almost all the states bordering Mexico. They are called "Empanaditas de Calabaza." The crust is rather spicy and requires a special preparation. Their sizes are about 2 to 2¼ inches in diameter.

The time of frying depends upon the heat of deep fat, but each pie should be golden brown, and one or two pies are served for each guest. Fine for a Buffet Party.

Dissolve cornstarch in cold water. Add all remaining ingredients except egg yolks and vanilla extract. Cook over hot water until mixture is thickened, stirring almost constantly. Stir in briskly the well-beaten egg yolks, then vanilla extract. Set aside to cool. Roll out crust very thin. Cut into circles about 2 to 2½ inches in diameter. Place 1 tablespoon cold filling in center of each; moisten edges slightly, fold up and crimp. Place in refrigerator to chill. Fry in hot deep fat (375° F.) until brown; drain on absorbent paper and serve very hot.

....

(306) PUMPKIN COTTAGE CHEESE PIE— MIDDLE WEST METHOD
ONE-CRUST PIE

For one 9-inch pie
- Sour cream (heavy): ¼ cup
- Milk (fresh): ½ cup
- Sherry wine: ¼ cup
- Sugar (brown): ½ cup
- Ginger (ground): ½ tsp.
- Cinnamon (ground): ½ tsp.
- Salt: 1 tsp.
- Pumpkin (canned, sieved): 2 cups
- Cottage cheese (drained, sieved twice): 1 cup
- Pastry: For 1 one-crust pie

For five 9-inch pies
- Sour cream (heavy): 1¼ cups or 10 ½ oz.
- Milk (fresh): 2½ cups or 1 lb. 4 oz.
- Sherry wine: 1¼ cups or 10 oz.
- Sugar (brown): 2½ cups or 13⅓ oz.
- Ginger (ground): 2½ tsps. or $^5/_{24}$ oz.
- Cinnamon (ground): 2½ tsps. or $^5/_{24}$ oz.
- Salt: 1⅔ Tbsps. or $^5/_6$ oz.
- Pumpkin (canned, sieved): 2½ qts. or 8 lbs. 2 oz.
- Cottage cheese (drained, sieved twice): 5 cups or 2½ lbs.
- Pastry: For 5 one-crust pies

Combine ingredients in order given, blending thoroughly. Pour mixture into well chilled unbaked pie shell and bake 10 minutes in a very hot oven (450° F.); reduce temperature to 350° F. and continue baking 30 minutes longer. Serve very cold.

(307) # PUMPKIN HONEY PIE
ONE-CRUST PIE

For one 9-inch pie

- Pumpkin (canned, sieved): 2 cups
- Honey (strained): 1 cup
- Ginger (ground): ½ tsp.
- Cinnamon (ground): ¾ tsp.
- Salt: 1 tsp.
- Whole eggs (slightly beaten): 3
- Milk (fresh): 1 cup
- Heavy cream (unwhipped): ½ cup
- Heavy cream (whipped): 1 cup
- Pastry: For 1 one-crust pie

For five 9-inch pies

- Pumpkin (canned, sieved): 2½ qts. or 8 lbs. 2 oz.
- Honey (strained): 5 cups or 3¾ lbs.
- Ginger (ground): 2½ tsps. or $5/24$ oz.
- Cinnamon (ground): 3¾ tsps. or $5/16$ oz.
- Salt: 1⅔ Tbsps. or $5/6$ oz.
- Whole eggs (slightly beaten): 15 or 1 lb. 14 oz.
- Milk (fresh): 5 cups or 2½ lbs.
- Heavy cream (unwhipped): 2½ cups or 1 lb. $4^{15}/16$ oz.
- Heavy cream (whipped): 5 cups or 2 lbs.
- Pastry: For 5 one-crust pies

Mix pumpkin, honey, ginger, cinnamon, salt, eggs, milk, and unwhipped cream in mixing bowl and blend thoroughly and smoothly; turn mixture into 9-inch unbaked pastry shell and bake 10 minutes in a very hot oven (450° F.); reduce temperature to 325° F. and continue baking 40 minutes longer, or until filling is firm. Cool. When cold top with whipped cream. Serve thoroughly chilled.

(308)

PUMPKIN MERINGUE PIE—
HOME METHOD
ONE-CRUST PIE, PRE-BAKED PIE SHELL

For one 9-inch pie

- Sugar (brown): 1 cup
- Sugar (granulated): ¼ cup
- Cinnamon (ground): 1 tsp.
- Cloves (ground): 1 tsp.
- Nutmeg (ground): ½ tsp.
- Pumpkin (freshly cooked): 2 cups
- Flour (pastry): ¼ cup
- Salt: 1 tsp.
- Milk: 1 cup
- Egg yolks (slightly beaten): 3
- Pastry: 1 baked pie shell
- Ginger meringue topping (No. 451)

For five 9-inch pies

- Sugar (brown): 5 cups or 1 lb. 10⅔ oz.
- Sugar (granulated): 1¼ cups or 9⁷/₁₇ oz.
- Cinnamon (ground): 1½ Tbsps. or ⅜ oz.
- Cloves (ground): 1½ Tbsps. or ⅜ oz.
- Nutmeg (ground): 2½ tsps. or ⁵/₂₄ oz.
- Pumpkin (freshly cooked): 2½ qts. or 8 lbs. 2 oz.
- Flour (pastry): 1¼ cups or 5 oz.
- Salt: 1½ Tbsps. or ¾ oz.
- Milk: 5 cups or 2½ lbs.
- Egg yolks (slightly beaten): 15 or 15 oz.
- Pastry: 5 baked pie shells
- Ginger meringue topping (No. 451)

Blend sugars, spices, freshly cooked, cooled pumpkin, which has been sieved, flour and salt. Gradually add milk combined with slightly beaten egg yolks, stirring constantly until mixture is smooth. Cook over hot water until thick and smooth, stirring almost constantly. Cool to lukewarm; turn into pre-baked 9-inch pie shell; top with a plain meringue, made in the usual way (No. 26), and bake 15 minutes in a moderately slow oven (325° F.), or until meringue is delicately brown. Serve cold.

(309) PUMPKIN PECAN PIE—TEXAS METHOD
ONE-CRUST PIE

For one 9-inch pie

- Pumpkin (freshly cooked, sieved): 1½ cups
- Sugar (brown): 1 cup
- Cinnamon (ground): 1 tsp.
- Ginger (ground): 1 tsp.
- Nutmeg (ground): ¼ tsp.
- Allspice (ground): ¼ tsp.
- Salt: ½ tsp.
- Molasses: 1 Tbsp.
- Orange juice: 2 Tbsps.
- Whole eggs (slightly beaten): 2
- Milk (rich): 1¼ cups
- Pastry: For 1 one-crust pie
- Butter (softened): ¼ cup
- Sugar (brown): 1 cup
- Pecans (halves): 1 cup

For five 9-inch pies

- Pumpkin (freshly cooked, sieved): 7½ cups or 6 lbs. 1½ oz.
- Sugar (brown): 5 cups or 1 lb. 10⅔ oz.
- Cinnamon (ground): 1½ Tbsps. or ⅜ oz.
- Ginger (ground): 1½ Tbsps. or ⅜ oz.
- Nutmeg (ground): 1¼ tsps.
- Allspice (ground): 1¼ tsps.
- Salt: 2½ tsps. or ⁵/₁₂ oz.
- Molasses: 5 Tbsps. or 3¾ oz.
- Orange juice: ⅝ cup or 5 oz.
- Whole eggs (slightly beaten): 10 or 1 lb. 4 oz.
- Milk (rich): 6¼ cups or 3 lbs. 2 oz.
- Pastry: For 5 one-crust pies
- Butter (softened): 1¼ cups or 10 oz.
- Sugar (brown): 5 cups or 1 lb. 10⅔ oz.
- Pecans (halves): 5 cups or 1 lb. 6⁶/₇ oz.

Combine the pumpkin, sugar, spices, and salt in mixing bowl; stir in the molasses, orange juice, beaten whole eggs, and milk. Blend thoroughly. Turn mixture into unbaked 9-inch pastry shell; place in a very hot oven (425° F.) and bake 10 minutes; reduce temperature to 325° F. and continue baking for 35 minutes longer, or until firm. Mix softened butter, sugar and pecan halves, spread over top of filling; place under the broiler long enough (about 4 or 5 minutes) to glaze or caramelize the top. Serve lukewarm or cold.

(310)   # PUMPKIN PINEAPPLE PIE—
CREOLE METHOD
ONE-CRUST PIE

For one 9-inch pie
- Sugar (brown): ½ cup
- Flour (pastry): 1 tsp.
- Ginger (ground): ¼ tsp.
- Cinnamon (ground): ½ tsp.
- Salt 1 tsp.
- Whole eggs (slightly beaten): 2
- Pumpkin (freshly cooked, or canned): 1½ cups
- Milk (rich): 1¼ cups
- Molasses: 4 tsps.
- Butter (melted): 1 Tbsp.
- Pineapple (canned, crushed, drained): 1 cup
- Pastry: For 1 one-crust pie

For five 9-inch pies
- Sugar (brown): 2½ cups or 13⅓ oz.
- Flour (pastry): 1⅔ Tbsps. or 5/12 oz.
- Ginger (ground): 1¼ tsps.
- Cinnamon (ground): 2½ tsps. or 5/24 oz.
- Salt: 1⅔ Tbsps. or 5/6 oz.
- Whole eggs (slightly beaten): 10 or 1 lb. 4 oz.
- Pumpkin (freshly cooked, or canned): 7½ cups or 6 lbs. 1½ oz.
- Milk (rich): 6¼ cups or 3 lbs. 2 oz.
- Molasses: 6⅔ Tbsps. or 5 oz.
- Butter (melted): 5 Tbsps. or 2½ oz.
- Pineapple (canned, crushed, drained): 5 cups or 3¾ lbs.
- Pastry: For 5 one-crust pies

Mix brown sugar, flour, spices, and salt. Beat eggs, and add pumpkin, rich milk, (top of bottle, or ½ cup water and ¾ cup of undiluted evaporated milk), and molasses and butter. Blend well. Combine with sugar mixture, and add pineapple, which has been well drained. Turn filling into unbaked 9-inch pastry shell and bake 10 minutes in a very hot oven (450° F.); reduce temperature to 350° F. and continue baking 30–35 minutes longer. Serve cold. You may substitute 1 cup of seedless raisins, parboiled and drained, for pineapple, if desired.

(311) PUMPKIN (PLAIN) PIE—HOME METHOD
ONE-CRUST PIE

For one 9-inch pie
- Pastry: For 1 one-crust pie
- Sugar (brown): 1 cup
- Ginger (ground): ½ tsp.
- Cinnamon (ground): 1 tsp.
- Cloves (ground): ¼ tsp.
- Salt: ½ tsp.
- Whole eggs (slightly beaten): 2
- Milk (cold): 1½ cups
- Cream (light): ½ cup
- Pumpkin (canned or cooked, cold): 1¾ cups

For five 9-inch pies
- Pastry: For 5 one-crust pies
- Sugar (brown): 5 cups or 1 lb. 10⅔ oz.
- Ginger (ground): 2½ tsps. or ⁵/₂₄ oz.
- Cinnamon (ground): 2½ Tbsps. or ⁵/₁₂ oz.
- Cloves (ground): 1¼ tsps.
- Salt: 2½ tsps. or ⁵/₁₂ oz.
- Whole eggs (slightly beaten): 10 or 1¼ lbs.
- Milk (cold): 7½ cups or 3¾ lbs.
- Cream (light): 2½ cups or 1¼ lbs.
- Pumpkin (canned or cooked, cold): 8¾ cups or 6 lbs. 9 oz.

Combine brown sugar, ginger, cinnamon, cloves, and salt. Blend well. Add slightly beaten eggs combined with milk, cream, and cooked or canned cold pumpkin; blend thoroughly. Turn filling into unbaked 9-inch one-crust pastry shell, spread as evenly as possible, and bake in a hot oven (425° F.) for 40–45 minutes, or until knife inserted in center comes out clean. Serve cold.

....

(312) RAISIN BUTTER PIE—HOME METHOD
ONE-CRUST PIE, PRE-BAKED PIE SHELL

For one 9-inch pie
- Egg yolks (well beaten): 3
- Sugar (granulated): 1 cup
- Butter: ½ cup
- Milk: 1¼ cups
- Salt: ¼ tsp.
- Meringue topping (optional)
- Raisins (seedless, stewed): 1¼ cups
- Pastry: 1 baked pie shell

For five 9-inch pies
- Egg yolks (well beaten): 15 or 15 oz.
- Sugar (granulated): 5 cups or 2½ lbs.
- Butter: 2½ cups or 1 lb. 4 oz.
- Milk: 6¼ cups or 3 lbs. 2 oz.
- Salt: 1¼ tsps. or ⁵/₂₄ oz.
- Meringue topping (optional)
- Raisins (seedless, stewed): 6¼ cups or 2 lbs. 1⅓ oz.
- Pastry: 5 baked pie shells

Beat egg yolks until creamy and lemon-colored; gradually beat in granulated sugar alternately with butter. Blend thoroughly. Scald milk; allow to cool a little, then beat it into the egg-sugar mixture, adding salt. Stir in stewed seedless raisins which have been thoroughly drained. Place mixture in top of double boiler and cook over hot water until thick, stirring constantly. Cool. When cold, turn into 9-inch pre-baked pastry shell; top or not with meringue. If meringue topping is spread over the top, bake 15 minutes in a moderately slow oven (325° F.), or until meringue is delicately browned.

....

(313)　RAISIN LEMON PIE
ONE-CRUST PIE, PRE-BAKED PIE SHELL

For one 9-inch pie
- Raisins (seedless): 1 cup
- Water (cold): Enough to cover
- Sugar (granulated): ¾ cup
- Salt: ½ tsp.
- Cornstarch: 5 Tbsps.
- Water (cold): 2 cups
- Egg yolks (slightly beaten): 3
- Lemon juice: 3 Tbsps.
- Lemon rind (grated): 1 tsp.
- Pastry: 1 baked pie shell
- Honey Meringue Topping No. 451

For five 9-inch pies
- Raisins (seedless): 5 cups or 1 lb. 10⅔ oz.
- Water (cold): Enough to cover
- Sugar (granulated): 3¾ cups or 1 lb. 14 oz.
- Salt: 2½ tsps. or ⁵/₁₂ oz.
- Cornstarch: 1 cup plus 9 Tbsps. or 8⅓ oz.
- Water (cold): 2½ qts. or 5 lbs.
- Egg yolks (slightly beaten): 15 or 15 oz.
- Lemon juice: 1 scant cup or 7½ oz.
- Lemon rind (grated): 1⅔ Tbsps. or ⅝ oz.
- Pastry: 5 baked pie shells
- Honey Meringue Topping No. 451

Cover raisins with cold water; boil 5 minutes; drain and chop very fine or put through food chopper. Combine granulated sugar, salt, and cornstarch, add the 2 cups of cold water and dissolve thoroughly. Cook over hot water, stirring constantly until mixture is clear and thick; gradually add slightly beaten egg yolks, stirring vigorously and constantly to prevent curdling; then stir in the combined lemon juice, lemon rind and raisins. Blend well. Pour mixture into pre-baked 9-inch pastry shell and bake 15 minutes in a moderate oven (350° F.). Cover with Honey Meringue Topping, made as indicated for recipe No. 451; return to moderately slow oven (325° F.) and bake 15 minutes, or until meringue is delicately brown. Serve cold.

....

(314) RAISIN-APPLE AND WALNUT PIE— WASHINGTON METHOD
ONE-CRUST PIE

For one 9-inch pie
- Raisins (seeded): 1½ cups
- Apples (tart, chopped): 1 cup
- Water (boiling): 1½ cups
- Quick-cooking tapioca: 1½ Tbsps.
- Sugar (granulated): ½ cup
- Salt: ¼ tsp.
- Lemon juice: 1 Tbsp.
- Lemon rind (grated): 1 tsp.
- Walnut meats (chopped): ½ cup
- Pastry: For 1 one-crust pie
- Walnuts meats (chopped): ½ cup
- Sugar (granulated): 1 Tbsp.

For five 9-inch pies
- Raisins (seeded): 7½ cups or 3 lbs.
- Apples (tart, chopped): 5 cups or 2½ lbs.
- Water (boiling): 7½ cups or 3¾ lbs.
- Quick-cooking tapioca: 7½ Tbsps. or 1⅞ oz.
- Sugar (granulated): 2½ cups or 1 lb. 4 oz.
- Salt: 1¼ tsps. or $5/24$ oz.
- Lemon juice: 5 Tbsps. or 2½ oz.
- Lemon rind (grated): 1⅔ Tbsps. or ⅝ oz.
- Walnut meats (chopped): 2½ cups or 13⅓ oz.
- Pastry: For 5 one-crust pies
- Walnut meats (chopped): 2½ cups or 13⅓ oz.
- Sugar (granulated): 5 Tbsps. or 2½ oz.

Wash and pick over the raisins; place in saucepan with apples and boiling water. Boil 10 minutes, or until tender; add tapioca combined with sugar and salt; cook, stirring constantly, until mixture is thickened, or about 10 minutes. Now add lemon juice and rind and first amount of chopped walnut meats. Turn mixture into unbaked 9-inch pie shell and bake 10 minutes in a very hot oven (450° F.); reduce temperature to 350° F. and continue baking 30 minutes longer, or until top is brown. Roll chopped walnut meats in remaining sugar and sprinkle over the baked filling while still hot. Allow to cool well before serving.

....

(315)   **RAISIN NUT PIE**
                ONE-CRUST PIE, PRE-BAKED PIE SHELL

Proceed as indicated for No. 312, Raisin Butter Pie, using the same amount of ingredients, adding ½ cup of chopped nut meats to the mixture before pouring it into the shell.

(316)

RAISIN PIE I
ONE-CRUST PIE

For one 9-inch pie
- Raisins (seedless): 2 cups
- Water (cold): 1½ cups
- Sugar (granulated): ¼ cup
- Sugar (brown, dark): ½ cup
- Corn syrup (dark): 2½ Tbsps.
- Salt: ¼ tsp.
- Cinnamon (ground): $1/8$ tsp.
- Nutmeg (ground): $1/8$ tsp.
- Cornstarch: 3½ Tbsps.
- Pastry flour: 2 tsps.
- Water (cold): 2 Tbsps.
- Lemon juice: ½ tsp.
- Butter (melted): 2 tsps.
- Pastry: For 1 one-crust pie

For five 9-inch pies
- Raisins (seedless): 2½ qts. or 3 lbs. $5^1/3$ oz.
- Water (cold): 7½ cups or 3¾ lbs.
- Sugar (granulated): 1¼ cups or 10 oz.
- Sugar (brown): 2½ cups or $13^1/3$ oz.
- Corn syrup (dark): 12½ Tbsps. or $9^3/8$ oz.
- Salt: 1¼ tsps. or $5/24$ oz.
- Cinnamon (ground): $5/8$ tsp.
- Nutmeg (ground): $5/8$ tsp.
- Cornstarch: 1 cup plus 1½ Tbsps. or $5^5/6$ oz.
- Pastry flour: $3^1/3$ Tbsps. or $5/6$ oz.
- Water (cold): $5/8$ cup or 5 oz.
- Lemon juice: 2½ tsps. or $5/12$ oz.
- Butter (melted): $3^1/3$ Tbsps. or $1^2/3$ oz.
- Pastry: For 5 one-crust pies

Into a saucepan, put raisins, water, sugars, corn syrup, salt, and spices and bring to a boil; immediately lower the heat and let this simmer for 30 minutes, or until raisins are tender, stirring frequently, with a wooden spoon. Then gradually add combined cornstarch and flour dissolved in remaining cold water, stirring constantly; allow the mixture to cook for 3 minutes until thick and clear. Bring to a boil; remove from the heat and spread into a shallow container to thoroughly cool. When cold, stir in the lemon juice alternately with butter. Turn mixture into unbaked 9-inch pastry shell and bake 10 minutes in a very hot oven (450° F.); reduce temperature to 350° F. and continue baking 20 minutes longer. Serve cold, or topped with either a meringue, which should then be baked in the usual way (No. 26), or with Streusel (No. 475).

(317)   # RAISIN PIE II—FRENCH METHOD
TWO-CRUST PIE

For one 9-inch pie
- White seedless raisins: 2 cups
- Orange juice: 1/3 cup
- Lemon juice: 2 Tbsps.
- Sugar (granulated): 1/2 cup
- Water (cold): 1/2 cup
- Flour (sifted): 2 Tbsps.
- Salt: 1/4 tsp.
- Sugar (granulated): 3 Tbsps.
- Water (cold): 2 Tbsps.
- Butter: 1 Tbsp.
- Pastry: For 1 two-crust pie

For five 9-inch pies
- White seedless raisins: 2½ qts. or 3 lbs. 1/3 oz.
- Orange juice: 1²/3 cups or 13¹/3 oz.
- Lemon juice: 5/8 cup or 5 oz.
- Sugar (granulated): 2½ cups or 1 lb. 4 oz.
- Water (cold): 2½ cups or 1 lb. 4 oz.
- Flour (sifted): 5/8 cup or 2½ oz.
- Salt: 1¼ tsps. or 5/24 oz.
- Sugar (granulated): 1 scant cup or 7½ oz.
- Water (cold): 5/8 cup or 5 oz.
- Butter: 5 Tbsps. or 2½ oz.
- Pastry: For 5 two-crust pies

Wash and drain raisins; put them into saucepan with orange and lemon juices, the ½ cup of sugar, and cold water. Mix well and place over low heat; let simmer gently, stirring frequently, until white raisins become plump, or about 15 minutes. Blend flour, remaining sugar and salt with remaining cold water to make a thin paste; gradually add to raisin mixture, stirring constantly until smooth and thickened. Add the butter and simmer gently for 5 minutes. Transfer filling to a shallow container to cool thoroughly. Fill pie pan lined with pastry with mixture; cover with top crust in the usual way, making a few slits to permit the escape of steam; brush the top with milk. Bake 10 minutes in a very hot oven (450° F.); reduce temperature to 350° F. and continue baking for 25 to 30 minutes longer, or until top is delicately brown. Serve cold with brandy hard sauce.

(318)
RAISIN RICE PIE—
NEW ORLEANS METHOD
ONE-CRUST PIE

For one 9-inch pie
- Rice (uncooked): ½ cup
- Raisins (seedless): 1 cup
- Milk (cold): 2 cups
- Whole eggs (slightly beaten): 2
- Sugar (brown): ½ cup
- Salt: ¼ tsp.
- Vanilla extract: ½ tsp. or $^1/_{12}$ oz.
- Pastry: For 1 one-crust pie

For five 9-inch pies
- Rice (uncooked): 2½ cups or 1 lb. 4 oz.
- Raisins (seedless): 5 cups or 1 lb. 10⅔ oz.
- Milk (cold): 2½ cups or 13⅓ oz.
- Whole eggs (slightly beaten): 10 or 1¼ lbs.
- Sugar (brown): 2½ cups or 13⅓ oz.
- Salt: 1¼ tsp. or $^5/_{24}$ oz.
- Vanilla extract: 2½ tsps. or $^5/_{12}$ oz.
- Pastry: For 5 one-crust pies

Wash rice thoroughly. Simmer rice and raisins in the milk 35 minutes, or until rice is soft. Add beaten eggs, sugar, salt and vanilla. Blend thoroughly. Turn mixture into pastry lined 9-inch pie pan and bake 10 minutes in a hot oven (425° F.); reduce temperature to 350° F. and continue baking for 25 minutes longer. Serve ice cold.

You may have to add more milk to mixture before turning it into pie crust, depending on age of rice. The ideal in rice is a cooked, plump, unbroken grain. You cannot get this with a soft rice, which will be soggy, glutinous, and heavy. Use the blue rose, which is not a brand, patua or fortuna. The Japanese rices are the undesirable types. They cook up soft and are impossible to handle with satisfactory results.

Use a fork for stirring rice while cooking, to prevent scorching. If you grease the bottom of the pot thoroughly before putting in the ingredients, the rice won't stick to the bottom.

(319) RASPBERRY COCONUT PIE— FRENCH METHOD
ONE-CRUST PIE, PRE-BAKED PASTRY SHELL

For one 9-inch pie
- Flour (sifted): 5 Tbsps.
- Sugar (granulated): ¼ cup
- Salt: ¼ tsp.
- Milk (cold): ½ cup
- Milk (scalded): 1½ cups
- Egg yolks (slightly beaten): 3
- Coconut (shredded): 1 cup
- Vanilla extract: ½ tsp.
- Almond extract: ¼ tsp.
- Lemon gratings: 1 tsp.
- Pastry: 1 baked pie shell
- Raspberries (fresh, washed, hulled): 1 cup
- Heavy cream (whipped): ½ cup

For five 9-inch pies
- Flour (sifted): 1 cup plus 9 Tbsps. or 6¼ oz.
- Sugar (granulated): 1¼ cups or 10 oz.
- Salt: 1¼ tsps. or $5/24$ oz.
- Milk (cold): 2½ cups or 1 lb. 4 oz.
- Milk (scalded): 7½ cups or 3¾ lbs.
- Egg yolks (slightly beaten): 15 or 15 oz.
- Coconut (shredded): 5 cups or 1 lb.
- Vanilla extract: 2½ tsps. or $5/12$ oz.
- Almond extract: 1¼ tsps. or $5/24$ oz.
- Lemon gratings: $1 2/3$ Tbsps. or $5/8$ oz.
- Pastry: 5 baked pie shells
- Raspberries (fresh, washed, hulled): 5 cups or 1 lb. $6 6/7$ oz.
- Heavy cream (whipped): 2½ cups or 1¼ lbs.

Combine flour, sugar, salt. Add cold milk and blend thoroughly. Add scalded milk gradually, stirring constantly until very smooth. Cook over boiling water until thickened, stirring constantly. Very slowly pour this hot mixture over the slightly beaten egg yolks; return to hot water and continue cooking for 3 minutes longer. Remove from hot water, add combined flavorings, and cool. When cold, turn mixture into pre-baked 9-inch pastry shell; cover with whipped cream forced through a pastry tube with a square tube; sprinkle coconut over whipped cream and make a border of fresh raspberries around the edges of the pie. Serve cold.

(320) RASPBERRY CREAM MERINGUE PIE
ONE-CRUST PIE, PRE-BAKED PASTRY SHELL

For one 9-inch pie
- Sugar (granulated): ¾ cup
- Salt: ¼ tsp.
- Milk (scalded): 1 cup
- Cornstarch: 3½ Tbsps.
- Orange juice: ¼ cup
- Egg yolks (slightly beaten): 2
- Vanilla extract: ¼ tsp.
- Butter: 1 Tbsp.
- Raspberries (fresh, washed, hulled): 1 cup
- Pastry: 1 baked pie shell
- Toffee Meringue Topping No. 451

For five 9-inch pies
- Sugar (granulated): 3¾ cups or 1 lb. 14 oz.
- Salt: 1¼ tsps. or $5/24$ oz.
- Milk (scalded): 5 cups or 2½ lbs.
- Cornstarch: 1 cup plus 1½ Tbsps. or $5^5/6$ oz.
- Orange juice: 1¼ cups or 10 oz.
- Egg yolks (slightly beaten): 10 or 10 oz.
- Vanilla extract: 1¼ tsps. or $5/24$ oz.
- Butter: 5 Tbsps. or 2½ oz.
- Raspberries (fresh, washed, hulled): 5 cups or 1 lb. $6^6/7$ oz.
- Pastry: 5 baked pie shells
- Toffee Meringue Topping No. 451

Mix sugar and salt, and gradually add to scalded milk, blending thoroughly. Combine cornstarch and orange juice, making a smooth paste, and add to milk mixture. Cook over hot water, stir constantly until mixture thickens. Allow to simmer very gently for 3 or 4 minutes, stirring frequently. Then gradually and slowly pour in the slightly beaten egg yolks, stirring briskly while pouring. Cook 2 minutes longer, stirring frequently. Remove from the heat, add vanilla extract and butter, and let cool; stir in raspberries. When cold, turn mixture into pre-baked 9-inch pastry shell; top with Toffee Meringue Topping, made as indicated for No. 451, and bake 15 minutes in moderately slow oven (325° F.), or until meringue is brown.

(321)

RASPBERRY CREAM PIE— FRENCH METHOD
ONE-CRUST PIE, PRE-BAKED PASTRY SHELL

For one 9-inch pie
- Raspberries (fresh or frozen): 1 qt.
- Orange juice (hot): ½ cup
- Sugar (granulated): 1 cup more or less
- Cornstarch: 2 Tbsps.
- Salt: ¼ tsp.
- Orange juice (cold): 3 Tbsps.
- Pastry: 1 baked pie shell
- Heavy cream (whipped): 1 cup
- Kirsch liqueur: 1 tsp.

For five 9-inch pies
- Raspberries (fresh or frozen): 5 qts. or 5 lbs.
- Orange juice (hot): 2½ cups or 1¼ lbs.
- Sugar (granulated): 5 cups, more or less or 2½ lbs.
- Cornstarch: ⅝ cup or 3⅓ oz.
- Salt: 1¼ tsps. or ⁵⁄₂₄ oz.
- Orange juice (cold): 1 scant cup or 7½ oz.
- Pastry: 5 baked pie shells
- Heavy cream (whipped): 5 cups or 2½ lbs.
- Kirsch liqueur: 1⅔ Tbsps. or ⅚ oz.

Pick and stem fresh raspberries; place in colander and pour lukewarm water over them several times to wash. Drain carefully. Turn into an enamelled saucepan, add hot orange juice and sugar, blend well and bring to a boil very slowly, stirring frequently; let simmer for 4 or 5 minutes, or until juice flows. Moisten cornstarch and salt with cold orange juice; add 4 or 5 tablespoons hot raspberry juice and mix well; pour into the raspberry mixture, stirring very gently. Bring to a boil and remove at once from the heat. Cool a little, then pour into pre-baked pastry shell brushed with butter. Cool. When cold, top with unsweetened whipped cream, flavored with Kirsch liqueur, forced through a pastry bag with a fancy tube, and decorate with a few, cleaned, stemmed, fresh raspberries dipped into melted currant jelly.

(322) RASPBERRY CREAM PIE CHANTILLY— PARISIAN METHOD
ONE-CRUST PIE

Proceed as indicated for recipe No. 355, Strawberry Cream Pie Chantilly, substituting fresh or frozen raspberries for fresh or frozen strawberries.

....

(323) RASPBERRY, STRAWBERRY CREAM PIE CHANTILLY—PARISIAN METHOD
TWO-CRUST PIE

Proceed as indicated for recipe No. 355, Strawberry Cream Pie Chantilly, using one pint (for each pie) of washed, hulled, and picked over fresh or frozen raspberries for the bottom filling, and one pint (for each pie) of washed, hulled, and picked over fresh or frozen strawberries for top filling.

Variations: (1) Have bottom filling made of canned, drained crushed pineapple and whipped cream, and top with fresh or frozen raspberries and whipped cream. (2) Have bottom filling made of cooked, sieved dried apricots mixed with whipped cream, and top with fresh or frozen raspberries and whipped cream. (3) Have bottom filling made of cooked, sieved dried peaches mixed with whipped cream, and top with fresh or frozen raspberries and whipped cream. (4) Have bottom filling made of fresh or frozen raspberries and whipped cream mixed with shredded, toasted, cooled almonds, and the top with fresh or frozen raspberries and whipped cream, or vice versa.

(324)
RASPBERRY PEACH PIE
TWO-CRUST PIE

For one 9-inch pie
- Pastry: For 1 two-crust pie
- Peaches (fresh or frozen, sliced): 8 or about 2 lbs.
- Raspberries (fresh or frozen): 3 cups
- Sugar (granulated): 1¼ cups
- Flour (pastry): 2 Tbsps.
- Cinnamon (ground): ¼ tsp.
- Nutmeg (ground): ⅛ tsp.
- Salt: ¼ tsp.
- Quick-cooking tapioca: 1 tsp.
- Plain whipped cream: about 1 cup

For five 9-inch pies
- Pastry: For 5 two-crust pies
- Peaches (fresh or frozen, sliced): 40 or about 10 lbs.
- Raspberries (fresh or frozen): 15 cups or 3¾ lbs.
- Sugar (granulated): 6¼ cups or 3 lbs. 2 oz.
- Flour (pastry): ⅝ cup or 2½ oz.
- Cinnamon (ground): 1¼ tsps.
- Nutmeg (ground): ⅝ tsp.
- Salt: 1¼ tsps. or ⁵⁄₂₄ oz.
- Quick-cooking tapioca: 1⅔ Tbsps. or ⁵⁄₁₂ oz.
- Plain whipped cream: about 5 cups or 2½ lbs.

Line a 9-inch pie plate with pastry rolled ⅛-inch thick and brush bottom and sides with slightly beaten egg whites. Let dry about 15 minutes. Fill with sliced peaches mixed with raspberries, sugar, flour, spices, salt, and tapioca. Thoroughly blend. Cover with top crust in the usual way, making a few slits for escape of steam; brush top crust with cold milk and bake 10 minutes in a hot oven (450° F.); reduce temperature to 350° F. and continue baking 25–30 minutes longer. Cool. Serve very cold with plain whipped cream.

....

(325)
RASPBERRY PINEAPPLE PIE GOURMET— FRENCH METHOD

Proceed as indicated for Strawberry Pineapple Pie Gourmet No. 362, substituting fresh or frozen raspberries for fresh or frozen strawberries.

(326)

RASPBERRY SPONGE PIE—
HOME METHOD
ONE-CRUST PIE

For one 9-inch pie
- Raspberries (fresh or frozen): 1 qt. or 1 lb.
- Egg whites (stiffly beaten): 2
- Sugar (powdered): ½ cup
- Sugar (brown, fine): ¾ cup
- Lemon juice: 1 Tbsp.
- Salt: ¼ tsp.
- Ginger (ground): ¼ tsp.
- Almond extract: ⅛ tsp.
- Pastry: 1 baked flaky pie shell (No. 47)
- Heavy cream (whipped): 1 cup
- Orange rind (grated): 1 Tbsp.
- Sugar (granulated): ¼ cup

For five 9-inch pies
- Raspberries (fresh or frozen): 5 qts. or 5 lbs.
- Egg whites (stiffly beaten): 10 or 10 oz.
- Sugar (powdered): 2½ cups or 11$^3/_7$ oz.
- Sugar (brown, fine): 3¾ cups or 1 lb. 4 oz.
- Lemon juice: 5 Tbsps. or 2½ oz.
- Salt: 1¼ tsps. or $^5/_{24}$ oz.
- Ginger (ground): 1¼ tsps.
- Almond extract: ⅝ tsp.
- Pastry: 5 baked flaky pie shells (No. 47)
- Heavy cream (whipped): 5 cups or 2½ lbs.
- Orange rind (grated): 5 Tbsps. or 1⅞ oz.
- Sugar (granulated): 1¼ cups or 10 oz.

Rinse and drain 3 cups of the prepared raspberries, reserving one cup for top garnishing. Crush slightly. To the stiffly beaten egg whites add combined powdered and brown sugar, lemon juice, salt, ground ginger, and almond extract. Now beat in the crushed raspberries until fluffy and spongy. Turn mixture into pre-baked 9-inch pastry shell, top with whipped cream to which has been added the orange rind and granulated sugar, and strew over the chilled, reserved whole raspberries. Serve very cold.

(327)   # A FEW FACTS ABOUT RHUBARB

Only the stems of rhubarb are used as stewed fruit, in pies and other desserts. The rhubarb leaves should never be eaten because they contain large amounts of oxalic acid. When the stalk seems too old, it is best to pour boiling water over the cut sections and allow to stand five minutes. Then pour off and cook at the lowest heat in order not to break the pieces. When cooking rhubarb, old or young, use as little water as possible, and when nearly done, add the sugar. This makes all the difference. It's rhubarb flavor you want, isn't it? And this is the way to get it all.

In cutting rhubarb use a very sharp knife to avoid stringing. It is not necessary to peel the fresh, young rhubarb. A good pointer about buying rhubarb is to select fresh-looking, thick stalks of bright coloring and buy by weight rather than by bunch, if possible. The bunches may vary in size because of the difference in length of stalks. Hot-house variety, or young rhubarb, is sold in 5-lb. boxes. There are 4 to 8 stalks to the pound. When rhubarb is cut into one-inch lengths, one pound will yield nearly a quart or four cups, which is enough for a 9-inch pie; when baked, one pound will yield 1 pint, or 5 generous portions. About half a cup of sugar is required per 12 oz. of rhubarb, depending on its tartness.

Rhubarb may be stored in a cool, dry place for a short time only. Or, it may be dried and kept indefinitely. When the dried rhubarb is soaked in water overnight it is almost as good as the fresh or canned fruit.

....

(328)   # RHUBARB BANANA PIE—
HOME METHOD
TWO-CRUST PIE

For one 9-inch pie
- Rhubarb (raw): 4 cups
- Salt: ¼ tsp.
- Nutmeg: ⅛ tsp.
- Sugar (granulated): ½ cup
- Sugar (brown): ⅓ cup
- Bananas (sliced): 2
- Pastry: For 1 two-crust pie

For five 9-inch pies
- Rhubarb (raw): 5 qts. or 5 lbs.
- Salt: 1¼ tsps. or $5/24$ oz.
- Nutmeg: ⅝ tsp.
- Sugar (granulated): 2½ cups or 1 lb. 4 oz.
- Sugar (brown): 1⅔ cups or $8 8/9$ oz.
- Bananas (sliced): 10 or 5 lbs.
- Pastry: For 5 two-crust pies

Wash rhubarb and cut in 1-inch pieces. Add salt, nutmeg, and sugars, which have been combined with sliced bananas. Line 9-inch pie pan with pastry rolled ⅛-inch thick; add fruit mixture and cover with top crust, making 3 or 4 slits for escape of steam; brush with milk. Bake in a very hot oven (450° F.) for 10 minutes; reduce temperature to 350° F. and continue baking for 25–30 minutes longer, depending on tenderness of rhubarb. Serve cold topped with plain whipped cream.

....

(329)

RHUBARB MERINGUE PIE— RHODE ISLAND METHOD
ONE-CRUST PIE

For one 9-inch pie
- Rhubarb (raw): 3 cups
- Egg yolks (well beaten): 3
- Sugar (granulated): 1 cup
- Flour (pastry): 2 Tbsps.
- Salt: ¼ tsp.
- Pastry: For 1 one-crust pie
- Egg whites (stiffly beaten): 3
- Sugar (granulated): 6 Tbsps.
- Angelica (chopped fine): 1 Tbsp.
- Almonds (shredded): ¼ cup

For five 9-inch pies
- Rhubarb (raw): 3¾ lbs.
- Egg yolks (well beaten): 15 or 15 oz.
- Sugar (granulated): 5 cups or 2½ lbs.
- Flour (pastry): ⅝ cup or 2½ oz.
- Salt: 1¼ tsps. or ⁵⁄₂₄ oz.
- Pastry: For 5 one-crust pies
- Egg whites (stiffly beaten): 15 or 15 oz.
- Sugar (granulated): 1⅞ cups or 15 oz.
- Angelica (chopped fine): 5 Tbsps. or 1⅞ oz.
- Almonds (shredded): 1¼ cups or 4 oz.

Wash rhubarb and cut in ½-inch pieces. Put in colander (unless using hothouse rhubarb), and pour boiling water over and let drain. Beat egg yolks; add combined flour and sugar and salt, which have been sifted together. Stir rhubarb into mixture and turn into 9-inch pie pan lined with pastry which has been thoroughly chilled. Bake in a moderate oven (350° F.) for 40–45 minutes. When cool, cover with a meringue made by adding sugar to stiffly beaten egg whites, angelica, and shredded almonds. Brown under low broiler heat (350° F.) for 1 to 2 minutes. Serve cold.

(330)

RHUBARB PIE I
TWO-CRUST PIE

For one 9-inch pie

- Rhubarb (raw): 1 qt. or 4 cups
- Sugar (granulated): 1 cup
- Flaky pastry: For 1 two-crust pie (No. 48)
- Drained juice from rhubarb: 3 Tbsps.
- Sugar (brown): 1/3 cup
- Corn syrup (light): 3 Tbsps.
- Salt: 1/4 tsp.

For five 9-inch pies

- Rhubarb (raw): 5 qts. or 5 lbs.
- Sugar (granulated): 5 cups or 2½ lbs.
- Flaky pastry: For 5 two-crust pies (No. 48)
- Drained juice from rhubarb: 1 cup or 7½ oz.
- Sugar (brown): 1²/₃ cups or 8⁸/₉ oz.
- Corn syrup (light): 1 cup or 11¼ oz.
- Salt: 1¼ tsps. or ⁵/₂₄ oz.

Wash rhubarb, drain and cut into ½-inch pieces; combine with granulated sugar and place mixture in a colander over a bowl. Allow to drain thoroughly about 2 hours. Have ready a 9-inch pie pan lined with long flaky pastry made as indicated for No. 48, and brushed with unbeaten egg white. Turn drained rhubarb pieces into the shell; which has been brushed with unbeaten egg white or butter, to prevent soaking of the crust. Have center of the pie higher than the edges, as during baking process the mixture has a tendency to shrink on account of the moisture of the fruit; cover with top crust in the usual way; make only one slash on the center of top crust; brush top crust with a mixture of water and molasses, and bake 10 minutes in a very hot oven (450° F.); reduce temperature to (350° F.) and continue baking 35 minutes longer. Remove the pie from the oven, and let stand 10 minutes before adding the following syrup through the hole made on the top of the pie. Into a saucepan, place the drained juice from the rhubarb and sugar, brown sugar, corn syrup, and salt. Stir until sugar is dissolved; let boil to the soft ball stage (240° F.) or until a drop in cold water flattens on removal. Remove from the heat and, using a funnel, pour about 1 cup through the hole on top of the pie. Let cool thoroughly before serving with plain whipped cream.

(331)

RHUBARB PIE II
TWO-CRUST PIE

For one 9-inch pie
- Rhubarb (canned, drained): 2½ cups or 1 #2½ can
- Drained rhubarb juice: 1 cup
- Sugar (granulated): ¾ cup
- Corn syrup (light): 2 Tbsps.
- Salt: ¼ tsp.
- Quick-cooking tapioca: 2½ Tbsps.
- Sugar (granulated): ⅓ cup
- Pastry: For 1 two-crust pie

For five 9-inch pies
- Rhubarb (canned, drained): 1 #10 can or 6 lbs. 1 oz.
- Drained rhubarb juice: 5 cups or 2½ lbs.
- Sugar (granulated): 3¾ cups or 1 lb. 14 oz.
- Corn syrup: (light): ⅝ cup or 7½ oz.
- Salt: 1¼ tsps. or $5/24$ oz.
- Quick-cooking tapioca: 12½ Tbsps. or 3¾ oz.
- Sugar (granulated): 1⅔ cups or 13⅓ oz.
- Pastry: For 5 two-crust pies

Turn canned rhubarb into a sieve, having a container underneath to receive the juice. There should be 1 cup juice; if not, add enough cold water to make up the difference. Place juice, sugar, corn syrup, and salt in a saucepan and stir well. Bring this to a rapid boil; then add combined tapioca and remaining granulated sugar; cook, stirring constantly, until mixture thickens. Let boil once briskly; remove from the heat and stir in, as gently as possible, the drained rhubarb. Turn mixture into a shallow pan or container and let cool thoroughly. When cold, turn into 9-inch pie pan lined with pastry; cover with top crust in the usual way; make several slits in top crust; brush with butter. Bake 10 minutes in a very hot oven (450° F.); reduce temperature to 350° F. and continue baking 35 minutes longer. Serve cold with either cheese or plain whipped cream.

(332)
RHUBARB PINEAPPLE PIE
TWO-CRUST PIE

Proceed as indicated for No. 331, Rhubarb Pie II, using only 2 cups of canned rhubarb, instead of 2½ cups, and combine drained rhubarb with 1 cup canned, crushed pineapple, also thoroughly drained, the juice mixed with that of the rhubarb to make the correct amount or weight.

....

(333)
RHUBARB PRUNE PIE
TWO-CRUST PIE

Proceed as indicated for No. 330, Rhubarb Pie I, using 3 cups of rhubarb and 1 cup of cooked, pitted prunes (cooked as indicated for No. 24, Dried Fruit Preparation). Serve cold, topped with whipped cream.

....

(334)
RHUBARB RAISIN PIE
TWO-CRUST PIE

Proceed as indicated for No. 330, Rhubarb Pie I, using 3 cups of fresh rhubarb and 1 cup of raisin filling made as indicated for No. 316, Raisin Pie I. Pour into 9-inch pie pan lined with pastry; cover with top crust in the usual way; make a few slits on top of crust for escape of steam and bake as indicated for Rhubarb Pie I, No. 330. Serve with whipped cream. A crisscross pie may be substituted for a two-crust pie, if desired; or a 9-inch pastry shell may be used with a meringue or Whipped Cream Topping.

(335)   RHUBARB AND STRAWBERRY PIE
TWO-CRUST PIE

For one 9-inch pie
- Rhubarb (raw): 2½ cups
- Sugar (granulated): ½ cup
- Salt: ¼ tsp.
- Quick-cooking tapioca: 2½ Tbsps.
- Lemon rind (grated): 1 tsp.
- Strawberries (fresh): 2 cups
- Pastry: For 1 two-crust pie

For five 9-inch pies
- Rhubarb (raw): 3¼ qts. or 3 lbs. 2 oz.
- Sugar (granulated): 2½ cups or 20 oz.
- Salt: 1¼ tsps. or $^4/_{24}$ oz.
- Quick-cooking tapioca: 12½ Tbsps. or 3¾ oz.
- Lemon rind (grated): 1$^2/_3$ Tbsps. or $^5/_8$ oz.
- Strawberries (fresh): 2½ qts. or 2 lbs. 13$^5/_7$ oz.
- Pastry: For 5 two-crust pies

Wash rhubarb; drain and cut into ¾-inch pieces. Mix sugar, salt, tapioca and lemon rind and combine with cut rhubarb. Let stand 10 minutes. Drain, then add strawberries. Line 9-inch pie pan with pastry; turn in the fruit mixture; cover with top crust in the usual way, making a few slits on top and brush with water mixed with a little molasses. Bake 10 minutes in a very hot oven (450° F.); reduce temperature to 350° F. and continue baking for 30–35 minutes longer, depending on tenderness of rhubarb. Serve cold with plain whipped cream.

NOTE: A crisscross pie or one-shell pie may be used in the same way, using the same amount of ingredients. You may top the one-crust pie with either a meringue or whipped cream topping, if desired.

(336)
RICE AND DRIED PEACH
MERINGUE PIE—CAMPER'S METHOD
ONE-CRUST PIE

For one 9-inch pie
- Egg yolks (well beaten): 4
- Milk (cold, rich): Enough to beat egg yolks light and frothy
- Cornstarch: 2 Tbsps.
- Milk (cold): 2 Tbsps.
- Peaches (dried, cooked, sieved, rather thick and cold): ¼ cup
- Rice (cooked): 1½ cups
- Butter (melted): 2 Tbsps.
- Salt: ¼ tsp.
- Vanilla extract: ¾ tsp.
- Almond extract: ¼ tsp.
- Egg whites (stiffly beaten): 4
- Salt: ⅛ tsp.
- Sugar (granulated): 6 Tbsps.

For five 9-inch pies
- Egg yolks (well beaten): 20 or 1¼ lbs.
- Milk (cold, rich): Enough to beat egg yolks light and frothy
- Cornstarch: ⅝ cup or 3⅓ oz.
- Milk (cold): 10 Tbsps. or ⅝ cup or 5 oz.
- Peaches (dried, cooked, sieved, rather thick and cold): 1¼ cups or 6⅔ oz.
- Rice (cooked): 7½ cups or 2¾ lbs.
- Butter (melted): ⅝ cup or 5 oz.
- Salt: 1¼ tsps. or ⁵/₂₄ oz.
- Vanilla extract: 1 Tbsp. plus ¾ tsp. or ⅝ oz.
- Almond extract: 1¼ tsps. or ⁵/₂₄ oz.
- Egg whites (stiffly beaten): 20 or 1¼ lbs.
- Salt: ⅝ tsp.
- Sugar (granulated): 1⅞ cups or 15 oz.

Beat egg yolks until thick and lemon-colored; then add enough cold rich milk to beat light and frothy. Dissolve cornstarch in remaining cold milk and gradually beat cornstarch into egg yolk-milk mixture, alternately with cold, cooked, sieved dried peaches, and add the rice, butter, salt, vanilla and almond extract. Blend thoroughly, adding a little more cold milk if batter seems too dry. Line a 9-inch pie pan with pastry, brush bottom and sides with melted butter, then sprinkle with a very little flour. Turn filling into pastry shell and bake 30–35 minutes in a hot oven (425° F.). Allow to cool a little, then top pie with a meringue made with stiffly beaten egg whites to which have been added the combined salt and sugar; bake 15 minutes in a moderately slow oven (325° F.). Serve cold.

(337) RICE AND DRIED APPLES MERINGUE PIE
ONE-CRUST PIE

Proceed as directed for No. 336, Rice and Dried Peach Meringue Pie, substituting cooked, dried, sieved apples. Should you desire a crunchy pie, reduce amount of rice to half and add ½ cup of finely chopped nut meats (any kind). You may brush bottom and sides of unbaked pastry shell with currant jelly, orange marmalade, or any other kind of jam desired.

....

(338) RICE AND DRIED APRICOT MERINGUE PIE
ONE-CRUST PIE

Proceed as directed for Rice and Dried Peach Meringue Pie, No. 336, substituting cooked, cold, sieved apricots for peaches.

....

(339) SHERRY CREAM PIE—FRENCH METHOD
ONE-CRUST PIE, PRE-BAKED PIE SHELL

For one 9-inch pie
- Pastry flour (sifted): ¼ cup
- Water (cold): 3 Tbsps.
- Salt: ⅛ tsp.
- Sugar (granulated): 1 cup
- Sherry: 3 Tbsps.
- Water (hot): 1½ cups
- Butter: 1 Tbsp.
- Pastry: 1 baked flaky pie shell, No. 47
- Apricot Cream Topping No. 450
- Strawberries (whole): 1 cup

For five 9-inch pies
- Pastry flour (sifted): 1¼ cups or 5 oz.
- Water (cold): scant cup or 7½ oz.
- Salt: ⅝ tsp.
- Sugar (granulated): 5 cups or 2½ lbs.
- Sherry: 1 cup or 7½ oz. (about)
- Water (hot): 7½ cups or 3¾ lbs.
- Butter: 5 Tbsps. or 2½ oz.
- Pastry: 5 baked flaky pie shells No. 47
- Apricot Cream Topping No. 450
- Strawberries (whole): 5 cups or 1 lb. 4 oz.

Stir pastry flour, cold water, and salt together until smooth; add sugar, sherry wine, and hot water, and stir until sugar is dissolved and mixture is smooth. Cook over hot water until thick and smooth, stirring constantly; let cook 3 or 5 minutes longer, stirring occasionally. Remove from hot water and stir in butter. Cool. When cold, turn filling into pre-baked 9-inch pastry shell, top with Apricot Cream, No. 450, and garnish with strawberries prepared as follows: Marinate equal-sized fresh or frozen strawberries (thawed) in good sherry for 30 minutes; then, before placing on top of whipped cream, dip each individual berry, which has been stemmed, in brown sugar.

....

(340)

SHOO-FLY PIE—
PENNSYLVANIA METHOD
ONE-CRUST PIE

For one 9-inch pie
- Flour (pastry): 1 cup
- Cinnamon (ground): ½ tsp.
- Salt: ¼ tsp.
- Sugar (dark brown): ½ cup
- Butter: 2 Tbsps.
- Molasses (dark): ½ cup
- Boiling water: ½ cup
- Baking soda: ¼ tsp.
- Pastry: For 1 one-crust pie

For five 9-inch pies
- Flour (pastry): 5 cups or 1¼ qts. or 1¼ lbs.
- Cinnamon (ground): 2½ tsps. or $5/24$ oz.
- Salt: 1¼ tsps. or $5/24$ oz.
- Sugar (dark brown): 2½ cups or $13^1/3$ oz.
- Butter: $5/8$ cup or 5 oz.
- Molasses (dark): 2½ cups or $1^7/8$ lbs.
- Boiling water: 2½ cups or 1¼ lbs.
- Baking Soda: 1¼ tsps.
- Pastry: For 5 one-crust pies

Sift flour once and mix with cinnamon, salt and sugar. Cut in butter. In another mixing bowl combine molasses and boiling water; add baking soda and blend thoroughly. Turn molasses mixture into 9-inch unbaked pastry shell; sprinkle flour and sugar mixture over the top and bake in a very hot oven (450° F.) for ten minutes; reduce temperature to 350° F. and continue baking for 20–25 minutes longer, or until top is firm.

(341)   SOUR CREAM DATE PIE—
HOME METHOD
ONE-CRUST PIE

For one 9-inch pie
- Whole egg (well beaten): 1
- Egg yolk (well beaten): 1
- Sugar (granulated): 1 cup
- Salt: ¼ tsp.
- Ginger (ground): ⅛ tsp.
- Evaporated milk (undiluted): 1½ cups
- Lemon juice: 2½ Tbsps.
- Lemon rind (grated): 1 tsp.
- Dates (pitted, chopped): 1½ cups
- Rich pastry: For 1 one-crust pie (No. 70)

For five 9-inch pies
- Whole eggs (well beaten): 5 or 10 oz.
- Egg yolks (well beaten): 5 or 5 oz.
- Sugar (granulated): 5 cups or 2½ lbs.
- Salt: 1¼ tsps. or ⁵/₂₄ oz.
- Ginger (ground): ⅝ tsp.
- Evaporated milk (undiluted): 7½ cups or 3¾ lbs.
- Lemon juice: ¾ cup plus ½ Tbsp. or 6¼ oz.
- Lemon rind (grated): 1⅔ Tbsps. or ⅝ oz.
- Dates (pitted, chopped): 7½ cups or 2 lbs. 13 oz.
- Rich pastry: For 5 one-crust pies (No. 70)

Beat whole egg and egg yolk together until fluffy; gradually add sugar, beating briskly after each addition; adding salt and ground ginger and mix well. Stir in the undiluted evaporated milk, to which has been added and thoroughly blended the lemon juice and lemon rind. Lastly stir in the pitted and chopped dates. Turn mixture into 9-inch pie pan lined with rich pastry, the bottom and sides of which have been brushed with softened butter, then sprinkled with a little flour. Bake 10 minutes in a hot oven (450° F.); reduce temperature to 350° F. and continue baking 25–30 minutes longer. When cold, top with sweetened and flavored whipped cream. Serve very cold.

NOTE: In this Sour Cream Date Pie, no sour cream is used, but you can have sour "cream" instantly by mixing lemon juice with undiluted evaporated milk— the lemon juice gives a pleasingly tangy flavor that is perfect with the mellow-sweetness of dates. The evaporated milk provides a rich creaminess of flavor and color and makes the filling superbly smooth, so that it sets beautifully.

(342)   SOUR CREAM FIG MERINGUE PIE— CALIFORNIA METHOD
ONE-CRUST PIE

For one 9-inch pie
- Figs (dried): 1 cup
- Sugar (brown): 1 cup
- Salt: 1/8 tsp.
- Quick-cooking tapioca: 1 Tbsp.
- Cinnamon (ground): 1/2 tsp.
- Ginger (ground): 1/2 tsp.
- Sour cream: 1 cup
- Egg yolks (well beaten): 2
- Pastry: For 1 one-crust pie
- Meringue or whipped cream topping

For five 9-inch pies
- Figs (dried): 5 cups or 1 lb. 10²/₃ oz.
- Sugar (brown): 1 cup or 1 lb. 10²/₃ oz.
- Salt: 5/8 tsp.
- Quick-cooking tapioca: 5 Tbsps. or 1¼ oz.
- Cinnamon (ground): 2½ tsps. or 5/24 oz.
- Ginger (ground): 2½ tsps. or 5/24 oz.
- Sour cream: 5 cups or 2 lbs. 9⅞ oz.
- Egg yolks (well beaten): 10 or 10 oz.
- Pastry: For 5 one-crust pies
- Meringue or whipped cream topping

Pour boiling water over dried figs, cover and let stand for 5 long minutes. Drain, clip stems and put through food chopper, using medium blade. Combine sugar, salt, tapioca and spices; mix in chopped figs and blend with sour cream and egg yolks. Pour into pastry-lined 9-inch pie pan and bake in a hot oven (400° F.) 30 to 35 minutes. If topping with meringue, bake 10 minutes longer at same temperature. If topping with whipped cream, after the pie is thoroughly cooled, you may garnish the cream with pecan or walnut halves, brushed with syrup, or molasses.

NOTE: If no sour cream is available you can turn the sweet cream into sour quite easily and effectively. Simply add 1 tablespoon vinegar to each cup of sweet cream. Proceed to use in the same way as regular sour cream.

SOUR CREAM PECAN PIE— KENTUCKY METHOD
ONE-CRUST PIE

(343)

For one 9-inch pie
- Pastry: For 1 one-crust pie
- Pecans or walnuts (broken): ¾ cup
- Egg yolks (well beaten): 2
- Sugar (granulated): ½ cup
- Sugar (brown): ½ cup
- Sour cream (heavy): 1 cup
- Flour (pastry): 1 tsp.
- Salt: ¼ tsp.
- Lemon rind (grated): 1 tsp. or ⅛ oz.
- Cinnamon (ground): ¼ tsp.
- Cloves (ground): ¼ tsp.

For five 9-inch pies
- Pastry: For 5 one-crust pies
- Pecans or walnuts (broken): 3¾ cups or 15 oz.
- Egg yolks (well beaten): 10 or 10 oz.
- Sugar (granulated): 2½ cups or 1¼ lbs.
- Sugar (brown): 2½ cups or 13⅓ oz.
- Sour cream (heavy): 5 cups or 2 lbs. 9⅔ oz.
- Flour (pastry): 1⅔ Tbsps. or $^{5}/_{12}$ oz.
- Salt: 1¼ tsps. or $^{5}/_{24}$ oz.
- Lemon rind (grated): 1⅔ Tbsps. or ⅝ oz.
- Cinnamon (ground): 1¼ tsps.
- Cloves (ground): 1¼ tsps.

Line 9-inch pie pan with pastry rolled ⅛-inch thick; cover with broken pecans or walnuts. Beat egg yolks until very light and lemon-colored; add combined sugars alternately with heavy sour cream, mixed with flour, salt, spices and lemon rind. Blend well. Turn filling into pastry shell gently, so as not to disturb the nut meats, and bake in slow oven (300° F.) for 40 minutes, or until filling is firm in center. Serve cold with or without plain whipped cream.

NOTE: Walnuts may be substituted for Pecans.

(344) SOUR CREAM PRUNE MERINGUE PIE
ONE-CRUST PIE

For one 9-inch pie

- Prunes (cooked, drained, chopped): 1 cup
- Egg yolks (well beaten): 4
- Sour cream: 1½ cups
- Sugar (granulated): ½ cup
- Salt: ¼ tsp.
- Nutmeg (ground): ¼ tsp.
- Cinnamon (ground): 1 tsp.
- Pastry: For 1 one-crust pie
- Egg whites (stiffly beaten): 3
- Salt: ⅛ tsp.
- Sugar (granulated): 6 Tbsps.
- Ginger (ground): ⅛ tsp.
- Lemon rind (grated): ½ tsp.

For five 9-inch pies

- Prunes (cooked, drained, chopped): 5 cups or 1¼ qts. or 1¼ lbs.
- Egg yolks (well beaten): 20 or 1¼ lbs.
- Sour cream: 7½ cups or 3¾ lbs.
- Sugar (granulated): 2½ cups or 1¼ lbs.
- Salt: 1¼ tsps. or $5/24$ oz.
- Nutmeg (ground): 1¼ tsps.
- Cinnamon (ground): $1^2/3$ Tbsp. or $5/12$ oz.
- Pastry: For 5 one-crust pies
- Egg whites (stiffly beaten): 15 or 15 oz.
- Salt: ⅝ tsp.
- Sugar (granulated): $1^7/8$ cups or 15 oz.
- Ginger (ground): ⅝ tsp.
- Lemon rind (grated): 2½ tsps. or $5/16$ oz.

Cook dried prunes in the usual way until tender (see No. 24, Dried Fruit Preparation); drain thoroughly, pit and chop. Beat egg yolks and add to sour cream; mix well. Combine first amount of sugar with salt, nutmeg and cinnamon and stir into egg yolks. Lastly stir in chopped prunes. Line 9-inch pie pan with rich pastry and pinch with finger to make a fancy edge. Pour mixture into pastry shell and bake 10 minutes in a hot oven (450° F.); reduce temperature to 325° F. and continue baking 25–30 minutes longer. Top with meringue made with stiffly beaten egg whites, salt, remaining sugar, ginger, and lemon rind in the usual way, and bake 15 minutes in a moderately slow oven (325° F.). Serve cold.

(345)   # SOUR CREAM RAISIN PIE—
                # HOME METHOD
                ### ONE-CRUST PIE

For one 9-inch pie

- Pastry: For 1 one-crust pie
- Egg yolks (slightly beaten): 3
- Sour cream (heavy): 1 cup
- Sugar (brown): 1 cup
- Raisins (seedless, chopped): 1 cup
- Cinnamon (ground): ¾ tsp.
- Cloves (ground): ¼ tsp.
- Salt: ¼ tsp.

For five 9-inch pies

- Pastry: For 5 one-crust pies
- Egg yolks (slightly beaten): 15 or 15 oz.
- Sour cream (heavy): 5 cups or 2 lbs. 9⅞ oz.
- Sugar (brown): 5 cups or 1 lb. 10⅔ oz.
- Raisins (seedless, chopped): 5 cups or 1 lb. 10⅔ oz.
- Cinnamon (ground): 3¾ tsps. or ⁵/₁₆ oz.
- Cloves (ground): 1¼ tsps.
- Salt: 1¼ tsps. or ⁵/₂₄ oz.

Line 9-inch pie pan with pastry rolled ⅛-inch thick, allowing ½ inch on edge of pan for a frill. Turn crust under and make a frill with thumb and forefinger or press with tines of fork. Brush bottom and sides of pastry with slightly beaten egg white; set in refrigerator to dry. Mix slightly beaten egg yolks with cream, sugar, chopped seedless raisins, spices, and salt. Blend thoroughly, then turn into pastry shell and bake 10 minutes in a very hot oven (450° F.); reduce temperature to 350° F. and continue baking 30 minutes longer, or until filling is delicately brown and firm. Serve cold. Or top with a meringue, return to moderately slow oven (325° F.) for 15 minutes, or until meringue is delicately brown.

Variation: Substitute ½ cup of broken nut meats (any kind) for ½ cup of raisins, and add ½ tsp. of vanilla extract.

(346)

SPICE MERINGUE PIE—
ALABAMA METHOD
ONE-CRUST PIE, PRE-BAKED PIE SHELL

For one 9-inch pie

- Sugar (fine granulated): ⅞ cup
- Cornstarch: ½ cup
- Salt: ¼ tsp.
- Water (boiling): 2 cups
- Egg yolks (well beaten): 3
- Cloves (ground): ½ tsp.
- Allspice (ground): ¼ tsp.
- Cinnamon (ground): ⅛ tsp.
- Nutmeg (ground): 1/16 tsp.
- Ginger (ground): A few grains
- Butter: 1½ tsp.
- Hot Water Pastry (No. 50): For 1 one-crust pie
- Egg whites (stiffly beaten): 3
- Sugar (granulated): 6 Tbsps.
- Almond extract: ⅛ tsp.

For five 9-inch pies

- Sugar (fine granulated): 4⅜ cups or 2 lbs. 1 oz.
- Cornstarch: 2½ cups or 13½ oz.
- Salt: 1¼ tsps. or 5/24 oz.
- Water (boiling): 2½ qts. or 5 lbs.
- Egg yolks (well beaten): 15 or 15 oz.
- Cloves (ground): 2½ tsps. or 5/24 oz.
- Allspice (ground): 1¼ tsps.
- Cinnamon (ground): ⅝ tsp.
- Nutmeg (ground): 5/16 tsp.
- Ginger (ground): a few grains
- Butter: 2½ Tbsps. or 1¼ oz.
- Hot Water Pastry (No. 50): For 5 one- crust pies
- Egg whites (stiffly beaten): 15 or 15 oz.
- Sugar (granulated): 1⅞ cups or 15 oz.
- Almond extract: ⅝ tsp.

Sift together fine granulated sugar, cornstarch, and salt. Stir in the boiling water and bring mixture to a boil, stirring constantly until thick and clear; let boil 2 or 3 times. Remove from the heat and gradually pour over the well-beaten egg yolks, stirring briskly. Return to the heat and boil once, stirring briskly. Remove at once from the heat, set in a pan of cold water, and when lukewarm, add combined spices and butter. Beat thoroughly. Turn filling into pre-baked 9-inch pastry shell and top with a meringue made with egg whites, remaining sugar, and almond extract. Bake 15 minutes in a moderately slow oven (325° F.), or until meringue is delicately brown.

(347)   # A FEW FACTS ABOUT SQUASH

All the methods of preparation of pumpkin may be adapted to the squash, and in piemaking it is wise after the squash is sieved or strained, or the canned squash is taken from the can, to place it in a heavy frying pan which has been well oiled or buttered. Stew down slowly over a very low flame, stirring often. Do this until every bit of moisture is out of the squash and it turns a little dark in color. The quantity diminishes by about one-half, but it is all squash and will absorb milk or cream in place of the missing water. The result will be worth a little extra time.

Squash is delicious served in pies. An interesting French recipe is a pie made by cutting through the side of the squash, extracting the seeds and filament, stuffing the cavity with cut and sliced apples and spices, baking it whole and serving it on a platter with heavy, fresh cream. For this recipe, which is a novelty and has never been published, here is how to proceed:

(348)   # SQUASH PIE—FRENCH METHOD

Take a large or as many small individual squashes as needed, preferably the bush scallops or patty pans, those disk-shaped with a scalloped edge, using either the white or yellow skinned variety. Wash carefully, sponge dry. Do not remove the blossom end, but cut it even with a sharp knife. Cut the top with a sharp knife, reserving it for a cover. Remove seeds and pulp, being careful not to break the walls. Select your favorite apple filling in this book. Brush the inside of the squash with butter, then sprinkle with flour. Fill the cavity with the chosen filling; dot generously with butter; replace the cut top, which has been brushed with butter, and bake in a slow oven (300° F.) for about 25–30 minutes, time depending on size of squash. Should the top brown too quickly, brush with butter or cover with buttered waxed paper.

(349)

SQUASH PIE DE LUXE— FRENCH METHOD
ONE-CRUST PIE

For one 9-inch pie

- Rich pastry: For 1 one-crust pie (No. 70)
- Egg white (slightly beaten): ½
- Macaroon crumbs (sieved): ¼ cup
- Squash (canned or cooked, sieved): 1 cup
- Heavy cream: 1 cup
- Sugar (light brown): ¾ cup
- Whole eggs (slightly beaten): 3
- Vanilla extract: ¾ tsp.
- Salt: ¼ tsp.
- Ginger (ground): ½ tsp.
- Nutmeg (ground): ¼ tsp.
- Mace (ground): ¼ tsp.
- Strained honey: ¼ cup
- Bread crumbs (sieved): ⅓ cup
- Salt: ⅛ tsp.
- Heavy cream (whipped): 1 cup

For five 9-inch pies

- Rich pastry: For 5 one-crust pies (No. 70)
- Egg white (slightly beaten): 2½ or 2½ oz.
- Macaroon crumbs (sieved): 1¼ cups or 5 oz.
- Squash (canned or cooked, sieved): 5 cups or 4 lbs. 1 oz.
- Heavy cream: 5 cups or 2 lbs. 9½ oz.
- Sugar (light brown): 3¾ cups or 1 lb. 5 oz.
- Whole eggs (slightly beaten): 15 or 1 lb. 14 oz.
- Vanilla extract: 3¾ tsps. or ⅝ oz.
- Salt: 1¼ tsps. or $^5/_{24}$ oz.
- Ginger (ground): 2⅔ Tbsps. or $^5/_{24}$ oz.
- Nutmeg (ground): 1¼ tsps.
- Mace (ground): 1¼ tsps.
- Strained honey: 1¼ cups or 15 oz.
- Bread crumbs (sieved): 1⅔ cups or 6⅔ oz.
- Salt: ⅝ tsp.
- Heavy cream (whippd): 5 cups or 2 lbs. 10 oz.

Line 9-inch pie pan with rich pastry and crimp edges. Brush bottom and sides with slightly beaten egg white, then sprinkle with sieved macaroon crumbs. Combine canned or freshly cooked squash (cold) with unwhipped cream and brown sugar. Beat slightly whole eggs and add to squash mixture. Combine vanilla, salt, and spices and blend with squash mixture, mixing thoroughly. Turn filling into pastry shell; bake 10 minutes in a hot oven (450° F.); reduce temperature to 350° F. and continue baking 30 minutes longer, or until center is firm. Cool. Spread pie filling with strained honey, using a wet spatula; and over the honey sprinkle sieved bread crumbs and salt as quickly as possible; cover the entire surface of the pie top with unsweetened, unflavored whipped cream, forced through a pastry bag with a fancy tube. Serve cold.

....

(350)

SQUASH RAISIN PIE—
SOUTHERN METHOD
ONE-CRUST PIE

For one 9-inch pie
- Squash (sieved): 2 cups
- Butter: 1½ Tbsps.
- Whole eggs (well beaten): 4
- Sugar (brown): ¾ cup
- Salt: ¼ tsp.
- Cinnamon (ground): 1 tsp.
- Cloves (ground): 1 tsp.
- Allspice (ground): ½ tsp.
- Raisins (parboiled, cooled): ½ cup
- Rich pastry: For 1 one-crust pie (No. 70)
- Whipped cream (plain): 1 cup

For five 9-inch pies
- Squash (sieved): 10 cups or 2½ qts. or 8 lbs. 2 oz.
- Butter: 7½ Tbsps. or 3¾ oz.
- Whole eggs (well beaten): 20 or 2½ lbs.
- Sugar (brown): 3¾ cups or 1¼ lbs.
- Salt: 1¼ tsps. or $5/24$ oz.
- Cinnamon (ground): $1 2/3$ Tbsps. or $5/12$ oz.
- Cloves (ground): $1 2/3$ Tbsps. or $5/12$ oz.
- Allspice (ground): 2½ tsps. or $5/24$ oz.
- Raisins (parboiled, cooled): 2½ cups or $13 1/3$ oz.
- Rich pastry: For 5 one-crust pies (No. 70)
- Whipped cream (plain): 5 cups or 1¼ qts. or 2½ lbs.

Simmer sieved squash until dry enough to stick together; add all the remaining ingredients in order given, except whipped cream. Turn filling into unbaked 9-inch pastry shell and bake 10 minutes in a hot oven (450° F.); reduce temperature to 350° F. and continue baking 25–30 minutes longer, or until center of filling is firm. Cool. Top with plain whipped cream. Serve very cold.

NOTE: If a crunchy squash pie is desired, substitute ½ cup chopped nuts, or use ¼ cup seedless raisins and ¼ cup chopped nuts, or ¼ cup nuts and ½ cup shredded coconut.

....

(351)   A FEW FACTS ABOUT STRAWBERRIES

Strawberries without caps should be carefully examined. They may have been roughly handled, or they may be over-mature. Such berries are likely to break down rapidly and are a wasteful buy. Conspicuous green or white tips are indicative of lack of flavor. Avoid sand; it is difficult to remove. Juice stains on surface of berries or on box may indicate over-ripeness or decay. Decay is easily detected through presence of mold on surface of berries. It may be found anywhere in container and is not always evident in top layer. Medium to large berries are best for eating raw. Medium-sized, tart flavored are best for canning and jam-making.

(352)
STRAWBERRY ANGEL PIE—
HOME METHOD
ONE-CRUST PIE

NOTE: Almost any kind of berry may be substituted for strawberries, such as raspberries, loganberries, blackberries, gooseberries, cherries (when pitted) either fresh, canned or frozen. The latter should be thawed.

For one 9-inch pie
- Pastry: For 1 one-crust pie
- Egg whites (stiffly beaten): 4
- Sugar (granulated): ½ cup
- Cream of tartar: ½ tsp.
- Salt: ⅛ tsp.
- Strawberries (quartered): 2 cups

For five 9-inch pies
- Pastry: For 5 one-crust pies
- Egg whites (stiffly beaten): 20 or 1 lb. 4 oz.
- Sugar (granulated): 2½ cups or 1 lb. 4 oz.
- Cream of tartar: 2½ tsps. or ⁵/₁₆ oz.
- Salt: ⅝ tsp.
- Strawberries (quartered): 2½ qts. or 2 lbs. 13⁵/₇ oz.

Line 9-inch pie pan with pastry and flute edges; bake 10 minutes in a very hot oven (450° F.) to set the crust, placing a small plate in bottom of pie to weight crust. While crust is baking, beat egg whites very stiff, beat in half of the sugar, cream of tartar and salt; then fold in the remaining sugar, alternately with the quartered, fresh, or frozen ripe strawberries. As soon as the pie crust is ready, remove from the oven, turn in the filling; return pie to the oven, having reduced temperature to 350° F., and continue baking 15 minutes longer, or until the top is brown as desired.

(353)   # STRAWBERRY ANGEL PIE DE LUXE
ONE-CRUST PIE, PRE-BAKED PASTRY SHELL

For one 9-inch pie

- Strawberries (fresh, canned or frozen): 2 cups
- Sugar (granulated): 1 cup
- Juice from the berries: about 1 cup
- Water (cold): 1½ cups
- Cornstarch: 3½ Tbsps.
- Salt: ⅛ tsp.
- Brandy, apple brandy or rum: 3 Tbsps.
- Sugar (powdered): 2 Tbsps.
- Egg whites (stiffly beaten): 4
- Pastry: 1 baked pie shell
- Heavy cream (whipped): 1 cup
- Coconut (shredded): ¼ cup

For five 9-inch pies

- Strawberries (fresh, canned or frozen): 2½ qts. or 2 lbs. 13⁵/₇ oz.
- Sugar (granulated): 5 cups or 2½ lbs.
- Juice from the berries: about 5 cups or 2½ lbs.
- Water (cold): 7½ cups or 3¾ lbs.
- Cornstarch: generous ¾ cup or 4¹/₆ oz.
- Salt: ⅝ tsp.
- Brandy, apple brandy or rum: 1 scant cup or 7½ oz.
- Sugar (powdered): ⅝ cup, or 3⅓ oz.
- Egg whites (stiffly beaten): 20 or 1 lb. 4 oz.
- Pastry: 5 baked pie shells
- Heavy cream (whipped): 5 cups or 2 lbs. 9⅞ oz.
- Coconut (shredded): 1¼ cups or 4 oz.

Crush the berries with the ½ cup granulated sugar in a mixing bowl. Let stand for one hour to allow the juice to draw. Drain off the juice (there should be 1 cup or thereabout) into a saucepan; add 1 cup of the cold water and the remaining granulated sugar. Stir well until sugar is dissolved. Bring this to a boil and when boiling, stir in the cornstarch and salt, mixed and dissolved with remaining cold water, stirring constantly until mixture thickens. Remove from the heat; cool. When cold, add the drained berry pulp and brandy. Blend thoroughly. Fold powdered sugar into the stiffly beaten egg whites, and fold in the strawberry mixture. Turn into pre-baked 9-inch pastry shell; cover with whipped cream forced through a pastry bag with a square tube, and sprinkle with coconut. Chill thoroughly (about 3 hours) before serving.

(354)   # STRAWBERRY CREAM CHEESE PIE—
PENNSYLVANIA METHOD
ONE-CRUST PIE, PRE-BAKED PASTRY SHELL

For one 9-inch pie
- Cream cheese: 1 (3-oz.) pkg.
- Heavy cream: 3 Tbsps.
- Pastry: 1 baked pie shell
- Strawberries (fresh or frozen): 1 qt.
- Sugar (granulated): ¾ cup
- Cornstarch: 2 Tbsps.
- Pineapple juice: (canned)
- Heavy cream: ⅓ cup
- Sugar (brown): 2 Tbsps.
- Vanilla extract: ⅛ tsp.

For five 9-inch pies
- Cream cheese: 5 (3-oz.) pkgs.
- Heavy cream: 1 cup or 7¹³/₁₆ oz.
- Pastry: 5 baked pie shells
- Strawberries (fresh or frozen): 5 qts. or 5 lbs. 11³/₇ oz.
- Sugar (granulated): 3¾ cups or 1 lb. 14 oz.
- Cornstarch: ⅝ cup or 3⅓ oz.
- Pineapple juice: (canned)
- Heavy cream: 1⅔ cups or 14⅙ oz.
- Sugar (brown): ⅝ cup or 3⅓ oz.
- Vanilla extract: ⅝ tsp.

Blend half the cream cheese with first amount of heavy cream until soft and smooth. With a spatula spread the cheese mixture over the bottom of pre-baked chilled pastry shell. Return to refrigerator and chill. Wash, hull strawberries. Select the largest and nicest ones to equal 1 pint. Slice them. Keep in refrigerator. Mash the remaining pint of berries, add granulated sugar and let stand for 1 hour. Force the mashed berries through a sieve until all liquid is extracted. Mix the thick juice and cornstarch to a smooth mixture and add enough pineapple juice to make 1½ cups of liquid. Cook this mixture over moderate heat until smooth, thick, and transparent, stirring constantly. When thick, remove from the heat and cool. Pour half of it over the cream cheese in the pie shell. Arrange the sliced strawberries in the sauce; pour the remaining sauce over the sliced berries and chill thoroughly. Top with remaining cream cheese, heavy cream, brown sugar and vanilla extract, mixed smooth and forced through a pastry bag with a square tube.

(355) STRAWBERRY CREAM PIE CHANTILLY— PARISIAN METHOD
TWO-CRUST PIE

For one 9-inch pie
- Semi-puff pastry: For 2 pie shells (No. 66)
- Strawberries (fresh or frozen): 1 qt.
- Sugar (powdered): ½ cup
- Heavy cream: 1 cup
- Salt: ⅛ tsp.
- Vanilla extract: ½ tsp.

For five 9-inch pies
- Semi-puff pastry: For 10 pie shells (No. 66)
- Strawberries (fresh or frozen): 5 qts. or 5 lbs. 11³/₇ oz.
- Sugar (powdered): 2½ cups or 11³/₇ oz.
- Heavy cream: 5 cups or 2½ lbs.
- Salt: ⅝ tsp.
- Vanilla extract: 2½ tsps. or ⁵/₁₂ oz.

Line 9-inch pie pan with pastry rolled ⅛-inch thick. Cut a 9-inch circle from another sheet of pastry, using a pie pan as a guide. Bake both pastry shell and pastry circle in a hot oven (450° F.) for 15 minutes. Cool thoroughly (not in refrigerator). Wash, hull, and pick over strawberries. Cut in halves; sprinkle berries with powdered sugar and toss so as to cover berries with sugar. Whip heavy cream with salt and vanilla extract. Combine halved, sweetened berries and whipped cream; place half of berry-cream mixture in bottom of pre-baked, cooled 9-inch pastry shell. Top with pre-baked 9-inch pastry circle, and top this circle with remaining berry-cream. Decorate or garnish edges with rosettes of plain whipped cream, forced through pastry bag with a small fancy tube.

Variation: You may spread any kind of jam, jelly or marmalade in bottom of pre-baked pastry shell before filling it, or you may use half of the berries, halved, for bottom and whole berries for top. For more variations, see No. 323, Raspberry, Strawberry Cream Pie Chantilly.

(356)
STRAWBERRY CREAM PIE—
HOME METHOD
ONE-CRUST PIE, PRE-BAKED PASTRY SHELL

For one 9-inch pie
- Sugar (granulated): 1 cup
- Water (cold): 1 cup
- Strawberries (fresh or frozen): 1 cup
- Cornstarch: 1 Tbsp.
- Salt: ⅛ tsp.
- Water (cold): 3 Tbsps.
- Strawberries (fresh or frozen): 1 cup
- Heavy cream (whipped): 1 cup
- Lemon rind (grated): 1 tsp. (optional)
- Pastry: 1 baked pie shell

For five 9-inch pies
- Sugar (granulated): 5 cups or 2½ lbs.
- Water (cold): 5 cups or 2½ lbs.
- Strawberries (fresh or frozen): 5 cups or 1 lb. 6⁶/₇ oz.
- Cornstarch: 5 Tbsps. or 1⅔ oz.
- Salt: ⅝ tsp.
- Water (cold): 1 cup or 7½ oz.
- Strawberries (fresh or frozen): 5 cups or 1 lb. 6⁶/₇ oz.
- Heavy cream (whipped): 5 cups or 13⅓ oz.
- Lemon rind (grated): 1⅔ Tbsps. or ⅝ oz. (optional)
- Pastry: 5 baked pie shells

Stir sugar and water together until sugar is dissolved; add the first cup of berries; cook 10 short minutes, or until berries are soft. Strain into a saucepan. To the syrup, add the cornstarch mixed to a paste with the salt and cold water; return to the heat and stir until thickened. Add the remaining whole, uncooked berries; blend well and cool. Spread half of the whipped cream, to which has been added the lemon rind, over the bottom of the cold pre-baked pastry shell. Pour the cold filling on top of the cream, spreading evenly so that no cream shows; and top with remaining whipped cream, using a pastry bag with a square tube. Chill thoroughly before serving

(357)   # STRAWBERRY JAM PIE
ONE-CRUST PIE, PRE-BAKED PASTRY SHELL

For one 9-inch pie
- Strawberry jam: 1 cup
- Sour Cream (heavy): 1 cup
- Sugar (granulated): ½ cup (more or less)
- Egg yolks (well beaten): 4
- Flour (pastry): 2 Tbsps.
- Vanilla extract: ½ tsp.
- Meringue Topping, No. 451, or
- Glazed Strawberry Topping, No. 465

For five 9-inch pies
- Strawberry jam: 5 cups or 3¾ lbs.
- Sour cream (heavy): 5 cups or 2 lbs. 9⅞ oz.
- Sugar (granulated): 2½ cups (more or less) or 1 lb. 4 oz.
- Egg yolks (well beaten): 20 or 1 lb. 4 oz.
- Flour (pastry): ⅝ cup or 2½ oz.
- Vanilla extract: 2½ tsps. or ⁵/₁₂ oz.
- Meringue Topping, No. 451, or
- Glazed Strawberry Topping, No. 465

Combine jam, sour cream, and sugar and bring to the boiling point, stirring occasionally. When boiling, gradually add combined egg yolks and flour, beating briskly until mixture thickens. Remove at once, add vanilla extract and spread filling in a shallow pan. When cold, fill cold, pre-baked 9-inch pastry shell with mixture. Top with either a meringue topping, made in the usual way and baked 15 minutes in a moderately hot oven (350° F.); or with Glazed Strawberry Topping No. 465, or with whipped cream. If topping with whipped cream, you may also arrange a border of fresh strawberries soaked in sherry, rum, brandy or apple brandy, drained, then rolled in brown sugar.

(358)   # STRAWBERRY MERINGUE PIE—
ENGLISH METHOD
ONE-CRUST PIE, PRE-BAKED PASTRY SHELL

For one 9-inch pie
- Pastry: 1 baked pie shell
- Apricot puree (or mashed cooked apricots or sieved apricot jam): ½ cup
- Egg whites (stiffly beaten): 3
- Salt: ¼ tsp.
- Vanilla extract: ½ tsp.
- Strawberries (fresh or frozen): 1 pint

For five 9-inch pies
- Pastry: 5 baked pie shells
- Apricot puree (or mashed cooked apricots or sieved apricot jam): 2½ cups or 1 lb. 14 oz.
- Egg whites (stiffly beaten): 15 or 15 oz.
- Salt: 1¼ tsps. or $5/24$ oz.
- Vanilla extract: 2½ tsps. or $5/12$ oz.
- Strawberries (fresh or frozen): 2½ qts. or 2 lbs. $13^5/7$ oz.

Brush pre-baked pie shell with melted butter; let this dry. Then spread bottom of shell with either apricot puree, mashed cooked dried apricots, or sieved apricot jam. Beat egg whites stiff with salt and vanilla extract and combine with washed, hulled berries. Fill pastry shell with mixture and brown in a moderate oven (350° F.) for 25–30 minutes. Serve as soon as cool.

(359)

STRAWBERRY, APPLE AND CRANBERRY PIE
TWO-CRUST PIE

For one 9-inch pie
- Strawberries (canned): 1½ cups
- Apples (pared, cored, ground): 1 cup
- Cranberries (raw, ground): 2¼ cups
- Sugar (granulated): 1 cup
- Salt: ¼ tsp.
- Nutmeg (ground): ⅛ tsp.
- Cinnamon (ground): ¼ tsp.
- Heavy cream (unwhipped): ¾ cup
- Pastry: For 1 two-crust pie

For five 9-inch pies
- Strawberries (canned): 7½ cups or 2 lbs. 2²/₇ oz.
- Apples (pared, cored, ground): 5 cups or 2½ lbs.
- Cranberries (raw, ground): 11¼ cups or 2¼ lbs.
- Sugar (granulated): 5 cups or 2½ lbs.
- Salt: 1¼ tsps. or ⁵/₂₄ oz.
- Nutmeg (ground): ⅝ tsp.
- Cinnamon (ground): 1¼ tsps.
- Heavy cream (unwhipped): 3¾ cups or scant 2 lbs.
- Pastry: For 5 two-crust pies

Combine all the above ingredients and blend thoroughly. Fill 9-inch pie pan, lined with pastry, with mixture; cover with top crust in the usual way, making 3 or 4 slits for escape of steam; brush with butter. Bake 10 minutes in a very hot oven (450° F.); reduce temperature to 350° F. and continue baking 30 minutes longer. Serve cold with additional whipped cream, flavored and sweetened to taste.

(360) STRAWBERRY PIE—HOME METHOD
TWO-CRUST PIE

For one 9-inch pie
- Pastry: For 1 two-crust pie
- Strawberries (fresh, washed, hulled): 1 qt.
- Sugar (granulated): 1¼ cups
- Salt: ⅛ tsp.
- Flour (sifted): 1 Tbsp.
- Cinnamon (ground): ¼ tsp.
- Nutmeg (ground): ¼ tsp.
- Butter: 1 Tbsp.

For five 9-inch pies
- Pastry: For 5 two-crust pies
- Strawberries (fresh, washed, hulled): 5 qts. or 5 lbs. 11³/₇ oz.
- Sugar (granulated): 6¼ cups or 2 lbs.
- Salt: ⅝ tsp.
- Flour (sifted): 5 Tbsps. or 1¼ oz.
- Cinnamon (ground): 1¼ tsps.
- Nutmeg (ground): 1¼ tsps.
- Butter: 5 Tbsps. or 2½ oz.

Line 9-inch pie pan with pastry rolled ⅛-inch thick; brush with butter and chill. Combine prepared berries with sugar, salt, flour, and spices and turn into pie shell. Dot with small pieces of butter. Prick tiny openings in the top crust and place on pie in the usual way. Crimp edges and bake 10 minutes in a very hot oven (450° F.); reduce temperature to 350° F. and continue baking for 30 minutes longer. Serve warm with brandy sauce. This pie may also be made crisscross fashion, served cold and à la mode.

(361)

STRAWBERRY PIE
TWO-CRUST PIE

For one 9-inch pie
- Cornstarch: ⅙ cup
- Water: ⅔ cup
- Sugar (granulated): ¾ cup
- Sugar (brown): ⅓ cup
- Salt: ¼ tsp.
- Nutmeg (ground): ⅛ tsp.
- Cinnamon (ground): ⅛ tsp.
- Ginger (ground): ⅛ tsp.
- Vanilla extract: ¼ tsp.
- Butter: 1 Tbsp.
- Red vegetable coloring: 2 drops
- Strawberries (fresh, washed, hulled): 1 qt.
- Pastry: For 1 two-crust pie

For five 9-inch pies
- Cornstarch: ⅚ cup or 4⁴/₉ oz.
- Water: 3⅓ cups or 1 lb. 10⅔ oz.
- Sugar (granulated): 3¾ cups or 1 lb. 14 oz.
- Sugar (brown): 1⅔ cups or 8⁸/₉ oz.
- Salt: 1¼ tsps. or ⁵/₂₄ oz.
- Nutmeg (ground): ⅝ tsp.
- Cinnamon (ground): ⅝ tsp.
- Ginger (ground): ⅝ tsp.
- Vanilla extract: 1¼ tsps. or ⁵/₂₄ oz.
- Butter: 5 Tbsps. or 2½ oz.
- Red vegetable coloring: 8 to 10 drops
- Strawberries (fresh, washed, hulled): 5 qts. or 5 lbs. 11³/₇ oz.
- Pastry: For 5 two-crust pies

Dissolve cornstarch in 2 tablespoons of the water and blend until smooth. Bring the remaining water to a boil with the combined sugars, salt, and spices and gradually stir in the dissolved cornstarch. Bring the mixture to a brisk boil, stirring rapidly from the bottom of the pan with a wire whisk until clear. Remove from the heat; stir in the vanilla extract, butter, and red vegetable coloring, adding just enough so as to obtain the reddish hue of fresh strawberries. Turn mixture into a shallow container to cool to lukewarm, then beat again with wire whisk until smooth; stir in the prepared strawberries. Turn into 9-inch pie pan lined with pastry, which has first been brushed with lightly beaten egg whites and allowed to dry; cover with top crust in the usual way; make a few slits on top of crust for escape of steam. Bake 10 minutes in a very hot oven (450° F.); reduce temperature to 350° F. and continue baking 30 minutes longer. Serve very cold with whipped cream, sweetened and flavored to taste.

(362)
STRAWBERRY PINEAPPLE PIE
GOURMET—FRENCH METHOD
ONE-CRUST (MERINGUE) PIE

For one 9-inch pie
Meringue Crust
- Egg whites (stiffly beaten): 6
- Salt: ¼ tsp.
- Ginger (ground): ⅛ tsp.
- Sugar (granulated): 1 cup
- Vanilla extract: ¾ tsp.
- Almond extract: ¼ tsp.
- Sugar (brown): ¾ cup
- Vinegar (cider): 1 Tbsp.

For five 9-inch pies
Meringue Crust
- Egg whites (stiffly beaten): 30 or 1 lb. 14 oz.
- Salt: 1¼ tsps. or ⁵/₂₄ oz.
- Ginger (ground): ⁵/₈ tsp.
- Sugar (granulated): 5 cups or 1¼ qts. or 2½ lbs.
- Vanilla extract: 3¾ tsps. or ⁵/₈ oz.
- Almond extract: 1¼ tsps. or ⁵/₂₄ oz.
- Sugar (brown): 3¾ cups or 1 lb. 4 oz.
- Vinegar (cider): 5 Tbsps. or 2½ oz.

Butter a 9-inch pie pan generously. Sprinkle with a complete coating of pastry flour, and shake off the excess. Beat egg whites with salt and ginger until stiff but not too dry; gradually add granulated sugar, beating briskly after each addition. Add vanilla and almond, then gradually beat in the brown sugar, alternately with cider vinegar. Line generously buttered 9-inch pie pan, bottom and sides, with the meringue, smoothing it out into a pile higher in center than at the edges. It should look more or less like a dome. Bake 30 minutes in a very slow oven (275° F.); increase oven temperature to 300° F. and continue baking 30 minutes longer. Cool. The meringue will settle in cooling and will be puffed and cracked.

Filling
- Pineapple (canned, drained, crushed): ¼ cup
- Heavy cream (whipped): 1 cup
- Salt: ⅛ tsp.
- Sugar (powdered): 3 Tbsps.
- Almond extract: ⅛ tsp.
- Vanilla extract: ¼ tsp.
- Lemon rind (grated): ½ tsp.
- Strawberries (whole, fresh or frozen): 1 pint (about)

Filling
- Pineapple (canned, drained, crushed): 1¼ cups or 15 oz.
- Heavy cream (whipped): 5 cups or 2½ lbs.
- Salt: ⅝ tsp.
- Sugar (powdered): 1 cup or 4²/₇ oz.
- Almond extract: ⅝ tsp.
- Vanilla extract: 1¼ tsps.
- Lemon rind (grated): 2½ tsps.
- Strawberries (whole, fresh or frozen): 2½ qts. (about)

When the meringue shell is cool and dry, spread canned, drained crushed pineapple in the bottom. Over the pineapple, force through a pastry bag with a fancy tube the whipped cream flavored with salt, sugar, almond and vanilla extracts and lemon rind, making a flat top and shaping in circles. Dot the whipped cream with cleaned, hulled strawberries soaked a few minutes in either orange or pineapple juice or brandy, rum or applejack. Serve very cold.

....

(363)   # A FEW FACTS ABOUT SWEET POTATOES

The versatility of this sweet, spongy-textured vegetable is perhaps seen at its apogee when it is translated, not into soup, as made down South, nor vegetable dishes, but into a perfect pie. Renowned, indeed, is the sweet potato pie, an evolution, if you will, of the sweet potato pone, encased in flaky pastry. Similar to, but tantalizingly different from, either pumpkin or squash pies, the sweet potato pie would seem well worth a trial as one of the favorite winter pies. Dug in October, the sweet is just in time to lend variety to early winter dinners. Its staying power is not great, however, and it is unwise to buy more than a few days' supply at one time. But those that are smooth and firm and of fairly symmetrical contour can be depended on to come up to specification.

Of the two well-known varieties, those that are firm and dry and light yellow in coloring are preferred by Northerners, while in the South the moist potato with the deep orange coloring is the favorite. The latter type, too, is chosen for candying and for making sweet potato pie.

The sweet potato is richer in minerals than the white potato, but to those who are interested it should be whispered that the sweets pack several more calories to the pound.

(364)

SWEET POTATO PIE I—
SOUTHERN METHOD
ONE-CRUST PIE

For one 9-inch pie

- Pastry: For 1 one-crust pie
- Mashed sweet potatoes (cooked): 1½ cups
- Sugar (granulated): 2 Tbsps.
- Sugar (brown, light): 3 Tbsps.
- Whole eggs (well beaten): 2
- Salt: ¼ tsp.
- Milk (fresh, rich): 2 cups
- Butter: 1 Tbsp.
- Lemon rind (grated): 2 tsps.
- Vanilla extract: ⅛ tsp.

For five 9-inch pies

- Pastry: For 5 one-crust pies
- Mashed sweet potatoes (cooked): 7½ cups or 3¾ lbs.
- Sugar (granulated): ⅝ cup or 5 oz.
- Sugar (brown, light): 1 cup or 5 oz.
- Whole eggs (well beaten): 10 or 1 lb. 4 oz.
- Salt: 1¼ tsps. or 5/24 oz.
- Milk (fresh, rich): 2½ qts. or 2½ lbs.
- Butter: 5 Tbsps. or 2½ oz.
- Lemon rind (grated): 3⅓ Tbsps. or 1¼ oz.
- Vanilla extract: ⅝ tsp.

Line 9-inch pie pan with pastry rolled ⅛-inch thick, allowing 2½ inches more than the diameter of the pan. Fold the rim of the pastry at the outer edge of pan, using forefinger of the left hand to make crinkly edge, and breaking off the surplus pastry. Prick pie shell; brush with butter and set in refrigerator to chill. To the cold mashed potatoes add combined sugar, well-beaten whole eggs, salt, and milk, and blend until smooth. Now beat in the butter, lemon rind and vanilla extract. Turn mixture into chilled pie shell as evenly as possible and bake 30 minutes in a moderate oven (350° F.). You may garnish the edge of pie with whipped cream; or top with a meringue, made in the usual way, and bake 15 minutes in a moderately slow oven (325° F.). Serve cold.

(365)

SWEET POTATO PIE II—
CALIFORNIA METHOD
ONE-CRUST PIE

For one 9-inch pie

- Sweet potatoes (cooked, mashed, cold): 1¾ cups
- Sugar (brown, light): ½ cup
- Salt: ⅓ tsp.
- Ginger (ground): ¼ tsp.
- Orange rind (grated): 1 tsp.
- Milk: 1¾ cups
- Whole eggs (well-beaten): 2
- Pastry: For 1 one-crust pie
- Heavy cream (whipped): ¾ cup
- Orange sections: 1 cup

For five 9-inch pies

- Sweet potatoes (cooked, mashed, cold): 2¾ qts. or 4 lbs. 6 oz.
- Sugar (brown, light): 2½ cups or 13⅓ oz.
- Salt: 1⅔ tsps. or ⁵⁄₁₈ oz.
- Ginger (ground): 1¼ tsps.
- Orange rind (grated): 1½ Tbsps. or ⁹⁄₁₆ oz.
- Milk: 2¾ qts. or 4 lbs. 6 oz.
- Whole eggs (well-beaten): 10 or 1 lb. 4 oz.
- Pastry: For 5 one-crust pies
- Heavy cream (whipped): 3¾ cups or 2 lbs.
- Orange sections: 5 cups or 1 lb. 14 oz.

Force cooked, cooled mashed potatoes through sieve; add sugar, salt, ginger, and orange rind. Blend well. Combine fresh milk and well-beaten eggs and blend with potato mixture until smooth and free from lumps. Line 9-inch pie pan with pastry rolled ⅛-inch thick; brush with melted butter and turn filling into it. Bake 10 minutes in a very hot oven (450° F.); reduce temperature to 325° F. and continue baking 30 minutes longer, or until custard is firm. Cool. When cold, top with whipped cream, using a pastry bag with a square tube, and decorate with orange sections, free from seeds and membranes. Serve very cold.

(366)   # SWEET POTATO PECAN PIE—
PLANTATION METHOD
ONE-CRUST PIE

For one 9-inch pie

- Sweet potatoes (cooked, mashed, cold): 1½ cups
- Sugar (brown): ½ cup
- Salt: ½ tsp.
- Cinnamon (ground): 1 tsp.
- Egg yolks (well beaten): 3
- Milk: 1 cup
- Butter (melted): 2 Tbsps.
- Pecans (chopped): ½ cup
- Pastry: For 1 one-crust pie
- Ginger Meringue Topping (No. 451), using brown sugar instead of white sugar

For five 9-inch pies

- Sweet potatoes (cooked, mashed, cold): 7½ cups or 3¾ lbs.
- Sugar (brown): 2½ cups or 13⅓ oz.
- Salt: 2½ tsps. or ⁵/₁₂ oz.
- Cinnamon (ground): 1⅔ Tbsps.
- Egg yolks (well beaten): 15 or 15 oz.
- Milk: 5 cups or 2½ lbs.
- Butter (melted): ⅝ cup or 5 oz.
- Pecans (chopped): 2½ cups or 13⅓ oz.
- Pastry: For 5 one-crust pies
- Ginger Meringue Topping (No. 451), using brown sugar instead of white sugar

You may use canned sweet potatoes, if desired. Mash potatoes until smooth and free of lumps. Add sugar, salt, cinnamon, well-beaten egg yolks, and milk. Beat well. Combine butter and pecans and add to potato mixture. Mix thoroughly. Turn mixture into unbaked 9-inch pastry shell, which has been brushed with melted butter and thoroughly chilled, and bake 10 minutes in a very hot oven (450° F.); reduce temperature to 350° F. and continue baking 25–30 minutes longer, or until top crust is evenly brown. Cover with Ginger Meringue Topping, made as indicated for No. 451, and serve cold.

(367)

SWEET POTATO RUM PIE—
HAITIAN METHOD
TWO-CRUST PIE

For one 9-inch pie
- Unbaked pastry: For 1 two-crust pie
- Sweet potatoes (medium-size, cooked in the skins): 3 (about)
- Sugar (brown): 1/3 cup
- Butter: 2 Tbsps.
- Orange juice (cold): 1¼ cups
- Ginger (ground): ¾ tsp.
- Rum: 1 wine-glassful

For five 9-inch pies
- Unbaked pastry: For 5 two-crust pies
- Sweet potatoes (medium-size, cooked in the skin): 15 (about) or about 5 lbs.
- Sugar (brown): 1⅔ cups or 8⁸/₉ oz.
- Butter: 10 Tbsps. or ⅝ cup or 5 oz.
- Orange juice (cold): 6¼ cups or 3 lbs. 2 oz.
- Ginger (ground): 3¾ tsps. or 5/16 oz.
- Rum: 5 wine-glassfuls or 1 lb. 4 oz.

Line 9-inch pie pan with pastry. Cover with a layer of thin slices of potatoes; sprinkle generously with sugar and dot with butter. Continue process until all potatoes are used. Then add orange juice (pineapple juice may also be used if desired), sprinkle with ginger and, lastly, the rum. Cover with top crust in the usual way; prick all over top crust with the tines of a fork, make a large slit in center for escape of steam, and brush with cold milk or slightly beaten egg yolk. Bake for 40–45 minutes in a slow oven (300° F.). Serve warm or cold with plain whipped cream.

(368) # TRANSPARENT COCONUT PIE—
CALIFORNIA METHOD
ONE-CRUST PIE

For one 9-inch pie
- Butter: ¾ cup
- Orange rind (grated): 1 tsp.
- Sugar (granulated): 1 cup
- Salt: ¼ tsp.
- Egg yolks: 5
- Pastry: 1 Western Pie Crust No. 69
- Coconut (medium shred): 1 cup
- Egg whites (stiffly beaten): 3
- Sugar (brown): 6 Tbsps.
- Salt: ⅛ tsp.
- Coconut (long shred): 1 cup

For five 9-inch pies
- Butter: 3¾ cups or 1 lb. 14 oz.
- Orange rind (grated): 1⅔ Tbsps. or ⁹⁄₁₆ oz.
- Sugar (granulated): 5 cups or 2½ lbs.
- Salt: 1¼ tsps. or ⅝ oz.
- Egg yolks: 25 or 1 lb. 9 oz.
- Pastry: 5 Western Pie Crusts No. 69
- Coconut (medium shred): 5 cups or 1 lb.
- Egg whites (stiffly beaten): 15 or 15 oz.
- Sugar (brown): 1⅞ cups or 10 oz.
- Salt: ⅝ tsp.
- Coconut (long shred): 5 cups or 1 lb.

Cream butter with orange rind; add granulated sugar gradually, creaming until light and flurry. Add salt to egg yolks and beat about 10 minutes, until eggs are almost white. Turn egg yolks into creamed butter mixture and beat again 2 minutes. Pour filling into 9-inch unbaked pastry shell, which has been brushed with melted butter, sprinkle with medium shred coconut, and bake in a very slow oven (300° F.) for 45 minutes. Beat egg whites until foamy; add brown sugar, 2 tablespoons at a time, beating after each addition until sugar is thoroughly blended. Then continue beating, adding salt, until meringue stands in peaks. Pile lightly on filling. Sprinkle with long shred coconut and bake 15 minutes in a moderately slow oven (325° F.). Serve cold.

(369) # TUTTI FRUTTI DRIED FRUIT PIE
TWO-CRUST PIE

For one 9-inch pie
- Raisins (seedless, chopped): ½ cup
- Figs (dried, chopped): ¼ cup
- Dates (pitted, chopped): ¼ cup
- Apples (pared, cored, chopped): 1 cup
- Sugar (granulated): ½ cup
- Sugar (brown): ½ cup
- Cinnamon (ground): 1 tsp.
- Allspice (ground): ¼ tsp.
- Salt: ¼ tsp.
- Lemon juice: 2 Tbsps.
- Orange juice: 2 Tbsps.
- Pecan nuts (crushed): ½ cup
- Pastry: For 1 two-crust pie

For five 9-inch pies
- Raisins (seedless, chopped): 2½ cups or 13$\frac{1}{3}$ oz.
- Figs (dried, chopped): 1¼ cups or 6$\frac{2}{3}$ oz.
- Dates (pitted, chopped): 1¼ cups or ½ lb.
- Apples (pared, cored, chopped): 5 cups or 2½ lbs.
- Sugar (granulated): 2½ cups or 1 lb. 4 oz.
- Sugar (brown): 2½ cups or 13$\frac{1}{3}$ oz.
- Cinnamon (ground): 1$\frac{2}{3}$ Tbsps. or $\frac{5}{12}$ oz.
- Allspice (ground): 1¼ tsps.
- Salt: 1¼ tsps. or $\frac{5}{24}$ oz.
- Lemon juice: $\frac{5}{8}$ cup or 5 oz.
- Orange juice: $\frac{5}{8}$ cup or 5 oz.
- Pecan nuts (crushed): 2½ cups or 15 oz.
- Pastry: For 5 two-crust pies

Place all the ingredients, except the nuts, in a saucepan. Let this simmer gently for 20–25 minutes. Cool to lukewarm and add the crushed pecan nut meats. Line 9-inch pie pan with pastry rolled ⅛-inch thick, pour in the mixture; cover with top crust in the usual way, making a few slits on top for escape of steam; brush with molasses diluted with warm water. Bake 30 minutes in a hot oven (400° F.), or until top is nicely brown. Serve as indicated, either warm or cold.

You may also make this pie one-crust with a meringue topping, a crisscross topping, or a whipped cream topping. It may be served hot or cold. If hot, serve with either brandy, rum or apple brandy hard sauce. If cold, you may serve à la mode, or with whipped cream. If topped with a meringue, serve cold without any side accompaniment.

(370) WALNUT PIE—CALIFORNIA METHOD
ONE-CRUST PIE

For one 9-inch pie
- Butter: ¼ cup
- Sugar (light brown): ⅔ cup
- Salt: ⅙ tsp.
- Maple Syrup: ¾ cup
- Whole eggs (well beaten): 3
- Vanilla extract: 1 tsp.
- Walnuts (broken): 1 cup
- Pastry: For 1 one-crust pie
- Walnut halves

For five 9-inch pies
- Butter: 1¼ cups or 10 oz.
- Sugar (light brown): 3⅓ cups or 1 lb. 1⅞ oz.
- Salt: ⅚ tsp.
- Maple syrup: 3¾ cups or 2 lbs. 13 oz.
- Whole eggs (well beaten): 15 or 1 lb. 14 oz.
- Vanilla extract: 1⅔ Tbsps. or ⅚ oz.
- Walnuts (broken); 5 cups or 1 lb. 6⁶⁄₇ oz.
- Pastry: For 5 one-crust pies
- Walnut halves

Cream butter, gradually add sugar, and continue creaming until thoroughly blended. Combine all the remaining ingredients, except walnut halves. Blend well. Turn into unbaked 9-inch pastry shell which has been brushed with softened butter and chilled, and bake 10 minutes in a very hot oven (450° F.); reduce temperature to 350° F. and continue baking 30–35 minutes longer, or until top is delicately brown. When cold, top with whipped cream and decorate with walnut halves. Serve very cold.

(371)

WALNUT CREAM PIE—
FRENCH METHOD
ONE-CRUST PIE

For one 9-inch pie

- Pastry: For 1 one-crust pie
- Quince jelly: 3 Tbsps.
- Milk (rich): 1¼ cups
- Sugar (granulated): ½ cup
- Salt: ¼ tsp.
- Milk (rich): ¼ cup
- Flour (sifted): 3 Tbsps.
- Cornstarch: 2 Tbsps.
- Whole egg (well beaten): 1
- Egg yolk (well beaten): 1
- Butter: 1 Tbsp.
- Vanilla extract: ¼ tsp.
- Almond extract: 1/6 tsp.
- Walnut meats (chopped, toasted): ½ cup
- Egg whites (stiffly beaten): 2
- Sugar (powdered): 2 Tbsps.
- Walnut halves for garnishing
- Marzipan Meringue Border No. 473

For five 9-inch pies

- Pastry: For 5 one-crust pies
- Quince jelly: 1 scant cup or 11¼ oz.
- Milk (rich): 6¼ cups or 3 lbs. 2 oz.
- Sugar (granulated): 2½ cups or 1 lb. 4 oz.
- Salt: 1¼ tsps. or $5/24$ oz.
- Milk (rich): 1¼ cups or 10 oz.
- Flour (sifted): 1 scant cup or 3¾ oz.
- Cornstarch: $5/8$ cup or $3^{1}/3$ oz.
- Whole eggs (well beaten): 5 or 10 oz.
- Egg yolks (well beaten): 5 or 5 oz.
- Butter: 5 Tbsps. or 2½ cups
- Vanilla extract: 1¼ tsps. or $5/24$ oz.
- Almond extract: $5/6$ tsp.
- Walnut meats (chopped, toasted): 2½ cups or $13^{1}/3$ oz.
- Egg whites (stiffly beaten): 10 or 10 oz.
- Sugar (powdered): $5/8$ cup or $2^{6}/7$ oz.
- Walnut halves for garnishing
- Marzipan Meringue Border No. 473

Line pie pan with pastry, allowing 2½ inches more than the diameter of top of pan; make a fluted rim. Brush bottom and sides of pastry with melted butter; allow to chill; then spread the quince jelly all over the bottom of crust. Chill first, then bake. Place the first amount of milk, the granulated sugar and salt in saucepan or top of double boiler; bring this to a boil, stirring occasionally. Combine remaining milk, flour, cornstarch and well-beaten whole egg and egg yolk, and blend to a paste. Gradually add to the boiling mixture, stirring briskly and constantly from the bottom of saucepan with a wire whisk until mixture is thick and smooth. Cook for 2 minutes, stirring constantly. Remove from the heat; add butter, flavoring extracts, and chopped walnuts. Stir—do not fold— the stiffly beaten egg whites, which have been beaten with powdered sugar, into the hot filling. Turn filling at once into chilled pastry shell. Cool. When cold, garnish with walnut halves as follows: Lay the walnut halves on the filling, starting first with a circle around the outside edge, not quite against crust, leaving space for the marzipan border. Make another row or circle, pressing the walnut halves up tightly against the first row or circle, and continue thus in toward the center. Lastly, using a pastry bag with a fancy tube, make a border of marzipan meringue and fill circle in center. Set the pie under the broiler and brown. Serve cold.

....

(372) WASHINGTON CHOCOLATE CREAM PIE
TWO-CRUST PIE

For one 9-inch pie
Pastry Circles
- Egg yolks: 3
- Lemon rind (grated): 1 Tbsp.
- Lemon juice: 1 Tbsp.
- Egg whites (stiffly beaten): 3
- Salt: ¼ tsp.
- Sugar (fine granulated): ½ cup
- Flour (cake): ½ cup

For five 9-inch pies
Pastry Circles
- Egg yolks: 15 or 15 oz.
- Lemon rind (grated): 5 Tbsps. or 1⅞ oz.
- Lemon juice: 5 Tbsps. or 2½ oz.
- Egg whites (stiffly beaten): 15 or 15 oz.
- Salt: 1¼ tsps. or $5/24$ oz.
- Sugar (fine granulated): 2½ cups or 1¼ lbs.
- Flour (cake): 2½ cups or 10 oz.

Beat egg yolks until thick and lemon-colored, then beat in the lemon rind and juice. Beat egg whites until stiff but not dry, fold in salt and sugar, one tablespoon at a time; then fold egg whites into egg yolks alternately with sifted cake flour, a little at a time. Turn into 9-inch pie pan and bake in a slow oven (325° F.) for 40 minutes. Invert pie pan on cooling rack until cold; remove from pan and split into two layers.

For one 9-inch pie
Filling
- Milk (scalded): 2¼ cups
- Chocolate (bitter, grated): 2 (1-oz.) squares
- Sugar (granulated): ⅓ cup
- Cornstarch: 3 Tbsps.
- Salt: ¼ tsp.
- Egg yolk (well beaten): 1
- Vanilla extract: 1 tsp.

For five 9-inch pies
Filling
- Milk (scalded): 11¼ cups or 5 lbs. 10 oz.
- Chocolate (bitter, grated): 10 (1-oz.) squares
- Sugar (granulated): 1⅔ cups or 13⅓ oz.
- Cornstarch: 1 scant cup or 5 oz.
- Salt: 1¼ tsps. or 5/24 oz.
- Egg yolks (well beaten): 5 or 5 oz.
- Vanilla extract: 5 tsps. or 5/6 oz.

To scalded milk add grated chocolate and stir until well blended. Combine sugar, cornstarch and salt and add to hot mixture. Cook, stirring constantly, until thick, or about 15 minutes; remove from the heat and at once beat in the well beaten egg yolk alternately with the vanilla. Cool. Spread between layers of pastry, trimming neatly, and sift confectioner's sugar over top. Serve cold, cut in pie-shaped wedges.

(373)   # WASHINGTON CREAM PIE
TWO-CRUST PIE

For one 9-inch pie
Pastry Circles
- Egg yolks (beaten): 2
- Sugar (granulated): ¾ cup
- Flour: ¾ cup
- Salt: ¼ tsp.
- Baking powder: 1 tsp.
- Milk: 1 Tbsp.
- Egg whites (stiffly beaten): 2
- Vanilla extract: ½ tsp.

Filling
- Whole egg (beaten): 1
- Egg yolk (beaten): 1
- Sugar (granulated): ⅓ cup
- Salt: ¼ tsp.
- Flour (pastry): 3 Tbsps.
- Milk (scalded): 1 cup
- Vanilla extract: ½ tsp.

For five 9-inch pies
Pastry Circles
- Egg yolks (beaten): 10 or 10 oz.
- Sugar (granulated): 3¾ cups or 1 lb. 14 oz.
- Flour: 3¾ cups or 15 oz.
- Salt: 1¼ tsps. or $5/24$ oz.
- Baking powder: 1⅔ Tbsps. or a scant $5/6$ oz.
- Milk: 5 Tbsps. or 2½ oz.
- Egg whites (stiffly beaten): 10 or 10 oz.
- Vanilla extract: 2½ tsps. or $5/12$ oz.

Filling
- Whole eggs (beaten): 5 or 10 oz.
- Egg yolks (beaten): 5 or 5 oz.
- Sugar (granulated): 1⅔ cups or 13⅓ oz.
- Salt: 1¼ tsps. or $5/24$ oz.
- Flour (pastry): scant cup or 3¾ oz.
- Milk (scalded): 5 cups or 2½ lbs.
- Vanilla extract: 2½ tsps. or $5/12$ oz.

Beat egg yolks slightly; add sugar gradually, beating constantly until sugar is dissolved; sift together twice flour, salt, and baking powder, and add to egg-sugar mixture with cold milk; mix well. Fold in the stiffly beaten egg whites, flavored with vanilla extract. Roll into a circle to ¼ inch thick to fit 9-inch pie pan and bake 15–20 minutes in a hot oven (450° F.). Remove from oven, let cool a little, then split in two. Cool thoroughly before using. For the filling, beat whole egg and egg yolk together with sugar, salt, and flour; stir in scalded milk and cook over hot water, stirring constantly, until mixture thickens; remove from the heat and stir in the vanilla extract. Cool; when cold, spread over one layer of baked pastry, then press the top layer over the filling. Trim neatly. Cool. When ready to serve, dust top with powdered sugar.

(374) # WASHINGTON FRUIT CUSTARD PIE
TWO-CRUST PIE

To the filling for Washington Cream Pie, No. 373, stir in 1 cup of canned, drained, chopped fruit salad or fruit cocktail.

....

(375) # WASHINGTON CUSTARD
MINCEMEAT PIE
TWO-CRUST PIE

To the hot filling for Washington Cream Pie, No. 373, stir in 1 cup of canned or home-made mincemeat.

....

(376) # WHITE HOUSE PECAN PIE—
WASHINGTON, D.C., METHOD
ONE-CRUST PIE

For one 9-inch pie
- Butter: 2 Tbsps.
- Sugar (granulated): ½ cup
- Maple (or other syrup): ¾ cup
- Egg yolks (well beaten): 2
- Egg whites (stiffly beaten): 2
- Salt: ¼ tsp.
- Vanilla extract: 1 tsp.
- Unbroken pecan meats: 1 cup
- Pastry: For 1 one-crust pie

For five 9-inch pies
- Butter: ⅝ cup or 5 oz.
- Sugar (granulated): ½ cup or 4 oz.
- Maple (or other syrup): 3¾ cups or 2 lbs. 13 oz.
- Egg yolks (well beaten): 10 or 10 oz.
- Egg whites (stiffly beaten): 10 or 10 oz.
- Salt: 1¼ tsps. or $5/24$ oz.
- Vanilla extract: $1\frac{2}{3}$ Tbsps. or $5/6$ oz.
- Unbroken pecan meats: 5 cups or 1¼ lbs.
- Pastry: For 5 one-crust pies

Cream butter until lemon-colored. Add sugar alternately with syrup, beating briskly after each addition; add the well-beaten egg yolks, stiffly beaten egg whites, beaten with salt and vanilla extract, and lastly the unbroken pecan nut meats; then beat briskly. Turn filling into 9-inch pie shell brushed with slightly beaten egg white and bake in a slow oven (275° F.) for 35–40 minutes. Serve cold, topped with unsweetened and unflavored whipped cream.

CHIFFON PIE
RECIPES

(377)   # A FEW POINTERS AND HINTS
ABOUT USING GELATIN

(a) Always place cold water or other liquid called for in recipe in mixing bowl and sprinkle amount of gelatin on top of liquid.

(b) Add sugar and hot liquid or liquids and stir until dissolved.

(c) If sliced or chopped fruits are to be added, and no special design is desired, allow mixture to thicken slightly and stir the prepared fruit through the congealing mixture.

(d) In order to utilize any fruit juices (fresh or canned) you have on hand, the gelatin may be soaked in cold fruit juices, or these fruit juices may be heated and substituted for the hot water in which the soaked gelatin is dissolved.

(e) It is always advisable to use real fruit juice if a real flavor is desired.

(f) If combining fresh pineapple juice or fruit with gelatin, always first scald juice or fruit. This is not necessary for canned pineapple, (see A Few Facts about Pineapple, No. 269).

(g) Gelatin mixtures will harden much more quickly if put in a shallow container.

(h) If you desire to use a meringue on top of chiffon pies, float spoonfuls of meringue mixture upon hot water in a shallow pan. Set pan in a slow oven (300°–325° F.) and bake until the meringues are lightly browned. Skim them off immediately and place on top of pie or pies.

(i) Two-toned, or three-toned chiffon pies may easily be made for special menus or parties and the top spread with either floated meringues or whipped cream topping.

(j) Any Bavarian cream may be served in chiffon pies, but the mixture must be very thick before turning into the baked pie or tart shell. Then garnish tops attractively with rosettes or pompoms of whipped cream, fruits, nuts, chocolate shots, tinted coconut or ground peanut or nut brittle.

(378) # ALMOND CHIFFON PIE
ONE-CRUST PIE, PRE-BAKED PASTRY SHELL

For one 9-inch pie
- Milk: 1¼ cups
- Sugar (granulated): ⅓ cup
- Salt: ¼ tsp.
- Cornstarch: 2 Tbsps.
- Flour (sifted): 2 Tbsps.
- Butter: 2 tsps.
- Vanilla extract: ½ tsp.
- Almond extract: 4 drops
- Egg whites (stiffly beaten): 3
- Sugar (granulated): 3 Tbsps.
- Toasted almonds (sliced or shredded): ½ cup
- Pastry: 1 baked flaky pie shell No. 47

For five 9-inch pies
- Milk: 6¼ cups or 3 lbs. 2 oz.
- Sugar (granulated): 1⅔ cups or 13⅓ oz.
- Salt: 1¼ tsps. or ⁵⁄₂₄ oz.
- Cornstarch: ⅝ cup or 3⅓ oz.
- Flour (sifted): ⅝ cup or 2½ oz.
- Butter: 3⅓ Tbsps. or 1⅝ oz.
- Vanilla extract: 2½ tsps. or ⁵⁄₁₂ oz.
- Almond extract: ⅓ tsp.
- Egg whites (stiffly beaten): 15 or 15 oz.
- Sugar (granulated): scant cup or 7½ oz.
- Toasted almonds (sliced or shredded): 2½ cups, or 8 oz. or ½ lb.
- Pastry: 5 baked flaky pie shells No. 47

Into saucepan place milk, ⅓ cup granulated sugar and salt; stir until sugar is dissolved, then bring to a boil, stirring occasionally. Thicken with cornstarch-flour mixture gradually, stirring constantly until mixture thickens. Allow to boil once or twice, remove from heat, and stir in butter and flavoring extracts. Beat egg whites stiff and add remaining sugar and the ½ cup of toasted, sliced or shredded almonds. Fold this into the cream mixture very gently, cool, and turn into pre-baked 9-inch flaky pastry shell. Cover with meringue or whipped cream topping and garnish with sliced almonds. Serve very cold.

(379) APPLE BAVARIAN GINGER CHIFFON PIE
ONE-CRUST PIE

For one 9-inch pie
Hot Water Gingerbread

- Whole egg: 1
- Sugar (granulated): ¼ cup
- Flour (bread): 1 cup
- Salt: ¼ tsp.
- Ginger (ground): 1 tsp.
- Molasses (dark): ¼ cup
- Baking soda: ½ tsp.
- Hot water: ½ cup
- Butter (melted): ¼ cup

For five 9-inch pies
Hot Water Gingerbread

- Whole eggs: 5 or 10 oz.
- Sugar (granulated): 1¼ cups or 10 oz.
- Flour (bread): 5 cups or 1 lb. 5¼ oz.
- Salt: 1¼ tsps. or $5/24$ oz.
- Ginger (ground): 1⅔ Tbsps. or $5/12$ oz.
- Molasses (dark): 1¼ cups or 15 oz.
- Baking soda: 2½ tsps. or $5/16$ oz.
- Hot water: 2½ cups or 1 lb. 4 oz.
- Butter (melted): 1¼ cups or 10 oz.

Beat egg until light; add sugar and continue beating until sugar is entirely dissolved. Sift flour, salt, and ginger together; add ⅓ of the flour mixture to egg mixture and beat until smooth. To this, add ⅔ of the molasses, alternately with remaining flour mixture. Add baking soda to remaining molasses and stir until foamy, then add hot water and blend thoroughly. Add melted butter to gingerbread mixture and stir until blended. Cover greased bottoms of 2 9-inch pie pans with circles of heavy greased paper cut ½ inch larger than the pans; spread mixture into paper-lined pie pans and bake 5 minutes in a moderate oven (375° F.). Remove from oven and cool.

For one 9-inch pie
Apple Bavarian Filling
- Egg yolk: 1
- Sugar (granulated): ⅜ cup
- Lemon juice: 1 Tbsp.
- Lemon rind (grated): ½ tsp.
- Cinnamon (ground): ¼ tsp.
- Nutmeg (ground): ¼ tsp.
- Ginger (ground): ½ tsp.
- Angostura bitters: 1 tsp.
- Apple sauce (tart, unsweetened): 1¼ cups
- Gelatin (granulated): 2¾ tsps.
- Cold water: ¼ cup
- Egg whites: 2
- Salt: ⅜ tsp.
- Sugar (granulated): ¾ cup
- Whipped cream: ¾ cup

For five 9-inch pies
Apple Bavarian Filling
- Egg yolks: 5 or 5 oz.
- Sugar (granulated): 1⅞ cups or 15 oz.
- Lemon juice: 5 Tbsps. or 2½ oz.
- Lemon rind (grated): 2½ tsps. or ⁵⁄₁₆ oz.
- Cinnamon (ground): 1¼ tsps.
- Nutmeg (ground): 1¼ tsps.
- Ginger (ground): 2½ tsps.
- Angostura bitters: 1⅔ Tbsps. or ⅚ oz.
- Apple sauce (tart, unsweetened): 1 qt. & 2½ cups or 3 lbs. 2 oz.
- Gelatin (granulated): 4 Tbsps. & 1¾ tsps. or 1¼ oz.
- Cold water: 1¼ cups or 10 oz.
- Egg whites: 10 or 10 oz.
- Salt: 1⅞ tsps. or ⁵⁄₁₆ oz.
- Sugar (granulated): 3¾ cups or 1 lb. 14 oz.
- Whipped cream: 3¾ cups or scant 2 lbs.

Beat egg yolk until thick and lemon-colored; add sugar and beat until sugar is dissolved. Combine lemon juice, lemon rind, spices, bitters and tart apple sauce; add to first mixture and beat until smooth. Add gelatin to cold water and dissolve over hot water. Beat egg whites until stiff, add salt and sugar and continue beating until mixture forms peaks. Fold dissolved gelatin into stiffly beaten egg whites, beat again until it forms moist peaks and add to first mixture. Lastly fold in the whipped cream. Pour into cooled pie shell and chill in refrigerator.

Glazed Apple Slices
- Apples (with red skin): 2
- Sugar (granulated): 1 cup
- Water: 1 cup
- Ginger (ground): ¼ tsp.
- Lemon slices: 2
- Salt: A few grains

Glazed Apple Slices
- Apples (with red skin): 10 or about 3¾ lbs.
- Sugar (granulated): 5 cups or 2½ lbs.
- Water: 5 cups or 2½ lbs.
- Ginger (ground): 1¼ tsps.
- Lemon slices: 10 or 2 medium-sized lemons
- Salt: ½ tsp. or ¹⁄₁₂ oz.

Select red-skinned apples that will hold their shape and become transparent in cooking, such as Greenings, Oldenberry (also called Duchess), Stayman, or Winter Banana apples. Do not remove the skin. Cut each apple into eight slices. Make sugar syrup by combining the remaining ingredients in a saucepan; bring to boiling point, stirring occasionally. When boiling, drop apple slices in syrup and cook very slowly without stirring, until transparent. Remove to absorbent paper and drain thoroughly. Do not try to glaze all the apple slices at once; add 4 or 5 slices to the syrup at a time, lest they stick together and turn into a mush. Cook as slowly as possible, so as to allow sugar to penetrate deep into slices and cook center thoroughly. Cool.

Arrange a rosette edge of whipped cream on pie with pastry bag, using a fancy tube. Sprinkle scraps of gingerbread, dried and rolled and sieved, in the center and place apple slices on pie so that each slice of apple will be in the center of each portion of pie when cut. Serve thoroughly chilled.

....

(380)
APRICOT CHIFFON PIE I— HOME METHOD
ONE-CRUST PIE, PRE-BAKED PASTRY SHELL

For one 9-inch pie
- Egg whites: 4
- Salt: ⅛ tsp.
- Apricots (dried, cooked, sweetened, sieved): 1 cup
- Almonds (blanched, toasted, shredded): ½ cup
- Pastry: 1 baked Cheese Pastry Shell (No. 52)

For five 9-inch pies
- Egg whites: 20 or 1 lb. 4 oz.
- Salt: ⅝ tsp.
- Apricots (dried, cooked sweetened, sieved): 5 cups or 3¾ lbs.
- Almonds (blanched, toasted, shredded): 2½ cups or 12 oz.
- Pastry: 5 baked Cheese Pastry Shells (No. 52)

Beat egg whites until stiff; add salt; carefully fold in the combined apricot puree and almonds. Turn mixture into pre-baked 9-inch cheese pastry shell, which has been fluted, and bake 12 to 15 minutes in a slow oven (300° F.); or until mixture is delicately browned on top. Serve cold with or without sweetened and flavored whipped cream.

(381)

APRICOT CHIFFON PIE II—
FRESH FRUIT METHOD
ONE-CRUST PIE, PRE-BAKED PASTRY SHELL

For one 9-inch pie
- Apricot (fresh, sieved): 1 cup
- Sugar (granulated): ⅞ cup
- Salt: ¼ tsp.
- Water (cold): ½ cup
- Cornstarch: 3 Tbsps.
- Flour (sifted): 2 Tbsps.
- Water (cold): 3 Tbsps.
- Egg whites (stiffly beaten): 4
- Sugar (powdered): ¼ cup
- Almond extract: 3 drops
- Pastry: 1 baked Rich Pie shell No. 70

For five 9-inch pies
- Apricots (fresh, sieved): 5 cups or 2½ lbs.
- Sugar (granulated): 4⅜ cups or 2 lbs. 3 oz.
- Salt: 1¼ tsps. or ⁵⁄₂₄ oz.
- Water (cold): 2½ cups or 1 lb. 4 oz.
- Cornstarch: 1 scant cup or 5 oz.
- Flour (sifted): ⅝ cup or 2½ oz.
- Water (cold): 1 scant cup or 2½ oz.
- Egg whites (stiffly beaten): 20 or 1 lb. 4 oz.
- Sugar (powdered): 1¼ cups or 5⁵⁄₇ oz.
- Almond extract: ¼ tsp. or ¹⁄₂₄ oz.
- Pastry: 5 baked Rich Pie shells No. 70

Pit fresh apricots and force through sieve. There should be 1 cup of sieved pulp. Combine apricot pulp, sugar, salt, and water in saucepan or top of double boiler and bring to boil. Blend cornstarch, flour and remaining cold water to a paste and add to boiling apricot mixture, stirring constantly until mixture is thick and smooth. Let this boil once or twice; remove from the heat and cool to lukewarm. Fold in the stiffly beaten egg whites, sweetened with powdered sugar and flavored with almond extract, mixing gently but thoroughly. Turn mixture into pre-baked 9-inch rich pastry shell, and when thoroughly cold, top with whipped cream, using a pastry bag; you may garnish the border with blanched, toasted, cooled and halved almonds, with small points toward center. Serve thoroughly chilled.

(382) BLACKBERRY BRANDIED CHIFFON PIE
ONE-CRUST PIE, PRE-BAKED PASTRY SHELL

For one 9-inch pie

- Apricots (cooked, sweetened, sieved): 1/3 cup
- Blackberries (fresh or canned): 3 cups
- Sugar (granulated): 3/4 cup
- Salt: 1/8 tsp.
- Muscatel: 1/4 cup
- Gelatin (granulated): 1 1/2 Tbsps.
- Pastry: 1 baked Semi-Puff Paste pie shell (No. 66)
- Heavy cream: 1 cup
- Sugar (powdered): 2 Tbsps.
- Brandy: 1 1/2 Tbsps.

For five 9-inch pies

- Apricots (cooked, sweetened, sieved): 1 2/3 cups or 1 lb. 4 oz.
- Blackberries (fresh or canned): 3 3/4 qts. or 2 1/2 lbs.
- Sugar (granulated): 3 3/4 cups or 1 lb. 14 oz.
- Salt: 5/8 tsp.
- Muscatel: 1 1/4 cups, or 10 oz.
- Gelatin (granulated): 7 1/2 Tbsps. or 1 7/8 oz.
- Pastry: 5 baked Semi-Puff Paste pie shells (No. 66)
- Heavy cream: 5 cups or 2 lbs. 9 7/8 oz.
- Sugar (powdered): 5/8 cup or 2 6/7 oz.
- Brandy: 7 1/2 Tbsps. or 3 3/4 oz.

If fresh blackberries are used, clean and wash them. Stew slowly until heated through in their own juice; then add apricots, sugar and salt. They should be quite sweet. If canned blackberries are used, a little less sugar may be needed. Next add the wine. Set aside, but keep hot. Soften gelatin in 1/4 cup of cold water, then dissolve it over steam. Add a little of the blackberry juice, stir and continue to cook over steam until gelatin is thoroughly dissolved. Then combine with apricot-berry mixture slowly, stirring constantly. Place over ice to cool, and when mixture begins to congeal, stir gently but thoroughly and turn mixture into pre-baked pastry shell. Place in refrigerator for 2 hours to chill thoroughly. When chilled, top with heavy cream, which has been whipped stiff, sweetened with powdered sugar, and flavored with brandy. Decorate top with whole, fresh blackberries or with chopped nuts. Serve cold.

(383) BLACKBERRY SPONGE CHIFFON PIE
ONE-CRUST PIE

For one 9-inch pie
- Cornflakes (crushed): 3 cups
- Sugar (light brown): ¼ cup
- Butter (melted): ⅓ cup
- Salt: ¼ tsp.
- Blackberries: 1 qt.
- Rum: 3 Tbsps.
- Gelatin (lime): 1 pkg.
- Orange juice (hot): 1¼ cups
- Lemon juice: 1 Tbsp.
- Heavy cream (whipped): 1 cup
- Sugar (granulated): ⅓ cup

For five 9-inch pies
- Cornflakes (crushed): 15 cups or 15 oz.
- Sugar (light brown): 1¼ cups or 6⅔ oz.
- Butter (melted): 1⅔ cups or 13⅓ oz.
- Salt: 1¼ tsps. or ⁵⁄₂₄ oz.
- Blackberries: 5 qts.
- Rum: 1 scant cup or 7½ oz.
- Gelatin (lime): 5 pkgs.
- Orange juice (hot): 6¼ cups or 3 lbs. 2 oz.
- Lemon juice: 5 Tbsps. or 2½ oz.
- Heavy cream (whipped): 5 cups or 2½ lbs.
- Sugar (granulated): 1⅔ cups or 13⅓ oz.

Combine crushed cornflakes, brown sugar, butter, and salt and mix thoroughly. Press mixture into bottom and sides of 9-inch buttered pie pan and bake in a moderate oven (350° F.) for 5 minutes.

Wash blackberries quickly; pick, hull, drain and sprinkle lightly with rum. Let stand 15 minutes. Drain and add remaining rum to orange juice. Dissolve lime gelatin in hot orange juice and stir until dissolved; add lemon juice, stir well and chill until mixture thickens and begins to set. Beat with rotary egg beater until fluffy and light in color. Fold in whipped cream, to which has been added the granulated sugar, and continue beating until thoroughly blended. Pour ¾ of the mixture into chilled cornflake pre-baked pastry shell and spread blackberries on top. Put remaining gelatin-cream mixture in a pastry bag and force a standing rim around the pie. Serve very cold.

(384)

BLACKBERRY CHIFFON PIE
ONE-CRUST PIE, PRE-BAKED PASTRY SHELL

For one 9-inch pie
- Gelatin (granulated): 1 Tbsp.
- Water (cold): ¼ cup
- Sugar (granulated): ½ cup
- Orange juice: ¼ cup
- Lemon juice: ¼ cup
- Water (hot): ½ cup
- Salt: ¼ tsp.
- Egg yolks (well beaten): 3
- Egg whites (stiffly beaten): 3
- Sugar (brown): ½ cup
- Blackberries (fresh or canned): 1¼ cups
- Pastry: 1 baked Rice Creole pie shell No. 71
- Red currant jelly (melted): ¼ cup (more or less)
- Whipped cream
- Blackberries (for garnishing): ½ cup
- Pineapple sticks (canned): 6 pieces

For five 9-inch pies
- Gelatin (granulated): 5 Tbsps. or 1¼ oz.
- Water (cold): 1¼ cups or 10 oz.
- Sugar (granulated): 2½ cups or 1 lb. 4 oz.
- Orange juice: 1¼ cups or 10 oz.
- Lemon juice: 1¼ cups or 10 oz.
- Water (hot): 2½ cups or 1 lb. 4 oz.
- Salt: 1¼ tsps. or $5/24$ oz.
- Egg yolks (well beaten): 15 or 15 oz.
- Egg whites (stiffly beaten): 15 or 15 oz.
- Sugar (brown): 2½ cups or 13$1/3$ oz.
- Blackberries (fresh or canned): 6¼ cups or 1 lb. 4 oz.
- Pastry: 5 baked Rice Creole pie shells No. 71
- Red currant jelly (melted): 1¼ cups (more or less) or 12½ oz.
- Whipped cream
- Blackberries (for garnishing): 2½ cups or 6$2/3$ oz.
- Pineapple sticks (canned): 30 pieces

Sprinkle gelatin over the ¼ cup of cold water. Let stand until mixture is thick. Combine granulated sugar, orange juice, lemon juice, hot water and salt; stir until sugar is dissolved and bring to the boiling point; then as slowly as possible pour in the well-beaten egg yolks, stirring briskly and constantly until mixture thickens to custard consistency. Remove from the heat, and stir in the thickened gelatin. Cool to lukewarm; fold in the stiffly beaten egg whites, sweetened with brown sugar, alternately with the 1¼ cups of blackberries. Turn mixture into pre-baked pastry shell brushed with red currant jelly. Set in a cool place until firm. Edge with a border of whipped cream, forced through a pastry bag, and place large tuft in center of pie, on which press the garnishing blackberries; arrange sticks of canned pineapple in equal distance in the open, ungarnished space, so as to have a stick of pineapple with each cut of pie. Serve very cold.

(385)
BLUEBERRY CHIFFON PIE
ONE-CRUST PIE, PRE-BAKED PASTRY SHELL

For one 9-inch pie
- Gelatin (granulated): 1½ Tbsps.
- Cold water: ¼ cup
- Sugar (granulated): ½ cup (more or less)
- Pineapple juice (canned): 1¼ cups
- Salt: ¼ tsp.
- Blueberries (fresh, frozen or canned): 1½ cups
- Heavy cream (whipped): ½ cup
- Pastry: 1 baked flaky pie shell No. 47

For five 9-inch pies
- Gelatin (granulated): 7½ Tbsps. or 1⅞ oz.
- Cold water: 1¼ cups or 10 oz.
- Sugar (granulated): 2½ cups (more or less) or 1 lb. 4 oz.
- Pineapple juice (canned): 6¼ cups
- Salt: 1¼ tsps. or $5/24$ oz.
- Blueberries (fresh, frozen or canned): 7½ cups or 2 lbs. $2^2/7$ oz.
- Heavy cream (whipped): 2½ cups or 1 lb. 5 oz.
- Pastry: 5 baked flaky pie shells No. 47

Sprinkle gelatin over cold water; let stand. Combine sugar, pineapple juice, and salt and bring to the boiling point; stir in the soaked gelatin and cool to lukewarm. Now add the blueberries, which have been washed and picked over if fresh or frozen, or thoroughly drained if canned, folding them in thoroughly alternately with the ½ cup cream, which has been whipped stiff. Turn into pre-baked, 9-inch flaky pie shell and chill for 2 hours. Garnish with a layer of sweetened, flavored whipped cream and then sprinkle with blueberries. Serve very cold.

(386)   # BLUEBERRY BAVARIAN CREAM
CHIFFON PIE
ONE-CRUST PIE, PRE-BAKED PASTRY SHELL

For one 9-inch pie
- Water (cold): ¼ cup
- Gelatin (granulated): 1 Tbsp.
- Blueberry juice and pulp: 1 cup
- Lemon juice: 2 tsps.
- Lemon rind (grated): 1 tsp.
- Sugar (granulated): ½ cup
- Salt: ¼ tsp.
- Whole blueberries (fresh, frozen or canned): 1 cup
- Heavy cream (whipped): 1½ cups
- Pastry: 1 Vanilla Wafer Pie Shell No. 65
- Boiled Meringue Topping for Chiffon Pie No. 451

For five 9-inch pies
- Water (cold): 1¼ cups or 10 oz.
- Gelatin (granulated): 5 Tbsps. or 1¼ oz.
- Blueberry juice and pulp: 5 cups or 3 lbs. 2 oz.
- Lemon juice: 3⅓ Tbsps. or 1⅔ oz.
- Lemon rind (grated): 1⅔ Tbsps. or ⅝ oz.
- Sugar (granulated): 2½ cups or 1 lb. 4 oz.
- Salt: 1¼ tsps. or ⁵⁄₂₄ oz.
- Whole blueberries (fresh, frozen, or canned): 5 cups or 1 lb. 6⁶⁄₇ oz.
- Heavy cream (whipped): 7½ cups or 3 lbs. ¹³⁄₁₆ oz.
- Pastry: 5 Vanilla Wafer Pie Shells No. 65
- Boiled Meringue Topping for Chiffon Pie No. 451

Pour cold water in mixing bowl and sprinkle with sparkling gelatin. Place bowl in boiling water and stir until gelatin is entirely dissolved; add blueberry juice and pulp, mixed with lemon juice and rind, sugar and salt, and stir until sugar is dissolved. Cool to lukewarm and fold in the whole, drained blueberries, alternately with the whipped cream. Turn mixture into prepared 9-inch vanilla wafers pie shell. Chill for 2 hours before topping with Boiled Meringue Topping for Chiffon Pie, made as indicated for No. 451. Serve very cold.

For Butterscotch Bavarian Cream Chiffon Pie, omit sugar, cook ¾ cup of brown sugar with 2 tablespoons of butter together for a few minutes and add this to the hot liquid before cooling to lukewarm. Serve thoroughly chilled, topped with either whipped cream or Boiled Meringue Topping for Chiffon Pie, No. 451.

(387)
BLACK BOTTOM RUM
CHIFFON PIE DE LUXE
ONE-CRUST PIE

For one 9-inch pie
Crust
- Ginger cookies (rolled, sieved): About 14
- Butter (melted): 5 Tbsps. or 2½ oz.
- Almond extract: 4 drops

For five 9-inch pies
Crust
- Ginger cookies (rolled, sieved): About 70
- Butter (melted): 1 cup plus 9 Tbsps. or 12½ oz.
- Almond extract: ⅓ tsp. or 20 drops

To sieved ginger cookies, add melted butter and almond extract and blend thoroughly. Pat out evenly in 9-inch pie pan and bake in slow oven (300° F.) for 10–12 minutes. Cool and place in refrigerator after brushing bottom and sides with melted chocolate.

Custard Filling
- Gelatin (granulated): 1 Tbsp.
- Water (cold): ¼ cup
- Milk (scalded): 2 cups
- Sugar (dark brown): ⅝ cup
- Salt: ¼ tsp.
- Butter: 1 tsp.
- Egg yolks (well beaten): 4
- Flour (pastry): 1½ Tbsps.

Custard Filling
- Gelatin (granulated): 5 Tbsps. or 1¼ oz.
- Water (cold): 1¼ cups or 10 oz.
- Milk (scalded): 2½ qts. or 5 lbs.
- Sugar (dark brown): 3⅛ cups or 1 lb. ⅔ oz.
- Salt: 1¼ tsps. or ⁵⁄₂₄ oz.
- Butter: 1½ Tbsps. or ¾ oz.
- Egg yolks (well beaten): 20, or 1 lb. 4 oz.
- Flour (pastry): 7½ Tbsps. or 1⅞ oz.

Sprinkle gelatin into cold water and let stand for 5 minutes; stir into scalded milk, combined with brown sugar, salt and butter; stir until sugar is entirely dissolved. Then add well-beaten egg yolks and flour which have been thoroughly blended together, gradually, stirring constantly from the bottom of the pan with a wire whisk. Place over hot water and cook, stirring constantly, for 15 minutes, or until mixture is thick and smooth and custard coats a spoon. Remove from hot water and place in pan of cold, not ice, water to prevent further cooking.

For one 9-inch pie
Chocolate Layer
- Sweet chocolate (melted): 3 Tbsps.
- Vanilla extract: ¾ tsp.
- Custard: 1 cup of the prepared custard (above)

For five 9-inch pies
Chocolate Layer
- Sweet chocolate (melted): 1 scant cup, or 7½ oz.
- Vanilla extract: 3¾ tsps. or ⅝ oz.
- Custard: 5 cups of the prepared custard (above)

Combine melted chocolate, vanilla extract and 1 cup prepared lukewarm custard and blend thoroughly.

Rum Layer (Meringue)
- Egg whites (stiffly beaten): 4
- Sugar (powdered): ½ cup
- Cream of tartar: ¼ tsp.
- Rum: 2 Tbsps.

Rum Layer (Meringue)
- Egg whites (stiffly beaten): 20 or 1 lb. 4 oz.
- Sugar (powdered): 2½ cups or $11^3/_7$ oz.
- Cream of tartar: 1¼ tsps. or $^5/_{24}$ oz.
- Rum: ⅝ cup or 5 oz.

To the stiffly beaten egg whites gradually add powdered sugar mixed with cream of tartar and rum, beating well after each addition until meringue holds its peaks.

Now gently fold meringue into chocolate mixture, and pour into bottom of prepared, cooled pie crust. Let remaining custard cool but not stiffen; then beat well. Pour custard over set chocolate in the pastry crust. Chill thoroughly before topping with either Boiled Ginger Meringue Topping for Chiffon Pie, No. 451 or plain whipped cream. Serve thoroughly chilled.

BRANDY CHIFFON PIE
(388)
ONE-CRUST PIE, PRE-BAKED PASTRY SHELL

For one 9-inch pie
- Gelatin (granulated): 1 Tbsp.
- Water (cold): ¼ cup
- Milk (scalded): 1½ cups
- Sugar (granulated): ¾ cup
- Salt: ⅛ tsp.
- Egg yolks (well beaten): 3
- Egg whites (stiffly beaten): 3
- Brandy: 3 Tbsps.
- Pastry: 1 baked Graham Cracker Pie Shell (No. 55)
- Whipped Cream Topping
- Angelica (chopped fine): 1 Tbsp.

For five 9-inch pies
- Gelatin (granulated): 5 Tbsps. or 1¼ oz.
- Water (cold): 1¼ cups or 10 oz.
- Milk (scalded): 7½ cups or 3¾ lbs.
- Sugar (granulated): 3¾ cups or 1 lb. 14 oz.
- Salt: ⅝ tsp.
- Egg yolks (well beaten): 15 or 15 oz.
- Egg whites (stiffly beaten): 15 or 15 oz.
- Brandy: 15 Tbsps. or 1 scant cup or 7½ oz.
- Pastry: 5 baked Graham Cracker Pie Shells (No. 55)
- Whipped Cream Topping
- Angelica (chopped fine): 5 Tbsps. or 1⅞ oz.

Place cold water in a mixing bowl; sprinkle with gelatin and let stand for 5 minutes. Combine scalded milk, sugar, salt, and blend well, stirring until sugar is dissolved. Gradually add well-beaten egg yolks, beating constantly from bottom of container; place mixture over hot water and cook until mixture thickens and coats the spoon, stirring constantly. Stir in the soaked gelatin until thoroughly dissolved. Cool until mixture starts to set, then fold in the stiffly beaten egg whites, alternately with the brandy. Turn mixture into prepared, pre-baked 9-inch graham cracker pie crust and chill thoroughly. When chilled, top with whipped cream, and sprinkle over the finely chopped angelica. Serve very cold. Apple brandy or rum may be substituted for brandy, if desired.

(389)   BUTTERSCOTCH CHIFFON PIE
ONE-CRUST PIE, PRE-BAKED PASTRY SHELL

For one 9-inch pie
- Plain gelatin: 1 pkg. or 1 Tbsp.
- Water (cold): ¼ cup
- Egg yolks (slightly beaten): 3
- Sugar (light brown): 1 cup
- Milk (scalded): 1 cup
- Butter: 2 Tbsps.
- Salt: ¼ tsp.
- Vanilla extract: ½ tsp.
- Egg whites (stiffly beaten): 3
- Sugar (granulated): ¾ cup
- Pastry: 1 baked rich pie shell (No. 70)
- Whipped Cream Topping

For five 9-inch pies
- Plain gelatin: 5 pkgs. or 5 Tbsps.
- Water (Cold): 1¼ cups or 10 oz.
- Egg yolks (slightly beaten): 15 or 15 oz.
- Sugar (light brown): 5 cups or 1 lb. 10⅔ oz.
- Milk (scalded): 5 cups or 2½ lbs.
- Butter: ⅝ cup or 5 oz.
- Salt: 1¼ tsps. or ⁵⁄₂₄ oz.
- Vanilla extract: 2½ tsps. or ⁵⁄₁₂ oz.
- Egg whites (stiffly beaten): 15 or 15 oz.
- Sugar (granulated): 3¾ cups or 1 lb. 14 oz.
- Pastry: 5 baked rich pie shells (No. 70.)
- Whipped Cream Topping

Soak gelatin in cold water for five minutes. Beat egg yolks slightly, and gradually add brown sugar, beating well after each addition. Add milk and butter, blend well, strain and cook in top of double boiler, stirring constantly, until custardlike. Now, add gelatin to hot milk mixture and stir until dissolved. Add salt and vanilla extract; fold in the stiffly beaten egg whites, sweetened with granulated sugar, adding a little at a time. Turn filling into pre-baked 9-inch pastry shell and when cold, top with whipped cream. Serve cold.

(390) CHERRY CHIFFON PIE—HOME METHOD
ONE-CRUST PIE, PRE-BAKED PASTRY SHELL

For one 9-inch pie
- Gelatin (granulated): 1 Tbsp.
- Water (cold): ¼ cup
- Egg yolks (well beaten): 4
- Sugar (granulated): ½ cup
- Cherry juice (from can): ½ cup
- Salt: ½ tsp.
- Lemon rind (grated): ½ tsp.
- Egg whites (stiffly beaten): 4
- Sugar (granulated): ½ cup
- Pastry: 1 baked Lemon Juice and Egg Pie Shell (No. 56)
- Whole cherries (canned, pitted)

For five 9-inch pies
- Gelatin (granulated): 5 Tbsps. or 1¼ oz.
- Water (cold): 1¼ cup or 10 oz.
- Egg yolks (well beaten): 20 or 1 lb. 4 oz.
- Sugar (granulated): 2½ cups or 1 lb. 4 oz.
- Cherry juice (from can): 2½ cups or 1 lb. 4 oz.
- Salt: 2½ tsps. or $5/12$ oz.
- Lemon rind (grated): 2½ tsps. or $5/16$ oz.
- Egg whites (stiffly beaten): 20 or 1 lb. 4 oz.
- Sugar (granulated): 2½ cups or 1 lb. 4 oz.
- Pastry: 5 baked Lemon Juice and Egg Pie Shells (No. 56)
- Whole cherries (canned, pitted)

Sprinkle gelatin over cold water in mixing bowl and let stand 5 minutes. Combine well-beaten egg yolks, ½ cup sugar, cherry juice, and salt, and blend well. Cook over hot water until thick and of custard consistency, stirring constantly; add the soaked gelatin and lemon rind and stir until gelatin is dissolved. Cool. When mixture begins to congeal, fold in the egg whites beaten with remaining sugar and turn into pre-baked 9-inch pastry shell. Chill for at least 2 hours before topping with whipped cream and garnishing with whole, pitted, canned cherries, all around the border of the pie. Serve very cold.

(391) CHOCOLATE BAVARIAN CREAM CHIFFON PIE
ONE-CRUST PIE, PRE-BAKED PASTRY SHELL

For one 9-inch pie
- Gelatin (granulated): 1 Tbsp.
- Water (cold): ¼ cup
- Milk (scalded): ½ cup or 4 oz.
- Cocoa: 6 Tbsps.
- Sugar (granulated): ⅓ cup
- Salt: ¼ tsp.
- Heavy Cream (whipped): 2 cups
- Vanilla extract: ¾ tsp.
- Pastry: 1 baked Peanut Butter Graham Cracker Pie Shell, No. 60
- Marshmallow Cream Topping (No. 470)

For five 9-inch pies
- Gelatin (granulated): 5 Tbsps. or 1¼ oz.
- Water (cold): 1¼ cups or 10 oz.
- Milk (scalded): 2½ cups or 1 lb. 4 oz.
- Cocoa: 1⅞ cups or 7½ oz.
- Sugar (granulated): 1⅔ cups or 13⅓ oz.
- Salt: 1¼ tsps. or $^5/_{24}$ oz.
- Heavy Cream (whipped): 2½ qts. or 5 lbs. 3¾ oz.
- Vanilla extract: 3¾ tsps. or ⅝ oz.
- Pastry: 5 baked Peanut Butter
- Graham Cracker Pie Shells, No. 60
- Marshmallow Cream Topping (No. 470)

Sprinkle gelatin over cold water in a mixing bowl and let stand 5 minutes. Combine scalded milk, cocoa, sugar and salt and stir until dissolved. Stir in the soaked gelatin thoroughly. Cook and when mixture begins to thicken, beat with rotary egg beater or electric mixer; fold in the whipped cream, to which has been added the vanilla extract. Turn into pre-baked pastry shell and chill for at least 2 hours. When well chilled, top with Marshmallow Cream Topping, No. 470. Serve very cold.

(392) A FEW FACTS ABOUT MARSHMALLOWS

Since marshmallows form a perfect starch, we cannot cook or heat them over direct heat without great danger of scorching and change in consistency. Hence marshmallows must be melted over hot water, as in a double boiler. And the heating or melting may not continue too long, else the marshmallows will return to their original colorless liquid. Heat or melt over hot water, but watch carefully, and remove when the marshmallows are only partially dissolved. Finish by beating them smooth.

The marshmallows may be cut into quarters for greater convenience and rapid melting. Use sharp shears, dipped first into cold water or flour. As mentioned, the consistency of the marshmallow is a spready or syrupy one, and thus is ideal for frostings and also for making all types of frozen desserts. A refrigerator mixture to which marshmallows have been added will never split or form ice crystals. If left to stand, the mixture will tend to become stiff and solid. If served or used as a baked meringue topping, serve instantly so as to allow the delicious burnt almond flavor to be enjoyed at its perfection. Watch the baking during melting—a few moments too long, or in a too-hot oven, and pouff!—the meringue will be a shade less perfect. The chef's technical term for this kind of quick oven browning is "to glaze in a hot oven."

Making Decorative Garnishes

Making decorative garnishes with such pliable material as marshmallows is both amusing and rewarding. Since it is only sensible to have all decorations on a cake or pie edible, and since sugar flowers are usually beyond the skill of anyone except a professional pastry cook, marshmallow flowers are the answer. To make dog-wood blossoms: Use marshmallows which are very slightly stale or hard. Cut thin slices crosswise and shape them with your fingers into petals. Drop them in granulated sugar to prevent stickiness. Then make a tiny slit on the tip end of each petal and touch with a bit of melted chocolate.

To make the stem cut round and round the marshmallow, using a very sharp knife, until a long slender strip is produced. Roll this in cocoa sugar.

To make leaves, cut lengthwise through the marshmallow and then pull each piece into a leaf shape. Sprinkle with green sugar or frost with green icing.

Other flowers may be taken for a pattern. The only skill required is with scissors and fingers. Sprays of apple blossoms, daisies, or pansies may be easily made and tinted with colored sugars or really painted with weak solutions of vegetable coloring.

An attractive variation of the Marguerite can be made as follows: Frost fresh, crisp salted crackers with confectioner's icing, and while still soft, press into each one a small flower shape made of bits of fresh marshmallow. Fill the centers with coarsely chopped nut meats and sprinkle the petals with colored sugars, if desired.

....

(393)
CHOCOLATE CHIFFON PIE
ONE-CRUST PIE, PRE-BAKED PASTRY SHELL

For one 9-inch pie
- Water (cold): $^2/_3$ cup
- Sugar (granulated): ¼ cup
- Salt: ¼ tsp.
- Bitter chocolate (grated): $^1/_6$ cup
- Cornstarch: $^1/_6$ cup
- Milk (cold): 2 Tbsps.
- Heavy cream (unwhipped): 3 Tbsps.
- Vanilla extract: ¼ tsp.
- Brandy, apply brandy, kirsch or rum: 1 Tbsp.
- Egg whites (stiffly beaten): 2
- Sugar (granulated): ¼ cup
- Pastry: 1 baked mealy pie shell (No. 49)
- Whipped Cream Topping
- Sweet chocolate (grated or shots)

For five 9-inch pies
- Water (cold): $3^1/_3$ cups or 1 lb. $10^2/_3$ oz.
- Sugar (granulated): 1¼ cups or 10 oz.
- Salt: 1¼ tsps. or $^5/_{24}$ oz.
- Bitter chocolate (grated): $^5/_6$ cup or $4^4/_9$ oz.
- Cornstarch: $^5/_6$ cup or $4^4/_9$ oz.
- Milk (cold): $^5/_8$ cup or 5 oz.
- Heavy cream (unwhipped): 1 scant cup or $7^{13}/_{16}$ oz.
- Vanilla extract: 1¼ tsps. or $^5/_{24}$ oz.
- Brandy, apple brandy, kirsch or rum: 5 Tbsps. or 2½ oz.
- Egg whites (stiffly beaten): 10 or 10 oz.
- Sugar (granulated): 1¼ cups or 10 oz.
- Pastry: 5 baked mealy pie shells (No. 49)
- Whipped Cream Topping
- Sweet chocolate (grated or shots)

Into a saucepan, place water, ¼ cup sugar, salt and grated chocolate. Blend well and bring this to a rapid boil, stirring occasionally until chocolate is thoroughly dissolved; then let it boil once or twice briskly. Lower the heat and gradually add the combined cornstarch and cold milk, blended to a paste. Stir constantly until mixture is thick and clear. Boil once more briskly and remove from the heat; stir in the combined heavy cream, vanilla and brandy (or other favorite spirit). Fold in gently but thoroughly the stiffly beaten egg whites, sweetened with remaining sugar. Turn mixture into pre-baked 9-inch pastry shell and chill thoroughly before topping with whipped cream and sprinkling with either grated chocolate, chocolate shots or decorettes. Serve very cold. Note that in this pie, there is no gelatin, the suspension being made with cornstarch. If the butterscotch flavor is desired, substitute ⅓ cup of dark brown sugar for granulated sugar, both with cooked mixture and meringue mixture, and stir in 2 teaspoons butter before folding in the meringue, and while mixture is hot.

....

(394) CHOCOLATE SUNDAE CHIFFON PIE
ONE-CRUST PIE, PRE-BAKED PASTRY SHELL

For one 9-inch pie
- Chocolate syrup: ¼ cup
- Almonds (ground, blanched, toasted): ¼ cup
- Milk (fresh): 1½ cups
- Egg yolks (well beaten): 3
- Sugar (dark brown): ⅓ cup
- Nutmeg (ground): ½ tsp.
- Cinnamon (ground): ¼ tsp.
- Vanilla extract: ⅝ tsp.
- Salt: ¼ tsp.
- Gelatin (granulated): 1 Tbsp.
- Water (cold): 3 Tbsps.
- Egg whites (stiffly beaten): 3
- Pastry: 1 baked Nut Pastry Shell (No. 57)
- Whipped cream topping
- Cocoa: ½ tsp.

For five 9-inch pies
- Chocolate syrup: 1¼ cups or 10 oz.
- Almonds (ground, blanched, toasted): 1¼ cups or 6⅔ oz.
- Milk (fresh): 7½ cups or 3¾ lbs.
- Egg yolks (well beaten): 15 or 15 oz.
- Sugar (dark brown): 1⅔ cups or 8⁸/₉ oz.
- Nutmeg (ground): 2½ tsps. or ⁵/₂₄ oz.
- Cinnamon (ground): 1¼ tsps.
- Vanilla extract: 3¾ tsps. or ⅝ oz.
- Salt: 1¼ tsps. or ⁵/₂₄ oz.
- Gelatin (granulated): 5 Tbsps. or 1¼ oz.
- Water (cold): 1 cup or 7½ oz.
- Egg whites (stiffly beaten): 15 or 15 oz.
- Pastry: 5 baked Nut Pastry Shells (No. 57)
- Whipped cream topping
- Cocoa: 2½ tsps. or ⁵/₁₂ oz.

Heat milk to the boiling point, but do not allow to boil; stir in the well-beaten egg yolks with dark brown sugar, nutmeg, cinnamon, vanilla, and salt. Blend thoroughly, and over hot water until mixture is consistency of rich cream, stirring constantly. Remove from the heat and add gelatin which has been soaked in cold water for 5 minutes. Cool. When mixture begins to set, fold in the stiffly beaten egg whites. Turn filling into prepared nut pastry, the bottom of which has been spread evenly with combined chocolate syrup and ground, blanched, toasted almonds. Chill. When thoroughly chilled, top with unsweetened and unfavored whipped cream and sprinkle cocoa over top. Serve cold.

....

(395)
COCONUT CHIFFON PIE
ONE-CRUST PIE, PRE-BAKED PASTRY SHELL

For one 9-inch pie
- Egg yolks (well beaten): 3
- Sugar (granulated): ½ cup
- Salt: ¼ tsp.
- Milk (cold): 1 cup
- Gelatin (granulated): 1 Tbsp.
- Water (cold): ¼ cup
- Egg whites (stiffly beaten): 4
- Coconut (shredded, moist): ½ cup
- Vanilla extract: 1 tsp.
- Lemon extract: $^1/_8$ tsp.
- Pastry: 1 baked Oatmeal Pie Shell (No. 58)
- Coconut (toasted): 1½ to 2 cups

For five 9-inch pies
- Egg yolks (well beaten): 15 or 15 oz.
- Sugar (granulated): 2½ cups or 1 lb. 4 oz.
- Salt: 1¼ tsps. or $^5/_{24}$ oz.
- Milk (cold): 5 cups or 2½ lbs.
- Gelatin (granulated): 5 Tbsps. or 1¼ oz.
- Water (cold): 1¼ cups or 10 oz.
- Egg whites (stiffly beaten): 20 or 1 lb. 4 oz.
- Coconut (shredded, moist): 2½ cups or ½ lb.
- Vanilla extract: $1^2/_3$ Tbsps. or $^5/_6$ oz.
- Lemon extract: $^5/_8$ tsp.
- Pastry: 5 baked Oatmeal Pie Shells (No. 58)
- Coconut (toasted): 7½ to 10 cups or 1½ lbs. to 2 lbs.

Into top of double boiler, put egg yolks, sugar, salt, and cold milk, and stir until sugar is dissolved and mixture is thoroughly blended; then cook over hot water until mixture is consistency of heavy cream, stirring constantly from the bottom of the pan. Add gelatin, which has been soaked in cold water for 5 minutes, and stir until gelatin is dissolved. Remove from the hot water and cool. When mixture begins to congeal, fold in the stiffly beaten egg whites alternately with moist coconut and combined flavoring extracts. Turn filling into pre-baked Oatmeal Pie Crust, and chill for at least 2 hours, Then sprinkle with freshly toasted, cooled coconut, using long thread coconut.

....

(396) COCONUT LEMON CHIFFON PIE
ONE-CRUST PIE, PRE-BAKED PASTRY SHELL

For one 9-inch pie
- Gelatin (granulated): 1 Tbsp.
- Water (cold): ¼ cup
- Egg yolks (slightly beaten): 3
- Sugar (brown): ¼ cup
- Sugar (granulated): ¼ cup
- Milk (scalded): 1 cup
- Salt: ⅛ tsp.
- Egg whites (stiffly beaten): 3
- Coconut (shredded): ½ cup
- Vanilla extract: ¾ tsp.
- Lemon extract: 1 tsp.
- Pastry: 1 baked Lemon Juice and Egg Pie Shell (No. 56)
- Whipped Cream Topping
- Coconut (shredded, toasted)

For five 9-inch pies
- Gelatin (granulated): 5 Tbsps. or 1¼ oz.
- Water (cold): 1¼ cups or 10 oz.
- Egg yolks (slightly beaten): 15 or 15 oz.
- Sugar (brown): 1¼ cups or 6⅔ oz.
- Sugar (granulated): 1¼ cups or 10 oz.
- Milk (scalded): 5 cups or 2½ lbs.
- Salt: ⅝ tsp.
- Egg whites (stiffly beaten): 15 or 15 oz.
- Coconut (shredded): 2½ cups or ½ lb.
- Vanilla extract: 3¾ tsps. or ⅝ oz.
- Lemon extract: 1⅔ Tbsps. or ⅚ oz.
- Pastry: 5 baked Lemon Juice and Egg Pie Shells (No. 56)
- Whipped Cream Topping
- Coconut (shredded, toasted)

Soften gelatin in cold water for 5 minutes. Beat egg yolks slightly and add combined sugars gradually, beating briskly. Slowly stir in scalded milk. Cook mixture in double boiler over hot water until custard is soft, stirring constantly. Then add softened gelatin and stir until dissolved. Add salt. Cool. When beginning to set, fold in stiffly beaten egg whites, alternately with plain shredded coconut, vanilla and lemon extracts. Turn into cooled, pre-baked 9-inch pastry shell as evenly as possible and top with sweetened, flavored whipped cream; sprinkle with cooled toasted coconut. Serve cold.

....

(397) COFFEE BAVARIAN CREAM CHIFFON PIE
ONE-CRUST PIE, PRE-BAKED PASTRY SHELL

Proceed as indicated for No. 391, Chocolate Bavarian Cream Chiffon Pie, substituting ½ cup strong boiled coffee for ½ cup scalded milk, and adding 1 tablespoon lemon juice. Use pre-baked Spiced Pastry Crust (No. 64) and top with Marshmallow Cream Topping, No. 470. Serve very cold.

(398) COFFEE CHIFFON PIE—HOME METHOD
ONE-CRUST PIE, PRE-BAKED PASTRY SHELL

For one 9-inch pie

- Prunes (cooked, sieved, sweetened): ½ cup
- Lemon rind (grated): ½ tsp.
- Gelatin (granulated): 1 Tbsp.
- Coffee (cold, strong): ¼ cup
- Egg yolks (slightly beaten): 4
- Sugar (granulated): ½ cup
- Salt: ½ tsp.
- Coffee (hot, strong): ½ cup
- Lemon juice: 1 Tbsp.
- Egg whites (stiffly beaten): 4
- Sugar (granulated): ¼ cup
- Pastry: 1 baked Cinnamon Bread Crumb Pie Shell, (No. 53)
- Whipped Cream Topping

For five 9-inch pies

- Prunes (cooked, sieved, sweetened): 2½ cups or 1 lb. 14 oz.
- Lemon rind (grated): 2½ tsps. or $^5/_{16}$ oz.
- Gelatin (granulated): 5 Tbsps. or 1¼ oz.
- Coffee (cold, strong): 1¼ cups or 10 oz.
- Egg yolks (slightly beaten): 20 or 1 lb. 4 oz.
- Sugar (granulated): 2½ cups or 1 lb. 4 oz.
- Salt: 2½ tsps. or $^5/_{12}$ oz.
- Coffee (hot, strong): 2½ cups or 1 lb. 4 oz.
- Lemon juice: 5 Tbsps. or 2½ oz.
- Egg whites (stiffly beaten): 20 or 1 lb. 4 oz.
- Sugar (granulated): 1¼ cups or 10 oz.
- Pastry: 5 baked Cinnamon Bread Crumb Pie Shells (No. 53)
- Whipped Cream Topping

Spread combined, lightly sweetened prune puree with lemon rind over the bottom and sides of pre-baked 9-inch Cinnamon Bread Crumb Crust. Chill. Prepare filling as follows: Soak granulated gelatin in cold coffee for 5 minutes. Beat egg yolks slightly, add the ½ cup granulated sugar, salt, and hot coffee; and cook over boiling water until of custard consistency, stirring constantly. Add the soaked gelatin and lemon juice, stir well and cool. When mixture begins to congeal, fold in the stiffly beaten egg whites to which has been added the remaining sugar. Turn filling into prepared 9-inch pastry shell and chill for at least 2 hours before topping with whipped cream. Serve very cold.

(399) CREAM CHEESE PINEAPPLE CHIFFON PIE
ONE-CRUST PIE

For one 9-inch pie

- Pastry: 1 baked Western Pie Shell (No. 69)
- Pineapple (canned, crushed, well drained): ½ cup.
- Gelatin (granulated): 2 tsps.
- Pineapple juice (canned): ¼ cup
- Boiling water: ½ cup
- Coffee infusion (hot, strong): 3 Tbsps.
- Cream cheese: ¾ cup
- Sugar (dark brown): $1/3$ cup
- Salt: $1/8$ tsp.
- Egg whites (stiffly beaten): 2
- Sugar (powdered): 2 Tbsps.
- Boiled Meringue Topping No. 451

For five 9-inch pies

- Pastry: 5 baked Western Pie Shells (No. 69)
- Pineapple (canned, crushed, well drained): 2½ cups or 1 lb. 14 oz.
- Gelatin (granulated): $3^{1}/3$ Tbsps. or $5/6$ oz.
- Pineapple juice (canned): 1¼ cups or 10 oz.
- Boiling water: 2½ cups or 1 lb. 4 oz.
- Coffee infusion (hot, strong): 1 scant cup or 7½ oz.
- Cream cheese: 3¾ cups or 1 lb. 14 oz.
- Sugar (dark brown): $1^{2}/3$ cups or $8^{8}/9$ oz.
- Salt: $5/8$ tsp.
- Egg whites (stiffly beaten): 10 or 10 oz.
- Sugar (powdered): $5/8$ cup or $2^{6}/7$ oz.
- Boiled Meringue Topping No. 451

Brush cold pre-baked pie shell with slightly beaten egg whites; let dry; then line bottom and sides with canned crushed pineapple which has been thoroughly drained. Place in refrigerator to chill while preparing the filling as follows: Soak gelatin in cold pineapple juice. Combine boiling water and coffee infusion, and heat to boiling point; add the soaked gelatin, stirring until dissolved. Beat cream cheese with fork until creamy; continue beating while adding sugar and salt until thoroughly blended. Gradually add the hot gelatin mixture. Blend well. Cool. When mixture begins to set or congeal, fold in the stiffly beaten egg whites sweetened with powdered sugar. Turn mixture into pre-baked, prepared, chilled pastry shell, and set in refrigerator to chill for 2 hours. Then top with Boiled Meringue Topping made as indicated for No. 451. Serve very cold.

(400)

CRANBERRY CHIFFON PIE—
HOME METHOD
ONE-CRUST PIE, PRE-BAKED PASTRY SHELL

For one 9-inch pie
- Cranberry sauce (canned, strained): 1¼ cups
- Water (cold): ⅜ cup
- Sugar (granulated): ½ cup
- Salt: ½ tsp.
- Cornstarch: 1 Tbsp.
- Flour (pastry): 1 Tbsp.
- Water (cold): ¼ cup
- Egg whites (stiffly beaten): 2
- Sugar (granulated): ¼ cup
- Pastry: 1 baked Gingersnap Pie Shell No. 54
- Whipped Cream Topping

For five 9-inch pies
- Cranberry sauce (canned, strained): 6¼ cups or 5 lbs.
- Water (cold): 1⅞ cups or 15 oz.
- Sugar (granulated): 2½ cups or 3 lbs. 2 oz.
- Salt: 2½ tsps. or ⁵⁄₁₂ oz.
- Cornstarch: 5 Tbsps. or 1⅔ oz.
- Flour (pastry): 5 Tbsps. or 1¼ oz.
- Water (cold): 1¼ cups or 10 oz.
- Egg whites (stiffly beaten): 10 or 10 oz.
- Sugar (granulated): 1¼ cups or 10 oz.
- Pastry: 5 baked Gingersnap Pie Shells No. 54
- Whipped Cream Topping

Combine canned, strained cranberry sauce with ⅜ cup cold water, ½ cup granulated sugar and salt and blend thoroughly with a wire whisk, beating until mixture is smooth; strain through a fine sieve to ensure smoothness. Place a pad under the saucepan to prevent scorching and bring to a rapid boil, stirring frequently with wire whisk. When boiling, gradually add combined cornstarch and flour dissolved with remaining cold water, stirring constantly until mixture is thick and clear. Give one or two brisk boils, remove from the heat and pour into shallow container to cool rapidly. When cold, fold in stiffly beaten egg whites sweetened with remaining sugar; turn into chilled, pre-baked pastry shell and chill well before topping with whipped cream, forced through a pastry bag with a square tube. Serve very cold.

(401)

EGGNOG CHIFFON PIE
ONE-CRUST PIE

For one 9-inch pie
- Gelatin (granulated): 1 Tbsp.
- Milk (cold): ¼ cup
- Milk (scalded): 1¼ cups
- Egg yolks (well beaten): 3
- Salt: ¼ tsp.
- Nutmeg (ground): ¼ tsp.
- Cinnamon (ground): ¼ tsp.
- Sugar (granulated): ½ cup
- Egg whites (stiffly beaten): 3
- Heavy cream (whipped): ¼ cup
- Sugar (powdered): ¼ cup
- Brandy, apple brandy or rum: 2 Tbsps. *or* vanilla extract: 1 tsp.
- Pastry: 1 Mealy baked pie shell No. 49
- Marshmallow Cream Topping for Chiffon Pie No. 470

For five 9-inch pies
- Gelatin (granulated): 5 Tbsps. or 1¼ oz.
- Milk (cold): 1¼ cups or 10 oz.
- Milk (scalded): 6¼ cups or 3 lbs. 2 oz.
- Egg yolks (well beaten): 15 or 15 oz.
- Salt: 1¼ tsps. or $5/24$ oz.
- Nutmeg (ground): 1¼ tsps.
- Cinnamon (ground): 1¼ tsps.
- Sugar (granulated): 2½ cups or 1 lb. 4 oz.
- Egg whites (stiffly beaten): 15 or 15 oz.
- Heavy cream (whipped): 1¼ cups or 10½ oz.
- Sugar (powdered): 1¼ cups or $5^5/7$ oz.
- Brandy, apple brandy or rum: ⅝ cup or 5 oz. *or* vanilla extract: $1^2/3$ Tbsps. or $5/6$ oz.
- Pastry: 5 Mealy baked pie shells No. 49
- Marshmallow Cream Topping for Chiffon Pie No. 470

Soak gelatin in cold milk for 5 minutes. Scald remaining milk. Combine well-beaten egg yolks, salt, spices and granulated sugar and beat together until thoroughly blended; gradually add to scalded milk, stirring constantly. Cook over boiling water until mixture coats spoon and is of the consistency of soft custard. Then stir in the soaked gelatin until entirely dissolved; cool. When cold, fold in the combined stiffly beaten egg whites, whipped cream and powdered sugar alternately with brandy or vanilla extract. Turn mixture into pre-baked 9-inch pastry shell and chill for at least 2 hours before topping with Marshmallow Cream Topping for Chiffon Pie, made as indicated for No. 470. Serve very cold, sprinkled with nutmeg.

(402)   # GOOSEBERRY CHIFFON PIE
ONE-CRUST PIE, PRE-BAKED PASTRY SHELL

For one 9-inch pie
- Pastry: 1 baked rich pie shell (No. 70)
- Gooseberries (fresh): 1¾ cups
- Water (cold): 1¾ cups
- Salt: ¼ tsp.
- Sugar (granulated): 1 cup
- Egg yolks (slightly beaten): 2
- Gelatin (granulated): 1 Tbsp.
- Water (cold): ¼ cup
- Egg whites (stiffly beaten): 3
- Whipped Cream Topping

For five 9-inch pies
- Pastry: 5 baked rich pie shells (No. 70)
- Gooseberries (fresh): 8¾ cups or 2 lbs. 3 oz.
- Water (cold): 8¾ cups or 4 lbs. 6 oz.
- Salt: 1¼ tsps. or $5/24$ oz.
- Sugar (granulated): 5 cups or 2½ lbs.
- Egg yolks (slightly beaten): 10 or 10 oz.
- Gelatin (granulated): 5 Tbsps. or 1$2/3$ oz.
- Water (cold): 1¼ cups or 10 oz.
- Egg whites (stiffly beaten): 15 or 15 oz.
- Whipped Cream Topping

Brush bottom and sides of pre-baked 9-inch pastry shell with butter; cool. Wash, clean, pick and drain fresh gooseberries and cook them in equal amount of water, until just soft—a little underdone. Force through sieve to remove skins and seeds. Add sugar and salt and bring to a boil. Stir in the slightly beaten egg yolks and continue cooking 1 or 2 minutes longer, stirring constantly from bottom of pan. Soak granulated gelatin in remaining cold water 5 minutes and pour into hot gooseberry mixture. Cool a little, then fold in the stiffly beaten egg whites. Turn filling into prepared pastry shell and chill well before topping with whipped cream, flavored and sweetened to taste and forced through a pastry bag with a fancy tube.

(403)
GRAPEFRUIT CHIFFON PIE— FLORIDA METHOD
ONE-CRUST PIE, PRE-BAKED PASTRY SHELL

For one 9-inch pie
- Gelatin (granulated): 1 Tbsp.
- Water (cold): 2 Tbsps.
- Orange juice (cold): 2 Tbsps.
- Egg yolks (well beaten): 4
- Sugar (granulated): ½ cup
- Grapefruit juice (canned): ½ cup
- Citron (candied, chopped): 1 tsp.
- Angelica (chopped): 1 tsp.
- Almonds (blanched, chopped, toasted): ¼ cup
- Egg whites (stiffly beaten): 4
- Sugar (powdered): $1/3$ cup
- Pastry: 1 Cinnamon Bread Crumb Pie Shell (No. 53)
- Whipped Cream Topping
- Grapefruit sections (fresh or canned): 1½ cups or 1 #2 can
- Maraschino cherries (red, drained)

For five 9-inch pies
- Gelatin (granulated): 5 Tbsps. or 1¼ oz.
- Water (cold): ⅝ cup or 5 oz.
- Orange juice (cold): ⅝ cup or 5 oz.
- Egg yolks (well beaten): 20 or 1 lb. 4 oz.
- Sugar (granulated): 2½ cups or 1 lb. 4 oz.
- Grapefruit juice (canned): 2½ cups or 1 lb. 4 oz.
- Citron (candied, chopped): $1^2/3$ Tbsps. or ⅚ oz.
- Angelica (chopped): $1^2/3$ Tbsps. or ⅝ oz.
- Almonds (blanched, toasted, chopped): 1¼ cups or $6^2/3$ oz.
- Egg whites (stiffly beaten): 20 or 1 lb. 4 oz.
- Sugar (powdered): $1^2/3$ cups or $7^1/7$ oz.
- Pastry: 5 Cinnamon Bread Crumb Pie Shells (No. 53)
- Whipped Cream Topping
- Grapefruit sections (fresh or canned): 7½ cups or 1 #10 can or 6 lb. 9 oz.
- Maraschino cherries (red, drained)

Soak gelatin in combined water and orange juice for 5 minutes. Beat egg yolks until light and add sugar; continue beating until sugar is dissolved and mixture is very light, adding, while beating, the grapefruit juice. Place in double boiler and cook over hot water until mixture is of creamy consistency, stirring constantly with a wire whisk. Add soaked gelatin, chopped citron, angelica and almonds and stir until well blended. Cool to lukewarm and add stiffly beaten egg whites, to which has been added the powdered sugar. Turn mixture into prepared Cinnamon Bread Crumb Crust. Chill for 2 hours. Then top with a thin layer of whipped cream with the grapefruit sections, thoroughly drained, arranged around the edges of the pie. Garnish center with halved, drained red maraschino cherries. Serve very cold.

......

(404) KENTUCKY CIDER CHIFFON PIE
ONE-CRUST PIE, PRE-BAKED PASTRY SHELL

For one 9-inch pie
- Gelatin (granulated): 1 Tbsp.
- Orange juice (canned or fresh): ¼ cup
- Water (hot): ¾ cup
- Whisky: 2 Tbsps.
- Lemon rind (grated): 1 tsp.
- Lemon juice: 1 Tbsp.
- Sugar (granulated): ⅓ cup
- Salt: ¼ tsp.
- Whole eggs (well beaten): 3
- Sweet cider: 1⅓ cups
- Pastry: 1 baked rich pie shell (No. 70)
- Whipped Cream Topping
- Fresh Mint: A few sprigs

For five 9-inch pies
- Gelatin (granulated): 5 Tbsps. or 1¼ oz.
- Orange juice (canned or fresh): 1¼ cups or 10 oz.
- Water (hot): 3¾ cups or 1 lb. 14 oz.
- Whisky: ⅝ cup or 5 oz.
- Lemon rind (grated): 1⅔ Tbsps. or ⅝ oz.
- Lemon juice: 5 Tbsps. or 2½ oz.
- Sugar (granulated): 1⅔ cups or 13⅓ oz.
- Salt: 1¼ tsps. or ⁵⁄₂₄ oz.
- Whole eggs (well beaten): 15 or 1 lb. 14 oz.
- Sweet cider: 6⅔ cups or 3 lbs. 5⅓ oz.
- Pastry: 5 baked rich pie shells (No. 70)
- Whipped Cream Topping
- Fresh Mint: A few sprigs

Soak gelatin in cold orange juice for 5 minutes and dissolve in combined hot water, whisky, lemon rind, lemon juice, sugar and salt; bring to a boiling point, stirring until gelatin is dissolved and mixture is thoroughly blended; beat in the well beaten eggs. Cook over hot water until mixture thickens, stirring constantly. Remove from the heat, add sweet cider and cool. When mixture begins to thicken, place in a pan of chopped ice and beat with rotary beater, or electric mixer set at medium speed, until very light. Turn filling into pre-baked 9-inch pastry shell; top with whipped cream, forced through pastry bag with a fancy tube, and garnish top of pie with a few sprigs of fresh mint. Serve cold. Rum, brandy or apple brandy may be substituted for whisky, if desired, or you may garnish top of pie with maraschino cherries, cut daisy-like, or you may sprinkle top with chopped, toasted nut meats.

....

(405) ## LEMON CHIFFON PIE I
ONE-CRUST PIE, PRE-BAKED PASTRY SHELL

For one 9-inch pie
- Gelatin (granulated): 1 Tbsp.
- Water (cold): ¼ cup
- Sugar (granulated): ½ cup
- Lemon juice: ½ cup
- Salt: ¼ tsp.
- Egg yolks (beaten light): 4
- Lemon rind (grated): 1½ tsps.
- Egg whites (stiffly beaten): 4
- Sugar (granulated): ½ cup
- Pastry: 1 baked Graham Cracker Pie Shell, (No. 55)

For five 9-inch pies
- Gelatin (granulated): 5 Tbsps. or 1¼ oz.
- Water (cold): 1¼ cups or 10 oz.
- Sugar (granulated): 2½ cups or 1 lb. 4 oz.
- Lemon juice: 2½ cups or 1 lb. 4 oz.
- Salt: 1¼ tsps. or $5/24$ oz.
- Egg yolks (beaten light): 20 or 1 lb. 4 oz.
- Lemon rind (grated): 2½ Tbsps. or 1 scant oz.
- Egg whites (stiffly beaten): 20 or 1 lb. 4 oz.
- Sugar (granulated): 2½ cups or 1 lb. 4 oz.
- Pastry: 5 baked Graham Cracker Pie Shells, (No. 55)

Soak gelatin in cold water for 5 minutes. Combine ½ cup sugar, lemon juice, salt, and egg yolks, beaten until light, in top of double boiler and cook, stirring constantly until smooth and creamy. Stir in the soaked gelatin alternately with lemon rind. Remove from hot water and cool. When mixture begins to congeal, fold in the stiffly beaten egg whites, to which has been added the remaining sugar. Fill pre-baked Graham Cracker pastry shell and chill for at least 2 hours. Top with whipped cream and serve very cold.

....

(406)   # LEMON CHIFFON PIE II
ONE-CRUST PIE, PRE-BAKED PASTRY SHELL

For one 9-inch pie
- Water (cold): 1 cup
- Sugar (granulated): ⅜ cup
- Salt: ¼ tsp.
- Lemon rind (grated): 2 tsps.
- Cornstarch: ¼ cup
- Lemon juice: ¼ cup
- Egg whites (stiffly beaten): 4
- Sugar (granulated): ½ cup
- Pastry: 1 baked Bread Crumb Pie Shell (No. 51)
- Whipped Cream Topping

For five 9-inch pies
- Water (cold): 5 cups or 2½ lbs.
- Sugar (granulated): 1⅞ cups or 15 oz.
- Salt: 1¼ tsps. or ⁵⁄₂₄ oz.
- Lemon rind (grated): 3⅓ Tbsps. or 1¼ oz.
- Cornstarch: 1¼ cups or 6⅔ oz.
- Lemon juice: 1¼ cups or 10 oz.
- Egg whites (stiffly beaten): 20 or 1 lb. 4 oz.
- Sugar (granulated): 2½ cups or 1 lb. 4 oz.
- Pastry: 5 baked Bread Crumb Pie Shells (No. 51)
- Whipped Cream Topping

Combine water, ⅜ cup sugar, salt, lemon rind (and if desired a drop of yellow vegetable coloring) in a saucepan or double boiler. Bring this to a boil, stirring occasionally until sugar is dissolved. Thicken with cornstarch dissolved in lemon juice, adding it very slowly, stirring constantly until mixture thickens; then boil twice. Remove from the heat and gradually pour hot mixture over stiffly beaten egg whites, which have been sweetened with remaining sugar, beating briskly and constantly with a wire whisk; turn hot filling into pre-baked 9-inch Bread Crumb Crust, made as indicated for No. 51, having center higher than edges. Cool thoroughly before topping with slightly sweetened whipped cream. Chill well before serving.

(407)

LIME CHIFFON PIE
ONE-CRUST PIE, PRE-BAKED PASTRY SHELL

For one 9-inch pie

- Gelatin (granulated): 1 Tbsps.
- Orange juice: ¼ cup
- Egg yolks (slightly beaten): 4
- Sugar (granulated): 1 cup
- Lime juice: ½ cup
- Salt: ½ tsp.
- Lime rind (grated): 1 tsp.
- Brandy: 1½ Tbsps.
- Egg whites (stiffly beaten): 4
- Pastry: 1 baked mealy pie shell (No. 49)
- Whipped Cream Topping

For five 9-inch pies

- Gelatin (granulated): 5 Tbsps. or 1¼ oz.
- Orange juice: 1¼ cups or 10 oz.
- Egg yolks (slightly beaten): 20 or 1 lb. 4 oz.
- Sugar (granulated): 5 cups or 2½ lbs.
- Lime juice: 2½ cups or 1 lb. 4 oz.
- Salt: 2½ tsps. or $5/12$ oz.
- Lime rind (grated): $1 2/3$ Tbsps. or $5/8$ oz.
- Brandy: 7½ Tbsps. or 3¾ oz.
- Egg whites (stiffly beaten): 20 or 1 lb. 4 oz.
- Pastry: 5 baked mealy pie shells (No. 49)
- Whipped Cream Topping

Soak gelatin in orange juice for 5 minutes. Beat egg yolks, add half of the granulated sugar, lime juice, and salt. Cook over boiling water until mixture is thick and smooth and coats the spoon. Add lime rind, brandy, and soaked gelatin; mix thoroughly. Cool. When mixture begins to thicken, fold in the stiffly beaten egg whites to which the remaining half cup sugar has been added. Turn filling into pre-baked, chilled pastry shell. Chill. Then top with plain whipped cream. Serve very cold.

(408)   # MACAROON CREAM CHIFFON PIE
ONE-CRUST PIE, PRE-BAKED PASTRY SHELL

For one 9-inch pie
- Gelatin (granulated): 1 tsp.
- Water (cold): 3 Tbsps.
- Egg yolks (slightly beaten): 3
- Sugar (granulated): ½ cup
- Milk (scalded): 1 cup
- Salt: ⅛ tsp.
- Macaroons (rolled fine): ¾ cup
- Vanilla extract: 1 tsp.
- Heavy cream (whipped): ½ cup
- Whipped Cream Topping
- Macaroon crumbs: ¼ cup or 1 oz.
- Pastry: 1 pre-baked Western Pie shell (No. 69)

For five 9-inch pies
- Gelatin (granulated): 1⅔ Tbsps. or ⁵/₁₂ oz.
- Water (cold): 1 scant cup or 7½ oz.
- Egg yolks (slightly beaten): 15 or 15 oz.
- Sugar (granulated): 2½ cups or 1 lb. 4 oz.
- Milk (scalded): 5 cups or 2½ lbs.
- Salt: ⅝ tsp.
- Macaroons (rolled fine): 3¾ cups or 15 oz.
- Vanilla extract: 1⅔ Tbsps. or ⅚ oz.
- Heavy cream (whipped): 2½ cups or 1 lb. 5 oz.
- Whipped Cream Topping
- Macaroon crumbs: 1¼ cups or 5 oz.
- Pastry: 5 pre-baked Western Pie shells (No. 69)

Soak gelatin in cold water 5 minutes; beat egg yolks, add sugar and beat again until light and lemon-colored; gradually stir in the scalded milk, to which salt has been added, and cook over hot water, stirring constantly, until mixture begins to thicken, then strain, and stir in the soaked gelatin. When mixture begins to congeal, stir in the macaroon crumbs and vanilla, alternately with the heavy whipping cream which has been whipped stiff. Turn into pre-baked chilled Western Pie shell. Chill for at least 2 hours before topping with whipped cream, forced through a pastry bag with a rose tube; sprinkle with remaining macaroon crumbs. Serve very cold.

(409) MAPLE BAVARIAN CREAM CHIFFON PIE
ONE-CRUST PIE, PRE-BAKED PASTRY SHELL

For one 9-inch pie
- Egg yolks (slightly beaten): 2
- Sugar (maple, shaved): ½ cup
- Salt: ¼ tsp.
- Milk (cold): 1 cup
- Gelatin (granulated): 1 Tbsp.
- Water (cold): ¼ cup
- Egg whites (stiffly beaten): 2
- Vanilla extract: ¼ tsp.
- Almond extract: ¼ tsp.
- Heavy cream (whipped): ½ cup
- Pecans (chopped): ½ cup
- Pastry: 1 baked pie shell

For five 9-inch pies
- Egg yolks (slightly beaten): 10 or 10 oz.
- Sugar (maple, shaved): 2½ cups or 13⅓ oz.
- Salt: 1¼ tsps. or ⁵/₂₄ oz.
- Milk (cold): 5 cups or 2½ lbs.
- Gelatin (granulated): 5 Tbsps. or 1¼ oz.
- Water (cold) 1¼ cups or 10 oz.
- Egg whites (stiffly beaten): 10 or 10 oz.
- Vanilla Extract: 1¼ tsps. or ⁵/₂₄ oz.
- Almond extract: 1¼ tsps. or ⁵/₂₄ oz.
- Heavy cream (whipped): 2½ cups or 1 lb. 5 oz.
- Pecans (chopped): 2½ cups or 11³/₇ oz.
- Pastry: 5 baked pie shells

Beat egg yolks with maple sugar, salt, and stir into cold milk. Place in top of double boiler and cook until of custard consistency, stirring constantly. Add gelatin, which has been soaked in cold water for 5 minutes, and stir until gelatin is dissolved. Remove from the heat and cool slightly, or until mixture just begins to thicken; fold in the combined stiffly beaten egg whites, flavoring extracts, whipped cream and chopped pecans. Turn mixture into pre-baked pastry shell and chill thoroughly. When chilled you may top the pie with either whipped cream, or Marshmallow Cream Topping, No. 470, if desired.

(410)   MAPLE RASPBERRY CHIFFON PIE— SOUTHERN METHOD
ONE-CRUST PIE, PRE-BAKED PASTRY SHELL

For one 9-inch pie
- Pastry: 1 baked Peanut Butter Graham Cracker Pie Shell (No. 60)
- Raspberry jam: ¼ cup
- Gelatin (granulated): 1 Tbsp.
- Milk (cold): ¼ cup
- Egg yolks (well beaten): 3
- Maple syrup: ½ cup
- Salt: ¼ tsp.
- Milk (scalded): 1 cup
- Egg whites (stiffly beaten): 3
- Sugar (brown): ¼ cup
- Whipped Cream Topping

For five 9-inch pies
- Pastry: 5 baked Peanut Butter Graham Cracker Pie Shells (No. 60)
- Raspberry jam: 1¼ cups or 12½ oz.
- Gelatin (granulated): 5 Tbsps. or 1¼ oz.
- Milk (cold): 1¼ cups or 10 oz.
- Egg yolks (well beaten): 15 or 15 oz.
- Maple syrup: 2½ cups or 1 lb. 14 oz.
- Salt: 1¼ tsps. or $5/24$ oz.
- Milk (scalded): 5 cups or 2½ lbs.
- Egg whites (stiffly beaten): 15 or 15 oz
- Sugar (brown): 1¼ cups or 6⅔ oz.
- Whipped Cream Topping

Spread chilled baked pastry shell with raspberry jam; return to refrigerator and let chill while preparing the filling. Soak gelatin in cold milk for 5 minutes. Beat egg yolks in top of double boiler, add maple syrup, salt, and scalded milk, and cook over hot water, stirring constantly, until mixture coats the spoon. Remove from hot water and stir in the softened gelatin. Cool; chill until mixture begins to congeal, then fold in the stiffly beaten egg whites, sweetened with brown sugar. Turn mixture into jam-lined pastry shell and chill until firm. Then top with a thin layer of whipped cream. Just before serving, drizzle a little maple syrup over the cream on each serving.

(411)   # MINCEMEAT CHIFFON PIE— WASHINGTON CREAM PIE STYLE

For one 9-inch pie
- Egg yolks (slightly beaten): 2
- Sugar (granulated): 1 cup
- Flour (pastry): 2 Tbsps.
- Salt: ¼ tsp.
- Milk (scalded): 1½ cups
- Gelatin (granulated): 1½ Tbsps.
- Water (cold): ¼ cup
- Mincemeat: 1 cup
- Heavy cream (whipped): 1 cup
- Vanilla extract: 1 tsp.
- Pastry: 2 baked round sponge cake layers

For five 9-inch pies
- Egg yolks (slightly beaten): 10 or 10 oz.
- Sugar (granulated): 5 cups or 2½ lbs.
- Flour (pastry): ⅝ cup or 2½ oz.
- Salt: 1¼ tsps. or $5/24$ oz.
- Milk (scalded): 7½ cups or 3¾ lbs.
- Gelatin (granulated): 7½ Tbsps. or 1⅞ oz.
- Water (cold): 1¼ cups or 10 oz.
- Mincemeat: 5 cups or 2½ lbs.
- Heavy cream (whipped): 5 cups or 2½ lbs.
- Vanilla extract: 1⅔ Tbsps. or ⅚ oz.
- Pastry: 10 baked round sponge cake layers

Combine in top part of double boiler the slightly beaten egg yolks, sugar, flour, and salt. Blend thoroughly. Add scalded milk slowly, then cook over hot water until mixture thickens, stirring constantly. Soak gelatin in cold water for 5 minutes, then add to hot custard, blending well. Chill, then beat with rotary egg beater or electric mixer. Fold in the mincemeat alternately with whipped cream, flavored with vanilla extract. Chill again and spread between layers of sponge or plain butter cake. Serve cold.

ORANGE CHIFFON PIE I
(412)
ONE-CRUST PIE, PRE-BAKED PASTRY SHELL

For one 9-inch pie

- Orange sections (free from seeds and membrane)
- Gelatin (granulated): 1½ Tbsps.
- Cold water: ¾ cup
- Orange juice: 1 cup
- Lemon juice: 2 Tbsps.
- Salt: ⅛ tsp.
- Sugar (granulated): ⅓ cup
- Egg whites (stiffly beaten): 2
- Sugar (granulated): ¼ cup
- Heavy cream (whipped): ½ cup
- Pastry: 1 baked mealy pie shell (No. 49)
- Whipped Cream Topping

For five 9-inch pies

- Orange sections (free from seeds and membrane)
- Gelatin (granulated): 7½ Tbsps. or 1⅞ oz.
- Cold water: 3¾ cups or 1 lb. 14 oz.
- Orange juice: 5 cups or 2½ lbs.
- Lemon juice: ⅝ cup or 5 oz.
- Salt: ⅝ tsp.
- Sugar (granulated): 1⅔ cups or 13⅓ oz.
- Egg whites (stiffly beaten): 10 or 10 oz.
- Sugar (granulated): 1¼ cups or 10 oz.
- Heavy cream (whipped): 2½ cups or 1 lb. 5 oz.
- Pastry: 5 baked mealy pie shells (No. 49)
- Whipped Cream Topping

Prepare orange sections. Soak gelatin in cold water for 5 minutes. Boil orange juice and lemon juice with salt and ⅓ cup sugar; add soaked gelatin and stir until dissolved. Cool. When mixture begins to congeal, stir in the stiffly beaten egg whites, to which has been added the remaining sugar, alternately with whipped cream. Turn mixture into cold pre-baked pastry shell and chill. Top with Whipped Cream Topping, sweetened and flavored to taste and forced through a pastry bag with a fancy tube; decorate with orange sections.

(413)
ORANGE CHIFFON PIE II
ONE-CRUST PIE, PREPARED PASTRY SHELL

For one 9-inch pie

- Pastry: 1 prepared Zwieback Pie shell (No. 67)
- Gelatin (granulated): 1 Tbsp.
- Water (cold): 2 Tbsps.
- Water (boiling): ½ cup
- Egg yolks (well beaten): 4
- Sugar (granulated): ½ cup
- Salt: ¼ tsp.
- Orange rind (grated): 1½ tsps.
- Orange juice: 1 cup
- Lemon juice: 3 Tbsps.
- Egg whites (stiffly beaten): 4
- Sugar (granulated): ¼ cup
- Whipped Cream Topping
- Glazed Orange Sections (No. 462)

For five 9-inch pies

- Pastry: 5 prepared Zwieback Pie shells (No. 67)
- Gelatin (granulated): 5 Tbsps. or 1¼ oz.
- Water (cold): ⅝ cup or 5 oz.
- Water (boiling): 2½ cups or 1 lb. 4 oz.
- Egg yolks (well beaten): 20 or 1 lb. 4 oz.
- Sugar (granulated): 2½ cups or 1 lb. 4 oz.
- Salt: 1¼ tsps. or ⁵⁄₂₄ oz.
- Orange rind (grated): 2½ Tbsps. or 1 scant oz.
- Orange juice: 5 cups or 2½ lbs.
- Lemon juice: ⅞ cup or 7½ oz.
- Egg whites (stiffly beaten): 20 or 1 lb. 4 oz.
- Sugar (granulated): 1¼ cups or 10 oz.
- Whipped Cream Topping
- Glazed Orange Sections (No. 462)

Prepare pastry and press over bottom and side of 9-inch pie pan; chill. Soak gelatin in cold water for 5 minutes; add boiling water and stir until dissolved. Beat egg yolks until very light, then gradually beat in first amount of sugar and salt and stir in hot gelatin. Add combined orange rind and fruit juices and cool until mixture begins to congeal; then fold in stiffly beaten egg whites beaten with remaining sugar. Turn filling into prepared pie shell and let stand in refrigerator until firm. Decorate with rosettes of whipped cream, forced through pastry bag with a square tube, and garnish with Glazed Orange Sections, made as indicated for No. 462. Serve very cold.

(414) ORANGE BLACK BOTTOM CHIFFON PIE
ONE-CRUST PIE, PRE-BAKED PASTRY SHELL

For one 9-inch pie
Black Bottom Filling

- Gelatin (granulated): 1½ tsps.
- Orange juice (cold): 2 Tbsps.
- Chocolate (grated): 1 1-oz square
- Water (boiling): ¼ cup
- Egg yolks (slightly beaten): 2
- Sugar (brown): 1/3 cup
- Salt: 1/8 tsp.
- Vanilla extract: ¼ tsp.
- Egg whites (stiffly beaten): 2
- Sugar (brown): 1/3 cup
- Pistachio nuts (chopped, toasted, cooled): ¼ cup
- Pastry: 1 baked Oatmeal Pie Crust (No. 58)

For five 9-inch pies
Black Bottom Filling

- Gelatin (granulated): 2½ Tbsps. or 5/8 oz.
- Orange juice (cold): 5/8 cup or 5 oz.
- Chocolate (grated): 5 1-oz. squares
- Water (boiling): 1¼ cups or 10 oz.
- Egg yolks (slightly beaten): 10 or 10 oz.
- Sugar (brown): 1 2/3 cups or 8 8/9 oz.
- Salt: 5/8 tsp.
- Vanilla extract: 1¼ tsps. or or 5/24 oz.
- Egg whites (stiffly beaten): 10 or 10 oz.
- Sugar (brown): 1 2/3 cups or 8 8/9 oz.
- Pistachio nuts (chopped, toasted, cooled): 1¼ cups or 5 5/7 oz.
- Pastry: 5 baked Oatmeal Pie Crusts (No. 58)

Soak gelatin in orange juice for 5 minutes. Mix grated chocolate with boiling water and blend until smooth and free from lumps, over hot water, stirring almost constantly; then add the soaked gelatin and stir until dissolved. To this add the combined slightly beaten egg yolks, brown sugar and salt, stirring briskly until smooth; add the flavoring extract. Cool. When mixture begins to thicken, fold in gently the stiffly beaten egg whites, to which have been added the remaining brown sugar and chopped, toasted pistashio nuts. Turn filling into pre-baked 9-inch pastry crust, spreading it evenly with a spatula. Set the half-filled pie in refrigerator to chill while preparing the second filling as follows:

For one 9-inch pie
Orange Filling
- Gelatin (granulated): 1½ tsps.
- Water (cold): 2 Tbsps.
- Sugar (granulated): ¼ cup
- Orange juice: ¼ cup
- Salt: ⅛ tsp.
- Egg yolks (slightly beaten): 2
- Orange rind (grated): 1½ tsps.
- Lemon juice: 1½ tsps.
- Egg whites (stiffly beaten): 2
- Sugar (granulated): ¼ cup
- Marshmallow Cream Topping
  (No. 470)

For five 9-inch pies
Orange Filling
- Gelatin (granulated): 2½ Tbsps. or
  ⅝ oz.
- Water (cold): ⅝ cup or 5 oz.
- Sugar (granulated): 1¼ cups or 10 oz.
- Orange juice: 1¼ cups or 10 oz.
- Salt: ⅝ tsp.
- Egg yolks (slightly beaten): 10 or 10 oz.
- Orange rind (grated): 2½ Tbsps. or
  1 scant oz.
- Lemon juice: 2½ Tbsps. or 1¼ oz.
- Egg whites (stiffly beaten): 10 or 10 oz.
- Sugar (granulated): 1¼ cups or 10 oz.
- Marshmallow Cream Topping
  (No. 470)

Soak gelatin in cold water 5 minutes. Combine first amount of sugar, orange juice, salt and slightly beaten egg yolks in top of double boiler, and cook over boiling water until mixture is creamy and smooth, stirring constantly. To the softened gelatin, add orange rind and lemon juice and stir this into the hot mixture, stirring briskly until dissolved. Cool, and when mixture begins to congeal, fold in the stiffly beaten egg whites, to which has been added, when beaten stiff, the remaining sugar. Be sure to fold gently, yet thoroughly, as follows: Empty the beaten, sweetened egg whites onto the top of the gelatin mixture and cut down through it with the edge of a large wooden spoon; bring the spoon along the bottom of the mixture and then up and over the egg whites, cutting down through the egg whites again; continue to cut and fold, as this is called, until the egg whites disappear into the mixture. Do not stir after egg whites have been added. Pour over the chocolate mixture in the prepared pie crust. Chill in the refrigerator for several hours before topping with Marshmallow Cream Topping, made as indicated for recipe No. 470, and forced through pastry bag with rose tube. Serve very cold.

(415) PEACH BAVARIAN CREAM CHIFFON PIE
ONE-CRUST PIE, PRE-BAKED PASTRY SHELL

For one 9-inch pie

- Gelatin (granulated): 1 Tbsp.
- Cold water: ¼ cup
- Water (boiling): ½ cup
- Peaches (fresh, sieved): 1 cup
- Lemon juice: 1 Tbsp.
- Salt: ¼ tsp.
- Sugar (granulated): ¼ cup
- Heavy cream (whipped): 1¾ cups
- Pastry: 1 baked short flaky pie shell (No. 47)
- Boiled Meringue Topping No. 451
- Glazed Sliced Peaches: 3 medium-sized peaches (No. 464)

For five 9-inch pies

- Gelatin (granulated): 5 Tbsps. or 1¼ oz.
- Cold water: 1¼ cups or 10 oz.
- Water (boiling): 2½ cups or 1 lb. 4 oz.
- Peaches (fresh, sieved): 5 cups or 3 lbs. 2 oz.
- Lemon juice: 5 Tbsps. or 2½ oz.
- Salt: 1¼ tsps. or $5/24$ oz.
- Sugar (granulated): 1¼ cups or 10 oz.
- Heavy cream (whipped): 2 qts. plus ¾ cup or 4 lbs. $9^{1}/_{8}$ oz.
- Pastry: 5 baked short flaky pie shells (No. 47)
- Boiled Meringue Topping No. 451
- Glazed Sliced peaches: 15 peaches (No. 464)

Soak gelatin in cold water for 5 minutes. Add boiling water and stir until gelatin is thoroughly dissolved. Add fresh, sieved peaches, combined with lemon juice, salt, and sugar, and stir until dissolved. Cool; when mixture begins to congeal, fold in the whipped cream. Turn into pre-baked 9-inch pastry shell and chill for at least 2 hours before topping with Boiled Meringue Topping, made as indicated for recipe No. 451, and garnishing (optional) the edge of the pie with Glazed Sliced Peaches No. 464. Serve very cold, as chilling gives it an ice cream taste and texture which makes it exceptionally delicious.

(416) PEACH CHIFFON PIE—HOME METHOD
ONE-CRUST PIE, PRE-BAKED PASTRY SHELL

For one 9-inch pie
- Peaches (fresh, sliced): 2 cups
- Sugar (granulated): ½ cup
- Salt: ¼ tsp.
- Gelatin (granulated): 1 Tbsp.
- Water (cold): ¼ cup
- Lemon juice: 1 Tbsp.
- Egg whites (stiffly beaten): 2
- Heavy cream (whipped): ¼ cup
- Pastry: 1 baked pie shell
- Whipped Cream Topping

For five 9-inch pies
- Peaches (fresh, sliced): 2½ qts. or 5 lbs.
- Sugar (granulated): 2½ cups or 1 lb. 4 oz.
- Salt: 1¼ tsps. or $5/24$ oz.
- Gelatin (granulated): 5 Tbsps. or 1¼ oz.
- Water (cold): 1¼ cups or 10 oz.
- Lemon juice: 5 Tbsps. or 2½ oz.
- Egg whites (whipped): 10 or 10 oz.
- Heavy cream (whipped): 1¼ cups or 10½ oz.
- Pastry: 5 baked pie shells
- Whipped Cream Topping

Measure sliced ripe peaches rather generously; place in saucepan, sprinkle with mixed sugar and salt and let stand until the juice begins to gather. Place over very low heat and let heat until the boiling point is reached, stirring gently; then remove from the heat and drain off the juice. It should measure one cup; if not, add sufficient cold water; stir juice into the gelatin which has been soaked in cold water. When dissolved, cool; then chill until mixture begins to congeal. Now lightly fold the peach slices, sprinkled with lemon juice, into gelatin mixture alternately with combined stiffly beaten egg whites and whipped cream, lightly yet thoroughly. Turn mixture into cold pre-baked pastry shell, and chill until firm. Then top with Whipped Cream Topping. You may, if desired, garnish the edge with sliced ripe peaches, dipped into powdered sugar. Serve very cold.

(417)
PEACH NUT CHIFFON PIE— HOME METHOD
ONE-CRUST PIE, PREPARED PASTRY SHELL

For one 9-inch pie

- Marshmallows (quartered): 10 or 2⅔ oz.
- Orange juice: ½ cup or 4 oz.
- Pastry: 1 Vanilla Wafer Pie Shell (No. 65)
- Peaches (canned, sliced, drained): 2 cups
- Heavy cream (whipped): 1 cup
- Nut meats (any kind, chopped): ½ cup
- Cherries (canned, drained, chopped): ¼ cup

For five 9-inch pies

- Marshmallows (quartered): 50 or 13⅓ oz.
- Orange juice: 2½ cups or 1¼ lbs.
- Pastry: 5 Vanilla Wafer Pie Shells (No. 65)
- Peaches (canned, sliced, drained): 2½ qts. or 3¾ lbs.
- Heavy cream (whipped): 5 cups or 2½ lbs.
- Nut meats (any kind, chopped): 2½ cups or 10 oz.
- Cherries (canned, drained, chopped): 1¼ cups or 7½ oz.

Quarter marshmallows and add orange juice. Let stand 15 minutes. Fill vanilla wafers pie crust with canned, drained, sliced peaches. Combine whipped cream, nut meats and canned, chopped, drained cherries, and spoon over the peaches. Place in refrigerator and allow to stand several hours. When ready to serve, pipe a "collar" of whipped cream, colored to taste with a few drops of vegetable coloring, around the edge of pie.

....

(418)
PINEAPPLE BAVARIAN CREAM CHIFFON PIE
ONE-CRUST PIE, PRE-BAKED PASTRY SHELL

Proceed as indicated for recipe No. 415, Peach Bavarian Cream Chiffon Pie, substituting canned, crushed pineapple for peaches.

(419)

PINEAPPLE CHIFFON PIE
ONE-CRUST PIE, PRE-BAKED PASTRY SHELL

For one 9-inch pie
- Pineapple (canned, crushed, drained): 1 #2 can
- Sugar (granulated): ½ cup
- Salt: ½ tsp.
- Cornstarch: ¼ cup
- Pineapple juice (cold): ¼ cup
- Egg whites (stiffly beaten): 4
- Sugar (granulated): ¼ cup
- Lemon juice: 1 Tbsp.
- Pastry: 1 baked mealy pie shell (No. 49)
- Whipped Cream Topping

For five 9-inch pies
- Pineapple (canned, crushed, drained): 1 #10 can or 6 lbs. 12 oz.
- Sugar (granulated): 2½ cups or 1 lb. 4 oz.
- Salt: 2½ tsps. or $^5/_{12}$ oz.
- Cornstarch: 1¼ cups or 6$^2/_3$ oz.
- Pineapple juice (cold): 1¼ cups or 10 oz.
- Egg whites (stiffly beaten): 20 or 1 lb 4 oz.
- Sugar (granulated): 1¼ cups or 10 oz.
- Lemon juice: 5 Tbsps. or 2½ oz.
- Pastry: 5 baked mealy pie shells (No. 49)
- Whipped Cream Topping

Drain pineapple; combine juice, sugar and salt and bring to a brisk boil; thicken with cornstarch dissolved in remaining cold pineapple juice, adding slowly, while stirring constantly until thick and clear; then add strained pineapple and blend thoroughly. Cool slightly, then fold in the stiffly beaten egg whites, sweetened with remaining sugar and flavored with lemon juice. Be sure you fold the beaten egg whites while mixture is hot, so that a spongy mixture results. Turn filling into pre-baked pastry shell, cool; when cold, top with Whipped Cream Topping, forced through a pastry bag with a rose tube. Serve very cold.

(420)   # PINEAPPLE SPONGE CHIFFON PIE
ONE-CRUST PIE, PRE-BAKED PASTRY SHELL

For one 9-inch pie
- Gelatin (granulated): 1 Tbsp.
- Pineapple juice (cold, canned): ¼ cup
- Egg yolks (well beaten): 3
- Sugar (granulated): ¼ cup
- Salt: ⅛ tsp.
- Ginger (ground): ⅛ tsp.
- Pineapple juice (canned, heated): ¾ cup
- Lemon Juice: 2 Tbsps.
- Egg whites (fluffy): 3
- Sugar (granulated): ½ cup
- Pastry: 1 baked pie shell
- Whipped Cream Topping
- Almonds (blanched, shaved, toasted, cooled): ¼ cup

For five 9-inch pies
- Gelatin (granulated): 5 Tbsps. or 1¼ oz.
- Pineapple juice (cold, canned): 1¼ cups or 10 oz.
- Egg yolks (well beaten): 15 or 15 oz.
- Sugar (granulated): 1¼ cups or 10 oz.
- Salt: ⅝ tsp.
- Ginger (ground): ⅝ tsp.
- Pineapple juice (canned, heated): 3¾ cups or 1 lb. 14 oz.
- Lemon juice: ⅝ cup or 5 oz.
- Egg whites (stiffly beaten): 15 or 15 oz.
- Sugar (granulated): 2½ cups or 1 lb. 4 oz.
- Pastry: 5 baked pie shells
- Whipped Cream Topping
- Almonds (blanched, shaved, toasted, cooled): 1¼ cups or 5⁵/₇ oz.

Soak gelatin in cold pineapple juice for 5 minutes. Beat egg yolks until light and lemon-colored; gradually add combined ¼ cup sugar and salt and continue beating until sugar is thoroughly dissolved; then stir in remaining pineapple juice, stirring vigorously until smooth and well blended. Strain through a double cheesecloth into top of double boiler, add lemon juice, and cook over boiling water until mixture is clear and thick, stirring constantly. Remove at once from hot water and stir in the soaked gelatin. Cool until mixture begins to congeal and fold in the stiffly beaten egg whites, sweetened with remaining sugar. Turn mixture into prepared, chilled pie shell. Chill. Top with slightly sweetened whipped cream and sprinkle with the prepared almonds. Serve cold.

(421)   PINEAPPLE SPONGE CHIFFON PIE—
FRENCH METHOD
ONE-CRUST PIE, PREPARED PASTRY SHELL

For one 9-inch pie
- Egg yolks (slightly beaten): 3
- Lemon rind (grated): 1 Tbsp.
- Lemon juice: 2 Tbsps.
- Sugar (granulated): ½ cup
- Salt: ¼ tsp.
- Gelatin (granulated): 1 Tbsp.
- Pineapple juice (canned, cold): ⅓ cup
- Pineapple (canned, crushed): ⅔ cup or 8 oz.
- Heavy cream (whipped): ½ cup
- Egg whites (stiffly beaten): 3
- Pastry: 1 prepared Cinnamon Bread Crumb Pie Shell, No. 53
- Pineapple (canned, drained): ⅔ to 1 cup
- Candied cherries (red or green)

For five 9-inch pies
- Egg yolks (slightly beaten): 15 or 15 oz.
- Lemon rind (grated): 5 Tbsps. or 1⅞ oz.
- Lemon juice: ⅝ cup or 5 oz.
- Sugar (granulated): 2½ cups or 1¼ lbs.
- Salt: 1¼ tsps. or ⁵⁄₂₄ oz.
- Gelatin (granulated): 5 Tbsps. or 1⅔ oz.
- Pineapple juice (canned, cold): 1⅔ cups or 13⅓ oz.
- Pineapple (canned, crushed): 3⅓ cups or 2½ lbs.
- Heavy cream (whipped): 2½ cups or 2½ lbs.
- Egg whites (stiffly beaten): 15 or 15 oz.
- Pastry: 5 prepared Cinnamon Bread Crumb Pie Shells, No. 53
- Pineapple (canned, drained): 3⅓ to 5 cups or 2½ to 3¾ lbs.
- Candied cherries (red or green)

Beat egg yolks slightly and add lemon rind, lemon juice, sugar, and salt. Cook over hot water, stirring constantly, until mixture thickens. Remove from heat and stir in gelatin which has been soaked in pineapple juice for 5 minutes; then stir in the well-drained crushed pineapple. Let cool; when mixture begins to thicken, add whipped cream alternately with stiffly beaten egg whites. Turn into prepared cinnamon bread crumb crust and decorate with sliced pineapple cut into fancy shapes, and cherries cut into daisy shape. Serve very cold.

(422)   # PRUNE CHIFFON PIE
ONE-CRUST PIE, PRE-BAKED PASTRY SHELL

Proceed as indicated for recipe No. 380, Apricot Chiffon Pie I—Home Method, substituting cooked prunes for apricots.

....

(423)   # PRUNE SPONGE CHIFFON PIE
ONE-CRUST PIE, PRE-BAKED PASTRY SHELL

Proceed as indicated for recipe No. 420, Pineapple Sponge Chiffon Pie, substituting canned, bottled or freshly cooked prune juice for pineapple juice.

(424)
PUMPKIN CHIFFON PIE I—
HOME METHOD
ONE-CRUST PIE, PRE-BAKED PASTRY SHELL

For one 9-inch pie
- Gelatin (granulated): 1 Tbsp.
- Water (cold): ¼ cup
- Egg yolks (slightly beaten): 3
- Sugar (granulated): ½ cup
- Pumpkin (canned): 1¼ cups
- Milk (cold): ½ cup
- Salt: ½ tsp.
- Cinnamon (ground): ½ tsp.
- Nutmeg (ground): ½ tsp.
- Egg whites (stiffly beaten): 3
- Sugar (granulated): ¾ cup
- Pastry: 1 baked Gingersnap Pie Shell (No. 54)
- Whipped Cream Garnish (optional)

For five 9-inch pies
- Gelatin (granulated): 5 Tbsps. or 1¼ oz.
- Water (cold): 1¼ cups or 10 oz.
- Egg yolks (slightly beaten): 15 or 15 oz.
- Sugar (granulated): 2½ cups or 1 lb. 4 oz.
- Pumpkin (canned): 1 #10 can or 6 lbs. 4 oz.
- Milk (cold): 2½ cups or 1 lb. 4 oz.
- Salt: 2½ tsps. or $5/12$ oz.
- Cinnamon (ground): 2½ tsps. or $5/24$ oz.
- Nutmeg (ground): 2½ tsps. or $5/24$ oz.
- Egg whites (stiffly beaten): 15 or 15 oz.
- Sugar (granulated): 3¾ cups or 1 lb. 14 oz.
- Pastry: 5 baked Gingersnap Pie Shells (No. 54)
- Whipped Cream Garnish (optional)

To slightly beaten egg yolks, add ½ cup sugar, pumpkin, milk, salt and spices. Blend well and cook over boiling water until thick, stirring constantly. Soak gelatin in cold water for 5 minutes. Stir in the soaked gelatin and mix thoroughly. Cool. When mixture begins to congeal, fold in the stiffly beaten egg whites to which has been added the remaining sugar, a small amount at a time. Turn mixture into chilled, pre-baked gingersnap pie crust and chill for 2 hours. Then garnish (or not) with small tufts of whipped cream forced through a pastry bag with a fancy tube. Serve very cold.

(425)   # PUMPKIN CHIFFON PIE II— SOUTHERN METHOD
ONE-CRUST PIE, PRE-BAKED PASTRY SHELL

For one 9-inch pie

- Sugar (light brown): $^2/_3$ cup
- Salt: ½ tsp.
- Cinnamon (ground): ½ tsp.
- Mace (ground): ½ tsp.
- Nutmeg (ground): ¼ tsp.
- Ginger (ground): ½ tsp.
- Egg yolks (slightly beaten): 3
- Pumpkin (cooked or canned, sieved): 1¼ cups
- Milk (heated): ½ cup
- Gelatin (granulated): 1 Tbsps.
- Water (cold): ¼ cup
- Egg whites (stiffly beaten): 3
- Sugar (granulated): $^1/_3$ cup
- Pastry: 1 baked mealy pie shell (No. 49)
- Heavy cream (whipped): ¼ cup

For five 9-inch pies

- Sugar (light brown): 3$^1/_3$ cups or 17$^7/_9$ oz.
- Salt: 2½ tsps. or $^5/_{12}$ oz.
- Cinnamon (ground): 2½ tsps. or $^5/_{24}$ oz.
- Mace (ground): 2½ tsps. or $^5/_{24}$ oz.
- Nutmeg (ground): 1¼ tsps.
- Ginger (ground): 2½ tsps. or $^5/_{24}$ oz.
- Egg yolks (slightly beaten): 15 or 15 oz.
- Pumpkin (cooked or canned, sieved): 6¼ cups or 5 lbs. 1¼ oz.
- Milk (heated): 2½ cups or 1 lb. 4 oz.
- Gelatin (granulated): 5 Tbsps. or 1¼ oz.
- Water (cold): 1¼ cups or 10 oz.
- Egg whites (stiffly beaten): 15 or 15 oz.
- Sugar (granulated): 1$^2/_3$ cups or 13$^1/_3$ oz.
- Pastry: 5 baked mealy pie shells (No. 49)
- Heavy cream (whipped): 1¼ cups or 10½ oz.

Combine brown sugar, salt, and spices in top of double boiler; add the slightly beaten egg yolks; slowly blend in the sieved pumpkin and heated milk. Cook over boiling water, stirring constantly, until filling thickens. Add the gelatin which has been soaked in the cold water for 5 minutes, and stir until dissolved. Set double boiler top in cold water and let stand until filling begins to congeal; then fold in the stiffly beaten egg whites, which have been beaten with remaining sugar, a small amount at a time, beating well after each addition. Pile mixture into cool, pre-baked 9-inch pastry shell. Chill until firm, or about 2 hours. Then top with heavy cream, which has been whipped and slightly sweetened with either brown or white sugar. Serve very cold.

(426)
RASPBERRY BAVARIAN CREAM CHIFFON PIE
ONE-CRUST PIE, PRE-BAKED PASTRY SHELL

Proceed as indicated for recipe No. 415, Peach Bavarian Cream Chiffon Pie, substituting fresh or canned raspberries for peaches and Vanilla Wafer Pie Crust, (No. 65).

....

(427)
RASPBERRY CHIFFON PIE I
ONE-CRUST PIE, PRE-BAKED PASTRY SHELL

For one 9-inch pie
- Gelatin (granulated): 1 Tbsp.
- Water (cold): ¼ cup
- Sugar (granulated): ¼ cup
- Water (hot): ½ cup
- Raspberries (fresh or canned, crushed): 1½ cups
- Lemon rind (grated): 1 tsp.
- Salt: ¼ tsp.
- Heavy cream (whipped): ½ cup
- Pastry: 1 Crumb Pie Shell (No. 51)
- Boiled Meringue Topping No. 451

For five 9-inch pies
- Gelatin (granulated): 5 Tbsps. or 1¼ oz.
- Water (cold): 1¼ cups or 10 oz.
- Sugar (granulated): 1¼ cups or 10 oz.
- Water (hot): 2½ cups or 1 lb. 4 oz.
- Raspberries (fresh or canned, crushed): 7½ cups or 2 lbs. $2^2/_7$ oz.
- Lemon rind (grated): $1^2/_3$ Tbsps. or $^5/_8$ oz.
- Salt: 1¼ tsps. or $^5/_{24}$ oz.
- Heavy cream (whipped): 2½ cups or 1 lb. 5 oz.
- Pastry: 5 Crumb Pie Shells (No. 51)
- Boiled Meringue Topping No. 451

Soak gelatin in cold water for 5 minutes. Combine sugar, hot water, raspberries, lemon rind, and salt and bring to the boiling point, stirring frequently. As soon as the boiling point is reached, remove at once from the heat and stir in the soaked gelatin until dissolved and mixture is thoroughly blended. Cool until mixture begins to congeal, then fold in the whipped cream (more sugar may be added, depending on sweetness of crushed raspberries). Turn filling into prepared, cold Crumb Pie Shell made as indicated for recipe No. 51 and chill thoroughly. When chilled, top with Boiled Meringue Topping No. 451. Serve very cold.

(428)   # RASPBERRY CHIFFON PIE II
ONE-CRUST PIE, PRE-BAKED PASTRY SHELL

For one 9-inch pie

- Water: $5/8$ cup
- Sugar (granulated): ½ cup
- Raspberries (fresh, washed, drained): 1¼ cups
- Cornstarch: ¼ cup
- Salt: ¼ tsp.
- Water (cold): ¼ cup
- Egg whites (stiffly beaten): 3
- Sugar (granulated): ½ cup
- Pastry: 1 baked Graham Cracker Pie Shell, No. 55
- Whipped Cream Topping

For five 9-inch pies

- Water: $3^1/8$ cups or 1 lb. 9 oz.
- Sugar (granulated): 2½ cups or 1 lb. 4 oz.
- Raspberries (fresh, washed, drained): 6¼ cups or 1¾ lbs.
- Cornstarch: 1¼ cups or $6^2/3$ oz.
- Salt: 1¼ tsps. or $5/24$ oz.
- Water (cold): 1¼ cups or 10 oz.
- Egg whites (stiffly beaten): 15 or 15 oz.
- Sugar (granulated): 2½ cups or 1 lb. 4 oz.
- Pastry: 5 baked Graham Cracker Pie Shells, No. 55
- Whipped Cream Topping

In top of double boiler combine water, sugar, and prepared fresh raspberries. Blend well and bring this to a boil over hot water. Dissolve cornstarch and salt in cold water and gradually add to raspberry mixture, stirring constantly, yet gently, so as not to mash the fruit, until mixture is thick and clear. Remove from the hot water and immediately fold in the stiffly beaten egg whites, to which has been added the remaining granulated sugar, two tablespoons at a time. Turn mixture at once into pastry shell. Place on a pastry rack to cool slowly, then chill and top with whipped cream topping. Serve very cold. You may garnish the cream with a border of fresh, steamed, washed, drained raspberries, if desired. Canned raspberries or frozen raspberries may be prepared in the same way, using the drained juice of the canned berries instead of water, and if not enough, adding enough water to complete the required amount.

(429)   # SHERRY CHIFFON PIE
ONE-CRUST PIE, PRE-BAKED PASTRY SHELL

For one 9-inch pie
- Pastry: 1 baked rich pie shell (No. 70)
- Apricots (dried, cooked, sieved): ¼ cup
- Sugar (granulated): ½ cup
- Milk (scalded): 1 cup
- Egg yolks (well beaten): 3
- Ginger (ground): ⅛ tsp.
- Nutmeg (ground): ⅛ tsp.
- Salt: ¼ tsp.
- Sherry: 1 cup
- Gelatin (granulated): 1 Tbsp.
- Milk (cold): ¼ cup
- Egg whites (stiffly beaten): 3
- Heavy cream (whipped): ½ cup
- Marshmallow Cream Topping, No. 470

For five 9-inch pies
- Pastry: 5 baked rich pie shells (No. 70)
- Apricots (dried, cooked, sieved): 1¼ cups or 15 oz.
- Sugar (granulated): 2½ cups or 1 lb. 4 oz.
- Milk (scalded): 5 cups or 2½ lbs.
- Egg yolks (well beaten): 15 or 15 oz.
- Ginger (ground): ⅝ tsp.
- Nutmeg (ground): ⅝ tsp.
- Salt: 1¼ tsps. or ⁵⁄₂₄ oz.
- Sherry: 5 cups or 2½ lbs.
- Gelatin (granulated): 5 Tbsps. or 1¼ oz.
- Milk (cold): 1¼ cups or 10 oz.
- Egg whites (stiffly beaten): 15 or 15 oz.
- Heavy cream (whipped): 2½ cups or 1 lb. 5 oz.
- Marshmallow Cream Topping, No. 470

Spread cooked dried apricots, which have been cooked as indicated for No. 24, Dried Fruit Preparation, over bottom and sides of pre-baked, cooled shell and keep in refrigerator while preparing the filling. Dissolve sugar in scalded milk over hot water, add well-beaten egg yolks, ginger, nutmeg and salt and cook until mixture just begins to thicken; slowly stir in the sherry, stirring briskly while pouring alternately with gelatin, soaked in cold milk; cook until mixture coats the spoon. Remove from hot water, cool slightly, then fold in the stiffly beaten egg whites alternately with whipped cream. Turn mixture over the apricots in the pre-baked pie shell, spreading evenly. Chill thoroughly before topping with Marshmallow Cream Topping, made as indicated for recipe No. 470. Serve very cold.

(430)
SPANISH CREAM CHIFFON PIE
ONE-CRUST PIE, PRE-BAKED PASTRY SHELL

For one 9-inch pie
- Milk: 1¼ cups
- Gelatin (granulated): 2 tsps.
- Egg yolks (slightly beaten): 3
- Sugar (granulated): ⅔ cup
- Salt: ⅛ tsp.
- Vanilla extract: 1 tsp.
- Egg whites (stiffly beaten): 3
- Heavy cream (whipped): 1 cup
- Pastry: 1 baked Zwieback Pie Shell No. 67
- Whipped Cream Topping

For five 9-inch pies
- Milk: 6¼ cups or 3 lbs. 2 oz.
- Gelatin (granulated): 3⅓ Tbsps. or ⅚ oz.
- Egg yolks (slightly beaten): 15 or 15 oz.
- Sugar (granulated): 3⅓ cups or 1 lb. 10⅔ oz.
- Salt: ⅝ tsp.
- Vanilla extract: 1⅔ Tbsps. or ⅚ oz.
- Egg whites (stiffly beaten): 15 or 15 oz.
- Heavy cream (whipped): 5 cups or 2 lbs. 9⅞ oz.
- Pastry: 5 baked Zwieback Pie Shells, No. 67
- Whipped Cream Topping

Reserve ¼ cup of the milk, and scald the remaining cup. Dissolve the gelatin in the reserved ¼ cup of cold milk. To the slightly beaten egg yolks gradually add combined sugar and salt, beating thoroughly until mixture is thick, light and fluffy; add the scalded milk slowly, beating briskly. Place over hot water and cook, stirring constantly, until mixture coats the spoon; remove from the hot water and stir in the soaked gelatin and vanilla extract. Set aside to chill until custard begins to congeal, then fold in the stiffly beaten egg whites alternately with the whipped cream. Turn filling into pre-baked, chilled pie crust and chill thoroughly before topping with a layer of whipped cream. Serve very cold.

(431)
STRAWBERRY BAVARIAN CREAM CHIFFON PIE
ONE-CRUST PIE, PREPARED PASTRY SHELL

Proceed as indicated for recipe No. 426, Raspberry Bavarian Cream Chiffon Pie, substituting fresh strawberry pulp and juice for raspberry pulp and juice.

(432)   # STRAWBERRY CHIFFON PIE I—
HOME METHOD
ONE-CRUST PIE, PRE-BAKED PASTRY SHELL

For one 9-inch pie
- Strawberries (fresh, crushed): 1½ cups or 1 lb. 2 oz.
- Sugar (granulated): 1 cup or 8 oz.
- Gelatin (granulated): 1 Tbsp.
- Water (cold): ¼ cup or 2 oz.
- Water (hot): ½ cup
- Salt: ⅛ tsp.
- Lemon juice: 1 Tbsp. or ½ oz.
- Egg whites (stiffly beaten): 3 or 3 oz.
- Heavy cream (whipped): ¾ cup
- Pastry: 1 baked flaky pie shell
- Whipped Cream Topping
- Fresh, whole strawberries

For five 9-inch pies
- Strawberries (fresh, crushed): 7½ cups or 5 lbs. 10 oz.
- Sugar (granulated): 5 cups or 2½ lbs.
- Gelatin (granulated): 5 Tbsps. or 1¼ oz.
- Water (cold): 1¼ cups or 10 oz.
- Water (hot): 2½ cups or 1 lb. 4 oz.
- Salt: ⅝ tsp.
- Lemon juice: 5 Tbsps. or 2½ oz.
- Egg whites (stiffly beaten): 15 or 15 oz.
- Heavy cream (whipped): 3¾ cups or 1 lb. 12⁴/₁₇ oz.
- Pastry: 5 baked flaky pie shells
- Whipped Cream Topping
- Fresh, whole strawberries

Sprinkle fresh crushed strawberries with granulated sugar and let stand 45 minutes to 1 hour—the longer the better—to draw the berry juice. Soak gelatin in cold water for 5 minutes. To the hot water, add salt and strawberry-sugar mixture and heat to the boiling point; then stir in the lemon juice alternately with the soaked gelatin. Let mixture cool until it begins to thicken, then beat briskly while folding in the stiffly beaten egg whites alternately with whipped cream. Turn mixture into pre-baked 9-inch flaky pastry shell and chill. When thoroughly chilled, top with whipped cream, forced through pastry bag with a fancy tube, and garnish the border with whole, washed, hulled fresh strawberries. Serve very cold.

(433)   **STRAWBERRY CHIFFON PIE II— HOME METHOD**
ONE-CRUST PIE, PRE-BAKED PASTRY SHELL

For one 9-inch pie
- Gelatin (granulated): 1 Tbsp.
- Water (cold): ¼ cup
- Egg yolks (slightly beaten): 3
- Sugar (granulated): ¼ cup
- Salt: ½ tsp.
- Lemon juice: 1 Tbsp.
- Strawberries (fresh or frozen, crushed): 1¼ cups
- Egg whites (stiffly beaten): 3
- Cream of tartar: ¼ tsp.
- Sugar (granulated): ½ cup
- Pastry: 1 baked Creole Rice Pie Shell No. 71
- Whipped Cream Topping
- Strawberries (fresh or frozen)

For five 9-inch pies
- Gelatin (granulated): 5 Tbsps. or 1¼ oz.
- Water (cold): 1¼ cups or 10 oz.
- Egg yolks (slightly beaten): 15 or 15 oz.
- Sugar (granulated): 1¼ cups or 10 oz.
- Salt: 2½ tsps. or $5/12$ oz.
- Lemon juice: 5 Tbsps. or 2½ oz.
- Strawberries (fresh or frozen, crushed): 6¼ cups or 1¾ lbs.
- Egg whites (stiffly beaten): 15 or 15 oz.
- Cream of tartar: 1¼ tsps. or $5/24$ oz.
- Sugar (granulated): 2½ cups or 1 lb. 4 oz.
- Pastry: 5 baked Creole Rice Pie Shells No. 71
- Whipped Cream Topping
- Strawberries (fresh or frozen)

Soak gelatin in cold water for 5 minutes. Slightly beat egg yolks in top of double boiler, then add ¼ cup of sugar and beat again until light and sugar is dissolved; add salt and lemon juice, blend and cook over hot water, stirring constantly until smooth and thickened (about 6 or 7 minutes). Combine soaked gelatin and crushed berries and beat with rotary egg beater 1 minute; add to hot mixture and continue beating 1 minute longer. Remove from heat. Cool. When mixture begins to congeal, beat again with rotary egg beater. Beat egg whites with the cream of tartar until meringue holds its peaks, then add sugar, and beat again until sugar is dissolved and meringue is glossy. Fold into gelatin-berry mixture; turn into pre-baked pastry shell and chill at least 2 hours before topping with whipped cream and garnishing with washed, hulled and halved fresh strawberries. Serve very cold.

(434)   STRAWBERRY JULEP CHIFFON PIE— KENTUCKY METHOD
ONE-CRUST PIE, PRE-BAKED PASTRY SHELL

For one 9-inch pie
- Strawberries (fresh): 3 cups
- Sugar (granulated): 1¼ cups
- Water (cold): 1½ cups
- Salt: ⅛ tsp.
- Gelatin (granulated): 1½ Tbsps.
- Water (cold): ¼ cup
- Mint flavoring extract: ½ tsp.
- Pastry: 1 baked flaky pie shell
- Whipped Cream Topping
- Mint leaves (fresh): 6

For five 9-inch pies
- Strawberries (fresh): 15 cups or 3¾ qts. or 4 lbs. 4⁴/₇ oz.
- Sugar (granulated): 6¼ cups or 3 lbs. 2 oz.
- Water (cold): 7½ cups or 3¾ lbs.
- Salt: ⅝ tsp.
- Gelatin (granulated): 7½ Tbsps. or 1⁷/₈ oz.
- Water (cold): 1¼ cups or 10 oz.
- Mint flavoring extract: 2½ tsps. or ⁵/₁₂ oz.
- Pastry: 5 baked flaky pie shells
- Whipped Cream Topping
- Mint leaves (fresh): 30

Wash, hull and drain fresh strawberries, reserving ½ cup for garnishing. Combine sugar, 1½ cups cold water, salt, and mint extract. Bring slowly to a boil, and let simmer gently 10 minutes. Soak gelatin in remaining cold water and add to syrup, stirring until dissolved. While syrup is still hot, pour over 2½ cups of prepared strawberries and stir gently, so as not to break or bruise the fruit. Let stand until gelatin just begins to congeal, then turn into pre-baked 9-inch pastry shell. Chill, then top with whipped cream and garnish with a border of remaining berries halved. Place 6 fresh mint leaves over the whipped cream at equal distance, so when the pie is cut, each portion has a mint leaf. Serve very cold.

(435) STRAWBERRY SPONGE CHIFFON PIE
ONE-CRUST PIE, PRE-BAKED PASTRY SHELL

For one 9-inch pie

- Strawberries (fresh or frozen): 1½ cups
- Sugar (granulated): ½ cup
- Gelatin (strawberry flavored): 1 pkg
- Water (hot): 1 cup
- Egg yolks (slightly beaten): 3
- Salt: ¼ tsp.
- Egg whites (stiffly beaten): 3
- Pastry: 1 baked Cheese Pie Shell, No. 52
- Whipped Cream Topping
- Whole strawberries

For five 9-inch pies

- Strawberries (fresh or frozen): 7½ cups or 2 lbs. $2^2/_7$ oz.
- Sugar (granulated): 2½ cups or 1¼ lbs.
- Gelatin (strawberry flavored): 5 pkgs.
- Water (hot): 5 cups or 1¼ qts. or 2½ lbs.
- Egg yolks (slightly beaten): 15 or 15 oz.
- Salt: 1¼ tsps. or $^5/_{24}$ oz.
- Egg whites (stiffly beaten): 15 or 15 oz.
- Pastry: 5 baked Cheese Pie Shells, No. 52
- Whipped Cream Topping
- Whole strawberries

Pick, wash, hull berries. Place in a bowl and sprinkle with half the sugar; let stand for 25 minutes. Dissolve strawberry-flavored gelatin in hot water. Drain ¼ cup juice from berries, add to egg yolks, and beat slightly. Cook over hot water until thickened, stirring constantly. Remove from heat; stir in gelatin, and chill until slightly thickened. Beat salt and remaining sugar into stiffly beaten egg whites and fold lightly into gelatin mixture. Pour into cold 9-inch, pre-baked cheese pastry shell. Chill until firm; top with sweetened and flavored whipped cream, making small circles, and garnish with whole berries.

(436) STRAWBERRY SUNDAE CHIFFON PIE— GEORGIA METHOD
ONE-CRUST PIE, PREPARED PASTRY SHELL

For one 9-inch pie

- Strawberries (fresh or frozen, crushed): 1½ cups
- Sugar (brown): ¾ cup
- Lemon juice: 2 Tbsps.
- Salt: ¼ tsp.
- Gelatin (granulated): 1½ Tbsps. or ⅜ oz.
- Water (cold): ⅓ cup or 2⅔ oz.
- Whole eggs (well beaten): 2 or 4 oz.
- Sugar (granulated): ½ cup
- Milk (evaporated): 1 cup
- Water (hot): ⅓ cup
- Ginger (ground): ⅛ tsp.
- Pastry: 1 prepared Nut Pie Shell, No. 57
- Whipped Cream Topping
- Whole strawberries

For five 9-inch pies

- Strawberries (fresh or frozen, crushed): 7½ cups or 2 lbs. 2²/₇ oz.
- Sugar (brown): 3¾ cups or 1 lb. 4 oz.
- Lemon juice: ⅝ cup or 5 oz.
- Salt: 1¼ tsps.
- Gelatin (granulated): 7½ Tbsps. or 1⅞ oz.
- Water (cold): 1⅔ cups or 13⅓ oz.
- Whole eggs (well beaten): 10 or 1 lb. 4 oz.
- Sugar (granulated): 2½ cups or 1 lb. 4 oz.
- Milk (evaporated): 5 cups or 2 lbs. 11½ oz.
- Water (hot): 1⅔ cups or 13⅓ oz.
- Ginger (ground): ⅝ tsp.
- Pastry: 5 prepared Nut Pie Shells No. 57
- Whipped Cream Topping
- Whole strawberries

If using frozen berries, thaw them before crushing. Crush berries with brown sugar, lemon juice, and salt. Let stand 30 minutes to draw the juice. Soak gelatin in cold water for 5 minutes. Beat whole eggs with granulated sugar and stir in the evaporated milk combined with the hot water and ground ginger; cook over hot water, stirring constantly, until mixture is thick and creamy. Remove from the heat and stir in the soaked gelatin. Cool. When mixture begins to congeal, beat until frothy, adding while beating, the crushed berries and juice. Turn mixture into prepared Nut Pastry, made as indicated for recipe No. 57, and chill for 2 hours. Then top with whipped cream, and garnish with washed, whole berries. Serve cold.

(437) TOKAY WINE CREAM CHIFFON PIE— CALIFORNIA METHOD
ONE-CRUST PIE, PRE-BAKED PASTRY SHELL

For one 9-inch pie
- Gelatin (granulated): 1 Tbsp.
- Water (cold): 1/3 cup
- Egg yolks (slightly beaten): 3
- Sugar (granulated): 1/2 cup
- Lemon juice: 2 Tbsps.
- Lemon rind (grated): 1/2 tsp.
- Tokay wine: 1/3 cup
- Salt: 1/4 tsp.
- Nutmeg (ground): 1/8 tsp.
- Mace (ground): 1/8 tsp.
- Egg whites (stiffly beaten): 3
- Sugar (granulated): 1/2 cup
- Heavy cream (whipped): 1/3 cup
- Pastry: 1 baked Gingerbread Crumb Pie Shell (No. 68)
- Whipped Cream Topping
- Tokay grapes: about 1/2 cup

For five 9-inch pies
- Gelatin (granulated): 5 Tbsps. or 1 1/4 oz.
- Water (cold): 1 2/3 cups or 13 1/3 oz.
- Egg yolks (slightly beaten): 15 or 15 oz.
- Sugar (granulated): 2 1/2 cups or 1 lb. 4 oz.
- Lemon juice: 5/8 cup, or 5 oz.
- Lemon rind (grated): 2 1/2 tsps. or 5/16 oz.
- Tokay wine: 1 2/3 cups or 13 1/3 oz.
- Salt: 1 1/4 tsps. or 5/24 oz.
- Nutmeg (ground): 5/8 tsp.
- Mace (ground): 5/8 tsp.
- Egg whites (stiffly beaten): 15 or 15 oz.
- Sugar (granulated): 2 1/2 cups or 1 lb. 4 oz.
- Heavy cream (whipped): 1 2/3 cups or 13 3/4 oz.
- Pastry: 5 baked Gingerbread Crumb Pie Shells (No. 68)
- Whipped Cream Topping
- Tokay grapes: about 2 1/2 cups

Soak gelatin in cold water for 5 minutes. Beat egg yolks slightly, add in the first amount of sugar and beat until light, and sugar is dissolved; add lemon juice and rind and continue beating until very foamy. Strain mixture into top of double boiler and add the Tokay wine combined with salt and spices. Blend well and cook over hot water until mixture is of the consistency of custard and coats the spoon, stirring constantly. Remove from hot water and stir in the soaked gelatin until dissolved. Cool. When mixture begins to congeal, beat vigorously with egg beater, folding in at the same time, the combined stiffly beaten egg whites, sweetened with remaining sugar, and whipped cream. Turn mixture into pre-baked 9-inch Gingerbread Crumb Crust (No. 68) and chill for at least 2 hours before topping with a thin layer of sweetened and vanilla-flavored whipped cream; garnish with a border of Tokay grapes. Serve cold.

(438)

TUTTI FRUTTI CHIFFON PIE I—
CALIFORNIA METHOD
ONE-CRUST PIE, PRE-BAKED PASTRY SHELL

For one 9-inch pie
- Fruit salad (canned, drained): 2¼ cups
- Juice from canned fruit: ¾ cup
- Sugar (granulated): ⅓ cup
- Salt: ¼ tsp.
- Cornstarch: ¼ cup
- Juice from canned fruit: ¼ cup
- Nutmeg (ground): ⅛ tsp.
- Egg whites (stiffly beaten): 3
- Sugar (granulated): 6½ Tbsps.
- Pastry: 1 baked flaky pie shell (No. 47)
- Whipped Cream Topping

For five 9-inch pies
- Fruit salad (canned, drained): 1 #10 can, or 6 lbs. 12 oz.
- Juice from canned fruit: 3¾ cups or 1 lb. 14 oz.
- Sugar (granulated): 1⅔ cups or 13⅓ oz.
- Salt: 1¼ tsps. or ⁵⁄₂₄ oz.
- Cornstarch: 1¼ cups or 6⅔ oz.
- Juice from canned fruit: 1¼ cups or 10 oz.
- Nutmeg (ground): ⅝ tsp.
- Egg whites (stiffly beaten): 15 or 15 oz.
- Sugar (granulated): generous 2 cups or 1 lb. ¼ oz.
- Pastry: 5 baked flaky pie shells (No. 47)
- Whipped Cream Topping

Drain canned fruit salad. To the ¾ cup of juice (if not enough, add cold water to make the required amount), add the first amount of sugar and salt, stir until sugar is dissolved and bring to a boil. When boiling, gradually add cornstarch, dissolved in the remaining fruit juice, and nutmeg, stirring constantly until mixture is creamy, thick and clear. Let this boil once briskly, remove from hot water and gently stir in the well-drained canned fruit. Fold in the stiffly beaten egg whites, to which has been added the remaining granulated sugar. Cool; when cold, turn filling into pre-baked 9-inch pastry shell and top with whipped cream. Serve very cold.

(439) TUTTI FRUTTI CHIFFON PIE II— FRESH FRUIT METHOD
ONE-CRUST PIE, PRE-BAKED PASTRY SHELL

For one 9-inch pie

- Sugar (granulated): ½ cup
- Water (cold): ¾ cup
- Salt: ¼ tsp.
- Nutmeg (ground): $\frac{1}{8}$ tsp.
- Cornstarch: ¼ cup
- Water (cold): ¼ cup
- Red cherries (fresh, pitted, halved): $\frac{1}{3}$ cup
- Apples (pared, cored, cubed): $\frac{2}{3}$ cup
- Peaches (ripe, firm, peeled, cubed): $\frac{1}{3}$ cup
- Strawberries (fresh, quartered): ½ cup
- Bananas (peeled, cubed): ¼ cup
- Pineapple (fresh or canned, cubed): $\frac{1}{3}$ cup
- Egg whites (stiffly beaten): 2
- Sugar (granulated): 6 Tbsps.
- Heavy cream (whipped): ½ cup
- Pastry: 1 baked flaky pie shell (No. 47)
- Whipped Cream Topping

For five 9-inch pies

- Sugar (granulated): 2½ cups or 1 lb. 4 oz.
- Water (cold): 3¾ cups or 1 lb. 14 oz.
- Salt: 1¼ tsps. or $\frac{5}{24}$ oz.
- Nutmeg (ground): $\frac{5}{8}$ tsp.
- Cornstarch: 1¼ cups or $6\frac{2}{3}$ oz.
- Water (cold): 1¼ cups or 10 oz.
- Red cherries (fresh, pitted, halved): $1\frac{2}{3}$ cups or 12 oz.
- Apples (pared, cored, cubed): $3\frac{1}{3}$ cups or 1 lb. $10\frac{2}{3}$ oz.
- Peaches (ripe, firm, peeled, cubed): $1\frac{2}{3}$ cups or $13\frac{1}{3}$ oz.
- Strawberries (fresh, quartered): 2½ cups or $11\frac{3}{7}$ oz.
- Bananas (peeled, cubed): 1¼ cups or 10 oz.
- Pineapple (fresh or canned, cubed): $1\frac{2}{3}$ cups or $13\frac{1}{3}$ oz.
- Egg whites (stiffly beaten): 10 or 10 oz.
- Sugar (granulated): $1\frac{7}{8}$ cups or 15 oz.
- Heavy cream (whipped): 2½ cups or 1 lb. 5 oz.
- Pastry: 5 baked flaky pie shells (No. 47)
- Whipped Cream Topping

Dissolve first amount of sugar in cold water, add salt and nutmeg and bring to a rapid boil. Dissolve cornstarch in remaining water and add to syrup; cook, stirring constantly, until mixture thickens and becomes creamy and smooth. Bring to a brisk boil, and remove from the heat. While still hot, stir in the combined fruits. Now fold in the stiffly beaten egg whites, sweetened with the remaining sugar and combined with the whipped cream. Cool to lukewarm, then turn into pre-baked pastry shell. Cool, chill, then top with whipped cream. You may, if desired, sprinkle a little chopped toasted nut meats over the whipped cream.

....

(440)   VANILLA CREAM CHIFFON PIE— HOME METHOD
ONE-CRUST PIE, PRE-BAKED PASTRY SHELL

For one 9-inch pie
- Sugar (granulated): ¼ cup
- Salt: ½ tsp.
- Milk (scalded): ¾ cup
- Egg yolks (slightly beaten): 4
- Gelatin (granulated): 1 Tbsp.
- Water (cold): ¼ cup
- Vanilla extract: 1 tsp.
- Egg whites (stiffly beaten): 4
- Sugar (granulated): ¼ cup
- Pastry: 1 baked mealy pie shell (No. 49)
- Whipped Cream Topping

For five 9-inch pies
- Sugar (granulated): 1¼ cups or 10 oz.
- Salt: 2½ tsps. or $5/12$ oz.
- Milk (scalded): 3¾ cups or 1 lb. 14 oz.
- Egg yolks (slightly beaten): 20 or 1 lb. 4 oz.
- Gelatin (granulated): 5 Tbsps. or 1¼ oz.
- Water (cold): 1¼ cups or 10 oz.
- Vanilla extract: 1⅔ Tbsps. or $5/6$ oz.
- Egg whites (stiffly beaten): 20 or 1 lb. 4 oz.
- Sugar (granulated): 1¼ cups or 10 oz.
- Pastry: 5 baked mealy pie shells (No. 49)
- Whipped Cream Topping

Combine first amount of sugar and salt into scalded milk until sugar is dissolved. Stir mixture slowly into slightly beaten egg yolks and cook over boiling water until mixture coats the spoon and is of the consistency of custard, stirring constantly. Remove from hot water and stir in the gelatin, which has been soaked in cold water for 5 minutes, stirring until entirely dissolved; stir in the vanilla extract. Cool until mixture begins to congeal, then fold in the stiffly beaten egg whites, to which remaining sugar has been added gradually. Turn filling into cold, pre-baked 9-inch pastry shell and chill for several hours before topping with whipped cream, forced through a pastry bag with a rose tube. Serve very cold.

....

(441) VELVET BANANA CREAM CHIFFON PIE
ONE-CRUST PIE, PRE-BAKED PASTRY SHELL

For one 9-inch pie
- Bananas (ripe): 4
- Orange juice: ½ cup
- Orange rind (grated): ½ tsp.
- Lemon juice: 1 Tbsp.
- Sugar (powdered): ¼ cup (more or less)
- Gelatin (granulated): 1 Tbsp.
- Water (cold): ½ cup
- Heavy cream (whipped): 1 cup
- Pastry: 1 baked pie shell

For five 9-inch pies
- Bananas (ripe): 20, or 6⅔ lbs.
- Orange juice: 2½ cups or 1 lb. 4 oz.
- Orange rind (grated): 2½ tsps. or ⁵/₁₆ oz.
- Lemon juice: 5 Tbsps. or 2½ oz.
- Sugar (powdered): 1¼ cups (more or less) or 5⅝ oz.
- Gelatin (granulated): 5 Tbsps. or 1¼ oz.
- Water (cold): 2½ cups or 1 lb. 4 oz.
- Heavy cream (whipped): 5 cups or 2 lbs. 9⅞ oz.
- Pastry: 5 baked pie shells

Peel bananas and force fruit through fine sieve. Immediately add orange juice and rind, lemon juice and powdered sugar (the amount of powdered sugar depends on sweetness of fruit and orange juice). Soak gelatin in cold water for 10 minutes (not less, and a few minutes longer will be better), then dissolve over hot water; combine gelatin and prepared fruit mixture, stirring briskly and rapidly. Place bowl containing mixture in a pan of cracked ice and stir until mixture begins to congeal, then fold in the whipped cream. Turn filling into pre-baked 9-inch pastry shell, chill thoroughly. Top, or not, with whipped cream, forced through a pastry bag with square tube, leaving a space in center to garnish with banana slices dipped in brown sugar. Serve very cold. Almost any kind of fruit that may be sieved, such as peaches, soft apples, pears, etc., may be prepared the same way.

....

(442)   # VELVET CREAM CHIFFON PIE
ONE-CRUST PIE, PRE-BAKED PASTRY SHELL

For one 9-inch pie
- Egg yolks (stiffly beaten): 4
- Sugar (granulated): $7/8$ cup
- Gelatin (granulated): 1 Tbsp.
- Water (cold): ½ cup
- Egg whites (stiffly beaten): 2
- Heavy cream (whipped): 2 cups
- Vanilla extract: 1 tsp.
- Currant jelly: ¼ cup
- Pastry: 1 baked Gingerbread Pie Shell (No. 68)

For five 9-inch pies
- Egg yolks (stiffly beaten): 20 or 1 lb. 4 oz.
- Sugar (granulated): $4^3/8$ cups or 2 lbs. 3 oz.
- Gelatin (granulated): 5 Tbsps. or 1¼ oz.
- Water (cold): 2½ cups or 1 lb. 4 oz.
- Egg whites (stiffly beaten): 10 or 10 oz.
- Heavy cream (whipped): 2½ qts. or 5 lbs. 3¾ oz.
- Vanilla extract: $1^2/3$ Tbsps. or $5/6$ oz.
- Currant jelly: 1¼ cups or 12½ oz.
- Pastry: 5 baked Gingerbread Pie Shells (No. 68)

Beat egg yolks until light; add sugar gradually, beating until sugar is entirely dissolved. Soak gelatin in cold water for 5 minutes, place over heat and let come to the boiling point; then pour over the beaten egg yolks, slowly, beating vigorously and constantly. Allow to cool until mixture begins to congeal, then beat briskly with rotary egg beater or in electric mixer and fold in the whipped heavy cream, to which has been added the vanilla extract and the currant jelly. Turn mixture into pre-baked pastry shell; chill thoroughly before topping with a thin layer of whipped cream, sweetened but unflavored. Serve very cold.

....

(443) VIENNESE NESSELRODE CHIFFON PIE
ONE-CRUST PIE, PRE-BAKED PASTRY SHELL

For one 9-inch pie
- Milk: 1¼ cup
- Sugar (granulated): ⅔ cup
- Salt: ¼ tsp.
- Egg yolks (slightly beaten): 4
- Gelatin (granulated): 1 Tbsp.
- Water (cold): ¼ cup
- Raisins (seedless, ground): ¼ cup
- Almonds (blanched, ground, toasted, cooled): ¼ cup
- Macaroons (crumbled, sieved): ¼ cup
- Brandy: 2 Tbsps.
- Vanilla extract: ⅛ tsp.
- Egg whites (stiffly beaten): 2
- Heavy cream (whipped): ½ cup
- Pastry: 1 baked Zwieback Pie Shell (No. 67)
- Whipped Cream Topping

For five 9-inch pies
- Milk: 6¼ cups or 3 lbs. 2 oz.
- Sugar (granulated): 3⅓ cups or 1 lb. 10⅔ oz.
- Salt: 1¼ tsps. or ⁵/₂₄ oz.
- Egg yolks (slightly beaten): 20 or 1 lb. 4 oz.
- Gelatin (granulated): 5 Tbsps. or 1¼ oz.
- Water (cold): 1¼ cups or 10 oz.
- Raisins (seedless, ground): 1¼ cups or 6⅔ oz.
- Almonds (blanched, ground, toasted, cooled): 1¼ cups or 5⁵/₇ oz.
- Macaroons (crumbled, sieved): 1¼ cups or 5 oz.
- Brandy: ⅝ cup or 5 oz.
- Vanilla extract: ⅝ tsp.
- Egg whites (stiffly beaten): 10 or 10 oz.
- Heavy cream (whipped): 2½ cups or 1 lb. 5 oz.
- Pastry: 5 baked Zwieback Pie Shells (No. 67)
- Whipped Cream Topping

Scald milk. Mix slightly beaten egg yolks with sugar and salt, then beat briskly until very light. Slowly add scalded milk, beating constantly. Place mixture over hot water and cook 5 minutes, stirring constantly from the bottom of the pan, until mixture begins to thicken; remove from the hot water. Soak gelatin in cold water for 5 minutes; add to milk-egg mixture, stirring rapidly, until gelatin is dissolved; then stir in the combined raisins, almonds, macaroon crumbs, brandy and vanilla extract stirring well. Cool until mixture begins to thicken; beat once or twice and fold in the combined stiffly beaten egg whites and the whipped cream. Chill for at least 2 hours, after turning mixture into pre-baked, chilled Zwieback Pie Crust, made as indicated for recipe No. 67. When thoroughly chilled, top with whipped cream forced through a pastry bag with a fancy tube. Serve cold.

(444) VISCOUNTESS RAINBOW CHIFFON PIE
ONE-CRUST PIE, PRE-BAKED PASTRY SHELL

For one 9-inch pie
- Apricot jam (sieved): ¼ cup
- Strawberry jam (sieved): ¼ cup
- Greengage plum jam (sieved): ¼ cup
- Milk (scalded): ⅔ cup
- Sugar (granulated): ⅔ cup
- Salt: ¼ tsp.
- Egg yolks (well beaten): 4
- Gelatin (granulated): 1 Tbsp.
- Water (cold): ⅓ cup
- Egg whites (stiffly beaten): 4
- Heavy cream (whipped): 1 cup
- Sugar (powdered): ⅓ cup
- Pastry: 1 baked Crunchy Semi-Puff Paste Flaky Pie Shell (No. 66)
- Whipped Cream Topping
- Chopped pistachio nuts: ¼ cup (about)

For five 9-inch pies
- Apricot jam (sieved): 1¼ cups or 15 oz.
- Strawberry jam (sieved): 1¼ cups or 15 oz.
- Greengage plum jam (sieved): 1¼ cups or 15 oz.
- Milk (scalded): 3⅓ cups or 1 lb. 10⅔ oz.
- Sugar (granulated): 3⅓ cups or 1 lb. 10⅔ oz.
- Salt: 1¼ tsps. or ⁵⁄₂₄ oz.
- Egg yolks (well beaten): 20 or 1 lb. 4 oz.
- Gelatin (granulated): 5 Tbsps. or 1¼ oz.
- Water (cold): 1⅔ cups or 13⅓ oz.
- Egg whites (stiffly beaten): 20, or 1 lb. 4 oz.
- Heavy cream (whipped): 5 cups or 2 lbs. 9⅞ oz.
- Sugar (powdered): 1⅔ cups or 7¹⁄₇ oz.
- Pastry: 5 baked Crunchy Semi-Puff Paste Flaky Pie Shells (No. 66)
- Whipped Cream Topping
- Chopped Pistachio nuts: 1¼ cups (about) or 5⁵⁄₇ oz.

Sieve the jams separately; there should be ¼ cup pulp each, rather thick. Chill. To the scalded milk, slowly add combined sugar, salt, and well-beaten egg yolks; stirring briskly. Cook over hot water until mixture thickens, stirring constantly; remove from the hot water and stir in the gelatin, which has been soaked in cold water for 5 minutes. Cool, and when mixture begins to thicken, fold in the combined stiffly beaten egg whites and whipped cream, to which has been added powdered sugar, a tablespoon at a time. Then proceed as follows to fill the chilled, pre-baked pastry shell: Spread bottom with a layer of apricot jam; over this arrange a layer of the cooled mixture, spreading evenly with a spatula; again, spread a layer of the strawberry jam, then another layer of the cooled filling mixture. On top of this second layer, spread the remaining greengage plum jam and top with remaining filling mixture. Chill for at least 2 long hours; then top with whipped cream, forced through a pastry bag with a rose tube, and sprinkle with chopped pistachio nuts. Serve very cold.

(445) WALNUT RASPBERRY CHIFFON PIE
ONE-CRUST PIE, PRE-BAKED PASTRY SHELL

For one 9-inch pie
- Gelatin (granulated): 1 Tbsp.
- Water (cold): ¼ cup
- Heavy cream (unwhipped): 1¼ cups
- Milk (cold): ¾ cup
- Sugar (granulated): ¾ cup
- Salt: ¼ tsp.
- Egg whites (stiffly beaten): 2
- Pineapple (crushed, canned, drained): ½ cup
- Raspberries (fresh or frozen): ½ cup
- Walnut meats (chopped): 1 cup
- Pastry: 1 baked Bread Crumb Pie Shell (No. 51) (using macaroon crumbs)
- Whipped cream (for garnishing)
- Raspberries (fresh or frozen): ½ cup

For five 9-inch pies
- Gelatin (granulated): 5 Tbsps. or 1¼ oz.
- Water (cold): 1¼ cups or 10 oz.
- Heavy cream (unwhipped): 6¼ cups or 3 lbs. 4½ oz.
- Milk (cold): 3¾ cups or 1 lb. 4 oz.
- Sugar (granulated): 3¾ cups or 1 lb. 14 oz.
- Salt: 1¼ tsp. or $^5/_{24}$ oz.
- Egg whites (stiffly beaten): 10 or 10 oz.
- Pineapple (crushed, canned, drained): 2½ cups or 1 lb. 14 oz.
- Raspberries (fresh or frozen): 2½ cups or 11$^3/_7$ oz.
- Walnut meats (chopped): 5 cups or 1 lb. 10$^2/_3$ oz.
- Pastry: 5 baked Bread Crumb Pie Shells (No. 51) (using macaroon crumbs)
- Whipped cream (for garnishing)
- Raspberries (fresh or frozen): 2½ cups or 11$^3/_7$ oz.

Sprinkle gelatin over the cold water in a mixing bowl and let stand five minutes; place over hot water and stir until dissolved. Mix the unwhipped cream, milk, sugar and salt in another mixing bowl and add the hot, dissolved gelatin. Blend thoroughly. Chill until mixture begins to congeal; fold in the stiffly beaten egg whites, combined with the pineapple and raspberries, alternately with the chopped walnut meats. Turn mixture into pre-baked chilled Macaroon Crumb Pie Crust and chill for at least 2 hours before forcing a border of whipped cream through a pastry bag with a fancy tube, and garnishing with whole raspberries. Serve very cold.

(446) WHIPPED CREAM MARSHMALLOW FLUFF CHIFFON PIE
ONE-CRUST PIE, PRE-BAKED PASTRY SHELL

For one 8- or 9-inch pie
- Egg yolks: 5
- Sugar (granulated): ½ cup
- Sugar (light brown): ¼ cup
- Salt: ¼ tsp.
- Milk (scalded): 1½ cups
- Red and white fresh currants (equal parts): ¾ cup
- Pastry: 1 baked mealy pie shell (square) (No. 49)
- Gelatin (granulated): 1 Tbsp.
- Water (cold): 2 Tbsps.
- Vanilla extract: 1 tsp.
- Marshmallows (quartered): 1 doz.
- Heavy cream (whipped): 1 cup
- Orange rind (grated): ½ tsp.
- Whipped Cream Topping
- Red and white currants (equal parts): ½ cup

For five 8- or 9-inch pies
- Egg yolks: 25 or 1 lb 9 oz.
- Sugar (granulated): 2½ cups or 1 lb. 4 oz.
- Sugar (light brown): 1¼ cups or 6⅔ oz.
- Salt: 1¼ tsps.
- Milk (scalded): 7½ cups or 3¾ lbs.
- Red and white fresh currants (equal parts): 3¾ cups or 17$\frac{1}{7}$ oz.
- Pastry: 5 baked mealy pie shells (square) (No. 49)
- Gelatin (granulated): 5 Tbsps. or 1¼ oz.
- Water (cold): ⅝ cup or 5 oz.
- Vanilla extract: 1⅔ Tbsps. or ⅚ oz.
- Marshmallows (quartered): 5 doz. or 1 lb.
- Heavy cream (whipped): 5 cups or 2 lbs. 9⅞ oz.
- Orange rind (grated): 2½ tsps. or ⁵⁄₁₆ oz.
- Whipped Cream Topping
- Red and white currants (equal parts): 2½ cups or 11$\frac{3}{7}$ oz.

Beat egg yolks until light; add sugars, combined with salt and beat again, until all sugar is dissolved; gradually add scalded milk. Cook slowly in top of double boiler, stirring constantly until custard coats the spoon. Spread the first amount of currants in bottom of pre-baked mealy pastry shell, which has been thoroughly cooled, and place in refrigerator while finishing the filling. Soften gelatin in cold water for 5 minutes and dissolve over boiling water; add it to the hot custard and stir well. Add vanilla and the quartered marshmallows and let soften. Place the bowl containing the custard in a bowl of ice water, and when mixture begins to congeal, fold in the whipped cream. Chill one or two minutes, then spoon very gently over the fruit in the square, pre-baked pie shell; chill for one hour. Top with whipped cream, forced through a pastry bag, making some circles, starting from center and finishing at the border. Sprinkle the remaining currants in the bottom of the circles and sprinkle the top of the circles with orange rind. Serve very cold in rectangular cuts.

(447)   # WINE JELLY CHIFFON PIE
ONE-CRUST PIE, PRE-BAKED PASTRY SHELL

For one 9-inch pie
- Gelatin (granulated): 1½ Tbsps.
- White wine (dry): ⅔ cup
- Whole eggs (slightly beaten): 3
- Sugar (granulated): ⅔ cup
- Salt: ⅛ tsp.
- Milk (scalded): 3 cups
- Lemon juice: 1 tsp.
- Orange rind (grated): 1 tsp.
- Heavy cream (whipped): ¼ cup
- Pastry: 1 baked Cheese Pie Shell (No. 52)
- Boiled Lemon Meringue Topping (No. 451)

For five 9-inch pies
- Gelatin (granulated): 7½ Tbsps. or 1⅞ oz.
- White wine (dry): 3⅓ cups or 1 lb. 10⅔ oz.
- Whole eggs (slightly beaten): 15 or 1 lb. 4 oz.
- Sugar (granulated): 3⅓ cups or 1 lb. 10⅔ oz.
- Salt: ⅝ tsp.
- Milk (scalded): 3¾ qts. or 7½ lbs.
- Lemon juice: 1⅔ Tbsps. or ⅚ oz.
- Orange rind (grated): 1⅔ Tbsps. or ⅝ oz.
- Heavy cream (whipped): 1¼ cups or 10½ oz.
- Pastry: 5 baked Cheese Pie Shells (No. 52)
- Boiled Lemon Meringue Topping (No. 451)

Soften gelatin in wine for 5 minutes. Combine slightly beaten whole eggs with sugar and salt and beat until light and creamy. Slowly pour the scalded milk over egg mixture, beating briskly and constantly. Strain this into top of double boiler, using a fine cloth or fine sieve, and cook over hot water, stirring constantly, until mixture coats the spoon; remove from hot water and stir in the wine-gelatin mixture to which have been added the lemon juice and orange rind, and beat with a wire whisk for 2 minutes. Cool and when mixture begins to congeal, fold in the whipped cream. Turn mixture into pre-baked 9-inch pastry shell and chill for at least 2 hours before topping with Boiled Lemon Meringue Topping made as indicated for recipe No. 451. Serve very cold.

(448)
ZABAGLIONE CHIFFON PIE
ONE-CRUST PIE, PREPARED PASTRY SHELL

For one 9-inch pie
- Egg yolks: 6
- Sugar (granulated): ½ cup
- Salt: ¼ tsp.
- White wine (dry): 2½ cups
- Lemon rind (grated): 1 tsp.
- Gelatin (granulated): 1¼ Tbsps.
- Water (cold): 3 Tbsps.
- Heavy cream (whipped): ¼ cup
- Almonds (shredded, toasted, cooled): ½ cup
- Pastry: 1 prepared Nut (Brazil) Pie Shell (No. 57)
- Whipped cream (for garnishing)
- Orange rind (grated): 1 Tbsp.

For five 9-inch pies
- Egg yolks: 30 or 1 lb. 14 oz.
- Sugar (granulated): 2½ cups or 1 lb. 4 oz.
- Salt: 1¼ tsps. or $5/24$ oz.
- White wine (dry): 3¾ qts. or 3¾ lbs.
- Lemon rind (grated): 1²/₃ Tbsps. or ⅝ oz.
- Gelatin (granulated): 6¼ Tbsps. or 1 scant oz.
- Water (cold): scant cup or 7½ oz.
- Heavy cream (whipped): 1¼ cups or 10½ oz.
- Almonds (shredded, toasted, cooled): 2½ cups or 11³/₇ oz.
- Pastry: 5 prepared Nut (Brazil) Pie Shells (No. 57)
- Whipped cream (for garnishing)
- Orange rind (grated): 5 Tbsps. or 1⅞ oz.

Beat egg yolks until light, add sugar and salt and continue beating until sugar is thoroughly dissolved. Heat wine and lemon rind in top of double boiler until mixture boils once; place over boiling water and slowly pour the egg yolk mixture into the hot wine, stirring briskly from the bottom of the pan with a wire whisk; let mixture boil once and begin to thicken slightly. Remove from hot water and stir in the gelatin, which has been soaked for 5 minutes in cold water. Blend thoroughly and allow to cool until filling begins to congeal; fold in the whipped cream alternately with the shredded, toasted, cooled almonds. Turn mixture into prepared, cooled Nut Pastry made of Brazil nuts. Chill thoroughly before forcing a large, flat ribbon of whipped cream through a pastry bag with a fancy tube, and sprinkle the orange rind over the whipped cream. Serve very cold.

Topping, Garnishing, and Glazing

(449) TOPPING, GARNISHING, AND GLAZING

The proof of the pie lies in its garnishing. Anything which will increase or add to appetite-appeal in the hot days of spring or midsummer is worth the attention of the chef and hostess.

What are the points on which any pie can be called a success or failure? Flavor—first, last, and all the time. Texture next, perhaps, because a well-made pie which is, however, "mushy," does not give the pleasing "bite" which everyone likes to meet in his foods. Color third, because even if the pie is tasty and also has contrasting texture, it will fail if it is unattractive to look at. Everyone knows how unappetizing is the pie which is dull and dry, with a discernible starchy taste and how much is gained by giving color-contrasts, pleasing garnishes, etc.

Whether or not the chef plans to make a special pie in connection with an approaching patriotic holiday, or for any kind of occasion, he should know his toppings, garnishings, and glazings, for these quite literally make the pie, and like effective cosmetic make-up do much to put a good outward appearance on what may be a rather plain surface. However, toppings, garnishings, and glazings and all their kindred intended for beautification, also aim at the final perfect touch of flavor and sweet contrast to the pie's firm or soft and distinctive texture.

Many pies and rich mixtures, like certain open-faced fruit pies and almost all the two-crust pies, do not actually require any topping, garnishing, or glazing. But most of the chiffon pies and small novelty pies, designed for almost any meal, should be finished with a topping, a garnishing, or a glazing which fulfills all the three requisites of *color, flavor, and texture.*

While a pure snowy-white topping is always delightful to look at, light pastel tints are appropriate and add novelty at times. Vegetable colors come in sets of tiny vials and a few drops of rose, green, or yellow, etc. will help the pie look like that of a first-class professional pastry chef's.

(450)   APRICOT CREAM TOPPING

Appropriate for almost any kind of one-crust fruit pie and chiffon pie.

For one 9-inch pie
- Sugar (granulated): 3 Tbsps.
- Flour (sifted): 3 Tbsps.
- Salt: ⅛ tsp.
- Apricot juice (canned): ¼ cup
- Apricot pulp (canned): ¼ cup
- Lemon juice: 2 Tbsps.
- Heavy cream (whipped): ¼ cup

For five 9-inch pies
- Sugar (granulated): 1 scant cup or 7½ oz.
- Flour (sifted): 1 scant cup or 3¾ oz.
- Salt: ⅝ tsp.
- Apricot juice (canned): 1¼ cups or 10 oz.
- Apricot pulp (canned): 1¼ cups or 10 oz.
- Lemon juice: ⅝ cup or 5 oz.
- Heavy cream (whipped): 1¼ cups or 10½ oz.

Combine sugar, flour and salt in top of double boiler; add apricot juice and mix thoroughly. Sieve well-drained apricots to obtain ¼ cup pulp and add gradually to flour mixture, stirring constantly. Remove from boiling water; add lemon juice. Chill. When well chilled, fold in the whipped cream. Spread over top of pie, through a pastry bag with a fancy tube.

....

(451)   BOILED MERINGUE TOPPING

Appropriate for almost any kind of one-crust pie, tart, and the like, especially for stripping, or crisscrossing open fruit pies, tarts, etc. This meringue is not browned.

For one 9-inch pie
- Egg whites (stiffly beaten): 2
- Water (cold): 2 Tbsps.
- Corn syrup (light): ½ Tbsp.
- Sugar (granulated): ½ cup
- Vanilla (or other flavoring): ¼ tsp.
- Lemon juice: ¼ tsp.

For five 9-inch pies
- Egg whites (stiffly beaten): 10 or 10 oz.
- Water (cold): ⅝ cup or 5 oz.
- Corn syrup (light): 2½ Tbsps. or 1⅞ oz.
- Sugar (granulated): 2½ cups or 1 lb. 4 oz.
- Vanilla extract (or other flavoring): 1¼ tsps. or ⅚ oz.
- Lemon juice: 1¼ tsps. or ⁵⁄₂₄ oz.

Beat egg whites by hand or with an electric mixer at medium speed, until they hold their peaks. Place water, corn syrup and sugar in a saucepan and stir until sugar is dissolved and syrup blended. Boil over high heat, without stirring, until syrup reaches 238° F., or if you have no thermometer, until syrup reaches the soft ball state, indicated when a small ball of syrup dropped in ice water loses its shape immediately. Remove from the heat at once and very slowly, in a thread-like stream, pour over stiffly beaten egg whites, beating briskly and constantly until syrup is all used up, then stir in the combined vanilla extract and lemon juice. The meringue is then ready to be placed over the pie.

Variations (For one pie):

(1) *Spongy Almond Extract Flavor:* Substitute ½ teaspoon almond extract for vanilla extract combined with lemon juice.

(2) *Angel Food Flavor:* Substitute ¼ teaspoon almond extract, combined with ¾ teaspoon vanilla extract and the lemon juice, for vanilla extract.

(3) *Apple Brandy Meringue Flavor:* Substitute 2 tablespoons of apple brandy for vanilla, and combined with the lemon juice, for vanilla extract.

(4) *Brandy Meringue Flavor:* Substitute 2 tablespoons good brandy (no extract), combined with lemon juice, for vanilla extract.

(5) *Chocolate Meringue Flavor:* Two methods may be used: (a) Substitute 3 tablespoons chocolate syrup for the vanilla extract, then fold in the lemon juice. (b) Substitute ¼ cup grated chocolate (bitter or sweet) for vanilla extract, then fold in the lemon juice. If using cocoa powder, use ½ cup of cocoa. For marble effect you may pour an extra tablespoon chocolate syrup in a thread-like stream over the chocolate meringue, just before placing into oven.

(6) *Coffee Meringue Flavor:* Substitute 2 teaspoons coffee essence, combined with lemon juice, for vanilla extract.

(7) *Ginger Meringue Flavor:* Substitute ¾ teaspoon ground ginger for vanilla extract, then fold in the lemon juice; or substitute 1 tablespoon crushed candied ginger for vanilla, then fold in the lemon juice.

(8) *Honey Meringue Flavor:* Substitute 1/3 cup (generous) strained honey, combined with lemon juice, for vanilla extract, adding honey mixture very slowly, 1 teaspoon at a time, and beating once or twice briskly after all the honey-lemon juice mixture has been added.

(9) *Lemon Meringue Flavor:* Substitute ¾ teaspoon lemon extract, combined with lemon juice, for vanilla extract; or, 1¾ teaspoons grated lemon rind added to the lemon juice.

(10) *Lime Meringue Flavor:* Proceed as for Lemon Meringue Flavor, substituting 1½ teaspoons grated lime rind and 1½ tablespoons lime juice for vanilla extract and lemon juice.

(11) *Maple Meringue Flavor:* Substitute maple sugar for granulated sugar, maple syrup for corn syrup, when making the syrup to be poured over stiffly beaten egg whites; or, proceed as directed and substitute 1½ tablespoons maple flavoring extract for vanilla extract, the maple extract combined with lemon juice.

(12) *Marzipan Meringue Flavor:* (usually used as a border meringue) see No. 473.

(13) *Orange Meringue Flavor:* Proceed as indicated for (9) above, substituting orange extract for vanilla extract; or use 2 tablespoons grated orange rind added to 2 tablespoons orange juice, instead of lemon juice.

(14) *Peppermint Meringue Flavor:* Substitute 1/3 teaspoon peppermint extract, or 3 or 4 drops of oil of peppermint, for vanilla extract, either combined with lemon juice.

(15) *Pineapple Meringue Flavor:* Substitute 1 teaspoon pineapple flavoring for vanilla extract and combine lemon juice with ¼ cup shredded, canned, well drained pineapple, to be blended last.

(16) *Rum Meringue Flavor:* Proceed as indicated for Apple Brandy (3) above, substituting rum for apple brandy.

(17) *Toffee Meringue Flavor:* Add 1½ tablespoons chopped toffee candy, folding gently into the ready meringue.

....

(452) BOILED MERINGUE TOPPING FOR CHIFFON PIE AND VARIATIONS

For one 9-inch pie
- Egg whites (stiffly beaten): 2
- Sugar (granulated): ¼ cup
- Salt: ⅛ tsp.
- Vanilla extract: 1 tsp.

For five 9-inch pies
- Egg whites (stiffly beaten): 10 or 10 oz.
- Sugar (granulated): 1¼ cups or 10 oz.
- Salt: ⅝ tsp.
- Vanilla extract: 1⅔ Tbsps. or ⅚ oz.

Beat egg whites until stiff; then gradually add sugar, combined with salt, and continue beating until sugar is entirely dissolved and meringue holds its peaks. Fold in the vanilla extract. Float either teaspoonfuls or tablespoonfuls, according to size of pie or tart to be covered, of meringue upon hot water (fruit juice may be used) in a shallow pan. Set pan in a slow oven (325° F.) and bake until brown. Skim off immediately, drain upon absorbent paper or a dry, clean towel and place on top of pie or tart.

NOTE: Same variations may be made as those indicated for No. 451, Boiled Meringue Topping. Besides being very attractive, these little meringues may be used to top almost any kind of cold dessert. They may be tinted according to occasion, as red for Washington's Birthday, green for St. Patrick's Day and so on. They keep several weeks, so they may be made in advance and kept in a cool, dry place.

....

(453)   **BROWN TOPPING**

Appropriate for almost any kind of one-crust fruit pies, cream and custard pies.

For one 9-inch pie
- Sugar (brown or granulated): 1/3 cup
- Butter or substitute: 1/4 cup
- Flour (pastry): 1/3 cup
- Cinnamon (ground): 1 tsp.
- Salt: 1/8 tsp.

For five 9-inch pies
- Sugar (brown or granulated): 1 2/3 cups or 8 8/9 oz. or 13 1/3 oz.
- Butter or substitute: 1 1/4 cups or 10 oz.
- Flour (pastry): 1 2/3 cups or 6 2/3 oz.
- Cinnamon (ground): 1 2/3 Tbsps. or 5/12 oz.
- Salt: 5/8 tsp.

Combine ingredients in order given and mix until it is crumbly. Sprinkle as even as possible over the pie or tart, when just removed from the oven and still very hot; return to oven and continue baking from 12 to 15 minutes longer, or until light brown. A fine substitute for a double-crust pie.

....

(454)   **BUNNY HEADS TOPPING**

For any amount.

Take fresh marshmallows and roll them in the palm of the hand until they become round. Pinch one side to form a head, then the opposite side to form a bit of a tail. Mark eyes with a toothpick dipped in chocolate. Cut ears from stiff writing paper, colored a delicate pink on one side, and insert just above the eyes.

(455)
CHEESE TOPPING
Appropriate for two-crust apple pie, and very simple to prepare.

When apple pie is two-thirds baked, sprinkle grated American Cheese over the top. It adds much to the flavor of the pie.

....

(456)
CINNAMON TOAST TOPPING
Appropriate for almost any open-face fruit pies, especially apple.

For one 9-inch pie
- Bread: 2 slices
- Soft butter
- Sugar (brown): 1 Tbsp.
- Cinnamon (ground): ½ tsp.

For five 9-inch pies
- Bread: 10 slices
- Soft butter
- Sugar (brown): 5 Tsps. or 1²/₃ oz.
- Cinnamon (ground): 2½ tsps. or ⁵/₂₄ oz.

Toast bread on both sides; spread with butter, sprinkle with brown sugar and cinnamon. Then cut into narrow strips and arrange strips, starting from center, over the baked pie, pinwheel fashion.

....

(457)
COCONUT MERINGUE TOPPING
Appropriate for almost any kind of one-crust pies, including chiffon pies.

Prepare a meringue as indicated for recipe No. 451, Boiled Meringue Topping; pile upon the open-face pie or pies; sprinkle, for each pie, ¼ cup shredded, long-thread coconut over the meringue and brown delicately in a slow oven (300°–325° F.). Cool before serving.

(458)   CHOCOLATE WHIPPED CREAM
TOPPING

Appropriate for almost any kind of one-crust pies, including chiffon pies or tarts.

For each pie use ¼ cup heavy whipping cream, whipped stiff, to which is added sugar to taste (about 3 tablespoons) and fold in 1 square of bitter chocolate, melted over hot water. Spread as you would any ordinary whipped cream topping, using pastry bag with a fancy tube.

....

(459)   FROZEN CREAM WHIP TOPPING

Appropriate for almost any kind of one-crust pies, including chiffon pies.

For one 9-inch pie
- Heavy cream: ½ cup
- Sugar (confectioner's): 2 Tbsps.
- Salt: ⅛ tsp.
- Vanilla extract (or other flavoring): ¼ tsp.
- Egg white (stiffly beaten): 1

For five 9-inch pies
- Heavy cream: 2½ cups or 1 lb. 5 oz.
- Sugar (confectioner's): ⅝ cup or 2⁶/₇ oz.
- Salt: ⅝ tsp.
- Vanilla extract (or other flavoring): 1¼ tsps. or ⁵/₂₄ oz.
- Egg whites (stiffly beaten): 5 or 5 oz.

Whip heavy cream until it begins to hold its shape; gradually beat in combined confectioner's sugar and salt, alternately with stiffly beaten egg white, to which has been added the flavoring extract. Turn mixture into freezing tray of automatic refrigerator and freeze for at least 2 hours, or a little longer if a hard topping is desired.

(460)   # GLAZED APPLE GARNISHING

Appropriate for open-face pie, including chiffon pies and tarts.

For one 9-inch pie
- Apples: 3
- Sugar (granulated): ½ cup
- Corn syrup (light): 2 tsps.
- Water (cold): ¾ cup
- Cloves (whole): 2 or 3 (heads removed)
- Salt: ⅛ tsp.

For five 9-inch pies
- Apples: 15
- Sugar (granulated): 2½ cups or 1 lb. 4 oz.
- Corn syrup (light): 3⅓ Tbsps. or 2½ oz.
- Water (cold): 3¾ cups or 1 lb. 14 oz.
- Cloves (whole): 10 to 15 (heads removed)
- Salt: ⅝ tsp.

Pare, core and cut raw apples into sections resembling orange sections; dropping sections into ice water to which has been added 1 tablespoon lemon juice for each pint of water. In a saucepan combine remaining ingredients and bring to a boil; when mixture is boiling, add a few apple sections at a time and let simmer gently for 4 to 5 minutes. Skim from the syrup and cool on absorbent paper; repeat glazing apples until all are done. When apple sections are cold, they are ready to use as a garnish.

....

(461)   # GLAZED CHERRY TOPPING
AND GARNISHING

Appropriate for cherry pies, open faced or chiffon pies, and pie tarts.

For one 9-inch pie
- Tapioca flour: ¾ Tbsp.
- Cherry juice from canned cherries (strained): ¼ cup
- Sugar (granulated): ¼ cup
- Corn syrup (light): 2 tsps.
- Cherries (canned, drained)

For five 9-inch pies
- Tapioca flour: 3¾ Tbsps. or 1 scant oz.
- Cherry juice from canned cherries (strained): 1¼ cups or 10 oz.
- Sugar (granulated): 1¼ cups or 10 oz.
- Corn syrup (light): 3⅓ Tbsps. or 2½ oz.
- Cherries (canned, drained)

Dissolve tapioca flour in a little cold cherry juice; to the remaining juice add sugar and corn syrup, stirring until sugar and syrup are dissolved. Bring to a boil and slowly stir in the tapioca flour mixture, stirring constantly; next add the thoroughly drained cherries. Do not let boil. The cherries are ready to use for topping an open cherry pie, as a garnish or as a filling for individual tarts.

....

(462)   # GLAZED ORANGE TOPPING
AND GARNISHING
Appropriate for open-face pies, including chiffon pies and tarts.

Proceed as indicated for No. 460, Glazed Apple Garnishing, substituting orange sections. When syrup reaches the soft ball state (238° F.), dip each section in the syrup and drain on rack or absorbent paper. They should be transparent with just a film of crystal. Tangerines may be prepared in the same way. Be sure to remove all the white skins from orange sections before dipping into the boiling syrup.

....

(463)   # GLAZED NUT TOPPING
AND GARNISHING
Appropriate for open-faced pies, including chiffon pies and tarts.

Prepare a syrup, as indicated for recipe No. 460, Glazed Apple Garnishing, substituting either shelled, halved and skinned pecans or walnuts. When syrup comes to the soft ball state (238° F.), dip prepared nuts in the syrup, which has been cooked over low heat. Drain on a rack; when cold, to be used as a garnish or a topping. They may be packed in sealed container, between layers of waxed paper, and kept in a cool, dry place. They will keep several months.

(464) ## GLAZED SLICED PEACH TOPPING
AND GARNISHING

Appropriate especially for open-faced peach pies, fresh or canned, chiffon pies and tarts.

Proceed as indicated for recipe No. 460, Glazed Apple Garnishing, substituting either fresh or canned sliced peaches, thoroughly drained. When syrup comes to the soft ball stage (238° F.), dip a few peach slices at a time into the hot syrup, let stand 2 minutes, skim and dry on a rack or on absorbent paper.

(465) ## GLAZED STRAWBERRY TOPPING
AND GARNISHING

Appropriate for open-faced strawberry pies, chiffon pies and tarts, as well as cream pies.

Use recipe for Glazed Cherry Topping (No. 461), substituting hulled, washed strawberries.

(466) ## GLAZED STRAWBERRY JUICE
FOR TOPPING

Appropriate for almost any kind of open-faced cream, strawberry, and chiffon pies as well as tarts and cakes.

For one 9-inch pie
- Water (cold): $2/3$ cup
- Corn syrup or glucose or maple syrup: 1 Tbsp. or ¾ oz.
- Sugar (granulated): 1 cup
- Red vegetable coloring: a tiny drop
- Tapioca flour: $2^2/3$ Tbsps.

For five 9-inch pies
- Water (cold): $3^1/3$ cups or 1 lb. $10^2/3$ oz.
- Corn syrup or glucose or maple syrup: 5 Tbsps. or 3¾ oz.
- Sugar (granulated): 5 cups or 2½ lbs.
- Red vegetable coloring: a few drops
- Tapioca flour: scant $7/8$ cup

Reserve a little cold water to dissolve the tapioca flour. Combine remaining ingredients, except the tapioca flour, in a saucepan and stir until blended. Bring to a boil and stir in as slowly as possible, so as not to stop the boiling process, the dissolved tapioca flour, stirring constantly from the bottom of the pan. Allow this to boil 2 minutes, stirring constantly until mixture is transparent. Have pie ready filled, and cover with the glaze while piping hot.

....

(467)   ## GLAZED FRESH OR FROZEN STRAWBERRIES FOR TOPPING AND GARNISHING

Appropriate for almost any kind of open-faced cream, fruit and chiffon pies and tarts.

Use the above glazed strawberry juice, dipping each berry into it, and arranging them according to fancy on top of filled pies or tarts. Or, dissolve some red currant jelly, but do not allow to boil, over hot water and dip each berry into the hot currant liquid; arrange the fruit on top of the filling, or topping, as you go along.

....

(468)   ## JELLY WHIPPED CREAM TOPPING AND GARNISHING

Appropriate for almost any kind of fruit or chiffon pie, and open-faced tarts.

To each ½ cup heavy whipping cream, whipped, fold in as thoroughly as possible 2 tablespoons any kind of fruit jelly. Force the mixture through a pastry bag with a fancy tube over the cold filling, or use as a border.

....

(469)   ## MAPLE WHIPPED CREAM TOPPING AND GARNISHING

Appropriate for almost any kind of fruit or chiffon pie, and open-faced tarts.

To each cup of heavy cream, which has been whipped, fold in 1/3 cup maple syrup, as thoroughly as possible. Force the mixture through a pastry bag with a fancy tube over the cold filling, or use as a border.

(470)   # MARSHMALLOW CREAM TOPPING AND GARNISHING I

Appropriate for almost any kind of open-faced pie, as fruit and chiffon, and tarts.

For one 9-inch pie
- Marshmallows (sliced): 12
- Heavy cream: 1 cup
- Salt: 1/8 tsp.

For five 9-inch pies
- Marshmallows (sliced): 60 or 1 lb.
- Heavy cream: 5 cups or 2 lbs. 8⅞ oz.
- Salt: ⅝ tsp.

Slice marshmallows as thinly as possible, using a floured pair of scissors; soak the slices in unbeaten heavy cream for at least 30 minutes; then beat with rotary egg beater, or electric mixer at second speed, until mixture holds its peaks. Force through a pastry bag with a rose tube, or pile loosely over the filling or use as a border or garnish.

NOTE: You may flavor the mixture with any desired flavoring extract, or apple brandy, brandy, rum or any kind of liqueur, using ¾ teaspoon flavoring extract (almond extract ½ teaspoon) and 1½ to 2 tablespoons liqueur, adding the flavoring after the cream mixture hold its peaks.

....

(471)   # MARSHMALLOW CREAM TOPPING AND GARNISHING II

Appropriate for almost any kind of open-face fruit or chiffon pies and tarts.

For one 9-inch pie
- Egg yolks: 2
- Sugar (granulated): 3 Tbsps.
- Salt: 1/8 tsp.
- Pineapple juice (strained): ⅔ cup
- Marshmallows: 12
- Egg whites (stiffly beaten): 2

For five 9-inch pies
- Egg yolks: 10 or 10 oz.
- Sugar (granulated): 1 scant cup or 7½ oz.
- Salt: ⅝ tsp.
- Pineapple juice (strained): 3⅓ cups or 1 lb. 10⅔ oz.
- Marshmallows: 60 or 1 lb.
- Egg whites (stiffly beaten): 10 or 10 oz.

Beat egg yolks until light, slowly add sugar, combined with salt, beating constantly; then add strained pineapple juice and blend thoroughly. Cook over hot water, stirring constantly, until thick and creamy, or about 7 or 8 minutes. Remove from hot water and transfer into a shallow pan to cool slightly. Cut marshmallows in small pieces or slices, using scissors dipped in water, and add to still hot mixture with a few drops of vanilla (optional) extract; blend well and chill. Then fold in the stiffly beaten egg whites. Keep in refrigerator until ready to use for topping or garnishing, forced through a pastry bag with a fancy tube.

··

(472) MARSHMALLOW MERINGUE TOPPING
Appropriate for almost any kind of cream or fruit pies and tarts.

For one 9-inch pie
- Egg whites (stiffly beaten): 2
- Sugar (granulated): 2 Tbsps.
- Salt: $\frac{1}{8}$ tsp.
- Marshmallows (cut into small pieces and softened near heat): 12 or 3$\frac{1}{5}$ oz.
- Vanilla extract: 4 drops

For five 9-inch pies
- Egg whites (stiffly beaten): 10 or 10 oz.
- Sugar (granulated): $\frac{5}{8}$ cup or 5 oz.
- Salt: $\frac{5}{8}$ tsp.
- Marshmallows (cut into small pieces and softened near heat): 60 or 1 lb.
- Vanilla extract: $\frac{1}{3}$ tsp.

Whip egg whites until stiff; gradually add sugar, mixed with salt, then the softened marshmallow pieces; beat again until mixture is stiff and holds its peaks; add the vanilla extract at the last minute. Spread, using a pastry bag with a fancy tube, over the cooled pie filling and bake in a slow oven (300°–325° F.) until delicately brown. Cool before serving.

(473)   # MARZIPAN MERINGUE BORDER

Very appropriate for open-faced cherry and berry pies, and tarts.

For 1 pound of marzipan

- Almond paste, No. 474: 2 cups
- Egg whites (unbeaten): 2
- Salt: ¼ tsp.
- Confectioner's sugar

For 5 pounds of marzipan

- Almond paste, No. 474: 2½ qts. or 5 lbs.
- Egg whites (unbeaten): 10 or 1 cup or 10 oz.
- Salt: 1¼ tsps. or $^5/_{24}$ oz.
- Confectioner's sugar

Combine almond paste and unbeaten egg whites thoroughly; gradually add salt and enough confectioner's sugar to stiffen mixture for easy handling. Knead the whole mass carefully upon a board, lightly sprinkled with confectioner's sugar, for 15 minutes. Put away for 24 hours in a covered earthenware or glass dish before using as follows:

For one 9-inch pie, take 4 ounces of prepared marzipan and beat it with 3 egg whites, stiffly beaten with a few grains of salt. The beating will be easier if the marzipan has been slightly softened. Force mixture through a strong pastry bag with a large fancy tube and arrange a border of the meringue around the edges of the pie or pies. Place in a slow oven (325° F.) to delicately brown; cool before serving. You may place the pie under the broiler a few minutes to brown quickly.

....

(474)   # ALMOND PASTE— EMERGENCY METHOD

For one pound

- Almonds (blanched, pounded or ground fine): 1½ cups
- Sugar (granulated): ¾ cup
- Water (cold): 1 cup
- Salt: ½ tsp.
- Almond extract: ½ tsp.

Put almonds, sugar and water in top of double boiler and stir to blend thoroughly. Cook, covered, over hot water for 20–25 minutes. Remove from the heat and stir constantly while adding salt and almond extract. Pack in container, cover, and keep in refrigerator for 24 hours to mellow and ripen before using.

This emergency almond paste may be tinted whole or in part with vegetable coloring. It will keep several weeks in refrigerator, when tightly covered.

....

(475)   **STREUSEL FOR TOPPING**

Appropriate for almost any kind of open-faced pies, and tarts.

For one 9-inch pie
- Butter (or margarine): ¼ cup
- Sugar (granulated): 2 Tbsps.
- Cinnamon (ground): 1 Tbsp.
- Flour (pastry): 1 cup

For five 9-inch pies
- Butter (or margarine): 1¼ cups or 10 oz.
- Sugar (granulated): ⅝ cup or 5 oz.
- Cinnamon (ground): 5 Tbsps.
- Flour (pastry): 5 cups or 1 lb. 4 oz.

To the creamed butter (or margarine) add combined sugar and cinnamon alternately with flour, and blend thoroughly until crumby texture. Sprinkle generously over filling before setting the pie in the oven.

....

(476)   **TARTS AND TORTES**

Tarts and tortes should be used more frequently than they are because they are both attractive and economical. As a rule, they take less filling than pies but look like a larger portion. When fruits are expensive, the wise chef or homemaker will make them go farther by using them in tarts rather than in pie fillings.

In making tarts or tortes, one may use cake crumbs, bread crumbs, oatmeal crumbs, rice crumbs, etc. Cooked cream fillings are usually the base. A fruit glaze, made from fruit juice, cooked to the "jell" stage, poured over the top prevents discoloration and adds to the appearance. Tart shells may be made of plain pastry or rich puff paste and may be baked over inverted pie pans or muffin pans; be sure to have the surface pricked. They may also be baked on the inside with another pan of the same size on top.

For pastry and tart shells, use either of the recipes found in Section II. Fit into tart pan; turn the edges under and pinch into scallops with the fingers. Prick all over with a fork and bake in a hot oven (450°–475° F.) about 8 to 10 minutes. A master recipe makes 4 tart shells.

Tarts and tortes may be covered with a meringue, if desired, selecting either one found in Section V, Topping, Garnishing, and Glazing, for pies and tarts.

In short, tarts are little pies daintily presented, pleasing to the eye and tempting to the appetite. They have a certain air of elegance that lends a festive note to the table and all the fillings used for pies, either two-crust, one-crust, or chiffon pies, may be used to great advantage in tarts and tortes.

An easy way to make attractive tart shells or patties is to shape them over backs of muffin pans. For 3-inch muffin pans, cut 5-inch rounds of pastry rolled thin and pricked all over with a fork. Fit dough snugly on pans, pinching into small pleats at regular intervals (about 7 pleats).

Tarts are sometimes baked with a filling and, in this case, the pastry is rolled thin and cut into rounds to fit the patty pans used. Line inside of pan with pastry, pressing it against sides to exclude air. Trim edges according to indication given in No. 47 and No. 48, Section II, Pastry and Crust Recipes. Fluted pans make professional-looking tarts or patties.

Tarts may be covered entirely or just bordered with whipped cream, either plain or sweetened and flavored to taste. For these toppings, see Section V; or one may use successfully a glazing made by cooking equal parts of strained fruit (strawberries or other fruit), apricots and corn syrup, boiling it down to a jelly consistency. Pour over the fruits while mixture is warm. Another suggestion is to melt strawberry jelly until it will pour easily and then pour over the fruit in the tart shells. This becomes firm when cooled and makes a glaze that is both simple to prepare and satisfactory.

As in pies, there are two kinds of tarts: (a) the tarts proper, which are diminutive pies of the one-crust kind; and (b) the chiffon tarts, or gelatin tarts, or as they are sometimes called, the refrigerator tarts. For these chiffon tarts, all the fillings indicated for chiffon pies may be used very satisfactorily, and either topped with whipped cream or special meringue mixture, as indicated for recipe No. 451, Boiled Meringue Topping for Chiffon Pies and Variations.